MOVING BEYOND SECTARIANISM

With best wishes

Cecelia

Joseph Liechty and Cecelia Clegg

Moving Beyond Sectarianism

RELIGION, CONFLICT, AND
RECONCILIATION IN NORTHERN IRELAND

the columba press

First published in 2001 by

the columba press

55A Spruce Avenue, Stillorgan Industrial Park,
Blackrock, Co Dublin

Cover by Bill Bolger
Origination by The Columba Press
Printed in Ireland by Colour Books Ltd, Dublin

ISBN 1 85607 318 1

Credits

Scripture quotations are from the *New Revised Standard Version*, copyright © 1989, by the Division of Christian Education of the National Council of the Churches of Christ in the United States of America. Used by permission. Earlier versions of some of the material in this book have already appeared in the following publications: Joseph Liechty and Cecelia Clegg, 'Moving Beyond Sectarianism: Religion, Conflict, and Reconciliation in Contemporary Northern Ireland' in *Toleration and Religious Identity: The Implications of the Edict of Nantes for France, Britain and Ireland,* eds Ruth Whelan and Carol Baxter (Dublin: Four Courts Press, forthcoming, 2001); Joseph Liechty, 'Four Religious Variations on the Theme of Sectarianism in Northern Ireland' in *National Questions,* eds Vincent Comerford and Enda Delaney (Dublin: Wolfhound Press, 2000); Joseph Liechty, 'Sectarianism and the Churches: The Legacy and the Challenge' in *Religion in Ireland: Past, Present and Future,* ed Denis Carroll (Dublin: The Columba Press, 1999); Joseph Liechty, 'Religion, Conflict and Community Relations' in *A Tapestry of Beliefs: Christian Traditions in Northern Ireland,* ed Norman Richardson (Belfast: Blackstaff Press, 1998); Joseph Liechty, 'The Nature of Sectarianism Today' and 'Historical and Theological Origins of Sectarianism' in *Sectarianism,* eds Alan Falconer and Trevor Williams (Dublin: Dominican Publications, 1995); Joseph Liechty, 'The Problem of Sectarianism and the Church of Ireland' in *As by Law Established: The Church of Ireland Since the Reformation,* eds Alan Ford, James McGuire and Kenneth Milne (Dublin: Lilliput Press, 1995); Joseph Liechty, '"But Is It Really Religious?" Religion and Conflict in Northern Ireland' in *Peace Section Newsletter* [of the Mennonite Central Committee] (Spring 1994), reprinted in *Conflict Resolution Notes,* vol 4, no 4 (April 1998); Joseph Liechty, *Roots of Sectarianism in Ireland: Chronology and Reflections* (Belfast: Irish Inter-Church Meeting, 1993); Joseph Liechty, 'Sectarianism' in *Doctrine and Life,* vol 43 (September 1993); Joseph Liechty, 'The Politics of Conversion in Ireland' in *Third Way,* vol 14 (February 1991).

Contents

ACKNOWLEDGMENTS

When we accepted appointment on the Moving Beyond Sectarianism project, we knew that we had to produce a 'final report'. We had no idea that the 'report' would turn out to be a book of this size and complexity. Though not fully adequate, it is our best effort at a reflection on a particular part of the story of the people of Northern Ireland. The graciousness and generosity with which so many people welcomed us, two strangers, into their lives and their communities will be an abiding memory and source of gratitude.

Six years of intense and close to constant collaboration on research and writing could well be a hazardous experience. How pleased we are, then, that we remain professional colleagues and have become friends. We have agreed in our analysis of sectarianism more often than we had a right to expect, and when we have differed, those differences have been fruitful, we like to believe, forcing us to reconsider inadequate viewpoints and leading us towards better and unanticipated positions.

We gratefully acknowledge enormous debts to many people. We begin by thanking Kenneth Kearon, director of the Irish School of Ecumenics (ISE), and the staff of the ISE in both Dublin and Belfast for their support, encouragement, and practical assistance. Being part of the ISE staff team has been an enriching and enjoyable experience for us. A special word of thanks is due to Geraldine Smyth OP, formerly director of the ISE and latterly supervisor to the project, for her unfailing interest, energy, encouragement, and challenges. We also need to mention the particular contributions of Sláine O Hogain and John Shiels, ISE librarian and fundraiser respectively. Sláine was so efficient at running down sources and finding material that she seemed at times like part of the research team. At a point in the project where we seemed to be spending almost as much time corresponding with funding agencies as we were actually doing research, John came along and took those matters out of our hands and into his own far more capable hands.

Working alongside Geraldine for specific events, David Stevens, general secretary of the Irish Council of Churches, and

David Porter. director of ECONI (Evangelical Contribution on Northern Ireland), have constituted an informal steering group that has given us time, insight, encouragement, friendship, and practical assistance. For their insightful comments on drafts of the chapters, heartfelt thanks are also due to our wider reference group: Lesley Carroll, William Crawley, Ciarán Dallat, Cathy Higgins, Brendan Keane, David McKittrick, Evelyn McKittrick, Johnston McMaster, John Morrow, Fran Porter, Keith Scott, Malcolm Scott, David Stevens, and Alwyn Thomson. More recently, Yvonne Naylor and Craig Sands have worked closely with the text, to our benefit. Another valued member of the MBS team for one year was Peter O'Reilly. Having planned and executed every detail of a conference in 1996, we said, 'Never again,' and it was Peter who delivered us by serving as the outstanding coordinator of the much larger Boundaries and Bonds conference in 1997.

We have at all times been conscious of being part of an informal community of people and groups working at reconciliation. Their support, encouragement, and insight have been of great benefit. We want especially to acknowledge ECONI, Corrymeela, and the Mediation Network for Northern Ireland.

We have no greater debt than to the many, many individuals and groups we worked with in consultations, conferences, workshops, interviews, and group work. We hope that they will see their stories reflected recognisably and honestly in what we have written.

Over the five years of its implementation, the Moving Beyond Sectarianism programme engaged in many activities and used many services. The combined outlay on salaries and allowances, facilitation, accommodation and subsistence for seminars and residential weekends, plus travel, materials, print, and other expenses was in excess of half a million pounds. Much of this support was used during the lifetime of the project, but some was earmarked for future work, for example, producing teaching materials based on our findings. The critical support of our financial contributors is gratefully acknowledged. We hope that this volume and the various outputs of the programme will help them to conclude that the effort was worthy of their generosity. Contributors fall into two parallel groups. The first comprises substantial donors institutionally committed to work of this kind, including the Community Bridges Programme of the International Fund for Ireland; the European Union Special

Support programme for Peace and Reconciliation; the Department of Foreign Affairs of Ireland; the Joseph Rowntree Charitable Trust in New York; the Northern Ireland Community Relations Council; the Northern Ireland Voluntary Trust; and the United States Institute for Peace in Washington.

The second group provided highly strategic help, particularly in terms of timing. They comprise church sources and other friends of the Irish School of Ecumenics, including the Bank of Ireland; Ms Betty O'Rawe; the Christendom Trust in Great Britain; Coventry Cathedral; the Council for World Mission in London; the Congregation of Dominican Sisters; Mr Eamon Flannighan; the Howard Foundation; the Irish Council of Churches; the Joseph Rank Benevolent Trust in London; a private donor; and the World Council of Churches in Geneva.

Sectarianism as a System: Basic Implications

In Northern Ireland, few interventions can raise the emotional temperature of a conversation so sharply as bringing up the topic of sectarianism. It is a harsh word, expressing a harsh reality and often hurled as an accusing, condemning weapon. In fact maintaining civil conversation usually means not discussing sectarianism at all, especially in mixed settings. Between these extremes of accusation and avoidance, people have painfully few tools for getting to grips with the problem of sectarianism in a constructive way.

Given the difficult and explosive nature of sectarianism, we want to begin by laying out as clearly and honestly as possible the basic elements of our approach. Readers can expect the following ideas, principles, and assumptions to pervade and guide the rest of this book.

Sectarianism as a system
While an understanding of sectarianism as a system has been part our work from the beginning, we have found it increasingly important to stress the systemic nature of sectarianism. We might pose the problem as follows: much thinking about sectarianism is faulty because we take a solely personal approach to a problem that is both personal and systemic. When thinking about sectarianism, we typically begin with personal attitudes and personal actions. Thus we absolve a person of responsibility, we think, when we say, 'She doesn't have a sectarian bone in her body.' In one sense, this concern with the personal is not only appropriate, we need more of it, not less. At the same time, however, a too exclusively personal approach fails to take seriously enough the systemic issues around sectarianism. To pose the problem another way: a sectarian system can be maintained by people who, individually, do not have a sectarian bone in their bodies. Some reflection on the nature and origin of the sectarian system will show how this paradox comes to pass.

Sectarianism is a system that works sometimes with sledge hammer directness and brutality, sometimes with great subtlety. We were struck by the juxtaposition of these modes in stories told in a Catholic group we worked with in the autumn of 1998. A priest told of his horror at standing across the street, power-less to intervene, while an IRA man pumped bullets into the head of an RUC man fallen at his feet. That is the sledge ham-mer. In the same session, a woman spoke of the effects of an annual Orange parade in the neighbourhood where she grew up. As she told the story, this was not a rowdy parade, and in-deed nothing particularly dramatic ever happened. And yet that annual event, always accompanied by her family staying in their house and quietly hoping that nothing would happen, generated in her an unspoken but ever-present sense of intimidation and limitation that shaped her life: where she would go, obviously, and whom she would befriend, but more subtle and internal limitations as well; a reserve and caution that did not always show, but that always shaped those encounters she did have with Protestants. As she spoke, however, what seemed to dis-tress her most was her sense, as a middle-aged mother of older children, that without ever intending or even realising it, she had somehow passed on the same limitations to her children. In one sense little or nothing happened, and yet the quietly de-structive effects could shape a life and pass silently to a new gen-eration. The system can be that subtle.

In its formative days, the 1500s and onwards, sectarianism knew little of subtlety. Sectarianism requires division, in partic-ular antagonised division, so in the beginning sectarianism worked with bold strokes: big hate, big violence, gross injustice. In the beginning, then, sectarianism generated and fed on events like the Elizabethan Wars in Ireland, plantation, the 1641 Rising, Cromwell, the Williamite Wars, penal laws, and so on. And since this is not just any antagonised division, it is sectarianism, it requires a religious contribution.[1]

It requires an English Protestant officer reflecting on a six-teenth-century military campaign in Ulster in these terms: 'how godly a dede it is to overthrowe so wicked a race [as the Irish] the world may judge: for my part I thinke there canot be a greater sacryfice to God.'

It requires that Catholic resistance to such logic should be framed in religious terms, so that when in 1579 James Fitzmaurice Fitzgerald returned to Ireland from four years on the continent to mount a campaign against the English crown, he should declare that the 'only object' of his campaign was to 'secure the administration of Christ's sacraments to a Catholic people in a Catholic rite', and his landing party should be led by two Franciscans bearing a banner blessed by the Pope, then by a bishop in full regalia, then by seven hundred soldiers paid for by the Pope. Fitzmaurice himself bore a letter from the Pope urging Irish Catholics to rise against the heretics and promising all who did 'the same plenary indulgence and remission of sins that those receive who fight against the Turks and for the recovery of the Holy Land.' These were the terms of holy war.

It requires that in the 1641 Rising, the Old English and the Irish parties, who could not unite under any other banner, should join together as the Confederate Catholics of Ireland, and that their leader, Owen Roe O'Neill, should return to Ireland with another letter from another pope, this one praising O'Neill's 'excelling fervour, that is, your constancy against the heretics' and offering a blessing to all 'who would help the cause of the Catholics'.

It requires in return that Oliver Cromwell should publicly defend his terrifying violence in Ireland as the righteous judgment of God, saying in response to a pamphlet issued by Catholic priests and bishops, 'You are a part of Antichrist, whose Kingdom the scripture so expressly speaks should be "laid in blood; yea, in the blood of the Saints." You have shed great store of that already: and ere it be long, you must all of you have "blood to drink"; even the dregs of the cup of the fury and the wrath of God, which will be poured out unto you!'

It requires that the Catholic, Presbyterian, and Anglican churches in the seventeenth century should each regard themselves as the one true church, that each should align itself with a political cause, and that each should, under the shared conviction that error has no right, seek victory and dominance over the other parties.

Neither can such matters be dismissed as distant history. These sixteenth- and seventeenth-century dynamics have been reflected in this century, even if in milder form.

Sectarianism requires, therefore, that Patrick Pearse's revolutionary thought should involve a heretical union of Christianity and nationalism.

It requires that Protestant resistance to home rule, sealed in the 1912 Solemn League and Covenant, should involve the church-blessed threat of violent resistance.

It requires that the two new states created by the partition of Ireland should function to a large extent as a Protestant state and a Catholic state.

It requires Cardinal MacRory announcing in the 1930s that the Protestant traditions really are not Christian churches at all.

It requires discrimination against Catholics in Northern Ireland, with Protestants turning a blind eye or supporting it.

It requires Pope Pius XII rejecting religious liberty and re-affirming error has no right in the 1950s, so that really until the Second Vatican Council opts for religious liberty in the 1960s, Protestant fears that 'home rule is Rome rule' have a rational basis in official Catholic doctrine.

While no match in ferocity for its reformation-era predecessors, this kind of sectarianism is still relatively direct and simple.

Nor is simple sectarianism dead today. Sectarianism still nurtures crude bigotry, injustice, and violence, and these remain its most potent fuels. The shock waves sent out by violence have a particular power to deepen and strengthen the sectarian divide. But the sectarian system, now long established, no longer requires large amounts of such comparatively exotic fuels to maintain itself. Just an occasional act of violence will do, because the sectarian system disposes us to judge others by the worst actions of the worst elements of 'their' community. Nor do motivations for the violence matter much. When accused of sectarianism, gross or subtle, most people turn first to their intentions and motivations to absolve themselves, but the victims or potential victims are not listening, and for good reason. Under threat, all we are interested in knowing is where the threat comes from. And this is a rational response to a real threat; we do not avoid some areas or situations at some times out of a paranoid fear that everyone is out to get us, but out of a reasonable fear that someone *might* be. This is no more than prudence, the self-preservation instinct at work.

Sectarianism, however, has become a system so efficient that it can take our sane and rational responses to a situation which it has generated and use them to further deepen sectarianism. For an example, we need look no further than one of the principle structural responses to the violence of the last thirty years, the increasing movement from mixed residential situations to living exclusively among our own. No one could in any way be faulted for doing so, and yet the corporate effect of these individually sensible and blameless movements is to reinforce sectarianism still further. This is only to look at the most obvious responses to sectarianism, of course. Others may have stopped short of physically withdrawing from mixed situations, whether residential, vocational, or social, while withdrawing in spirit. Our trust has been violated, so we redraw the boundaries and hold ourselves back from unseen but effective limits. This too is an entirely understandable response to sectarianism. And here we might pause to marvel, for a system that can maintain itself by feeding on logical responses to situations it has created is a wonder of adaptation.

In fact the efficiency of the sectarian system goes at least two steps further. First, sectarianism does not really require any direct, active response at all from most of us, it simply requires that we do nothing about it. 'Comparative sectarianism' is the simple and efficient mechanism the sectarian system has established for keeping us passive or at least keeping our protests ineffectual. We are inclined to approach sectarianism by drawing lines between them and us, and since we can always find a 'them' out there whose actions can be plausibly construed as worse than ours, we can justify ourselves in identifying 'them' as the real sectarian problem. While distinctions between levels and grades of sectarianism are important, the problem is that everyone can find someone worse than themselves, so no one is ever responsible. This buck never stops passing. We may even rail against sectarian abuses and therefore regard ourselves as anti-sectarian, but because they are always someone else's abuses we are attacking, the sectarian system can readily absorb our criticisms and carry on undisturbed. In the meantime, the comparative sectarianism approach means that the systemic features of sectarianism are rarely even addressed.

Second, the sectarian system can sometimes use even our best efforts to build itself up. Given the church-related concentration of our work in the Moving Beyond Sectarianism project, we see this most crucially in the way that sectarianism feeds on Christians' religiously-motivated boundary maintenance. We choose to worship, educate, and marry almost exclusively among our own. Our motivation is not to be sectarian, it is to build strong communities, but because our efforts fall within the boundaries set by sectarianism, our best pastoral efforts can end up strengthening the sectarian divide. Ironically, strong communities are and will be crucial to challenging sectarianism. And yet so long as the churches see challenging the sectarian divide as a marginal responsibility, or no responsibility at all, or a responsibility we will address when everything else has been settled, the sectarian system will go on employing well-intentioned, positive, community-building activities as sustenance for itself.

So it is that the sectarian system, born from gross violence and what most people would now see as unapologetic injustice, can now maintain itself on a diet consisting largely of our rational responses, understandable comparisons, good intentions, and positive actions. A system so impressively efficient is not going to disappear simply because we are now enjoying paramilitary ceasefires, more or less, and a measure of political progress, however fragile. It will need to be challenged, by Christians, their churches, and others, in a range of creative ways and for a long time to come.

Reflections

This meditation on sectarianism as a system became a standard feature in virtually every presentation we gave or group work session we led, whether for a local cross-community group or a national gathering of church leaders. It proved to be a useful tool. Some significant part of its utility had to do with a feature readers may have noticed: throughout this sectarianism-as-a-system passage we consistently and strongly reify sectarianism, treating it as a living and even wilful entity. We may initially have done this occasionally and casually, but for several reasons it soon became a deliberate approach.

Probably our primary reason was that a reified presentation of sectarianism seemed to reflect people's experience. Take, for example, the setting from which this reflection on sectarianism as a system first emerged. We were working for two weekends with a Catholic religious order and some of their key lay collaborators in a review of their ministry, thinking particularly about how they could address issues of sectarianism. An early session involved the group of fifteen to twenty people relating their personal experiences of sectarianism. As story after story revealed the contours, complexity, and sinister power of sectarianism, a numinous atmosphere settled over the group. Regrettably, however, the divinity evoked was a dark one, and the awe it inspired was enervating. Near the end of the session Joe made some fumbling, reifying remarks about the nature of the beast we were confronting. It sparked some recognition and interest, and after the session some people asked Joe to elaborate. That night he wrote out an initial, cruder version of the reflection on sectarianism as a system offered in this chapter, and the next morning he shared it with the group. What he said met with quiet but firm assent, and the mood changed. Having evoked, recognised, and named sectarianism, we could now get on, it seemed, with the business of challenging it. For virtually every group we worked with after that weekend, this reflection on sectarianism as a system served, at least to some degree, a similar function: a mix of focusing, bonding, and energising.

Second, by reifying sectarianism we mean to connect it to the biblical concept of principalities and powers, especially as mediated to us by Walter Wink's work on the powers, principally *Engaging the Powers: Discernment and Resistance in a World of Domination*.[2] While we only make explicit use of the language of the powers in a few places in our written work, it consistently undergirds our thinking about sectarianism, as it does in this sectarianism-as-a-system passage. While sectarianism generates both concrete institutions and a correlating malign spirituality, the spiritual aspect is probably less apparent to modern sensibilities. It is most useful, therefore, to embrace a perspective that allows us to see that the struggle against sectarianism is 'against the rulers, against the authorities, against the cosmic powers of this present darkness, against the spiritual forces of evil in the heavenly place'. (Eph 6:12) For many, Wink's treatment will help to bridge the gap between biblical and modern worldviews.

Third, reifying sectarianism provides a form of what is so very difficult to come by in Northern Ireland: an agreed and shared enemy that we can struggle against together. People returning to Northern Ireland after long experience of the struggle against apartheid in South Africa bemoan the absence in Northern Ireland of a broad and identifiable movement one can join to oppose a broad and identifiable evil. Reflecting in 1998 on her observations of sectarianism and inter-church relations in Northern Ireland, a Reformed pastor from Romania commented that what the North requires is a Communist dictatorship. A shared oppressor, not least through providing inter-church experiences in prison, would encourage mutual respect and collaboration among estranged religious parties in society, as happened in Romania. In the absence of such an unlikely blessing, a reified sectarianism goes some way toward meeting the need.

Fourth, a reified sectarianism helps us in the delicate task of thinking about responsibility for sectarianism in ways that go beyond finger-pointing exercises in blame. The response we hoped to evoke in those we work with might be put like this: we face a problem of awesome power and subtlety; there is no hiding from it and little innocence in the face of it; it implicates us collectively and individually; let us join together to face it. Sometimes this happened, and sometimes this sectarianism-as-a-system reflection seemed to help it happen.

In addition to the reification of sectarianism, readers may also have noticed a slippery use of 'we'. Sometimes 'we' refers to Cecelia and Joe. Sometimes 'we' refers to something larger and more vague, perhaps the people of Northern Ireland, perhaps those who wish to challenge sectarianism. Sometimes it is unclear which use of 'we', the narrow or the broad, we intend. Such ambiguity does not work well in print, and through the remainder of this book, 'we' will almost always refer solely to Joe and Cecelia. During the course of the Moving Beyond Sectarianism project, however, what may have begun as an unconscious ambiguity soon became deliberate. We are both outsiders, Cecelia as a Scot with an English accent and Joe as an American, a Mennonite, and a Dubliner. Outsider status was in some ways crucial to our work, and if we had not had it, we might have been tempted to cultivate it. Being outsiders is not an unmixed blessing, however, so we also needed to find ways to temper it. We have been continually alert to what we came to think of as 'the shock of recognition' – those occasions when the experience of Northern Ireland is not only what we observe but also a mirror in which we see ourselves and our communities, perhaps in unexpected ways. As 'the shock of recognition' became more 'the expectation of recognition', a many-layered and ambiguous use of 'we' came to seem an honest indication of the ways we are both outsiders and insiders. It was also, and it remains, one more way of cultivating that crucial sense of standing together, all of us implicated and yet determined to challenge a formidable opponent.

Why Moving Beyond Sectarianism matters

Reflection on sectarianism as a system reveals just how high are the costs attached to it. The pervasive nature of sectarianism means that social relations are too often tainted and stunted, sometimes in obvious ways, sometimes subtly. The persistent, rooted nature of sectarianism means that hard-earned political progress could be damaged or undone by a sectarian society not fully capable of living at peace in new political structures. The religious aspect of sectarianism means that personal faith, the life of church communities, and church structures can be twisted in ways that run counter to, even mock, basic Christian tenets. The systemic nature of sectarianism means that well-meant actions and understandable silences can be poisoned so that they contribute to the social conditions in which lethal violence erupts.

If the costs exacted by the sectarian system are great, so too are the potential benefits of addressing sectarianism in a sustained and purposeful way. Such work will make its most immediate impact at the level of social and civic life, undermined and limited by sectarianism. Among social and civic institutions, the churches have a particular interest in tackling sectarianism. Standing implicated as one contributor to sectarianism, action by the churches is in effect their repentance, and repentance is the strongest possible root of renewal, whether personal or corporate. As post-Troubles Northern Ireland casts about for who and what was to blame, the churches are likely to be on the receiving end of accusations, sometimes justly, sometimes not. Commitment to deal with sectarianism will be the churches' most effective response, and finally the only one that matters. Not least, work on sectarianism, much of it of apparently modest and local significance, will make an indirect but substantial contribution to preventing a return to the killing that tore Northern Ireland asunder for many years. The future stakes are as high as the past costs.

Responsibility and blame

One of the challenges our work has consistently presented is how we can name sectarianism as clearly and honestly as possible, including dealing with issues of responsibility, without, as Fran Porter put it to us, 'apportioning paralysing chunks of blame'. This is especially a problem because one of our emphases will be to challenge typical and simple assumptions about the innocent majority and the guilty few. Responsibility for sectarianism is too easily assigned to everyone but oneself and one's own people, and especially to the relatively few people directly and obviously involved in violence, intimidation, and provocation.

Given that sectarianism builds and relies on a culture of blame, our response has been to find ways of promoting a culture of taking responsibility. One crucial step is for people to move beyond a focus on good intentions, which are almost universally proclaimed and which we by and large accept, to think about consequences and implications, even where these are not intended. Another step, at least useful and probably necessary, is to broaden definitions of responsibility. Too much talk about responsibility, we find, is implicitly based on a quasi-judicial understanding of guilt: when considering their responsibility, people are often asking, in effect, if I was taken to court and charged with sectarianism, would there be enough direct evidence to convict me? For most people the answer is no, of course not. But taking responsibility means asking other questions, about unintended consequences certainly, and about what has been left undone, what has gone unchallenged, what has been allowed or acquiesced in; it means people considering whether they might meaningfully accept responsibility for corporate acts, even when they have not participated directly, even when they could avoid responsibility.

These are the questions necessary for moving from a culture of blame to a culture of taking responsibility, which is, we are convinced, the fundamental, Copernican revolution necessary for moving beyond sectarianism. The sectarianism a group suffers at the hands of others still matters, of course, and it may truly be worse than anything the group inflicts. Redress may and should be sought. One's own sectarianism is the only kind one can necessarily do anything about, however, which makes it a natural and appropriate starting point. Furthermore, taking responsibility for one's own sectarianism may do more to encourage others to do the same than any amount of blame might do. Ironically, the culture of blame inures everyone to charges of sectarianism, even when they are well-grounded.

Because we judge the culture of blame to be a pernicious force that entrenches sectarianism, we try not to indulge in blame, even as we talk about responsibility. Some may find this a spurious distinction, or at least that we have failed to live up to it. Others, however, are likely to find this an objectionably 'softly, softly' approach to a problem so severe that it might seem to warrant and require some blasts, if not of blame, at least of prophetic judgment. Our decision not to take this approach has several bases. One concerns our position as outsiders. Whatever the role of hard prophetic judgment for insiders, it would seem arrogant and presumptuous for us. If we are to have anything at all to say about sectarianism in Ireland, as we have been asked to do, it seems right to us that we should proceed from a basic stance of getting alongside, asking questions, and listening. We imagine, however, that even if we were insiders, we would be inclined to take the same approach, which seems to us what the times require. In a divided, weary society recovering from decades of conflict, the prophetic and the pastoral are both necessary, and neither should be divorced from the other. If the prophetic cannot be framed in pastorally sensitive ways, it may be blame dressed up in righteous clothing and better left unsaid; if pastoral utterances and actions have no prophetic edge, they may soothe but they are unlikely to heal.

If we must at points discuss responsibility to do our job properly, our purpose is not to act as judge and jury, it is only to raise awareness and stir to action. If instead we deliver those paralysing chunks of blame, we will have failed. Our hope is that readers will gain a new understanding of the extent and ways of the sectarian system, see ways in which they and their communities may have been implicated in sectarianism even though in all likelihood never intending or desiring it, and come away with a will and ideas to address sectarianism in all its manifestations, but especially those closest to home.

Hope and expectation
On telling people that our work from 1995-2000 was to examine sectarianism, we have come to expect that one likely response will be pity. Delving into the workings of sectarianism, week after week and year after year, would seem to be a sure formula for frustration and depression. Although at times the extent of sectarianism and the strength of its grip can bring despondency, most of the time our work felt like a privilege and it was energising, not enervating. This arises naturally from the way sectarianism works and what it means, therefore, to challenge it. Sectarianism induces a sense of powerlessness, overwhelming

people with the immensity of the problem and making them feel isolated and insignificant in the face of it. When people start to address sectarianism, however, even the first small steps, especially when taken alongside others, begin to lift that aura of powerlessness and isolation. Hope and expectation begin to take root, not immediately displacing fear, anger, and depression, but at least tempering them. While nothing can make working on sectarianism easy, our experience of working with and among such people so consistently involved a sustaining positive spirit that we came to approach sectarianism with something of the same hope and expectation. That is the spirit we mean to be undergirding this book, and we hope that readers, who are by definition addressing the problem of sectarianism, can share in it.

Focus and audience
After years of research, we are more keenly aware than ever of the magnitude of the issue of sectarianism, of how wide and deep it spreads. Consequently, we are aware also of all the things we might have studied and might have done, but did not. In fact many advised us to take a particular focus. Give an account of the working class people who have suffered most from sectarianism, some suggested. Or emphasise the crudest forms of sectarianism: bigotry, hatred, violence. Or study particular institutions or issues: education, policing, paramilitaries, and the loyal orders probably head the most-frequently-mentioned list. All of these are legitimate concerns and require serious attention, and some will feature to some extent in this book. We have needed to make choices, however, and our focus will lie elsewhere.

Our consistent emphasis will be on the role of Christians and the Christian churches in fostering, nurturing, sustaining, and allowing sectarianism, as well as their contributions, actual and potential, to moving beyond sectarianism. Along the way we will look at elements of history, where sectarianism fits in the context of conflict in Northern Ireland, what sectarianism is and is not, the variety of ways sectarianism is expressed, how sectarianism might be overcome, the nature of reconciliation. Religion will not always be explicitly to the fore, and we hope that what we have learned may be relevant in situations where religion plays little or no role. The responsibilities of Christians and their churches, however, is the thread that will run through the whole, and they are our primary audience.

Working with this constituency leaves us in the position, some fear, of preaching to the converted. After all, few of the people we have worked with are bigots in any obvious way, and few have been active stone-throwers, bomb-planters, rioters, gun-wielders, knee-cappers, marchers, or barricade-setters. So what is the point?

Applied to sectarianism in Northern Ireland, the phrase 'preaching to the converted' is not just useless, it is destructively misleading. 'Preaching to the converted' suggests two main lies about sectarianism. The first is that a clear line can be drawn between the guilty, who are responsible for sectarianism, and the converted, who are no longer subject to the problem of sectarianism. If one were to attempt to name people who might qualify as genuinely 'converted', however, based on evident changes in their lives and on their commitment to working on the problem of sectarianism, one thing they would have in common, in our experience, is the conviction that no such clear line between guilt and innocence exists. They are, in effect, recovering sectarians, who know that sectarianism is not the kind of problem one ever leaves entirely behind. Ironically, those who show most evidence of being converted would be the first to challenge the idea of labelling themselves or any group of people as 'the converted'. The second lie suggested by 'preaching to the converted' is that this is in some way a coherent group of people who share a positive way of dealing with sectarianism. Nothing could be further from the truth. Many of those imagined, by others and sometimes by themselves, to be among 'the converted' are simply moderate people who, in relation to sectarianism, share little more than the fact that they do not throw stones, and who vary in the face of sectarianism between ineffectual hand-wringing and apathy inspired by hopelessness. In Northern Ireland, those among the moderate majority, the supposedly 'converted', often feel marginalised, ineffectual, alone, and powerless, which cannot be the basis for making an effective contribution to moving beyond sectarianism. We hope that this book can help such people to develop a constructive, active consensus about how best to challenge sectarianism. Such consensus building among moderates is an essential resource for establishing a durable and meaningful peace.

We chose the general topic of sectarianism and a church-orientated approach to it partly due to straightforward research considerations. Sectarianism is widely recognised as a significant aspect to conflict in Northern Ireland, and yet very little of the voluminous literature on the Troubles has given serious attention to sectarianism. And when sectarianism is discussed, the role of religion receives little attention; remarkably little, given that the popular understanding of sectarianism associates it with a destructive mingling of religion and politics. A church-focused approach to sectarianism addresses an important gap in understanding conflict in Northern Ireland.

We chose our topic and approach for more than academic reasons, however. Institutional and personal religious commitments also played an important part. Moving Beyond Sectarianism is a project of the Irish School of Ecumenics, identified in its mission statement as 'Christian in its inspiration and ethos,' and committed to pursuing 'the unity of Christians, dialogue between religions, and work for peace and justice in Ireland and abroad'. These are commitments shared by us as project researchers. Cecelia is a member of La Retraite, a Roman Catholic religious congregation, and Joe is a long-time worker for Mennonite Board of Missions, an agency of the Mennonite Church in North America. Thus while we are obviously outsiders, as a Scot and an American, we are as Christians also insiders of a sort, and we intend our work as a service to the Christian church in Ireland.

Research methodology
When we began the Moving Beyond Sectarianism project in January 1995, we understood our work as a fairly standard academic research project. While it might involve a measure of immediately relevant, practical application, we anticipated that we would do the research and analysis first and practical application would follow. With this in mind, we committed ourselves to:

(a) gather, evaluate, and synthesise previous literature on religion and conflict in Northern Ireland;
(b) design and conduct an appropriate form of group work;
(c) conduct interviews with a wide range of people in Northern Ireland;
(d) hold two conferences;

(e) hold a series of smaller, focused consultations; and
(f) develop a social science survey to test attitude change in group work participants.

With the exception of the attitude survey, which fell through after initial explorations, these things took place more or less as planned. At the beginning of the project, we held four regional consultations to gather responses to our projected approach. Cecelia designed and implemented an innovative form of group work for mixed groups wishing to address sectarianism in a deliberate, systematic way. Joe conducted approximately fifty interviews. We organised two conferences, the first, in 1996, confined to Northern Ireland speakers and participants, and a second, in 1997, which had largely local participants, but speakers who came from international situations with some similarity to Northern Ireland. Finally, we read widely, although less comprehensively and systematically than we originally hoped.

What came to dominate MBS, however, was a kind of work not even mentioned in our original job description. Early in the project, groups started to ask if we would say something to them about sectarianism or help them think about how they could address sectarianism. While it did not fit our initial understanding of our work, we did not feel free to say to people who were willing, even eager, to tackle so crucial an issue as sectarianism, 'Give us a few years to finish the research, and we'll get back to you.' Such assignments snowballed and soon occupied more of our time than any other single element. By the end of MBS, we had led hundreds of sessions, sometimes a single session intended largely for information, more often multiple sessions for one group with some practical outcome in mind. Those we worked with included church or church-based groups such as clergy groups, local inter-church groups, and congregations and parishes, as well as regional or national bodies such as the Irish Council of Churches, the Council of Churches of Great Britain and Ireland, the Irish Inter-Church Meeting, the National Conference of Priests of Ireland, gatherings of clergy from two (mostly) Northern Ireland dioceses, Catholic religious orders, the Northern Ireland branch of the Conference of Religious in Ireland, the Friends' Ireland Yearly Meeting, and the Presbyterian Peace and Peacemaking Committee; theological and historical societies; cross-community groups; secondary school teachers; women's groups; RUC trainers and recruits;

secondary school, university, teacher-training, seminary, and international students; a probation services group; and groups of our peers involved in partner organisations working at some combination of mediation, reconciliation, community relations, and church renewal. In a large majority of cases, these were groups that had never tackled sectarianism directly or in depth.

Making a virtue of necessity, we came to regard these sessions not as a diversion from our work, but as a form of research in their own right. Every session involved some opportunity for feedback, and it was often extensive. We used these responses to shape and re-shape our understanding of sectarianism and consequently our material, gradually coming to understand what kinds of material worked best with different kinds of groups. Some of our ideas and exercises survived more or less intact through the course of MBS; some were much modified; a few that we favoured at the beginning were rarely used by the end; and some of those we came to value most were created in response to issues and ideas raised by groups.

The final form of this book reflects the dominance of our work with such groups. We might originally have anticipated that Cecelia's group work and Joe's interviews would be the most direct and obvious influence on what we wrote. In the end, however, due in part to problems of uneven and ambiguous confidentiality requirements surrounding group work and interviews, but even more to the natural course of our work, we decided that it would be best to let group work and interviews inform our work indirectly, though powerfully, rather than make frequent direct references. As a result, most of the text of this book, though much expanded in many cases, grows directly from ideas and exercises presented many times to a wide range of groups.

Non-sectarianism, anti-sectarianism,
and moving beyond sectarianism
Readers may better situate our approach to sectarianism if we compare it to two others, non-sectarianism and anti-sectarianism. The three seem to have developed in a particular historical order, and perhaps each does follow logically as a response to the previous, but today all three approaches are practised in different settings.

The first approach is non-sectarianism. Non-sectarianism

judges sectarianism to be at least a problem and probably an evil, and responds by working around it: people choose to deal with sectarianism by avoiding it, which they accomplish by carefully avoiding certain topics, above all religion and politics, in mixed settings. This has been the strategy, and often a successful strategy, of many a workplace, club, and social event in Northern Ireland. Non-sectarianism is the typical strategy of the middle class and above, and its characteristic images are work around, avoid, divert.

The weakness of the non-sectarian approach is exposed in times of crisis: having operated by means of avoidance, non-sectarianism has no positive response when a crisis makes sectarianism unavoidable. The result, if the relationship or institution in question survives at all, is deepened, more fixed division, and a greater hesitation to cross it. What has been a cordial avoidance can become wary, suspicious avoidance.

Observing this inherent limitation of non-sectarianism, anti-sectarianism takes a nearly opposite tack. Sectarianism is not to be avoided, people must name it, confront it, expose it, and they will not wait for a crisis to do so, they will address sectarianism now and vigorously. The characteristic images of anti-sectarianism are confront, fight, smash, destroy.

But anti-sectarianism has its typical failings, also. In the first instance, in the anti-sectarian approach, sectarianism is typically out there, an external problem, someone else's problem. More generally, much of what passes for anti-sectarianism is actually a mirror image of sectarianism; in fact, we could go further and say that anti-sectarianism can easily become a form of sectarianism. The process works like this. When sectarianism encounters difference, that encounter often runs in a sequence something like this:

    encounter - judge - condemn - reject - demonise - separation/antagonism.

This sequence would be one way of naming the dynamics of sectarianism. But note what can all too easily happen when liberalism encounters what it regards as sectarian. The content of the judgment is different, but the process often looks much the same:

    encounter - judge - condemn - reject - demonise - separation/antagonism.

In other words, the dynamics of supposedly rejecting sectarianism can be identical to the dynamics of sectarianism, although the person rejecting sectarianism is likely to be totally unaware of this. This is one source of what we call liberal sectarianism.

In the absence of a better name, our own approach is left with the rather cumbersome title of the moving-beyond-sectarianism approach. We share with anti-sectarianism the inclination to name and confront sectarianism, but observing that no one is entirely innocent in relation to sectarianism, and that sectarianism is generally a distortion of something good, we reject the strategy of destroying or smashing sectarianism; these risk destroying what is good along with its distortion. We opt instead for an approach characterised by strategies of transforming, redeeming, healing, and converting sectarian distortions.

If we occasionally imagine that we have identified the approach that will supersede non-sectarianism and anti-sectarianism, we know in our better moments that this is not true. First, there are the potential or probable weaknesses. Identifying these is more likely to be others' work than our work, but we can at least make a start by recognising that a strategy which reflexively seeks to transform and redeem may lack an adequate scheme for discerning what movements and institutions, though never individuals, are better bound for oblivion than for transformation. Even apart from its possible weaknesses, the moving-beyond-sectarianism approach is probably better seen as a complement to non- and anti-sectarianism rather than as a replacement. Non-sectarianism relies essentially on the merits of good manners and a basic civility, and if they are limited in what they can accomplish, they are not to be despised; sometimes just getting on with things rather than tackling them head on is entirely appropriate. As for anti-sectarianism, its forthrightness and vigour will often be necessary traits. Understood as a complement, however, the moving-beyond-sectarianism approach does offer some new insights and strategies for dealing with sectarianism. The purpose of this book is to develop them.

Generosity of judgment
If we intend this book as a service to the Christian church in Ireland, some may wonder how much of a service we are performing by consistently arguing that the churches are deeply implicated in the evils of sectarianism. Many readers, we suspect, will be angered by some part of what they read in these pages.

Speaking in 1995 at the Belfast launch of the Moving Beyond Sectarianism project, the late Eric Gallagher, a Methodist minister whose work was a life-long challenge to sectarianism, called us to 'speak the truth in love' as we learned more about sectarianism. That charge has been an ideal never far from our minds. To the extent that we have succeeded in living up to it, our readers' angry response may reflect the fact that the truth about sectarianism is sometimes hard and unfamiliar truth. But anger may also reflect a just judgment on the ways we have failed to see the truth adequately or to address our audience in a respectful and generous way. Where readers disagree with our findings, we hope they will tell us so. The Moving Beyond Sectarianism project is over. Our interest in and concern about these matters is ongoing, however, and being challenged is one of the ways we learn. But we also hope that our readers will read generously, not dismissing everything we say because we have made mistakes, but reflecting on what is of value even where we have expressed it imperfectly or mixed truth and error. In so doing they will model an essential dynamic in moving beyond sectarianism, an enterprise that will be stunted and perhaps doomed without acts of generosity from those who may have plausible reasons for withholding generosity.

CHAPTER 1

Understanding Sectarianism:
Some Ground-Clearing Exercises

It is entirely possible, we have discovered, to have a vigorous discussion about sectarianism, only to find that the people involved are talking past each other because they do not share a common understanding of what they mean by sectarianism. Disagreement will be with us always, of course, but much disagreement is based on unnecessary confusion and misunderstanding, we believe, so we are devoting this chapter to some basic ground-clearing and ground-preparing work. We begin by looking at some of the different ways that scholars understand the role of religion in conflict in Northern Ireland. Although conflict in Northern Ireland ranks as one of the world's most extensively written-about and interpreted situations, experts still put forward sharply different interpretations, not least concerning the role of religion in conflict. We then go on to explain how we are using some basic terms necessary for thinking about sectarianism: religion, politics, ethnicity and nationality, Protestant and Catholic, sectarianism, and reconciliation. In some cases we will say most of what we are going to say about the topic in this book, in others we will just introduce ideas we will discuss much more fully in later chapters. Finally, we will discuss the problem of reductionist logic, which makes it impossible to think soundly about sectarianism and the role of religion in society generally.

Religion and conflict: contradictory interpretations
In the course of an excellent overview of thinking from scholars, church leaders, and others about the role of religion in the Troubles, educator Brian Lambkin sees an 'emerging consensus on the interpretation of the conflict' which will 'give central importance to ... religion'.[1] While he amply demonstrates that a religion-based interpretation is gaining some support, any notion of a consensus seems premature. In fact the evidence points

more toward a full spectrum of opinion, ranging from those who see religion as primary to those who dismiss it utterly.

Lambkin rightly cites sociologists John Hickey, Steve Bruce, and John Fulton as leaders in stating the case for the significance of religion in the Troubles.[2] Bruce, whose work has been especially influential and contested, states baldly at the beginning of his concluding chapter in *God Save Ulster! The Religion and Politics of Paisleyism* that 'the Northern Ireland conflict is a religious conflict.'[3] Bruce immediately qualifies his statement, however, by adding that 'economic and social differences are also crucial', and it is in this modified form that his work is most likely to have ongoing influence. This is compatible, for example, with John Whyte's conclusion, in his masterly *Interpreting Northern Ireland*, a comprehensive and wise overview of the literature on and interpretations of conflict in Northern Ireland up to 1990. Whyte wrote: 'The sharpness of the divide varies from one place to another. The mix of religious, economic, political, and psychological factors which underpins it varies from one place to another.'[4] In 1993 the Opsahl Commission, a well-balanced group of local people and outsiders representing enormous experience and expertise, published conclusions of their long and intense 'citizens' inquiry' throughout Northern Ireland. Concerning religion they wrote, 'religion may or may not be the prime cause of the conflict', but 'it is certainly a potent component of it. ... It simply comes to this: the Northern Ireland conflict is in part economic and social, in part political and constitutional, and also in part religious, and damagingly so.'[5] Séamus Dunn, director of the Centre for the Study of Conflict at the University of Ulster, Coleraine, takes such logic one step further, arguing that conflict in Northern Ireland is not so much a single, multi-faceted problem 'as a set of interlocked and confused problems. ... So the sort of arcane debates that try to establish, for example, whether it is a religious problem, or an economic problem, or a social problem, or a political problem are thought to be pointless, since it is all of these, and others as well.'[6] In a fine study of sectarianism in Ireland, sociologist Robbie McVeigh takes a similarly integrating approach to the problem of sectarian identity. '[T]here is no essence of "Protestantness" or "Catholicness",' he writes. 'Rather, in Ireland at least, what makes a Protestant a Protestant and a Catholic a Catholic is the interaction of a number of factors: historical, religious, social, cultural, and political.'[7]

By no means, however, are all analysts of conflict in Northern Ireland prepared to grant that religion is a factor of even partial significance, let alone primary. For example, Lambkin correctly cites John Darby, a political scientist and for over two decades an influential interpreter of Northern Ireland, as making a place for religion in his interpretative framework. In a chapter of Séamus Dunn's book, *Facets of the Conflict in Northern Ireland,* Darby recognises 'a problem of religious difference' as one of six in a 'tangle of interrelated problems'. '[N]one can claim dominance. Each affects the others. Any approach to change needs to take into account all elements of the problem.'[8] For the most part, however, religion has not had much part in Darby's analysis. In a recent overview of the conflict, although he continues to view conflict in Northern Ireland as 'a multi-larered problem',[9] religion figures little, and he mentions the 'popular view that the conflict is essentially religious' only to dismiss it in a single phrase as 'a view shared by only a small number of academic commentators, notably Bruce'[10] – the scholar who, Lambkin has hoped, might be providing the basis for a new interpretative consensus. But perhaps no other current commentator is so witheringly and systematically dismissive of religion as the prolific team of political scientists, John McGarry and Brendan O'Leary, whose 1995 work, *Explaining Northern Ireland: Broken Images,* is the most comprehensive overview of interpretations since John Whyte. While we will argue that in crucial ways their chapter on religious interpretations, 'Warring Gods? Theological Tales', is not well reasoned, it does represent wide reading. At the end of their forty-three page critique they conclude, 'Explanations which emphasise the primacy of religion … need to be exposed to strong light. When that happens, they evaporate, leaving little residue.'[11] Given such wildly contradictory claims about the role of religion, consensus appears a long way off.

While we will not resolve these interpretative conflicts about the role of religion, we do hope at least to move the debate forward toward greater clarity. In our view, however, greater clarity paradoxically means accepting and working with some blurring, even confusion. Interpreters may be able to lay out some matters decisively – perhaps the issues and choices that people face and the dynamics of conflict and peace. But categories like religion, politics, economics, and psychology are arbitrary divisions of human experience, so being clear about them means recognising the way they blend into one another. For understanding sectarianism, accepting a degree of blurring is a necessary part of an appropriate clarity.[12]

Definitions

Religion: Some discussions of the role of religion in conflict operate on the assumption that religion can be equated with religious doctrine. The equation is a problem in two ways: it is always too simple, and it is likely to be based on a misunderstanding of doctrine.

The first problem with equating religion and doctrine is that religion involves much more. In this book, for example, we will also take seriously religion as shaper of individual and communal worldview, religion as church institutions, religion as a community-building dynamic and as communities, religion as social institution and agent of socialisation, religion as a source of moral formation. Conversely, we will also consider ways in which political ideology and commitments sometimes parallel and mimic religion, effectively becoming religious in nature. Making sense of the role of religion in conflict must begin with an expansive understanding of religion that can take into account its varied functions and meanings.

The equation of religion and doctrine can be further misleading when it is based on a too narrow understanding of doctrine. Specifically, too many people assume a definition of doctrine as intellectual propositions about religion or faith to which the believer gives rational assent. That is one kind or function of doctrine, but doctrine can have broader and more dynamic meanings as well. In 1984 the theologian George Lindbeck, for example, sparked a fruitful debate, still ongoing, about the meaning of religious doctrine through his short book, *The Nature of Doctrine: Religion and Theology in a Postliberal Age.* Working with a far-reaching understanding of religion as 'a kind of cultural and/or linguistic framework or medium that shapes the entirety of life and thought', Lindbeck then assigns doctrine the role of grammar in this framework: doctrine functions as 'communally authoritative rules of discourse, attitude, and action'.[13] Such an understanding of religious doctrine includes intellectual propositions, but goes far beyond.

Politics: Politics too can have a variety of meanings. Broadly speaking, politics can be understood as the organisation and conduct of public life. This definition takes in the most common meaning of politics, as governmental institutions and the various groupings and activities built up around them. But it also includes a wider understanding of politics, one that recognises the political role and impact of other groups and institutions in society that are not ordinarily thought of as directly political. Politics can also mean the ways different groups in society handle power relations, internally or between themselves. Some of the issues we discuss will involve politics in this latter sense, even though we will not necessarily use the word.

Politics and religion: Broad definitions of religion and politics make it clear that religion and politics are not discrete spheres, they intersect. Religion, for its part, is likely to have a vision for what constitutes a good society and a healthy public life, while every state will have an understanding of the proper role of religion, especially religious institutions. In a smoothly functioning western society, the intersection of religion and politics may often be invisible. In Ireland, however, North and South, the intersection is frequently apparent, often when a church or religious grouping has taken a contentious public stance. Understanding that politics and religion are overlapping spheres is essential for understanding sectarianism, because sectarianism, as we will develop in chapter three, typically involves a negative mixing of religion and politics.

Ethnicity and nationality: Of the many ways that groups of people organise themselves into communities, ethnicity and nationality are two of the most common.[14] They are also closely related and overlapping concepts. Ethnicity indicates shared culture – often including religion – as well as shared language and communal memory. Nationality adds to these some combination of a territorial sense or claim, a shared political goal, or a shared state. In Northern Ireland, the religious communities demarcated as Protestant and Catholic cannot be easily or neatly distinguished from ethnicity and nationality. In terms of ethnicity, a long and sometimes turbulent process beginning in the seventeenth century eventually saw Gaelic Irish and Old English ethnic identities subsumed into an overarching Catholic identity, while in the nineteenth century, a variety of religious groups, comprising people of Scottish and English ethnic origin, gathered together under the heading of Protestant. In the process, the terms Protestant and Catholic have come to indicate ethnic as well as religious identity. For many people, these terms indicate both ethnic and religious allegiance; for a growing number, they are solely or predominantly ethnic labels; for a few, they are solely religious and unrelated to ethnicity.

National identity also falls along Protestant/Catholic lines. In fact shared political goals were a key factor that assisted in subsuming ethnic identities into Protestant and Catholic identities. Catholic political goals have varied over the centuries, but they have always involved either a degree of independence from England or Britain, or they have been in opposition to Protestant political goals, or both. In Northern Ireland today, many Catholics favour an all-Ireland republic, while a similar number favour, and virtually all Catholics will settle for the kind of arrangement, crucially featuring power-sharing and cross-border bodies, laid out in the 1998 Good Friday Agreement. Protestants have consistently and often overwhelmingly – though not always or unanimously – favoured a close political arrangement with England or Britain. This remains true today, although many, perhaps a majority, accept the Good Friday Agreement as an adequate expression of such a relationship, while the remainder oppose the Agreement for reasons that include fearing that it will dilute the British connection and lead ultimately to a united Ireland. A small number of Catholics are unionist in their politics, while an even smaller number of Protestants are nationalists. It is worth noting that since 1998 majority cross-community support for the Good Friday Agreement, however slim at times, may well be the first time so many Irish Catholics and Protestants have agreed on common political arrangements.

Throughout the world, religion and ethnicity are often closely aligned. At least for Christianity and Judaism, this close relationship of religion and ethnicity is complex. In different ways for the two religions, the religious-ethnic bond is part of their nature, and yet a problem, also. Judaism is the more strongly and obviously ethnic in nature, beginning not with a teacher, teachings, or a particular moral code, but with God's promise to make Abraham and Sarah's descendants a great 'nation', a biblical term probably better understood as 'people' or 'ethnic group', given the modern tendency to associate nation and state. This ethnic base has remained through the millennia. In fact, according to Marc Gopin, Orthodox Jewish rabbi and conflict resolution scholar, 'There has been a discouragement of conversion to Judaism since the beginning of rabbinic Judaism almost two thousand years ago.'[15] The relatively small number of people from outside the Jewish community who have chosen to become Jews were and are proselytes, in the strict and neutral sense of the term, meaning that they integrate into all the religious and ethnic ways of Jewish faith and culture, rather than adapting some core religious vision to their own culture. And yet this Jewish nation does not exist solely for itself. Old Testament scholar Walter Brueggeman finds three key Old Testament traditions in which 'Israel's obligation to Yahweh reaches well beyond justice in the community and holiness in the sanctuary. Indeed, *Israel is said to have as part of its vocation and destiny a role in the well-being of the world.*'[16] [Brueggeman's emphasis] Already in God's original call to Abram, God says, 'In you all the families of the earth shall be blessed.' (Gen 12:3) At another critical juncture in Israel's history, as Moses approaches God on Mount Sinai after the Israelites have been delivered from Egyptian captivity, God says to Israel through Moses, 'Indeed, the whole earth is mine, but you shall be for me a priestly kingdom and a holy nation.' (Ex 19:5-6) And in the prophetic vision of Isaiah, Israel's destiny and call is to serve beyond its own boundaries. God says to Israel, 'It is too light a thing that you should be my servant to raise up the tribes of Jacob and to restore the survivors of Israel; I will give you as a light to the nations, that my salvation may reach to the end of the earth.' (Is 49:6) According to Gopin, Judaism struggles to this day with the tension between the call to be a separate people, consecrated to God, and the call to be deeply involved in the world, 'teaching the world "the path of God"'.[17]

In Christianity, the religious-ethnic tension takes a different balance. A community-building dynamic is present from the beginning, as Jesus does not simply travel from town to town preaching to whoever will hear him, he gathers and builds a community of disciples to carry on his work. In fact, one of those disciples, Peter, appropriates the old Jewish language of chosenness and nationhood as the ideal for the new Christian reality: 'But you are a chosen race, a royal priesthood, a holy nation,

God's own people, in order that you may proclaim the mighty acts of him who called you out of darkness into his marvellous light. Once you were not a people, but now you are God's people.' (1 Pet 2:9-10) And yet the break with Jewish ethnicity is one of the defining moments in the emergence of the new Christian movement. The move was marked by Peter's vision from God concerning the Jewish purity code, from which Peter drew the conclusion that 'God has shown me that I should not call anyone profane or unclean', (Acts 10:28) and by Peter's subsequent visit with Cornelius, a Roman centurion and a spiritual seeker, which led Peter to declare: 'I truly understand that God shows no partiality, but in every nation anyone who fears him and does what is right is acceptable to him.' (Acts 10:34-35) At the same time, Christianity does not abolish ethnicity or replace Jewish ethnicity with a new Christian ethnicity. In the words of the Croatian theologian Miroslav Volf, 'Christians are not some cosmopolitan third race, equally distant from their own culture and every other. The proper distance from a culture *does not take Christians out of that culture.*'[18] [Volf's emphasis] John's apocalyptic vision from Jesus makes a similar point. Near the end of the book of Revelation – in which the 'nations', translated from the Greek *ethnos,* have been shown to be capable of the most horrific actions – John sees that the nations will ultimately be redeemed. John is shown a 'new Jerusalem', set in 'a new heaven and a new earth'. (Rev 21:1-2) Those who have entered the holy city have come not merely as individuals, but also as 'nations'. 'People will bring into it [the new Jerusalem] the glory and the honour of the nations', (Rev 21:26) John reports. There they will find 'the tree of life ... and the leaves of the tree are for the healing of the nations.' (Rev 22:2) Ever since these early days, the Christian notion of conversion, in which the gospel seed is planted in new cultures to take new forms, has been one of Christianity's key distinguishing features.[19]

The Christian ideal might be stated as embracing particular ethnicities, while subordinating them to a higher and shared loyalty. The balance is wonderfully captured in the day of Pentecost, when the presence of the Holy Spirit among the believers of the earliest church, drawn from many nations and speaking many languages, miraculously enabled them to communicate with one another. This was not achieved through a single tongue, however. Instead, they 'began to speak in other languages, as the Spirit gave them ability', (Acts 2:4) and each person understood the others in his or her own language. "Are not all these who are speaking Galileans? And how is it that we hear, each of us, in our own native language?"' (Acts 2:7) Thus Christians are bound together in a new community, and yet the ethnic particularity of each is embraced.[20]

The ideal is beautiful and powerful, but also hard to live out faithfully. Sometimes Christians, stressing unity, have failed to recognise and respect ethnicities sufficiently. Sometimes they have elevated particular ethnicities at the expense of recognising the shared Christian bonds that subordinate every ethnicity. And sometimes the two dynamics feed each other in destructive ways: the elevation of one ethnicity to some special role in God's plan involves the suppression of others; a failure, especially by dominant elites, to respect ethnicity leads to an exaggerated, perhaps even violent, assertion of ethnicity.

Protestant and Catholic: Given our emphasis on religious issues, we will most often use the terms Protestant and Catholic to refer to the parties on different sides of Northern Ireland's fundamental divide, while sometimes using unionist and nationalist when the context is primarily political. The use of 'two traditions' language and logic is sometimes criticised for oversimplifying or ignoring the actual complexity of interests and identities in Northern Ireland. Two examples of particular force and clarity are Simon Lee's contribution to the Opsahl Commission and *Them and Us? Attitudinal Variations Among Churchgoers in Belfast,* by Fred Boal, Margaret Keane, and David Livingstone. For all their sophisticated and telling criticisms, however, these scholars notably fail to provide an alternative language to the two traditions language they criticise.[21] We are left thinking that a chastened 'two traditions' logic remains a necessary tool for thinking about Northern Ireland. Crucial categories of gender, class, region, and age cut across the Protestant/Catholic divide, and each religious grouping is divided within itself. This is particularly true of Protestantism, with its many denominations, and these internal tensions will figure in our analysis at several points. When every qualification and complication is recognised, however, they do not dissolve the Protestant/Catholic division, which in many ways remains the big one, though it is neither the only division nor absolute.

Contrary to still common usage in Northern Ireland, Catholicism and Protestantism are not different religions. Hinduism and Islam are different religions, Christianity and Judaism are different religions, but Catholicism is a church or denomination and Protestantism a grouping of churches or denominations within one religion, Christianity. Parallels might be the relationship of Theravada and Mahayana Buddhism and Shia and Sunni forms of Islam. In some ways, referring to Protestants and Catholics as different religions is understandable – such has been the division and animosity between them that they have seemed to think of themselves as separate religions. Moving beyond sectarianism must mean dealing as honestly and precisely as possible with difference, however, neither exaggerating difference, as sectarianism typically does, nor minimising difference, which can be a natural but generally unhelpful reaction. Thinking of Protestantism and Catholicism as different religions overstates their difference, while referring to them as a grouping of churches and a church respectively gets the difference about right.

If Catholicism and Protestantism are not different religions, still less are they 'opposite religions', a phrase sometimes used in Northern Ireland.[22] Although those who use the phrase rarely intend to be sectarian, the notion of opposite religions is a striking and chilling sign of a culture's customary mindset becoming infested by sectarianism, which typically seeks to magnify difference as far as possible. 'Opposite' is not an especially helpful idea for understanding any aspect of human life, least of all religion. People can be astonishingly different, but they cannot be opposite – they will always share fundamental qualities. Protestantism and Catholicism, in their most contradictory and antagonistic extremes, still share a great deal.

Sectarianism: We will be defining and describing sectarianism at considerable length in a later chapter. If pressed, however, we would be willing to stand over this short definition: sectarianism is a complex of problems – including dividing, demonising, and dominating – which typically arise from malignant intersections of religion and politics and which are characteristic of the kind of religiously-shaped ethno-national conflict experienced in Northern Ireland. While 'sectarian' and 'sectarianism' are used in analysis of other conflict situations, usually ones that involve both politics and religion, we are applying our definition, here and in chapter three, to Ireland alone. It may be useful in other situations, but we have developed it solely with reference to Ireland. Of the many implications that follow from such a definition, we will name just three here. We will also discuss the origin of the Irish usage of the terms 'sectarian' and 'sectarianism', as well as one common approach to sectarianism that we believe is misguided.

'Sectarianism' and 'sectarian' always refer to something bad, a problem
This reflects ordinary usage of the term in Northern Ireland, but some kinds of usage, especially of 'sectarian', are ambiguous, so that 'sectarian' might be understood as either neutral or bad. One might read references, for example, to 'sectarian division'. The writer might be referring merely to religious division, a neutral statement with no judgment implied; or she might mean that this particular religious division is bad, and thus the term sectarian is used as a negative judgment; or she might mean that all religious division is bad and hence sectarian. We do not believe that all religious division is inherently problematic, so in our usage, 'sectarian division' will mean only division that is in some way a problem, while we would use 'religious division' as a descriptive term implying no particular judgment.

We have also heard some people distinguish between good sectarianism and bad sectarianism. They are operating on the basis that 'sectarianism' should be regarded as a neutral term indicating a strong group identity, so that 'good sectarianism' describes a situation in which such identities are working in a healthy way, and 'bad sectarianism' describes destructive applications or elements of group identity. We fully accept the reasoning behind such usage – that strong group identities, and even conflict between them, are by no means necessarily problematic – but we find the good sectarianism/bad sectarianism distinction needlessly paradoxical. In our judgment, 'sectarian' and 'sectarianism' are clearer and more useful terms when used as negative terms, and this will be our practice.

Sectarianism always involves religion
Religion is the factor that makes an attitude, an action, a belief, or a structure specifically sectarian – as opposed to being simply generally bad or destructive. Thus an act of discrimination

against a Chinese person and an act of discrimination against a Catholic might be identical in general structure and in the consequence for the individual discriminated against, but the first would be called racial or ethnic discrimination, the second sectarian discrimination. The role of religion may be direct and immediate or diffuse and distant, but it must be present if something is to be described as sectarian. Sectarian violence, for example, might be committed by people of little or no religious conviction against people of little or no religious conviction. But it would still be called sectarian violence if perpetrators and victims both came from communities demarcated and defined in part by religion, i.e. Catholic and Protestant communities. Clear thinking about sectarianism depends on holding together two ideas: while the role of religion makes sectarianism distinct from other destructive patterns of relating, it is also true that sectarianism is similar to other destructive patterns of relating in significant ways.

Good religion, bad sectarianism?

In one of the best studies on religion and conflict in Ireland, the sociologist John Fulton criticises Irish Christians and churches for distinguishing between 'good religion and bad sectarianism' for the sake of 'saving religion from disrepute'.[23] 'There is therefore little theory of bad religion', he says, 'except of that religion which other churches and religions might possess.'[24] Not all religion is sectarian, and not all sectarianism can be attributed solely to religion. On the whole, however, we agree with Fulton: the distinction between good religion and bad sectarianism is spurious. Much of sectarianism can be thought of as bad religion, religion gone wrong, as we will seek to demonstrate in this book. If Irish Christians wish to save religion from disrepute, the way to do it is not to deny the relationship between sectarianism and religion, but to recognise the link and to change accordingly.

The roots of Irish usage of 'sectarian' and 'sectarianism'

A central feature of the sociology of religion, originating in the work of Max Weber in the early 1900s, is a distinction between church and sect.[25] At its most basic, the difference between church and sect can be seen in terms of membership: one is born into a church, while one chooses to join a sect as an adult. Thus in Ireland, 'churches', according to the sociology of religion, would include Catholicism, the Church of Ireland, and Presbyterianism, while 'sects' would include groups such as Baptists, the Brethren, and Pentecostals. Methodists represent another classic application of church-sect typology: originating in the eighteenth century as a sect, they became, in time, a church. Since Weber's work, scholars have developed many variations on the church-sect theme. Although this scheme has been challenged in part and in whole by some sociologists and theologians,[26] any introduction to the sociology of religion is likely to include a discussion of church-sect typology.[27]

We mention church-sect typology only to dismiss it as irrelevant to Irish usage of 'sectarian' and 'sectarianism'. To apply church and sect categories directly would be to blame sectarianism on Ireland's relatively sect-like groups – Pentecostals, Baptists, Free Presbyterians, Brethren, and others. These no doubt make their contribution to sectarianism, and it can be a particularly blatant and flamboyant contribution at times, but it would be difficult to argue that their contribution is much out of proportion to their numbers, which are very small. In fact sectarianism is as much a problem of what are classically churches – Presbyterian, Catholic, and Church of Ireland – as of these 'sects'. This is most obvious when one looks at the Reformation and counter-Reformation roots of Irish sectarianism, but it remains true today, although in more subtle ways. One could perhaps make use of church-sect typology by arguing that Ireland is a place where churches act like sects, i.e. they contribute to sectarianism by exhibiting some of the negative characteristics usually attributed to sects, especially defensiveness and a dualistic, oppositional outlook. While this approach might be satisfying to the ironically inclined, this is to use the typology by standing it on its head, and probably does more to challenge the validity of church-sect typology than to illuminate sectarianism. The apparent relevance of church-sect analysis proves to be little more than a linguistic accident.

Searching for a useful definition of 'sectarian' and 'sectarianism', we have found none that does much to illuminate characteristic Irish usage. The *Oxford English Dictionary* definition of sectarianism is as good as any: 'The sectarian spirit; adherence or excessive attachment to a particular sect or party, esp. in religion; hence often, adherence or excessive attachment to, or undue favouring of, a particular "denomination".'[28] Although 'excessive attachment' points in the right direction, it is too pallid a phrase to convey the hard, even explosive implications the word can have in Ireland. While we know of no effort to trace the history of Irish usage of 'sectarian' and 'sectarianism', the *Oxford English Dictionary* examples of early usage of 'sectarian' are suggestive. The first known use of the word 'sectarian' was during the mid-seventeenth-century English civil war, a context in which politics and religion could not have been more closely aligned. Thus 'sectarian' was a term of abuse applied by one party to its politico-religious enemies, first by Presbyterians to Independents, later by Anglicans to Nonconformists.[29] This would be a plausible root of much Irish usage.

Sectarianism is not solely or primarily a state problem
Because this book focuses primarily on the responsibilities of Christians and their churches in relation to sectarianism, state responsibilities are addressed only occasionally and in passing. We recognise, however, that the state has been deeply implicated in establishing and nurturing sectarianism and that moving beyond sectarianism involves political and legal actions that only the state can accomplish.

One fairly common line of reasoning, however, most often found among nationalists, in our experience, contends that the state is not merely one contributor to sectarianism, the state is solely or primarily responsible for sectarianism. The argument, distilled from many conversations, seems to run something like this. Sectarianism, in its many and varied expressions, has its roots in the artificial creation by the British government of the artificial Northern Ireland state. Get the state and its laws right, therefore, and sectarianism will disappear. From this perspective, community relations work – work on sectarianism between communities and within – appears either harmless but largely irrelevant, or else politely, insidiously dangerous, because it obscures the state's primary responsibility for dealing with sectarianism.

In our judgment, this kind of reasoning is both bad history and bad current affairs. Concerning history, the creation of the Northern Ireland state was a landmark in the development of sectarianism, giving it a particular shape and institutional expression and generating particular results. In terms of the basic

impulses of sectarianism, however, the Northern Ireland state
created nothing. One of the more obvious ways of demonstrating this is to examine the Home Rule issue from 1886 onward, in
which the basic sectarian dynamics and issues, a tangle of political,
economic, and religious factors, are already present and active.
The creation of Northern Ireland is itself one consequence of
those sectarian dynamics, not the source of them.

Concerning current affairs, pinning responsibility for sectarianism solely or primarily on the state involves overlooking and
denying obvious areas of communal responsibility. The sociologist Robbie McVeigh, for example, argues that anti-sectarian
work in Northern Ireland has been fundamentally flawed because it has been sponsored and funded by the state. 'But the
same state is also the key sectarian actor – it controls the sectarian
security policy, it segregates housing on a sectarian basis, it
builds and polices "peacelines", it supports an education system
which is sectarian and so on.'[30]

McVeigh is certainly right to call attention to the potential
contradictions arising when the state – which is part of the sectarian problem, not above it – controls the flow of much of the
money that goes into anti-sectarian and community relations
work. To make the state 'the key sectarian actor' is to go much
too far, however. To demonstrate this we need go no further
than McVeigh's four examples of state culpability, three of
which actually show the flaw in his argument rather than support it. He is on solid ground with his first example, security
policy. The state is responsible for security policy and therefore
must take primary responsibility for the ways in which it is sectarian. But housing is segregated in Northern Ireland because the
threat of violence has made people feel more secure when living
in their own communities, not because of state policy. State efforts to integrate public housing on a voluntary basis have failed
because undersubscribed by the public, and any state attempt to
dictate integration as a matter of policy would surely be flatly
refused. As for peacelines dividing Protestant and Catholic communities, many have been built at the request of embattled communities, not imposed by the state on unwilling citizens. Some
government initiatives to remove peacelines since the paramilitary ceasefires of 1994 have been resisted by the people immediately affected, because they believed that the danger was still too
great to warrant the dismantling of peacelines. As for education,

the existence of Catholic schools, state schools largely used by Protestants, and integrated schools, reflects the desires of different groups in Northern Ireland. In 1923 the new Minister of Education, Lord Londonderry, proposed an education act stipulating no religious instruction in school hours, guaranteeing that religion played no part in hiring teachers, and mixing Catholic and Protestant children. 'With a rare ecumenical spirit,' writes John Darby, 'all the churches opposed the act.'[31] We have no reason to believe that the church leaders who resisted the government's proposal did so without the approval of the vast majority of their church members. Catholics opted out, Protestants rendered the act unworkable by 1925, and in 1930 a new education act, more in accordance with what the churches wanted, i.e. guaranteeing segregation, was implemented. While the state is indeed a key sectarian actor, McVeigh's own evidence demonstrates that the public is also a key sectarian actor.

People concerned to address sectarianism in Northern Ireland may legitimately approach it from many angles. McVeigh and others who stress the responsibility of the state do others a service – as we do a service, we like to believe, by focusing on the responsibilities of Christians and their churches. But what is required of everyone tackling sectarianism is that they recognise the complexity and sweep of the problem. Approaches that make the state solely or primarily responsible for sectarianism, denying or minimising the responsibility of Northern Ireland's divided communities, oversimplify sectarianism and make it difficult, even impossible, to address the full extent of the problem of sectarianism.

Reconciliation: Reconciliation, although it will not be constantly in the foreground, is the cornerstone of our understanding of the main goal and dynamics of moving beyond sectarianism. The concept of reconciliation is criticised from at least two main angles: some politically-orientated critics see reconciliation as a weak-minded, establishmentarian alternative to the real task of justice and structural change, while its conservative religious critics condemn reconciliation as a matter of crying peace where there is no peace. Although both viewpoints are often overstated, they are also at least partially just, and we hope that the conception of reconciliation on which we base our work and which we occasionally articulate will meet their criticisms. To meet the

political critique, we work from an understanding of reconciliation as necessarily built on the interlocking dynamics of forgiveness, repentance, truth, and justice, understood in part as religiously-rooted virtues, but also as basic dynamics (even when
unnamed or unrecognised) of human interaction, including
public life and therefore politics. In response to conservative religious critics, we adopt an understanding of reconciliation as
for all Christians a desirable goal, which will not necessarily
diminish difference but will always allow difference to live in
harmony and mutual respect and may lead to unity. We also
recognise, however, that not all differences can be reconciled, so
we have worked at developing ways of dealing with difference,
short of reconciliation, that at least avoid sectarian antagonism
and may allow honest, respectful relationships.

Reductionism: Anyone seeking to understand the nature and dynamics of conflict in Northern Ireland must beware of four common forms of reductionism likely to distort understanding of
how religion connects with other factors. In discussing these
varieties of reductionism, we will give examples from books or
articles on Northern Ireland. We must stress that in each case we
have chosen extracts not because they come from bad sources,
but precisely because they are from good sources with much to
offer. That our examples come from valuable writings emphas-
ises just how widespread are distorting, reductionist assumptions about the role of religion. We need also to say that even
though we are working with written examples from academic
texts, reductionism is a problem for more than academics alone.
These four types of reductionism find their way into ordinary
conversation about conflict in Northern Ireland, and the effect is
just as distorting there as in academic circles.

Either/Or: the reductionism of false choices

The first and probably the most common form of reductionism
is to impose a false either/or choice between religion and other
factors. Too much analysis of conflict in Northern Ireland,
whether in a pub conversation or a scholarly journal, poses
some form of the question, are the Troubles really religious, or
are they political (or colonial, ethnic, economic, national, or
whatever else might be the analyst's preferred explanation)?
The answer is usually, no, the Troubles are not really religious,

religion is merely a mask, a marker, a flag of convenience waving distractingly over the real causes.

The answer could hardly be adequate, however, because the question is fundamentally flawed. As generally presented, the question imposes a crude and unnecessary choice, thereby obscuring the much more subtle and fruitful – and difficult – task of understanding how these factors relate to each other and how the relationship has shifted over time and in different situations. Of course weighing the relative significance of religion and other categories might be a valid task. All too often, however, what purports to be assessing significance – religion is contrasted to that which is 'primary', 'fundamental', or 'essential' – is actually a premature, simplistic, and ill-informed choice. If relative significance is to be assigned, that step must come at the end of a process in which all the relevant factors have been given the most careful attention.

One example of this either/or reductionism is Michael MacDonald's *Children of Wrath: Political Violence in Northern Ireland*. MacDonald is a political scientist interested in analysing Northern Ireland as a colonial problem. Before turning entirely to that theme, he devotes ten pages to considering the role of religion in conflict in the north of Ireland, past and present. Although his analysis is exceptionally insightful in parts, his intermittent and eventually conclusive use of either/or logic finally renders his treatment of religion confused and unsatisfactory.

Early on MacDonald writes:

Religion obviously plays a paramount role in fostering and sustaining Northern Ireland's conflict, but if the importance of religion is beyond dispute, the same cannot be said of its meaning. ... [S]omething more than religious affiliation forges the communities opposing each other in Northern Ireland. What is this 'more' and why does it result in endemic conflict?[32]

This sounds promising – MacDonald recognises the significance of religion along with other factors. He continues in a similar vein.

[R]eligion might express as well as foster Northern Ireland's divisions. ... [I]t is clear that religion has developed its meaning in a context that associated it with deeply secular interests and identities. The two 'religious' communities are separated by political, socio-economic, and cultural as well as religious differences.[33]

In the language of 'as well as' lies the possibility of a both/and approach that will illuminate connections between the whole range of named factors. But that possibility is denied already on the same page, as MacDonald makes his choice as to what is really significant.

> What counts is, in a word, colonialism: Protestants were colonisers, while Catholics were colonised. The conflict that appears as simply religious is at heart colonial, with the colonial actors donning religious attire to contest an order that systematically favours one and subordinates the other.[34]

So despite his earlier talk about the 'paramount role' of religion along with other factors, MacDonald has now decided that only colonialism counts. Religion is mere appearance and masking.

Having earlier recognised the significance of religion, however, MacDonald cannot extricate himself so easily. For several pages he shifts back and forth between either/or logic and both/and logic. In the passage following the previous quotation, he returns immediately, thoughtfully, and at some length to both/and logic, finally concluding that

> [t]he point ... is not that religion has no importance other than distinguishing settlers from natives – it does – but that because each community shares more than religion, each is more than a religious community. ... They are colonial as well as religious.[35]

But already in the next passage, he reverts to what amounts to either/or logic, with the effect of diminishing the significance of religion.

> [T]he actors, stakes, and logics [sic] of the conflict in Northern Ireland are shaped by the legacy of colonialism. The actors are Protestant 'settlers' versus Catholic 'natives'; the stakes involve power and privilege and not merely religion. ... Religion serves, therefore, to reproduce the original and dominant conflict between the native and settler populations.[36]

The key phrase is: 'the stakes involve power and privilege *and not merely* religion.' [our emphasis] Had he here retained the language of 'as well as', we would remain on course to understanding how religion relates to power and privilege, but once religion is reduced to 'merely religion', it is unlikely to be taken seriously.

The following section has MacDonald adjudicating between the dismissive approach to religion typical of what he calls the 'socialist interpretation' and the strongly religious interpretation of the political scientist Richard Rose. MacDonald resolves the conflict with his clearest articulation of both/and logic.

The problem, of course, is that Northern Ireland's divisions are neither only religious nor only national; they are both. Religion and nationality do not exist as two independent variables that sometimes correlate, but rather as two halves of one identity welded together by history.[37]

One would expect that an author who has recognised religion as playing a 'paramount role' in conflict and as inseparably 'welded together' with nationality, would have set himself the task of teasing out the relationship of religion, nationality, and colonialism. Instead religion fades away over the next few pages, disappearing from the book as a vital factor and reappearing only rarely and in the severely reductionist form on which MacDonald has finally settled.

MacDonald's dismissing of religion mars his analysis of colonialism. Because either/or logic finally prevails, he misses some of the interesting questions a both/and approach might have inspired. He does not ask, for example, how did the role of religion differ between various efforts at plantation? He does not bother placing seventeenth-century colonialism in the context of the wars of religion and European geopolitics; he is interested in comparing seventeenth- and eighteenth-century Irish penal laws to twentieth-century South African apartheid[38] but not to a similar mix of religious, economic, and political penal laws in seventeenth- and eighteenth-century France. He does not look at the anti-Catholicism so fundamental to the outlook of settlers, nor does he test the significance of Counter-reformation progress among Ulster Catholics. Apart from a single sentence,[39] he does not consider, as some scholars have, the role of religious difference and conflict in perpetuating the plantation settlement, especially by way of inhibiting the intermarriage that might have undermined ethnic distinctions.[40] Having opted for an either/or choice between religion and colonialism, MacDonald was never likely to entertain such questions about intersections and combinations.

While the distorting effects of reductionism always involve some form of falsely imposed either/or logic, some variations on the reductionism theme are common or distinctive enough to merit separate attention. We turn now to three such varieties of reductionism: reducing religion to doctrine, dismissing religion as a mere boundary marker, and the pursuit of the fundamental.

Reducing religion to doctrine
The second form of reductionism, reducing religion to doctrine, originates in the common but false assumption that religion and politics are entirely discrete spheres of human life. In fact religion and politics are intersecting spheres. For most purposes this might be a merely pedantic point, because this is a more subtle form of reductionism and not necessarily distorting. Scholars and their readers have workable ideas about what they mean by religion and politics, and any confusion is usually made clear by usage and context. But greater precision is required for the study of sectarianism, which is all about understanding how politics and religion intersect and to what effect.

While the intersection of religion and politics can be defined in several ways, two simple but fundamental examples will serve to illustrate the point. In its broadest sense, politics can be defined as the organisation of public life, and this formulation suggests the first intersection: religion also has a vision for the organisation and conduct of public life, as any observer of Irish history or current affairs can testify. Although the visions may be diverse and even contradictory, every church will cultivate a vision for the conduct of public life (more likely several visions), at least implicitly. The intersection of politics and religion is most visible when political and religious models for public life are in conflict, but it is always there.

The second intersection is that both religion and politics make claims on loyalty, even ultimate loyalty, and these claims are sometimes in conflict. In Irish history, the loyalty issue has been a problem for those outside the establishment – for dissenting Protestants, but especially for Catholics. The loyalty theme has been a near constant for post-Reformation Catholics, as they sometimes put the claims of religion over the claims of the state and sometimes sought a way to be religiously loyal to their church and politically loyal to the state, always in the face of Protestant conviction that Catholics were inherently disloyal. As with so many themes in the history of sectarianism, the contemporary echoes of the loyalty issue in Northern Ireland are deafening.

While fundamental intersections between politics and religion have been more persistently and recently troubling in Ireland than elsewhere in the western world, it is important to remember that these intersections are not accidents of Irish history; they are inherent to both modern states and Christian churches. The first of the ten commandments to the children of Israel – 'I am the Lord your God, who brought you out of the land of Egypt, out of the house of slavery; you shall have no other gods before me' (Ex 20:2-3) – established a principle of primary loyalty. It would give the Hebrew people and the faiths that emerged from them a qualified and potentially problematic relationship with the claims on loyalty of every state they encountered, not least modern states, with their extensive powers and claims. Many of the remaining commandments, indeed the entire Old Testament witness of both priests and prophets, established equally that God cared deeply about the organisation of public life. Because this core conviction is always likely to shape how people within Jewish and related traditions think about politics, religion and politics will never be neatly separable categories for any version of Christian faith that is true to its roots.

When people treat religion and politics as discrete spheres, they are indulging in a fiction. It is a seductive fiction because it is so widely believed and assumed. In fact a mark of a peaceful, modern, western society is an intersection of religion and politics so smooth and conflict-free that people can comfortably believe the fiction. In Ireland, however, the fiction is exposed with uncomfortable regularity, whether by the latest constitutional referendum or by a host of historical incidents. David Hempton and Myrtle Hill, in their outstanding book *Evangelical Protestantism in Ulster Society, 1740-1890,* make the point particularly well in their discussion of the first home rule crisis of 1886. They show how British Nonconformists, pressed hard by their Irish counterparts for support against home rule, looked reflexively to solve their problem by drawing 'boundaries between religion and politics'. 'The trouble with the Irish Question', say Hempton and Hill, 'was that no such boundary existed',[41] and this they amply demonstrate.

Treating politics and religion as discrete spheres becomes

reductionist and distorting when the distinction is used to reduce religion to those aspects which are outside the intersection,
which are purely or narrowly religious. By this logic, religion is
frequently equated with religious doctrine, so that when analysts of Northern Ireland announce that the conflict is not really
religious, they frequently mean that it is not a doctrinal dispute.
The equation of religion with doctrinal statements is an absurd
reduction, and when it is used to dismiss religion, it distorts
analysis.

A passage from Edward Moxon-Browne's *Nation, Class and
Creed in Northern Ireland*, an important analysis of the 1978
Northern Ireland Attitude Survey, which was supervised by
Moxon-Browne himself, illustrates the tendency to reduce religion to doctrine. He writes, 'It is easy ... to slip into the illusion
that the conflict is basically a religious one because the most
commonly used labels for the protagonists – Protestants and
Catholics – imply a doctrinal dispute.'[42] In fact the terms
Protestant and Catholic imply this only if one comes to the problem with a narrow understanding of religion that reduces it to
doctrine; if one has a broader understanding, in which doctrine
is just one element of religion, no such implication follows. Even
where Moxon-Browne concedes the significance of religion, the
wording of his concession indicates his tendency to equate religion and doctrine. He sees the conflict as 'essentially political
and nationalistic', but he accepts that

> it would be a gross oversimplification to state that there were
> no *doctrinal disputes* between Protestants and Catholics in
> Ulster. On the contrary, there are elements in the *teachings* of
> both major denominations that tend mutually to alienate and
> inflame, although probably not to an equal extent in each
> community ... It is also possible that pseudo-religious slo-
> gans and an undue emphasis on *theological differences* serve to
> preserve group solidarity in a divided society.[43] [our em-
> phases]

However, Moxon-Browne immediately brings this passage to a
conclusion that is jarringly singular in emphasis, given even the
limited religious element he has acknowledged: 'Northern
Ireland society is divided by a fundamental disagreement: the
appropriate state for the society to belong to.'[44] This analysis has
no room for religion. In a book on nation, class, and creed, religion largely disappears after page three.

If the fiction that religion and politics are entirely separate categories can sometimes distort analysis, it is also an occasionally useful fiction, or at least an unavoidable one. People reinforce it every time they use the language of religion and politics, and while we find ourselves trying to work around it by using terms like 'purely political' and 'narrowly religious' to indicate areas outside the intersection of politics and religion, occasional adjectives do little to modify the essential categories. Even if the fiction is unavoidable, however, those seeking to understand sectarianism will need to maintain a steady awareness that the fiction is not reality if they wish to avoid reductionist conclusions.

The reductionism of dismissing religion
as a mere boundary marker

The third common form of reductionism is to treat religion as a mere boundary marker, without significant content. In this view, religion arbitrarily marks conflicting parties, which are actually divided by more fundamental and truly meaningful issue or issues. Martin Marger's *Race and Ethnic Relations: American and Global Perspectives* is a popular textbook that has gone through five editions since 1985. Although Marger's chapter on Northern Ireland, one of many test cases from around the world, is generally competent, it also illustrates the tendency to reduce religion to the status of a mere boundary marker. Marger understands conflict in Northern Ireland as 'an ethnic conflict in which religious identities mark off the boundaries of the two major ethnic groups ... Regarding the role of religion in the conflict, Harold Jackson and Anne McHardy write that it is simply "the handiest identifying mark available to the two sides".'[45] That religion, through the categories of Protestant and Catholic, provides boundary markers for conflicting parties is obviously and undeniably true. To suggest, however, that this is the sole or primary role of religion in conflict is grossly reductionist.

Religion is just one possible boundary marker from a group which includes at least race, language, nationality, ethnicity, and ideology. Not only is each a marker, each is a *mere* marker to the extent that it is an accident of birth, and undoubtedly a substantial element of accident of birth is inherent in each of these categories. At the same time, however, each is much more than an accident of birth: each has a content that commands loyalty, and

in some cases demands it. For religion, ethnicity, and ideology
the element of content is obvious, but perhaps less so for race,
language, and nationality, if construed as mere skin colour,
mere words, and mere place of birth. But even to state the possibility of so construing them is to expose the absurdity of it, because race, language, and nationality connote a complex cultural
content. For all our possible markers, including religion, the
content they stand for is likely to include elements that will
conflict with the content of other markers, and the content will
certainly include assumptions that will shape conflict: when
compromise is appropriate, what it means, the significance of
violence, the possibility and meaning of forgiveness, and so on.
The content of the various markers means they will not be mere
markers of conflicting parties, they will be an integral part of the
conflict equation.

It is true that a conflict in full flow will tend to crush all distinctions of content and impose a single, relentless logic. Frank
Wright develops this idea in his book *Northern Ireland: A
Comparative Analysis*. He writes, 'Representative violence creates
deterrence communities and the symbols which denote them
[i.e. their markers] are ultimately of little consequence: all that
matters is their mutually threatening character and the dissolution of all politically transcendent values or institutions which
might bind them together.'[46] Anyone who has worked with
Wright's carefully developed understandings of 'representative
violence' and 'mutual deterrence communities' will feel the
force of his argument. Note, however, that Wright is not describing a situation in which merely ephemeral markers are burned
away to reveal a solid core of truly political reality: along with
the markers or symbols, the conflict has destroyed politics as
well, by dissolving 'all politically transcendent values or institutions'. Elsewhere Wright speaks of 'crises which are about
everything and nothing at the same time and which can develop
into a chaos which makes a nonsense of everything they are os-
tensibly about'.[47] But both Wright's statements are about conflicts that have developed to an advanced state of crisis. The content of our various markers will have shaped the path to this
crisis, and in the slow and difficult struggle to restore 'politically
transcendent values or institutions' the content of markers, including religion, will figure once again, whether to impede or to
advance the process. When a boundary marker has a cultural

content, as does religion, it is likely to figure in the conduct of conflict and in progress toward peace.

The reductionism of seeking the fundamental

As noted above, either/or reasoning often operates by attempting to tear away the false, the apparent, the ephemeral, and to find beneath it the essential or the fundamental. The pursuit of the fundamental takes at least two main forms. The first form works to establish relative significance – a particular factor in a conflict may be understood as fundamental, i.e. as of greatest significance, but that does not necessarily mean that other factors are insignificant or that the fundamental can necessarily be understood apart from the other factors of lesser significance. This stance is easily abused, with distorting consequences. Those things assigned lesser significance can be simply those things the author does not really understand or care about and therefore is not really qualified to speak about. At least in theory, however, this form of seeking the fundamental can have real integrity. Different factors may have different degrees of significance in a conflict; one or several may be so pivotal as to be called fundamental, and some factors of apparent significance, we want to allow, may actually be insignificant. Done well, distinguishing between fundamental and lesser significance is a valuable exercise.

Our focus is on a second form of seeking the fundamental. This one makes sharper choices, distinguishing not relative significance but between what is fundamentally significant and what is insignificant. Thus when the fundamental has been established, it can be focused on to the exclusion of all other factors, because those are insignificant. Perhaps there exists somewhere a conflict where such distinctions between the fundamental and the insignificant can be fruitfully made. In the case of Northern Ireland, however, we find that this sharp distinction between the fundamental and the insignificant always distorts by oversimplifying. It is this cruder form of the pursuit of the fundamental that we wish to challenge.

At the beginning of this chapter, we introduced political scientists Brendan O'Leary and John McGarry as the authors of *Explaining Northern Ireland,* a far-reaching overview, informed by wide reading, of explanations of conflict in Northern Ireland. They are experts in what they call ethno-national conflict, and when they apply this analysis to Northern Ireland, the results are sophisticated and insightful. Regrettably, however, they are also relentlessly reductionist in their methodology. Not only do they focus on ethno-national dynamics to the exclusion of other approaches, as is typical with pursuit-of-the-fundamental reductionism, they go one step further and rubbish alternative approaches. In fact they only get around to their own analysis in a concluding section headed 'Synthesis and Futures'. They do not have much left to synthesise, however, as they have spent the first 307 pages of the book attempting the systematic demolition of rival interpretations, first external explanations (nationalist, unionist, and Marxist) and then internal explanations under the headings of religion, culture (including history), and economics.

Their treatment of internal explanations, especially religious and cultural explanations, is of particular interest and concern to us. We will give it more attention than we did previous examples by MacDonald, Moxon-Browne, and Marger, because those authors are social scientists eager to get on with discussing their areas of specialisation, so religion is dismissed more or less in passing. O'Leary and McGarry attempt something of an entirely different order. Their goal, pursued at great length, is a comprehensive, systematic dismissal of religious and cultural explanations of conflict in Northern Ireland, which, in turn, requires a more substantial critique from us.

Although O'Leary and McGarry do not make explicit use of the language of the fundamental, the logic behind their efforts to discredit other interpretations is consistently the pursuit of the fundamental. According to O'Leary and McGarry, conflict in Northern Ireland is ethno-national in character,[48] that conflict can be successfully resolved or managed through appropriate political institutions,[49] and '[t]o create a constructive peace, rather than the peace of exhaustion, requires intelligent and informed statecraft from all parties in Northern Ireland, the Republic and Great Britain.'[50] So far, so good: we agree that conflict in Northern Ireland is ethno-national and that appropriate political institutions, developed through brave and thoughtful statecraft, will be crucial for a meaningful peace. For O'Leary and McGarry, however, these factors are not a starting point or a framework in which to integrate other elements, they are the fundamental, whole, and exclusive truth about the situation, and other explanations and factors are not merely insignificant, they obscure the fundamental truth and must therefore be dismissed. In their efforts to eliminate other elements and explanations, O'Leary and McGarry do some indirectly useful work that helps, at least implicitly, to establish the limits of the interpretations they are analysing. They are not interested in setting limits, however, they are interested in dismissing, which leads them into a variety of errors of reasoning. We will begin by discussing examples of their approach to religion, but in seeking to understand their logic we will actually turn to their arguments about culture, because it is in this context that they discuss their reductionist methodology most clearly.

Our disagreements with McGarry and O'Leary's understanding of the role of religion in conflict are too numerous, for the purposes of this chapter, to go through point-by-point. Instead we will focus on one kind of argument they seem to find compelling and on the general logic behind their dismissal of religion.

At the beginning of their chapter on religious interpretations, McGarry and O'Leary note that 'significant numbers of journalists, historians and social scientists place religion at the heart of the conflict' in Northern Ireland, and '[m]uch of the British public shares this verdict.'[51] If this is true, they say,

> important implications follow. Socio-economic inequalities, cultural or national differences, inter-state relations, and political institutions must be of secondary or no importance. The conflict must be pre-modern, with essentially endogenous roots. Policy-implications also follow: 'religious' solutions have to be canvassed such as secularisation, ecumenism, or integrated education. Alternatively despair may be encouraged, because the devout are not famous for tolerance.[52]

The last paragraph of the chapter sees them returning to the same logic, as they lay out a similar list of policy and interpretative disasters that follow from '[e]xplanations which accord primacy to religion'.[53]

But these 'important implications' do not follow anywhere outside the rigidly reductionist world of O'Leary and McGarry. From other points of view, one can see how 'socio-economic inequalities, cultural or national differences, inter-state relations, and political institutions' contribute to conflict along with religion or perhaps intersect with religion; policy implications involving religion can work alongside other kinds of policy approaches. The oppositions they set up are unnecessary and false. True, they do cover themselves with a kind of logical fig leaf by talking not about arguments that *include* religion but about arguments that emphasise the *primacy* of religion. Of course giving 'primacy to religion' does not necessarily mean giving sole or exclusive significance to religion. Recognising, however, that 'primacy' might be misused in this way, we acknowledge that if any scholar or school actually did insist that conflict in Northern Ireland was about religion only or that only religion really mattered, then O'Leary and McGarry's argument would be reasonable – the implications they cite would indeed follow from such a stance. But we know of no such argument, and they do not refer to one. And if they were really interested in dethroning religion from a role of primacy rather than dismissing it entirely, then they would still be left with the task of thinking about how religious explanations, once no longer seen as primary, fit as part of a larger explanation. But they do no such thing. They are interested solely in dismissing.

In between these beginning and ending dismissals of religion, O'Leary and McGarry operate with a logic that amounts to the pursuit of the fundamental, although they do not use that term. A few quotes will illustrate their approach. In each case, the italics are ours.

(1) Arguing against suggestions that the Catholic doctrine of just war provides backing for IRA activists, they write,

It is possible to explain – though not justify – republican violence strictly through reference to nationalist ideology, the suppression of economic, cultural and political rights, and the historically widely dispersed lesson that "force can work".[54]

(2) Arguing against analysts who see religious reasons for Protestant resistance to a united Ireland, they say that economic, cultural, and political fears, without any reference to religion,

are sufficient to explain – though they do not justify – why so many Protestants are unwilling to accommodate nationalists.[55]

(3) Unionists' reasons for resisting accommodation with Catholics obviously include religious motivations, but apart from fundamentalists, these reasons are not paramount or widespread. There is a simpler reason: for unionists accommodating Catholics means accommodating nationalists.[56]

(4) The "chosen people" theme in the history of Ulster

> Protestantism is therefore *capable of being interpreted in a much*
> *more hard-headed manner* than that customary amongst histo-
> rians and sociologists of religion. [57]

'It is possible to explain', 'are sufficient to explain', 'there is a
simpler reason', 'capable of being interpreted in a much more
hard-headed manner'. Behind all such phrases (and examples
could be multiplied) lies a logic that we find radically misguided
and destructive of sound reasoning. These phrases point to a set
of interpretative principles that O'Leary and McGarry believe
are truly fundamental: if any situation *can* be interpreted in
terms of these principles, then that situation *must* be interpreted
in those terms, and any other possible explanation can safely be
dismissed, perhaps even must be dismissed.

Exactly what constitutes this arena of core logic is not easily
named, but one way of identifying it, which O'Leary and
McGarry develop in their chapter on culture, might be the conviction that human activities can always be explained as the
actions of *rational agents*, which they contrast with the idea that
people are *cultural agents*.[58] 'Each school', rationalist and culturalist, 'plainly ... has its merits',[59] they admit, and '[s]ynthesis between rationalist and culturalist interpretations ... is, of course,
possible.'[60] If rationalist and culturalist approaches both have
merits and may be synthesised, readers might expect that the
authors will attempt to do so, but this rare admission is never
acted upon. In practice, their commitment to rationalism and
their habit of constructing their work around false and needless
oppositions are so dogmatic, fixed, and limiting that they always
choose and never synthesise – cultural explanations are always
depicted as having no merit. In one of their clearest statements
of methodological assumptions they say, 'our parsimonious
methodological principle suggests that unique cultural explanations should only be resorted to in the last instance, rather than
in the first instance.'[61] If their 'parsimonious principle' is to be
more than an arbitrary choice – parsimony, or simplicity, being
very much in the eye of the beholder – it must be based on the
notion that there is a realm of rationality that lies outside culture
and can expose and judge culture. But no such realm exists. As
the philosopher Alasdair McIntyre has so powerfully demonstrated, rationality is not beyond culture, it is an expression of
culture, it operates within culture.[62] In at least one crucial instance, O'Leary and McGarry admit as much: 'we believe that

many cultural norms can be seen as rational when the context in which they flourish is properly specified.'[63] Since the context which must be specified is of course a cultural context, they are here recognising the way in which culture and rationality are linked. Again, however, they return immediately to argue the priority of rational over cultural explanations, failing to recognise or act on the significance of what they have just stated.

The conception of rationality employed by O'Leary and McGarry can be judged by the results that follow when they apply it to Northern Ireland. In fact it consistently yields unnecessary choices and occasionally produces silly arguments. Both are in evidence throughout, and not least where they most explicitly attempt to defend their commitment to rationalism. They discuss, for example, the 1994 IRA ceasefire.

> The culturalist school which sees the IRA as an offshoot of Gaelic, romantic, Catholic culture can be usefully contrasted with that which sees republican paramilitaries as rational agents pursuing strategic objectives, namely a united Ireland. The recent announcement [1994] of a complete cessation of violence by the IRA does not represent the abandonment of Gaelic, romantic, or Catholic culture, but rather the calculation that unarmed struggle is more likely to be successful, in the long run, than continuing the long war. Whether that calculation proves correct is less important than the fact that culturalists have no easy way of interpreting it.[64]

If the 'it' culturalists supposedly have 'no easy way of interpreting' is 'the calculation that unarmed struggle is more likely to be successful, in the long run, than continuing the long war', then O'Leary and McGarry are simply wrong. We know of no individual and no school of interpretation which believes that people do not calculate and reason! Cultural interpretations simply argue that culture provides some or all of the material on which people reason and that culture may also shape how people reason. O'Leary and McGarry's critique of 'the culturalist school' seems to be in part a response to Padraig O'Malley's *Biting at the Grave: The Irish Hunger Strikes and the Politics of Despair*, most of their argument here being taken from O'Leary's review of the book.[65] In the extreme case of the ten republican prisoners who died on hunger strike in 1981, O'Malley wrote, 'Their actions, ultimately, were not the actions of autonomous individuals, but rather a reflexive embrace of the way in which political prison-ers throughout Irish history were presumed to have behaved. ... In the end, they were the victims of our myths.'[66] O'Leary dis-liked this quote, and we agree that it is overstated. But even if it is an overstatement, this is not sufficient reason to dismiss en-tirely the significance of cultural influences on the hunger strik-ers, as O'Leary seems to do, and still less to dismiss all cultural explanations.

If O'Leary and McGarry mean to be making a broader point, that culturalists have no easy way to explain the 1994 ceasefire, then they are right. Considerations of culture cannot explain why a ceasefire should take place at a particular time. It is equally true, however, that rationalists have no easy way of interpreting the ceasefire. If the use or abandonment of violence is to be inter-preted solely in terms of rationality, then what made violence irrational in 1994 when it had been rational before? If rational decisions on their own can explain the ceasefire, then who is rational here: the many nationalists who always believed that violence was an irrational way of pursuing a united Ireland? The mainstream republicans who believed it was rational until 1994 and then ceased to be rational? Or the die-hard republicans who still believe that violence is a rational means of seeking a united Ireland? If all are rational, then of what explanatory value is rationality? In fact narrow considerations of rationality, as of culture, explain nothing here.

But the main problem in this passage and with their general approach is the way they needlessly set up a choice between rationality and culture. The IRA decision to abandon violence no doubt involves hard reasoning on hard experience. It also in-volves a shift in political culture, from one in which a united Ireland is a fixed goal in which the end justifies the means to one in which a united Ireland is a deeply desired goal, but subject to other considerations, especially of consent; from a culture in which compromise is a curse to one in which compromise is a possibility, perhaps even a political virtue; from a culture of vic-tory to a culture of negotiation. Not only does making a choice between rationalist and culturalist interpretations offer no posi-tive interpretative help, it ignores the fruitful possibilities of thinking about human beings as both rational and cultural agents – a possibility, as we said before, that O'Leary and McGarry allow but never pursue. Culture shapes reason, reason shapes decisions, decisions shape culture. Sound methodologies allow us to trace the connections between different factors, bad methodologies force us to choose between them.

A final example. O'Leary and McGarry wish to argue that the 1981 hunger strikers are better understood as rational actors rather than as culturally influenced.

> The prisoners knew what they were doing. In some cases they seem to have literally weighed the benefits of political martyrdom (damage to the enemy and personal posthumous reputation) against the costs of serving out a life sentence.[67]

This is an outstanding example of the close relationship between rationality and culture, not an example of rationality over against culture. If your culture tells you that damage to a personal and collective political enemy and enhancement of your personal posthumous reputation are potentially worth dying for, then freely chosen political martyrdom can be a rational choice. Change the cultural context, however, to one in which the personal is valued over the collective and getting on in this life trumps any posthumous considerations, temporal or eternal, and then starving to death over a set of political symbols appears the height of absurdity. Rationality and culture simply are not discrete concepts. They go on:

> The key question is why were some nationalists more disposed than others to behave in the manner of the hunger-strikers? Was it because they had imbibed more of the relevant cultures? If so, why had they done so? An easy explanation exists. ... The hunger-strikers had experienced oppression at the hands of Protestants or the state authorities.[68]

Their 'easy explanation' is probably part of a full and complex explanation, but by itself it explains nothing. Oppression had also been experienced by paramilitaries who chose not to go on hunger strike, by nationalists who were rendered apolitical by the experience, and by nationalists who responded by committing themselves to the nonviolent pursuit of justice. Each outcome is equally rational, so rationality, by itself, explains nothing. No direct correlation exists between the level of oppression experienced and particular political outcomes for individuals.

What ought to be apparent by now is that every attempt at single-cause explanation – political, religious, cultural, or any other – will fail to account for the complex actions of individuals and societies. Far from justifying their 'parsimonious method-ological principle', O'Leary and McGarry's efforts to do so demonstrate its weakness. The solution, it seems to us, lies in seeking complex explanations, involving multiple causes and consistently looking to the possibility of integrating and synthes-ising rather than making unnecessary choices. What disappears as so much vapour when exposed to strong light is efforts to establish a single-factor explanation of conflict in Northern Ireland, including McGarry and O'Leary's own attempts.

Returning from culture in general to religion in particular, we try to imagine what would constitute a religious conflict in terms of O'Leary and McGarry's parsimonious method. First, it would have to be about religion *qua* religion, religion narrowly conceived. One can imagine Catholic and Protestant parish-ioners, heated by sermons on doctrinal difference, emerging from their churches on a Sunday morning and shouting Reformation and Counter-reformation slogans while battering each other with rosary beads and bibles. But even this would not necessarily meet the required standards. The combatants must also be divided by religion *qua* religion only. If, for example, these people had economic and political differences as well as religious differences, then those would constitute 'simpler' ex-planations in O'Leary and McGarry's terms, so religion could be dismissed as irrelevant.

Have we caricatured O'Leary and McGarry's position? Perhaps, but if so it is the kind of caricature naturally generated by any attempt to meet their impossible criteria. By these crite-ria, we cannot think of any conflict anywhere that could ever be classified as religious. In fact, we can go further and speculate that by their criteria no long-term conflict anywhere has ever been about anything, because none is ever reducible to a single factor narrowly conceived. Operating as a strict system then, O'Leary and McGarry's criteria are useless to explain conflict in Northern Ireland.

Given the interpretative problems to which the pursuit of the fundamental so easily leads, we want to suggest that situations of endemic conflict, as in Northern Ireland, are best thought of as analogous to ecosystems. In studying an ecosystem the pur-suit of the fundamental would be a nonsense, because the focus is on relationships between parts in the context of the whole sys-tem. Conceived of in this way, conflict in Northern Ireland would leave scholars with interpretative work running on a continuum between two extremes. At one end, a few master synthesisers can concentrate on considerations of the whole, the parts in relationship to one another, and the dynamics that bind them together. At the other end, those of us not ready for so grand a work will focus on particular elements of conflict. But even those of us working at this more mundane end of the continuum will be constantly aware of the contributions of others and how their work may impinge on our own. Our efforts will always be directed toward a critical integration of elements, and we will maintain a steady awareness that the integrity of our work depends on remembering that our part is not the whole.

Conclusion

Perhaps these four forms of reductionism are so pervasive because denying the role of religion in sectarian conflict suits such diverse and even contradictory purposes. Denying the role of religion can suit the churches, because if religion is not really a significant factor, then Christians and their churches are not really responsible. Anyone influenced by Marxism will be ideologically predisposed to minimise the role of religion, because if religion is all false consciousness, it cannot be taken seriously in its own right, but must be interpreted in economic terms. While there are outstanding exceptions, relatively few scholars formed by the secular assumptions of modern social science training will acquire there a sensitivity to religion and its varied roles and meanings. The intellectually lazy from all walks of life will always find it easier to avoid the complexities of both/and logic and instead embrace either/or logic, make a choice as to which is the real cause of conflict in Northern Ireland, and then deal exclusively with that one factor. And tragically, once either/or logic is embedded as the normative way of analysing conflict in Northern Ireland, it becomes necessary to dismiss religion in order to take other factors seriously: if one want to stress politics, one must deny or ignore religion; if one want to stress economics, one must deny religion. No such choice should be necessary. Sectarianism is so complex a problem because it involves religion and politics and economics and a host of other factors. Only approaches that can take in this whole range stand a chance of understanding sectarianism and moving beyond it.

CHAPTER 2

Where Does Sectarianism Come From?
Historical Perspectives

When did sectarianism begin in Ireland? While this question can legitimately be answered in various ways, we encounter some historical misconceptions that are likely to stunt contemporary understanding of sectarianism and how to deal with it. Some believe, for example, that partition was the font of all sectarianism; undo partition, therefore, and sectarianism will wither and fade. Others see sectarianism as effectively a result of the Troubles, which suggests that peace might be sought by a return to the way things were. While both partition and the Troubles did give new impetus and expression to sectarianism, all the essential elements of sectarianism already had a long history by the beginning of the twentieth century.

An account of the historical roots of sectarianism has the obvious purpose, then, of correcting a short-sightedness that can distort thinking about how to respond to sectarianism. Put positively, a longer look at the sources of sectarianism may give people new insights and new ways of seeing their responsibilities, personal and communal, for sectarianism and for moving beyond sectarianism. At very least, we intend this chapter to suggest the complexity and persistence of sectarianism's tangled roots, and therefore the sobering immensity of the task taken on by those who would find a better way.

The events and ideas discussed in this chapter do not represent anything like a comprehensive treatment of the history of sectarianism. In fact anyone interested in Irish history is likely to notice things that might have been, perhaps should have been, included. We do intend, however, that the sketch presented here should be sufficiently accurate that any additions would serve to flesh it out rather than to contradict it or to alter it in any substantial way.

The first three sections provide background. The first considers the sometimes tense relationship between the past as interpreted by historians and as perceived by communities, while the next two look at doctrinal roots of sectarianism and the European context out of which Irish sectarianism arises. The remaining six sections are organised around key themes. 'The Barbarous Irish' recognises one of the ways in which colonialism has shaped sectarianism. 'The Role of Religion in Conflict, Violence, and Catastrophe' gives a few examples of crises, by definition exceptional events, that have nonetheless seared scars on conflicting communal memories. Situations of long-term conflict easily lead to 'Identity in Opposition' to one's opponents, the subject of the next section. 'Conversion' has been a fraught issue, shot through with religious and political implications, since the Reformation in Ireland. Sectarianism requires and sustains antagonised division, to which the Christian churches in Ireland have made a substantial contribution; 'Separation' presents one cameo, based on the difficult issue of inter-church marriage. 'Sacred Violence, Politics as Religion' examines how religion and politics, in both unionist and nationalist traditions, have sometimes combined to produce sectarianism of the most destructive kind and most enduring influence. While we might have covered much more, we hope these themes and examples will be sufficient to demonstrate how deep run the roots of sectarianism.

History and communal memory
An account of the roots of sectarianism needs to acknowledge a theme which will shape how some readers understand what we write: the complex and sometimes difficult relationship between history, that is the past as understood by professional historians, and communal memory, the past as remembered by communities – in Ireland, communities in conflict. Communal memory corresponds with myth, which the *Concise Oxford Dictionary* defines as a 'widely held but false notion of the past'.[1] Should we accept such a definition, it would certainly simplify the historian's task in relation to myths: correct them. The actual relationship between history and myth is more complex than such a definition allows, however, and not nearly so convenient for historians. The function of myths is to embody, in story form, truths that help us understand who we are as a community, where we came from, and where we stand in relationship to other groups. The story may or may not be historically verifiable, but this is never

the main point. What really matters with myth is the way we understand a story, the meaning we take from it, not the literal, factual truth of the story, nor even the variety of different ways the story might be interpreted. When communal myths are derived from the way communities understand the past, as is frequently the case in Ireland, and communities believe these understandings to be history, conflict is all but inevitable between communities and historians. The tension arises because historians are likely to lay out a range of possible interpretations of a given historical event, including events of great mythic significance, and these interpretations may not correspond with the primary meaning assigned to that event by a particular community. The debate about historical revisionism which flared up from time to time in the 1980s and 1990s is in part the result of this tension between the way historians and communities read the past.[2]

Joe, who trained as an historian, had his most direct experience of this tension while serving from 1991 to 1993 as a member of an ecumenical Working Party on Sectarianism sponsored by the Irish Inter-Church Meeting. This group managed to produce consensus documents on a range of topics. Discussions were tense at times, especially on education and security issues, and compromises meant that final positions did not suit everyone equally well. But the group achieved a working consensus on every issue except one, resulting in a publication that all were willing to stand over, even where it said less or more than some members might have wished. The single exception, and the document that generated the most explosive meeting of the Working Party, was a chapter on the history of sectarianism. On this topic, the group simply could not come to agreement. As the author of that chapter, Joe likes to think that failure to reach consensus reflects the difficulty of the topic more than the competence of the author. When it became apparent that agreement would be difficult, he met twice with some of his sharpest critics, each time bringing a revised and substantially expanded draft for consideration. Finally, however, the best efforts of all concerned came to nothing, and everyone had to accept that an agreed history was work for another day.[3]

Some of the most contentious issues explored occupy that ground where communal memory and academic history clash and the demarcation between past and present is elusive. Joe came to imagine a continuum with personal identity at one end, communal memory in the middle, and formal, academic history at the other end. In most modern, western societies, personal identity might be connected with communal memory – although not necessarily, given the power of individualism – but a conscious link between personal identity and academic history would be rare indeed, at least in mainstream society.[4] For Joe's critics, however, all of them living and working in difficult, frontline situations in Northern Ireland, the three points on the continuum were frequently related, and certain issues effectively collapsed the continuum into a single point. At this nexus of contention, the ordinary stakes of historical scholarship are raised dramatically – evaluating a reading of history as wrong is received as both an intellectual and a moral judgment, and an offending account can have the impact of an affront to both corporate and personal identity. The novelist William Faulkner had one of his characters say of the American south, 'The past is not dead and gone; it isn't even past.'[5] Much the same applies to how some Irish people see the past, and, as a general rule, the more nearly one approaches the epicentre of conflict in Northern Ireland, the more frequently this sense of the past can be seen to operate.

This tension between communal memory and history has important implications for both historians and communities. Historians, for their part, must abandon the self-serving idea that a myth is a 'widely held but false notion of the past'. The relationship between myth and truth is much more complicated than that. Communal memory of a past event may in fact be true in every detail, in some details, or in none, but the main point to bear in mind is that communities will be searching the past for its meaning for that particular community, not for narrative accuracy or breadth of interpretation. If historians really wish to communicate with an audience, therefore, they will need to know the meaning communities attach to the events they are studying and thus how historians' work is likely to be received. They need not defer to that meaning, they may even wish to challenge it, but they cannot arrogantly assume that communal memory is false merely by being communal memory. Furthermore, in the matter of interpretation, historians must accept that they have no privileged role. They speak with authority at other levels of understanding, but when it comes to interpreting meaning, they are one voice among many.

Rendering the past truly past requires more than historians can do alone. The boundary between past and present becomes badly blurred in situations where the pressing problems of the present are easily and plausibly interpreted as just the latest manifestation of old and enduring themes, as is so often the case in Ireland. In such circumstances, an altered view of the past requires an altered view and experience of the present, a change requiring work that is primarily pastoral and political rather than historical.

Historians do have a contribution to make, however, and communities need to accept that what historians have to say may challenge their understanding of the past. The most basic historical contribution will be to foster a more complex sense of the past, especially one that can acknowledge and account for both the connections and the discontinuities between history and communal memory. Aspects of history touching on sectarianism present historians with striking challenges. No topic is more likely to trigger the collapse of the boundary between past and present than sectarianism, because its central themes are so easily understood as constants in Irish history. And so they are in many cases. Contextualising the history of Irish sectarianism may occasionally involve asserting that continuities perceived and asserted by communal memory are false, but more often it will require showing that the continuity is only partial, that the course travelled from past to present has been more tortuous than usually recognised, that the continuity is not inexorable, it is shaped in part by contingencies. Such an interpretation may challenge some communal myths, but it also holds out hope: change is genuinely possible. The past need not dictate the future, as sectarianism likes us to believe.

Historical and theological roots of sectarianism
The historical roots of sectarianism in Ireland can be traced back to the Reformation era of the 1500s and 1600s. In this period the state-established Church of Ireland, the Catholic Church, and eventually the Presbyterian Church were each closely linked with a particular political option, and these were locked in a bitter struggle for ascendancy. In this age the churches shared a combination of three doctrines which fostered sectarian attitudes and actions:
    providence;

one true church, outside of which is no salvation; and
error has no right.

The doctrine of *providence* is the simple, basic teaching that God
is at work in the world. Building on this conviction, some believe – as was certainly commonplace in the Reformation period
– that a faithful Christian observer of the world can discern
God's will and purpose by reading the signs of the times in
human events and the natural world. *One true church* is largely
self-explanatory – our church is the only true church, the implication being that if you are outside this church, your chances of
salvation are much diminished, at best. *Error has no right* is less
well known. This doctrine was developed in the fourth and fifth
centuries by St Augustine to justify the use of state coercion to
suppress his heretical opponents, the Donatists: because they
are radically in error, they have no right to express or hold their
beliefs. Ever since, the doctrine has been put to similar use,
whether explicitly or implicitly, as the principle behind every
use of coercion, especially state coercion, for religious purposes.
Error has no right is the doctrine behind penal laws, inquisitions, forced conversions, and similar episodes in Christian history.

Specifically, the origin of sectarianism lies in two combinations of these three doctrines. The first combination is *one true
church* with *error has no right*. One true church is a truth claim
and therefore automatically carries with it the danger of arrogance and imposition. But these are only dangers, not necessary
outcomes – everything depends on how the truth claim is made,
and if made consciously and humbly, it does not have to impose
on others. If you believe that error has no right, however, then
the chances are your truth claim will be made disastrously, because if your church is the one true church and error has no
right, then it is your duty to see that error is suppressed by whatever means necessary. From this viewpoint tolerance is no
virtue – tolerance is a deadly vice. Commenting on the Edict of
Nantes of 1598, which granted religious liberty to French
Protestants, Pope Clement VIII grumbled that it was 'the worst
edict that can possibly be imagined. ... An edict that permits liberty of conscience, the worst thing in the world.'[6] At that time
Pope Clement's viewpoint was by no means peculiarly Catholic;
it was widely shared by pious, zealous leaders, whether
Protestants or Catholics, in church and state. The whole idea of

religious toleration was only slowly coming to be accepted, and at first acceptance was mostly a matter of pragmatic, weary bowing to ugly, pluralist reality – no matter how we try, we cannot seem to beat our enemies, so we will have to find a way to live with them. It took hundreds of years for the idea of toleration to be widely embraced as a positive principle.

The other doctrinal combination behind sectarianism begins with *one true church* and *providence*. Again, providence simply teaches that God is at work in the world, which is not necessarily a problematic doctrine. If providence is interpreted in light of one true church, however, it is very easily reduced to 'God is on our side.' If combined with *error has no right* again, 'God is on our side' is likely to mean, 'God wants us to suppress others.' The disastrous consequences are obvious, as can be observed from episodes in Irish history and elsewhere.

Several key points about sectarianism follow from these doctrines and combinations. First, in the case of both combinations, note that error has no right is the most dangerous element. For intellectual and spiritual reasons, some people may wish to object to exclusive truth claims and to over-confidence about knowing God's ways and purposes, and those who hold such beliefs may indeed do so in ways contemptuous of others. But these are not necessarily damaging positions to hold, and in cases where they are damaging, the damage can be as much to the holder as to others. In the notion of error has no right, however, imposition on others is an inherent, ineradicable element. Oppression is the natural outcome of error has no right, unless those who believe it lack the power or will to act on it.

Second, these doctrines are much more than intellectual propositions about Christian faith. For the 1500s and 1600s, we might do better to think of these not as mere doctrines but as elements of worldview – these were categories in which people thought, a mental framework, standard assumptions about how the world worked. As such, these doctrines deeply shaped Christian identity.

Third, these doctrines did not emerge from small fringe groups, they were shared by the three main churches in Ireland, first Catholic and Church of Ireland and later Presbyterian, which simply differed as to which was the true church, who was in error, and whose cause God favoured. Thus sectarianism is rooted in the Irish mainstream, not the margins.

Fourth, these doctrines were not obscure teachings from musty, neglected confessions of faith; they were actively affirmed. They come from the centre of mainstream Christian teaching, not from the fringe.

Finally, taken together these conclusions about the roots of sectarianism mean that each of the three main churches was historically either an established church or an establishment in waiting. Given the disproportionate share of power the Church of Ireland held in its traditional role as the established church until 1870, it was all but inevitable that the Church of Ireland would be responsible for a disproportionate share of actions with sectarian implications. This hard fact should not be dodged, but at the same time we must be clear that this is a question of power, not of principle – there is little reason to think Catholics or Presbyterians would have behaved any better as an establishment, because they were animated by the same principles. A striking case in point is seventeenth- and eighteenth-century France, where Protestants in a Catholic state lived under restrictions and penal laws much like those experienced by Catholics in Britain and Ireland. The Jesuit scholar Fergus O'Donoghue pithily summarises the attitude of *all* governments, whether Catholic or Protestant, in the post-Reformation era: 'when practicable, persecute.'[7] An Irishman, the Duke of Ormond, knew as much at the time. Justifying tough actions against Presbyterians in the aftermath of a failed rebellion in 1683, the Duke of Ormond noted that Nonconformists were quick to cry persecution 'if they had not liberty to persecute others, even those that come nearest to their principles'.[8]

European context
While most of the story of sectarianism in Ireland involves the way Reformation and Counter-reformation clashed from the sixteenth century onward, we need to remember elements of context that are older in Ireland and both wider and older in Europe. In fact, searching for the roots of sectarianism involves looking at developments that occurred long before sectarianism was named or even recognised as a problem. The broad framework for interpreting the origin of sectarianism is to see it as one aspect of the break-up of medieval christendom and the working out of Reformation/Counter-reformation conflict. In medieval Europe, the doctrines of providence, one true church, and

error has no right did not cause internal conflict, with the exception of an occasional unusually large or stubborn heretical
group. Applied externally to infidels and internally to Jews and
dissenters – groups usually too weak and small to offer much resistance – these doctrines identified the enemy and weeded out
dissent, thus promoting unity in the mainstream society. The
Reformation divided Europe into mini-christendoms organised
on a state-by-state basis, but once again one true church, error
has no right, and providence could maintain their unifying function, only on a smaller scale, within each state. Problems arose,
however, when rival contestants for ascendancy arose within a
state and victory was impossible or long delayed. In these circumstances, the doctrines central to sectarianism continued to
unify, but they unified factions within a single state that were
themselves in conflict with each other. The potential for conflict
was particularly great in Ireland, where not only did rival
claimants challenge the legitimacy of the established church, but
the Church of Ireland failed even to achieve the minimum requirement of a state church, that it be the church of the majority.
This potential for conflict has been all too fully realised, and its
legacy is sectarianism. The history of Irish sectarianism is the
story of how a medieval norm became a modern problem, first a
practical problem as the establishment of the Church of Ireland
led not to general acceptance but to protracted conflict, and finally
a problem in principle, as the old norm was rejected and replaced
by new standards of religious liberty, tolerance, and related concepts.

'The barbarous Irish'
Sectarianism did not arise solely from post-Reformation divisions
in Irish society, it developed in part by transmuting elements of
long established conflict between Irish and Anglo-Irish into the
terms of conflict between Catholic and Protestant. One such element was the 'barbarous Irish' theme enunciated so influentially
by the twelfth-century Welsh-Norman priest and scholar,
Giraldus Cambrensis.

   In 1188 and 1189 Giraldus completed two works on Ireland
and the first years of the Norman presence there, *Topographia
Hibernica* and *Expugnatio Hibernica*. A prominent feature of these
books was his criticism of the Irish as primitive and immoral.
'This people is, then, a barbarous people, literally barbarous. ...

Their natural qualities are excellent. But almost everything acquired is deplorable.'[9] Barbarism was the key to Giraldus' understanding of the Irish, which he applied to many aspects of their society. Ultimately he identified this supposed Irish barbarism as not merely primitive backwardness, but as a moral condition: '[t]his is a filthy people, wallowing in vice'; 'above all other peoples they always practise treachery.'[10] Even a supposedly high rate of physical deformity Giraldus traced to moral perversity, saying, '[I]t is not surprising if nature sometimes produces such beings contrary to her ordinary laws when dealing with a people that is adulterous, incestuous, unlawfully conceived and born, outside the law, and shamefully abusing nature herself in spiteful and horrible practices.'[11]

This kind of studied contempt on encountering a new and different culture is a feature of many a colonial enterprise: dehumanising, even demonising, the natives seems to be a necessary prelude to dominating them. What matters most for the history of sectarianism, however, is that these ideas became conventional wisdom in the Anglo-Irish community. According to historian Nicholas Canny, the efforts of the English interest in Ireland, right down to the eve of the Reformation, were shaped by a Giraldus-influenced conviction that 'the struggle being pursued in Ireland between Anglo-Norman and Gael was a conflict between the forces of good and evil.'[12] When most of these Anglo-Irish families eventually opted for Counter-reformation Catholicism, and recent English settlers came to dominate Irish Protestantism, the 'barbarous Irish' theme and its 'superstitious' variant survived these shifts by taking on a powerfully confessional note – now the Irish were barbarous not only because they were Irish, but because they were Catholics.

The barbarism/civility dichotomy influenced many aspects of Protestant thought. The historian Toby Barnard notes that in the seventeenth and eighteenth centuries, 'clerical propagandists … regularly contrasted … civility in language, dress, diet and housing, with barbarism.'[13] Some of the sharpest expressions of the barbarism/civility theme can be found in political sermons of the same period. In 1708, for example, preaching a sermon commemorating the rebellion of 1641, Ralph Lambert was particularly concise in arguing that 'a False and Idolatrous Religion, does naturally produce Bloodshed, Barbarity, Wasting, and Destruction', and specifically that 'the Doctrine and Practice of the Church of Rome do allow and justify such Barbarous Massacres'[14] as the rebellion of 1641. But the same basic idea was repeated over and over,[15] along with more mundane evidences of supposed barbarism. Although twentieth-century manifestations of the barbarity theme generally pale before the ferocity of earlier years, traces are everywhere, in sources as diverse as the mainstream Protestant historiography of G. V. Jourdan and the politico-religious pronouncements of Ian Paisley.[16] In 1983, Seamus Deane went so far as to argue that '[t]he language of politics in Ireland and England, especially when the subject is Northern Ireland, is still dominated by the putative division between barbarism and civilisation.'[17] While Deane probably overstates the significance of the theme, anyone sensitised to it will see its ongoing influence.

The role of religion in conflict, violence, and catastrophe
From the sixteenth century onward, sectarianism has been nurtured by the influence of religion in catastrophic events of violence and death. Whether interpreting the course of events, naming sources of motivation, or justifying actions, conflicting parties turned to religion as one explanation.

During the reign of Queen Elizabeth I, the years from 1558 to 1663 marked a significant hardening of an already troubled situation. Up to the mid-1500s, the English and Anglo-Norman perception of the native Irish as barbaric was alive and well, but it was limited – Irish culture might be barbaric, but the people themselves were reformable. About this time English attitudes began to change. Influenced by the literature spawned by increased European contact with very different cultures (the Spanish colonial experience in the Americas in particular) and by contemporary infatuation with the example of ancient Rome, some leading English adventurers and thinkers came to regard Irish culture and the Irish as so fundamentally barbaric and pagan that they could not be directly reformed. The native Irish must first be subdued by the sword and trained by the yoke of colonisation before they could accept English standards of civility (meaning a properly ordered society) and the mild precepts of the Christian faith. At the same time, the English government was coming to realise that given the intensely local nature of the Gaelic political structure, government plans to centralise authority would require military subjugation, not just the earlier, more pacific policy of surrender and regrant.

This combination of forces was a formula for a kind of total war unprecedented in Ireland: atrocities, despoliation of land, the slaughter of noncombatants, including women and children. The Irish committed counter atrocities, and there is evidence of intensified hatred of the English, an attitude which was increasingly shared by the more gaelicised of the Catholic Old English lords. In 1575 the earl of Kildare, whose ancestors had recently been pillars of the English interest in Ireland, was reported to have declared 'that if the callioght [hag] of Englande [meaning the queen] were once dead, they in England wolde be with their horns one against another and that then the Erle of Kyldare and they his followers wolde kill all the Englisshe churles or dryve them to the sea; and that so the worlde be all theirs.'[18]

A good number of the architects and implementers of the new English policy were fiercely committed to Protestantism and regarded their efforts as directed to godly ends. Reflecting on an Ulster military campaign in 1574 which was marked by atrocities against Irish and Scottish inhabitants, one English officer concluded, 'how godly a dede it is to overthrowe so wicked a race the world may judge: for my part I thinke there canot be a greater sacryfice to God.'[19] In the government's repertoire of strategies for subduing the Irish, reformed religion became linked to colonisation and brutal military campaigns.

Protestants had no monopoly on linking violence and religion. From 1534, all armed resistance to the Tudors' increasing efforts to extend the crown's authority in Ireland was accompanied by some raising of the banner of religion in support of the Pope and the old religion and in opposition to the reformed religion. But according to Catholic historian Canice Mooney, it was the expedition led by James Fitzmaurice Fitzgerald in 1579 that 'partook more of the nature of a religious crusade than any other Irish movement of the century'.[20] Beginning in 1575 Fitzmaurice spent four years on the continent, busily negotiating with Spain, France, and Rome for support for a military expedition to Ireland. In July 1579 Fitzmaurice and an armed company finally landed in Kerry to mount a campaign against the crown in Ireland. Fitzmaurice returned to Ireland as a convinced holy warrior in the cause of the Counter-reformation. Although many of his compatriots in arms had distinctly more secular goals, and perhaps his own motives were more complex than he admitted, he protested that the 'only object' of his military efforts was 'to secure the administration of Christ's Sacraments to a Catholic people in a Catholic rite'.[21] Disembarking at Dingle, the first ashore were two banner-bearing Franciscans (one banner, marked by the image of Christ on the cross, had been blessed by the Pope). They were followed by a bishop in mitre and crozier, and only then by Fitzmaurice and seven hundred soldiers paid for by Pope Gregory XIII.

Fitzmaurice was also armed with a letter of support from the Pope to the bishops and faithful of Ireland. In 1570 Elizabeth had become the first post-Reformation English monarch to be excommunicated and deposed by Rome, and now Pope Gregory reminded the people of Ireland that 'these last few years we have encouraged you by our letters to regain your liberty and defend and preserve it against the heretics.' He urged people to support the Fitzmaurice campaign in whatever way possible, offering in return 'to all who confess and communicate ... the same plenary indulgence and remission of sins that those receive who fight against the Turks and for the recovery of the Holy Land'.[22]

Fitzmaurice's campaign was a failure. He died in a minor skirmish in August 1579, and after the campaign had been put down, the huge Munster lands of his cousin, the earl of Desmond, who joined the cause after Fitzmaurice's death, were forfeited to the state and planted with English colonists. What might have galled Fitzmaurice most was the very limited response to the religious exhortations he presented to the Irish people. Nonetheless, the tone and content of the Pope's letter was significant: war against the heretical Protestants was couched in the concepts of the crusades.

Subsequent Irish history provided many more examples of religious links to violence, hatred, and oppression: further Elizabethan wars, plantation, the 1641 Rising, the Williamite wars, penal laws, and so on. In terms of sectarianism, what mattered as much as these events in and of themselves was the way they were incorporated into communal memory. The 1640s, as savage a decade as Ireland has ever experienced, illustrate the point.

During the first half of the seventeenth century, Europe was wracked by wars of religion, and Ireland did not escape. From the beginning of the Irish rising of 1641, one prominent Protestant line of interpretation understood it as a priest-inspired and priest-ridden rebellion, intended to exterminate Protestants. The initial reality was very different, but religion was a factor from the beginning and soon a prominent one. Some of the atrocities suffered by Protestants had a religious motivation or aspect. The insurgents were riddled with cultural and political divisions, most fundamentally between Irish and Old English parties; they joined together under the only banner that could unite them, calling themselves the Confederate Catholics of Ireland. After three decades on the continent, the Irish leader Owen Roe O'Neill returned to Ireland bolstered by a letter of support from the Pope praising O'Neill's 'excelling fervour, that is, your constancy against the heretics and mind of true faith' and offering his blessing to all 'who would help the cause of Catholics'.[23]

The bitterly sectarian disposition of the times was captured in extreme form by the exhortations of Cornelius O'Mahony, a Jesuit. Writing from Portugal in 1645, he urged the Confederate forces to 'kill your heretic adversaries.' He believed that they had killed up to 150,000 between 1641 and 1645, 'as the heretics themselves, mooing like cows, openly say and you do not deny, and I believe that more of the heretic enemy were killed, and I wish they all were.' The task before the Confederates was 'to kill the rest of the heretics or expel them from the territory of Ireland'.[24] When O'Mahony's book got to Ireland, it was roundly condemned by the Confederate Catholics, who had it burned by the common hangman. The source of scandal, however, seems to have been more O'Mahony's politics – he called for not only a Catholic king, but a native Catholic king, and he refused to recognise a heretical king as a legitimate sovereign – than his sectarianism. It should also be noted that O'Mahony's estimate that 150,000 or more Protestants had been killed by 1645 was wildly inaccurate. The best contemporary account estimates that 112,000 of English extraction and 504,000 Irish died from sword, plague, and famine between 1641 and 1652, so the number of Protestants killed by 1645 could not have been close to 150,000.

Such hugely exaggerated numbers were common at the time. The first exaggerations were deliberate propaganda by Protestants, designed to magnify outrage against Irish Catholics. In this they succeeded, and in the process, inflated numbers became widely circulated and widely accepted. 'At this date, towards the end of the religious wars', writes Patrick Corish, 'men were ready to believe the worst.'[25]

The autumn of 1649 brought more savage sectarianism, as

Oliver Cromwell's blend of religious and military ferocity found expression in slaughters of Catholics at Drogheda (where a good number of English Catholics were among the victims) and Wexford. His victims were not only surrendered soldiers but civilians, including clergy, women, and children. Even Edmund Ludlow, who was for a time leader of the parliamentary army in Ireland and was not squeamish about harsh measures, judged Cromwell's actions to be 'extraordinary severity', and all resistance collapsed in the face of it. Cromwell was in Ireland to prevent a royalist resurgence and to guarantee the confiscation of Irish land he needed to pay off his army and his financial backers, but he publicly defended his deeds as godly vengeance for Catholic massacres of Protestants at the beginning of the rising, thus imparting a bloody symmetry to the decade.

The bloodshed of 1641 and 1649 exerted a long influence in Irish history. For Catholics, Cromwell's extreme violence (and confiscations) were the source of long and bitter anger, becoming not only a key component in their communal memory of domination and victimisation, but a symbol of what they saw as the genocidal intentions of the English in Ireland. Protestant memories of 1641 were equally potent. In 1662 the first restoration Irish parliament passed an act establishing 23 October, the date for a foiled conspiracy to seize Dublin at the beginning of the rising, as a national holy day. The act anathematised the plot as 'a conspiracy so generally inhumane, barbarous and cruel, as the like was never before heard of in any age or kingdom', fomented by 'many malignant and rebellious papists and Jesuits, fryers, seminary priests and other superstitious orders of the popish pretended clergy'.[26] For more than a century the holy day was widely observed, and in Dublin with great pomp and circumstance. The Irish administration and the House of Lords processed to Christ Church Cathedral, where they worshipped according to the form of a specially composed liturgy and heard a sermon by a Church of Ireland dignitary, usually a bishop. These sermons, which were often published, rarely strayed far from the themes of: why Catholics cannot be trusted, why the nature of Catholicism inevitably yields barbarous acts like the massacre being remembered, and why Protestants must be eternally vigilant if 1641 was not to be visited upon them again. The Protestant community understood itself as perpetually under siege.

Both sets of memories, of 1641 and of 1649, served exactly the same function for their communities, passing from generation to generation a graphic image of the true nature of the enemy. The memories were also mutually exclusive. Protestants remembered 1641 and Catholics remembered 1649, but neither community remembered the other event (except sometimes to diminish the exaggerations of the other side). In this way the purity of communal pain and the consequent righteousness of the communal cause were preserved unsullied. A divided society produced divided memories, thus widening the divisions which were their source. The Scottish poet Ian Crichton Smith writes,

The anthology of memories of the other
is a book I hadn't reckoned on …[27]

In Ireland, 'the anthology of memories of the other' remains a book that is rarely even opened.

Identity in opposition
Although widespread theological controversy was relatively slow to develop in Reformation-era Ireland, it was in full flow by the early 1600s. In these combative, conflictual times, theology, and even one's Christian identity, seemed to depend as much on knowing what beliefs one rejected as on what one accepted. This situation corresponds to what theologian Alan Falconer calls 'theologies-in-opposition' and rabbi Marc Gopin refers to as 'negative identity'.[28] To a degree this is natural and inevitable: at a basic and primitive level, a person or group always knows, in part, what it is by what it is not. Taken too far, however, negative identity quickly becomes a trap. Our group resists taking a certain stance or course of action, however apparently sensible, because it is identified with your group; our group cannot allow your group to change, or admit that it has, because our identity is locked into yours. By such misshapen logic, negative identity serves to distort identity, prevent change, and perpetuate conflict.

When Trinity College Dublin, then a Church of Ireland institution, established its chair of divinity, the holder was called Professor of Theological Controversies. The men who held the post between 1607 and 1641 lived up to the title, focusing their lectures on refuting Cardinal Bellarmine, the foremost Catholic apologist of the time, who himself once held the chair of Controversial Theology at the Jesuit college in Rome. From 1600

to 1614, the Jesuit Henry Fitzsimon and the Church of Ireland
Bishop of Killaloe, John Rider, conducted a running debate that
produced five publications and prefigured numerous similar
contests. In *The Irish Catholic Experience,* Patrick Corish says of
early-seventeenth-century Catholics, 'to be a Catholic now was
to know why one was not a Protestant.'[29] Alan Ford's work on
the Protestant Reformation in Ireland demonstrates that the
same dynamic was operating in the contemporary Church of
Ireland, as Protestant controversialists, '[i]n rebutting Catholicism
... helped to create for members of the church a new consciousness of their own beliefs and their distinctiveness'.[30] Probing the
identity of the Irish churches in any post-Reformation period,
including today, is likely to reveal some variation on this theme.

Alan Falconer has done particularly important work in this
area, arguing that 'the role of the churches ... in the situation of
conflict in Ireland has been to reinforce the alienation of the different communities by developing theologies-in-opposition.'[31]
He notes the twentieth-century survival of this mode of thinking in *The One Hundred Texts,* first published in one volume in
1939 by T. C. Hammond, a former leader of Irish Church
Missions.[32] Each text was accompanied by about forty questions
divided into four or five sections, along with a section of comments and background information. Most of the questions were
positive in orientation, but the final section was always called
'Error Condemned', and the errors were always Roman. The errors cited for Acts 4:12 – 'Neither is there salvation in any other:
for there is none other name under heaven given among men,
whereby we must be saved' – were typical in content, though
unusually brief:

36. What is the one necessity of salvation?
    That it be in the Name of our Lord.

37. What necessity does Rome add?
    Union with the Pope.

38. Of what sin is she thus guilty?
    Of the sin of putting another name beside that of our
    Lord Jesus.

39. How does our text condemn all such teaching?
    'Neither is there salvation,' etc.[33]

None of this was Hammond's innovation; he was codifying the
Irish Church Mission's traditional approach to teaching con-

verts, in practice at least since 1862.[34] Catechism involved not
only what to believe, but what not to believe.

Falconer also discovered a different version of the same dynamic in a much more surprising place, a pamphlet called
Anglican and Irish: What We Believe, published in 1976 and written by Victor Griffin, then Dean of St Patrick's Cathedral, who
was widely regarded during his tenure as the very image of
Irish Protestant liberalism. Griffin's purpose may have been
eirenic, as Falconer says,[35] but his method was proportionately
more oppositional than Hammond's. Chapter two, 'The Bishop
of Rome in the Early Church,' makes no mention of Anglicanism,
but is devoted solely to proving that papal supremacy in the
early church was the result of Rome's political preeminence
rather than innate spiritual authority.[36] Chapter three, on 'The
Petrine Texts', argues that Catholic understandings of these texts
are false and that 'Anglicans ... are in complete agreement with
the early fathers and teachers of the church in taking these three
texts plainly and obviously as referring personally to St Peter
and having no bearing whatever on the claims of the Bishop of
Rome';[37] chapter four contends that 'monarchical episcopacy',
in the Anglican manner, 'is a legitimate development in the life
of the church',[38] but that the development of the papacy is not
equally legitimate. Only then, more than halfway through his
pamphlet, does Griffin begin to develop an essentially positive
account of an Anglican approach to the Christian faith.

It almost seems that Griffin did not so much choose this combative method as have it thrust upon him by the oppositional
assumptions of Irish society. He is clearly exasperated, even
angry, with a society in which a (presumably Catholic) news-
paper letter-writer can blame the Troubles on Henry VIII and
the Reformation, and a Catholic priest on television can 'justify
the claims of the church of Rome to be the one true church by ...
detailing the persecution of Roman Catholics by Protestants' but
with no acknowledgement of Catholic persecution of Protestants.'[39] 'Such ignorance of the elementary facts of history,' he
says, 'would be laughable if it were not so widespread and so
tragic.'[40] He rightly, and eirenically, concludes that '[r]eligious
persecution is a stain on the history of Christianity, an evil out of
which no denomination should seek to make capital but for
which all should be penitent before God and ask forgiveness one
of another.'[41]

Christian identity was not always posed in oppositional terms. Historian Ian Green has discovered particularly important evidence on this matter in his work on catechesis in the Church of Ireland from 1560 to 1800. His exhaustive study leads him to conclude that the polemics of identity-in-opposition did not usually extend to catechisms themselves: 'instruction at the elementary level tended to avoid the negative, and to focus on the positive message contained in the staple items of catechetical teaching.'[42] Green also notes occasional increases in controversial material and even some straightforward polemics, however, and one of the latter, the anonymously-written *A Protestant Catechism: Shewing the Principal Errors of the Church of Rome*, went through eleven Dublin editions between 1740 and 1785 – more Irish editions than all but one of the 75 Protestant catechisms Green identified.[43] With sectarianism, what is typical is not the only measure of significance.

Conversion
The conversion theme in Irish history is most often associated with the nineteenth-century evangelistic efforts known as the Second Reformation or the Protestant Crusade. While this is the period when conversion efforts were most visible and most openly contentious, an adequate understanding of how conversion came to be so explosive an issue requires that we look back to the Reformation era in Ireland.

In most of Europe, the Protestant Reformation worked on many levels of society. The state was involved; church leaders engaged in intense debate and church structures were altered; and many ordinary people participated and declared their loyalties. In Ireland, however, the Reformation was almost entirely a state phenomenon – few church leaders were committed to reform, and their efforts were largely ineffectual, while common people showed virtually no interest in or commitment to reformation. In these circumstances the concerns of the state naturally took priority, and the Irish priority of the energetic Tudor monarchs was to subdue and gain political control over the Irish people, which four centuries of English rule had notably failed to accomplish. As a result the Irish Reformation became another English method – along with colonisation, warfare, and anglicisation – for subjugating and civilising Ireland.

With the Irish Reformation labouring in this unequal yoke,

the results were sometimes quite at odds with typical Reformation values. In most places, for example, a basic Reformation
method and goal was to make religious literature, especially the
Bible, widely available in vernacular languages. But in Ireland
one state method of gaining political control was to suppress
Irish culture, in particular the Irish language. This conflict of interests was resolved very much in favour of the political needs
of the state and against the religious needs of the Reformation:
translation of religious literature into Irish only came in tiny
quantities and late in time. By the end of the sixteenth century,
the Reformation had made very little progress in Ireland, but the
connection between conversion to Protestantism and the political control of the Irish had been well established.

Historians have been inclined to underestimate the potency
of the conversion theme in seventeenth- and eighteenth-century
Ireland. David Miller's assessment of eighteenth-century Ulster
can be extended to all of Ireland for at least the period 1660-1800,
and it probably expresses a rough consensus among historians:
each of the three largest churches, Catholic, Church of Ireland,
and Presbyterian, 'was a church ministering to a pre-assigned
community – none was a sect seeking converts.'[44] This judgment
has much to commend it since combinations of political circumstance and under-resourced churches meant that simply ministering to one's own community was more than an enough challenge. So sweeping a generalisation as Miller's cries out for some
qualification, however, as he recognised himself without pursuing the matter – the situation he described obtained only 'generally', and the churches accepted it only 'for the time being'.[45]

A collection of essays published in 1995, *As By Law
Established: The Church of Ireland Since the Reformation,* begins to
give shape to the necessary qualification, at least for the Church
of Ireland. Whenever Protestants considered strategies for the
conversion of Catholics, education and translation of religious
literature into Irish were sure to figure. Throughout his essay on
charity schools, David Hayton tests the waning and waxing of
the conversion theme between 1690 and 1730. Ian Green, in his
work on catechisms, finds that four Irish or English/Irish catechisms published between 1680 and 1722, along with separate
publications of Old and New Testaments, 'remind us that concern about catechising in Irish was far from dead' – 'a not incon-
siderable number of episcopalians … still thought it best to carry
the fight to the Catholic majority in their own tongue.'[46]

Perhaps the most distinctive contribution of essays in *As By Law Established* is a more nuanced sense of the range of Reformation-advancing techniques, how they related to each other, and how they might ultimately connect to conversion. Working internally toward Protestant reform or externally toward conversion of Catholics might seem like opposite ideals, but while they may have been in immediate tension, they could also be sequential rather than contradictory. This sequential approach is apparent in John McCafferty's study of 'John Bramhall and the Church of Ireland in the 1630s'. The legal machinations and epic court battles conducted by Lord Deputy Wentworth and Bishop Bramhall in the 1630s do not immediately present themselves as the stuff of Reformation, but so they were conceived. Their efforts were designed to improve the finances of the church, a church on a stronger financial footing could support a resident clergy, and through these, said a petition to the king from the Convocation of 1634, 'barbarism and superstition will be expelled, and the subject shall learn his duty to God and to his Sovereign and true religion be propagated.'[47] According to McCafferty, this sequence was the internal logic of the Irish church policy of Wentworth, Bramhall, and Laud.[48]

A similar sequence is apparent in David Hayton's work on Protestant charity schools from 1690 to 1730. He points out that while pietist-inspired reformers of the early 1700s directed most of their energy to charity schools for Protestant children, they

> were by no means 'soft' on popery. In essence they were paring the forces of Reformation to a sharper point. ... The first concern of 'reforming' initiatives ... was to haul in backsliders from the Protestant community, so that progress might be made from a sure foundation. [49]

References to converting the Irish 'ran like a thread through the texture of charity-school sermons', he finds, and if this was 'a secondary consideration in reforming enterprises, an argument to catch contributions rather than an internal dynamic',[50] how interesting and significant – in an age when the Church of Ireland was supposedly a church ministering to a pre-assigned community, not a sect seeking converts – that the logic of converting Catholics should be a consistently attractive, and presumably productive, fundraising appeal! In any case, Hayton shows that the balance between reforming Protestants and converting Catholics had begun to shift toward conversion by 1711-

12. By the advent of the Protestant charter schools in 1733, the shift was complete, with proselytising taking first priority and other purposes a subordinate place.

Toby Barnard's work on 'Improving Clergymen 1660-1760' extends the range of reform efforts that can plausibly be related to advancing the Reformation. Raising clerical standards was the pivot point of the reform process. A reformed clergy would 'improve Ireland and the Irish',[51] but before this could happen, material conditions needed to improve to allow a consistently resident clergy. Therefore the Reformation cause was advanced not only by parliamentary efforts to strengthen the church's finances, but by agricultural reform, which would increase the income of those clerics who farmed and of the parishioners from whom Church of Ireland clergy took a tithe, and by architectural reform, which would not only provide the clergy with suitable housing, but stand as a civilised example and suitable alternative to the 'barbaric' housing of the Irish. 'Indeed, housing and architecture were part of the English and Protestant mission in Ireland',[52] Barnard argues. 'It was hardly chance that a cleric, determined to raise standards through the Charter School project, also schemed to publish rational house plans.'[53] If the culture of improvement sometimes seems to represent a mindset desiring little more than to enhance the status quo, having lowered its aims far beneath converting the nation, Barnard cautions us not to '[play] down the doubt and dismay that beset thoughtful Protestants. Some clergymen still entertained grander aspirations.'[54]

If conversion in seventeenth- and eighteenth-century Ireland is often remembered primarily as Protestant efforts to convert Catholics, there was also a reverse flow, though hard to quantify, of Protestants to Catholicism. Jacqueline Hill has observed that Fr Cornelius Nary, an influential Catholic priest in early eighteenth-century Dublin, retained hopes and advanced strategies for the conversion of Protestants. This may seem perfect folly in the context of an Irish Catholic Church staggering under the penal laws, but Hill argues that it made good sense in light of larger European trends, in which Protestants had fallen from about half of European population around 1600 to a northern fringe of twenty percent by 1700.[55] Observing the same trend, David Hayton comments that 'the contemporary description applied to many of the penal laws as acts "to prevent the growth of popery" was no mere trope.'[56] Similarly complex signs of Catholic conversion hopes and Protestant defensiveness can be observed into the nineteenth century.

Larger European trends toward a numerically reduced and geographically marginalised Protestantism were not the only reason for Irish Protestant anxiety. Irish Protestants were a small minority in a nominally Protestant country, an especially worrying situation for the Church of Ireland as the established church – the only minority established church in Europe. European and Irish marginality exacerbated Irish Protestant fears that a number of Catholic religious and political doctrines made Catholics innately disloyal, and in Catholic actions during the wars of the 1640s and then in the Williamite Wars of 1689-91, Protestants saw the proof of their fears. One result was the ferocious penal laws the eighteenth-century Irish Protestant parliament enacted against Catholic land, power, and religion (and to a lesser extent against Presbyterians and other Dissenters, also, but that is a different story). Although the exact motivation for these penal laws remains a disputed topic, one reason for the penal laws was that Protestants intended to remove the problem of what they saw as Catholic treachery by removing the basis of Catholic political power and destroying the Catholic religion. The connection between Protestantism and the political control of Irish Catholics could not have been more crudely or forcibly demonstrated. At the end of the 1700s, however, despite a century of penal laws, Catholics remained a large majority. For Irish Protestants, this Catholic majority always seemed an intractable problem.

The French revolution era, beginning in 1789, was one of those periods in human history when it seemed that the world had been turned upside down and old certainties no longer counted for anything. Ireland had experienced its own local version in the rebellion of 1798, the bloodiest episode in Irish history with 30,000 people killed in three months. Among Protestants, sectarian aspects and sectarian interpretations of the rebellion reawakened or confirmed fears about the Catholic majority. Protestants were terrified by what had happened and anxious about the future, but unsure what measures could guarantee safety. In the wake of the rebellion, three forces converged to dictate one kind of Protestant attempt at a solution to the problem.

(1) The solution was certain to involve religion. One deep-

rooted political and social assumption in eighteenth-century Ireland was the necessity of subordination for a stable social order. Each person must accept his or her place in society, neither envying those above nor abusing those below. A corollary was that only sound religion could guarantee the necessary subordination. Without religion, subordination would be based only on coercion and could not last; but if people understood that God had ordained the social hierarchy and put each person in the place intended, then they would submit willingly and the social order would be secure. Protestants, certain that theirs was the only sound religion, could only conclude that a great extension of Protestantism was the necessary foundation of a peaceful Ireland.

(2) By 1800 penal laws were no longer considered a valid way of creating a Protestant society. On the issue of coercion *versus* persuasion in religion, the eighteenth century had brought a fundamental shift in mental framework. In the early part of the century, some Protestant preachers could speak of penal laws and the light of the gospel in the same breath, as if they were acceptable and compatible paths to the same destination.[57] By mid-century, however, John Wesley, on one of his frequent and long visits to Ireland, noted in his journal that it was no 'wonder that those who were born Papists generally live and die such, when the Protestants can find no better way to convert them than Penal Laws and Acts of Parliament'.[58] Others came to ask similar questions, until by 1800 all shades of Protestant opinion had come to accept Wesley's viewpoint as irrefutable conventional wisdom: coercion for religious purposes was out. Not even the horrors of 1798 could revive interest in penal laws.[59]

(3) If penal laws were out, evangelical Protestantism was definitely in. In 1800 evangelicalism was still a relatively young reform movement, bursting with the kind of energy and drive that would be necessary to take on the task of extending Protestantism in Ireland. Even more important, evangelicals had nothing but contempt for the notion that compulsion could be used to establish Christianity. Instead they put their faith in evangelism and conversion. At the founding of the Evangelical Society of Ulster in 1798, George Hamilton preached from Luke 14:23, 'And the lord said unto the servant, Go out into the highways and hedges, and compel them to come in that my house may be filled', a text that has been tragically abused in Christian history.

Hamilton, however, condemned as 'carnal' and 'antichristian' the idea that 'external force or violence' or 'the arm of civil power' could ever make Christian disciples. 'Gospel compulsion', he maintained, could only mean evangelism.[60]

By 1800 these converging developments and assumptions had dovetailed tightly together. The need for social stability in Ireland (and the whole of Europe) had never been greater; sound religion was widely accepted as the necessary basis of a peaceful social order; coercion and penal laws were no longer credible as a means of establishing religion; evangelicals' conversion emphasis made them least reliant on coercion, and their energy made them most likely to act. These forces and beliefs pointed to an all but inevitable conclusion: Irish Protestants, with evangelicals prominent among them, must mount a campaign to convert Irish Catholics to Protestantism. In fact 'campaigns' may be more accurate than 'campaign', because these efforts, gradually gaining momentum until they were running at full throttle by the 1820s, came from diverse origins and had no over-all coordination, but taken together they were a formidable force.

While these events are sometimes called the Second Reformation, one contemporary participant, William Magee, Church of Ireland Archbishop of Dublin, saw things differently. 'In truth,' he said in 1825, 'with respect to Ireland, the Reformation may, strictly speaking, be truly said only now to have begun.'[61] Although 'Second Reformation' remains a useful term, Magee made a valid point. Explicitly religious, even theological, conflict became a commonplace of Irish public life as never before, and the contest may justly be called a struggle for the hearts and minds of the Irish people, partly because the quest for religious supremacy was never far removed from the quest for political supremacy.

No issue was more explosive than conversion. Stories of conversions were the very lifeblood of Protestant efforts; denying the stories, or countering them with tales of death-bed returns to Catholicism, were essential for Catholic morale. Most sensitive of all were stories of priests converting. In 1827, after one huge public theological debate (some of these debates ran for days and were attended by thousands, although only a few could actually hear what was said), the Catholic priest involved, Fr Tom Maguire, claimed that the Church of Ireland Archbishop of

Tuam, Power le Poer Trench, had offered him £1000 plus £800 a year if he would convert. The archbishop, denouncing this as an absurd lie, sued Maguire and won £50 damages. As in all such cases, however, ordinary Protestants and Catholics no doubt believed what it suited them to believe.

In 1826 a satirical Catholic publication congratulated a Catholic priest who had converted to the Church of Ireland. 'I hear you have obtained a chaplaincy of £300 a year. A fine thing this – a capital price for an old "turn-coat".' But the author had some advice for the converted priest: do not bother hoping for higher or richer office.

> No, no, these are fat things which good Protestants want for themselves; and though the church *endures* such apostates as you, believe me that it suspects their sincerity. ... Enjoy yourself for awhile, and never forget that, like hundreds of your predecessors, you will one day be likely to seek refuge in the church you have abandoned.[62]

Here were the classic Catholic responses to conversions to Protestantism: the conversion was likely insincere, perhaps for reasons of material advantage, and in any case the so-called convert (sometimes called 'perverts') had probably only temporarily lapsed and would eventually return. To live a Protestant and die a Catholic, that was the best of both worlds.

In all this controversy, conversion and the political control of Catholics were unashamedly linked. Of course evangelicals were not alone in making this connection nor, as we have seen, was it a new idea, but neither were they able to see beyond this conventional wisdom of their day. 'Those who are most under the influence of the word of God,' said Peter Roe, a prominent evangelical preacher, 'are most anxious that its [government's] administration should proceed steadily and uninterrupted – while, on the contrary, those who are unacquainted with, or neglect, or oppose that word, are dissatisfied, turbulent, and rebellious.'[63] The implications for dissatisfied, turbulent, and rebellious Irish Catholics were obvious: they would continue in their disaffected state until brought more 'under the influence of the word of God', meaning Protestantism.

Sometimes the connection between conversion and politics could be crude and direct. In 1827, Archbishop Magee required all converts from Catholicism in his diocese to take the oaths of allegiance and supremacy. Lord Farnham, a leading lay evangelical who founded the Cavan Association for Promoting the Reformation, argued this way:

1. The claims of Irish Catholics must be conceded if they continue in their present strength of numbers.
2. If conceded, the Church Establishment must fall.
3. The separation of Ireland and Britain would follow.[64]

Because maintaining the political status quo depended, from this point of view, upon converting Catholics to Protestantism, conversion inevitably became an explosive politico-religious issue. In 1851 the respected Church of Ireland evangelical leader Henry Irwin expressed his satisfaction with a confirmation service in County Limerick for two hundred converts from Rome, who at the close of the service 'joined in singing an appropriate hymn to the air of our national anthem, which was most judiciously chosen to cast a beam of loyalty over their minds'.[65] Sound religion and sound politics had become all but indistinguishable in many Protestant minds, and Catholics bitterly resented the political intentions of evangelism. 'The Bible, without note or comment,' said one Catholic pamphleteer, 'is not less a means of Protestant dominion than the Orange Yeoman's military array.'[66]

Efforts to convert Catholics to Protestantism coincided with the Irish famine of 1845-49, to tragic effect. Ironically, if the famine, viewed from a historical perspective, was to have a religious legacy, it probably ought to have been a happy one on balance, insofar as a tragedy of this magnitude can leave any positive legacy. Christians of several churches, Catholic and Protestant, worked heroically and indefatigably – and frequently cooperatively – to relieve suffering. Even though their efforts could not possibly match the scale of need, the consequences of the famine would have been worse without their work.

A conjunction of two factors ensured that cooperative efforts would not be the remembered legacy of famine. First, famine hit hardest in poor, agricultural, and overwhelmingly Catholic regions of the west which were most dependent on the potato, while more prosperous and predominantly Protestant Ulster, with its more diverse economy, was relatively unaffected. This difference in experience of the famine, coming at the same time as intense Protestant efforts to convert Catholics, ensured that service and cooperation would take second place in popular memory to 'souperism': the charge that some Protestants offered food (usually soup, hence 'souperism') or other material aid to desperate Catholics only on the condition that they convert or, more likely, fulfill some religious condition, perhaps attending a Bible class or worship service. Desmond Bowen's study, *Souperism: Myth or Reality*, demonstrates that clerical cooperation was the norm and that charges of souperism were exaggerated. But they were also extremely difficult to prove or disprove, one person's souperism being another's disinterested benevolence. In 1847 James Collins, Church of Ireland Dean of Killala and a diligent co-worker with the Catholic priest of Killala in the cause of famine relief, was accused of souperism by another Catholic priest in the area. While admitting that Catholics had joined his church, Collins denied souperism, saying that conversions were 'a consequence and not a condition of the relief afforded'.[67] Such ambiguous stories allowed whatever interpretation the interpreter was inclined to give them.

The characteristic outlook of the evangelical party among Protestants left them particularly wide open to charges of souperism. The 1847 annual report of the Baptist Irish Society affirmed that its primary work was evangelism, not famine relief, and described how the two were related.

> Large numbers of the peasantry have offered to join our churches, supposing that thereby they would be provided for. In all such cases they have been told the entrance into the church of Christ is by sincere repentance and faith in Jesus Christ and in him alone. Having first corrected the mistake, the agents have not allowed these children of want to go unrelieved. And, while carefully abstaining from any effort to proselytise, they have not, through fear of misrepresentation, refrained from making known the truth as it is in Jesus, while distributing the bounty of the British churches.[68]

This typically evangelical effort to distinguish between proselytising and evangelising would almost inevitably lead to charges of souperism –as the Baptists apparently realised, judging by the 'fear of misrepresentation' remark – and yet famine relief was far from being merely an occasion to make converts. British churches that gave nothing to the Baptist Irish Society for evangelism gave generously for famine relief. Grey areas abounded in both doctrine and practice.

What can be said with certainty is that resentful memories of souperism long outlived the famine era. From the Reformation onwards, conversion to Protestantism often held the promise of some material benefit, and long before the famine Catholics were reflexively suspicious that greed was the motive for conversion. The notion of souperism summed up this tradition in an image invested with particular potency because of the total vulnerability of its victims.

The census of 1861 demonstrated that Protestant conversion efforts had failed to alter the religious demography of Ireland – after half a century of intensive labour, the denominational balance remained much as before. Why the Second Reformation failed to make more numerical difference is not clear; some converts no doubt returned to the Catholic Church, others emigrated. What is certain, however, is that conversion efforts did not fail before having considerable impact. Specifically religious conflict became a common feature of Irish public life, and conversion was more contentious than ever. Hoping to convert large numbers of Catholics, the Protestant campaigners were far more successful at revitalising their own Protestant churches; hoping to bequeath to future generations a legacy of social peace, they left behind instead an intensified sectarian animosity.

Separation
Sectarianism both creates and requires separation, to which the Christian churches have contributed greatly. One of the principal areas of separation has been marriage and family life – for the most part Catholics marry Catholics and Protestants marry Protestants. Those who marry across these boundaries have sometimes done so against the wishes of their churches and families, and some have suffered degrees of tension, rejection, and abuse for it. In Ireland, these matters have never been more in the public eye than in the aftermath of Pope Pius X's *Ne Temere* decree of 1907.

Pope Pius issued the decree in order to tidy up some inconsistencies in Catholic marriage law. Among other provisions, *Ne Temere* reaffirmed and applied universally the teaching that 'only those marriages are valid that are contracted before the parish-priest ... and at least two witnesses', and it also added that this condition of validity applied even if one partner was not Catholic. *Ne Temere* came into effect quietly enough in 1908, but it soon became the occasion for enormous sectarian controversy. 'In simple terms,' summarises Fr Eoin de Bhaldraithe in a study of *Ne Temere,* 'a mixed marriage in Ireland would not be valid in Roman Catholic eyes after *Ne Temere* unless witnessed by the Parish Priest. In practice the Catholic clergy would not officiate unless both parties had promised that all the children would be Catholic.'[69]

In 1910 the implications came to public attention in the celebrated McCann case in Belfast. Alexander McCann was Catholic, his wife Agnes a Presbyterian. They married in her Presbyterian church and had two children before he left with the children in 1910. Protestant and Catholic accounts of the situation had that much in common, but little else.

The Protestant interpretation first came to public attention through the intervention of Agnes McCann's minister, William Corkey, in November 1910. According to Corkey, a happy marriage had been ruined by a meddling priest who told the McCanns that their marriage was invalid in light of *Ne Temere* and would require a proper Catholic ceremony; when Mrs McCann refused, her husband became abusive and finally left her. This story became the subject of sermons, pamphlets, debates in Westminster, and public rallies through Ireland and Scotland. Protestants understood it as confirming their every fear about priestcraft and Romanism: the Catholic church was a domineering, manipulative institution, insinuating itself into all areas of life; since *Ne Temere* allowed for national exceptions which had been granted for Germany but not for Ireland, the McCann case represented the attempt of a hostile foreign power to undermine British law. To Protestants, the whole story provided a cautionary, prophetic parable about life in a home rule Ireland, and Presbyterian historian John Barkley argues that the McCann case was the final nail in the coffin of Presbyterian support for home rule.

Catholics disputed some of the basic facts and derived from them a totally different interpretation. According to a letter from Alexander McCann which was read out in the House of Commons by nationalist MPs, the marriage was always unhappy because Agnes McCann was a sectarian shrew who 'cursed the Pope and sang hymns all day'.[70] Furthermore, he left her of his own volition and without any prompting from any priest, a claim that gained additional credence when Mrs McCann and her supporters failed to name the priest supposedly involved. Joseph Devlin, nationalist MP for West Belfast, dismissed

Protestant hysteria not only as totally unfounded, but as the manipulation of an unfortunate event for political purposes – he claimed that election posters in his constituency read, 'Will you vote for Devlin and have your Protestant children kidnapped by the Priest?'[71] All parties involved found suitable facts and interpretations, and the effect of the whole affair was to deepen pre-existing convictions and divisions.

Long after the McCann furore died down, *Ne Temere* remained a contentious issue because of its effect on Protestant numbers in the south of Ireland, where Protestants made up only 10 per cent of the population at the time of partition. It was always likely that some Protestants would want to marry Catholics, and the effect of *Ne Temere*'s requirement that the Protestant partner consent to raising the children as Catholics was to reduce the Protestant population. Because several factors contributed to declining Protestant numbers, it is difficult to calculate the exact role of *Ne Temere*, but in 1974 a study by Garret FitzGerald, then Foreign Minister of the Irish government, concluded that from 1946 to 1961 the effects of the *Ne Temere* decree caused Protestant population to fall at the rate of 1 per cent per year. In 1970, however, the situation was dramatically improved when the papal decree *Matrimonia Mixta* removed any requirement that the Protestant partner promise that children would be raised Catholic. In 1983 tension was further eased, though far from eliminated, when the Irish Catholic bishops specifically applied *Matrimonia Mixta* to the Irish situation, saying, 'The religious upbringing of the children is the joint responsibility of both parents. The obligations of the Catholic do not, and cannot, cancel out, or in any way call into question, the conscientious duties of the other party.'[72] The situation of mixed marriages remains difficult, however, both in terms of social pressures and in specifically religious areas such as sharing communion.

Sacred violence, politics as religion
Religion and politics, we have argued in chapter one, are inherently intersecting categories. That intersection need not be problematic and can, we believe, be an enormously positive force. Examples are many, but we would cite the role of religion in the US Civil Rights Movement of the 1950s and 1960s as a particularly important one. Sociologist David Martin's recent book, *Does Christianity Cause War?*, analyses religion working as a positive

political force in various modes of operation and political contexts.[73] The intersection of religion and politics can also be destructive, however, and sectarianism typically involves such an intersection.

No matter how people may define their religion or lack of it, their effective religion is the things they give highest priority, especially those things held as non-negotiable, which will not or cannot be compromised. These commitments may or may not be formally identified as religious, but to the extent that they are non-negotiable, they effectively constitute one's 'religion' – in Christian terms, idolatrous religion, which supplants loyalty appropriately given only to God. This is how political commitments which are not inherently religious or sectarian can come, first, to take on a sacred character in the lives of adherents and, second, to be sectarian when they divide along sectarian lines. One way of measuring the strength of such political commitments is to observe whether they are backed by violence or the threat of violence. In terms of the development of sectarianism in Irish history, the significance of these reflections is that events and ideas leading to the foundation of Northern Ireland and the Irish Free State involved both absolutised politics and the use or threat of violence.

For much of the nineteenth century, the political desire of most Irish nationalists had been for home rule for Ireland – effectively a local parliament for local affairs, but still within a United Kingdom framework. Irish unionists had been resisting home rule under the slogan 'Home Rule is Rome Rule.' By 1911, however, home rule legislation was inevitable. In December 1910 a tight general election left Irish nationalists holding the balance of power at Westminster, and the price they exacted for supporting the Liberals was, as always, home rule. Before home rule could be enacted, the House of Lords' veto power had to be removed, because the Lords had vetoed the second Home Rule Bill in 1893, and they certainly would have done so again. With nationalist support and the King's consent, the Lords' veto was duly abolished in August 1911. In April 1912 a third Home Rule Bill began its slow, but this time inexorable, course through parliament.

The years since 1886 and the first Home Rule Bill had done nothing to diminish Ulster unionist opposition to home rule. The issue now was, how far would they go in resisting the legal imposition of home rule? In 1886 and 1893 the anti-home rule formula had involved an all but seamless joining of political, economic, and religious factors. In the 1910s these remained as before, but now unionists upped the stakes by declaring an absolute commitment to opposing home rule and backing it by threatening and planning for violence.

Already by the autumn of 1911, unionist leader Edward Carson announced to a wildly enthusiastic crowd of over 50,000 Ulster Protestants that he would lead them into self-government should home rule become law. Winston Churchill, then a Liberal cabinet minister, spoke for many when he disdained 'these frothings', believing that 'when the worst comes to the worst we shall find that civil war evaporates in uncivil words.'[74] As events unfolded, however, Protestant resolve to resist home rule became increasingly undeniable. In addition to providing the personnel for resistance, the Protestant churches also helped to provide legitimacy. On Easter Tuesday 1912, in anticipation of the imminent introduction of the Home Rule Bill, the Unionist Council organised another mass protest rally, this one attended by more than 100,000 people. The event began with prayers offered by the Presbyterian moderator and the Church of Ireland Archbishop of Armagh, thus blessing resistance with the support of the two largest Protestant churches. The course of events was heating popular passions, which in the summer of 1912 sometimes spilled over into the well-worn groove of sectarian antagonism. The single worst incident, at a Celtic-Linfield football match in Celtic Park, sent sixty casualties to hospital.

In addition to finding such actions personally abhorrent, Carson thought that they were a waste of energy and politically counter-productive, as they would diminish the unionist cause in the eyes of the world, especially in the eyes of British Conservatives and others whose support the unionists urgently needed. Unionist leaders sought to channel the passions behind sectarian riots by elevating and focusing home rule resistance, casting it in the rubric of the ancient Scottish covenanting tradition. The idea of covenanting enjoyed unrivalled cachet among Presbyterians, because in the 1500s and 1600s, national covenants had been the form whereby Scottish Calvinists joined together, under God, the causes of church and nation in resistance to popery and prelacy, i.e. Catholicism and Anglicanism. These covenants were central to Presbyterian memory and identity.

Now the unionists, Church of Ireland and Nonconformist alike, joined together in the astonishing Presbyterianisation of Ulster Protestantism, formulating the basis of their resistance to home rule in a Solemn League and Covenant for Ulster, which had been submitted to the Protestant churches for editing and approval. For Ulster Protestants, Covenant Day, Saturday, 28 September 1912, was essentially a holy day: work ceased, the day began with congregations meeting for worship, and many processed from worship to the centres where they signed the Covenant. About noon in Belfast City Hall, Carson was the first to sign the Covenant, followed by Lord Londonderry and church representatives. When it was all over 218,206 Ulstermen had signed the Covenant, 228,991 women had signed a parallel Declaration, and resistance to home rule was firmly cast as the cause of God and Ulster.

Seeking in part to circumvent sectarian rioting, unionist leaders had at the same time cast their entire movement in sectarian terms. In the midst of all the overt mingling of politics and religion, perhaps the most chilling element was a single phrase from the Covenant, which committed those who signed it to 'using all means which may be found necessary to defeat the present conspiracy to set up a Home Rule Parliament in Ireland'.[75] This was not merely a commitment to the union as a high ideal, or to resisting home rule by any *lawful* means, but resistance *by all means which may be found necessary.* At one stroke, this phrase makes a particular political arrangement absolute and non-negotiable and threatens violence.

The threat was not mere words. Military drilling began spontaneously among some Orange Order lodges, but in January 1913, all the separate efforts were harnessed together in an Ulster Volunteer Force. At first, all this enthusiastic but ill-equipped drilling was the source of mirth for outsiders, but the UVF rapidly became a large, committed, and well-organised force. After April 1914, when a carefully plotted gun-running effort brought in 20,000 rifles and 2,000,000 rounds of ammunition, it was also a well-armed force.

The extent of Ulster Protestant military organisation was an innovation observed with great interest by Irish nationalists, who soon responded in kind. In the midst of a violent labour dispute in the summer of 1913, union leader James Larkin suggested that Dublin workers should follow the Ulster Protestant example, and one of his deputies organised a UVF-inspired citizen army. The arming of Ulster coincided with Patrick Pearse's transformation from cultural and constitutional nationalist to physical force republican, and the autumn of 1913 found him enthusing about the UVF.

> I am glad that the Orangemen have armed, for it is a goodly thing to see arms in Irish hands. ... I should like to see any and every body of Irish citizens armed. We must accustom ourselves to the thought of arms, to the sight of arms, to the use of arms. We may make mistakes in the beginning and shoot the wrong people; but bloodshed is a cleansing and a sanctifying thing, and the nation which regards it as the final horror has lost its manhood.[76]

That same autumn, a force of National Volunteers emerged, explicitly following the UVF example and soon flourishing. In the summer of 1914, the National Volunteers once again followed the UVF example, this time with their own gun-running effort into Howth harbour. In 1916 most UVF members and many from the National Volunteers fought in the British forces against Germany. The Irish Volunteers, a radical splinter group from the National Volunteers, took over the GPO and declared an Irish republic.

Consistent with the French revolution roots of Irish republicanism, the proclamation of a republic on Easter Monday 1916, drafted by Patrick Pearse, was impeccably secular and nonsectarian. On another level, however, Pearse's revolutionary thought throbbed with religious rhetoric and imagery, a heretical union of Christianity and nationalism. In Pearse's thought national freedom was 'like a divine religion' bearing 'the marks of unity, of sanctity, of catholicity, of apostolic succession'; the message of Irish republicanism was a gospel, and the four advocates he admired most – Wolfe Tone, Thomas Davis, John Mitchel, and James Fintan Lalor – were its four evangelists, prophets who spoke the word of the Lord; three deaths resulting from a gun-running episode were a national rebaptism by blood; the impending rising was the exulted 'day of the Lord'. He gave liturgical expression to the 'religion of Irish nationality' in an oath-prayer.[77]

> In the name of God,
> By Christ His only Son,
> By Mary His gentle Mother,

By Patrick the Apostle of the Irish,
By the loyalty of Colm Cille,
By the glory of our race,
By the blood of our ancestors,
By the murder of Red Hugh,
By the sad death of Hugh O'Neill,
By the tragic death of Owen Roe,
By the dying wish of Sarsfield,
By the anguished sigh of Fitzgerald,
By the bloody wounds of Tone,
By the Noble blood of Emmet,
By the Famine corpses,
By the tears of Irish exiles,
We swear the oaths our ancestors swore,
That we will free our race from bondage,
Or that we will fall fighting hand to hand.
Amen.[78]

None of Pearse's compatriots matched the intensity or consistency of his revolutionary mysticism, and some had no faith at all. But a general Catholic piety – mostly more orthodox than Pearse's – was common among the idealist revolutionaries gathered in the General Post Office. One of Pearse's first acts in the GPO was to summon a priest to hear confession, and the last act of the surrendered men was to say the rosary, beads in one hand, rifles in the other. And Pearse's fusion of Christ's sacrifice and national sacrifice was seductive. Even James Connolly, always the rigorous socialist, required the Pearsean language of Calvary, blood, and redemption to express the meaning of the imminent rising. Such imagery could be applied to the trivial and the profound. In the confusion after the rising, when the mayor of Dublin, a moderate member of the Irish Parliamentary Party suffered a brief false arrest, he 'could use the incident to compare himself to Christ',[79] observes historian Roy Foster. Terence MacSwiney, the lord mayor of Cork who would die on hunger strike in 1920, reflected on the significance of those republican martyrs who preceded him in dying for the cause of Irish freedom.

[It] is because they were our best and bravest that they had to die. No lesser sacrifice would save us. Because of it our struggle is holy – our battle is sanctified by their blood, and our victory is assured by their martyrdom. We, taking up the

work they left incomplete, confident in God, offer in turn sacrifice from ourselves. It is not we who take innocent blood,
but we offer it, sustained by the example of our immortal
dead and that Divine example which inspires us all – for the
redemption of our country.[80]

No wonder that political scientist Frank Wright argued that
'nationalisms are not merely "like" religions – they are religions.'[81]
What might seem a startling claim is transparently plausible in
light of the Pearsean tradition of Irish republicanism, and visible
as well in other nationalisms. Seán Farrell Moran, author of a
study of republican martyrdom, concludes that the influence of
Pearse's ideas is the key to understanding IRA violence, which
'is hardly inexplicable terrorism; it functions in a tradition in
Western culture which, out of a deep sense of grievance and a
hope to institute a new age, will not surrender its notion of the
holy and the true.'[82] The founding events of the modern Irish
state found religion, politics, and bloodshed mingled once
again.

If the 1920 Government of Ireland Act divided Ireland into
two political entities in 1920, it was by no means a clean split or a
final settlement. A majority of Irish nationalists could accept the
1921 Anglo-Irish Treaty as providing a significant measure of
immediate benefit and as a basis for pursuing the ideal of a 32-
county republic, but a large minority refused to accept the
treaty. Sinn Féin, the anti-treaty party, had first lost the treaty
vote in the Dáil, then they lost an election divided along
treaty/anti-treaty lines, then they lost another election, then
they lost a civil war between pro- and anti-treaty forces. But still
they persevered in refusing to recognise the Free State government and in maintaining a counter government which they understood as the legitimate government of Ireland. Countess
Constance Markiewicz was one Sinn Féin member pragmatic
enough to wonder how, despite the elections, despite the civil
war, they could claim to be the real, legitimate government of
Ireland. Sinn Féin leader Éamon De Valera's answer was concise: 'The people have never a right to do wrong.'[83] The voice of
the people will matter only when they get the right answer.

This assertion is significant in at least two ways. First, De
Valera was a devout and theologically well-informed Catholic,
and he could hardly have failed to notice the close similarity
between 'the people have never a right to do wrong' and the

doctrine that 'error has no right', the Augustinian notion at the heart of sectarianism in Irish history. Here De Valera transmuted 'error has no right' into a directly political principle. Second, by invoking 'the people have never a right to do wrong', De Valera put the goal of a thirty-two county republic beyond negotiation. The longed for republic thus became a quasi-religious object, a political commitment on equal standing with unionism's absolute rejection of home rule, 'by all means which may be found necessary'. Such a view of the republic would have a long life. If the IRA never used the words 'the people have never a right to do wrong', the logic was ever-present, behind the archaic insistence that the IRA army council is the legitimate government of Ireland and above all, until 1994, behind the maintenance of a violent campaign without a popular mandate.

'The people have never a right to do wrong', 'by all means which may be found necessary': similar and absolutist rationales for contesting political ideals, and the roots of a sectarian political culture which finds compromise a difficult skill to learn.

Conclusion

By such means – subtle and crude, direct and convoluted – were the roots of sectarianism propagated in Irish history. If an account of them suggests the weight of history, it should also suggest hope. First, an historical account shows that sectarianism, while the product of powerful forces, was not inevitable. It resulted from concrete choices people made, and which they might have made differently. We cannot undo the past, but we can make different choices now to shape a different future. Understanding those past choices can suggest what it might mean to choose differently now. Second, while one can draw links, more and less direct, between the historical roots of sectarianism and their current manifestations, in no case is the same dynamic present in precisely the same way today. In every case, in fact, the current situation is an improvement on the past cases presented here. We pointed to the poisonous influence of the doctrine that 'error has no right'; over the past century, almost all Christian churches have repudiated that doctrine. One can still see examples of 'identity in opposition', but the ecumenical movement and other vehicles for improved relations between churches have significantly undermined it. While the kind of absolutised politics that yields nationalism-as-religion is still visible, developments in both religion and politics have pushed it off centre stage. Ordinary Catholics and Protestants are far less likely to endorse such stances than they were a century ago. These and other changes are reasons for gratitude and hope. They are also reasons to seek further what it will mean and require to move beyond sectarianism.

CHAPTER 3

What is Sectarianism? A Working Definition

Introduction

The task of saying what sectarianism 'is' becomes complex because the system of sectarianism is itself one of extraordinary complexity. It has both inner and outer aspects. Sectarianism is about what goes on in people's hearts and minds, and it is about the kind of institutions and structures created in society. It is about people's attitudes to one another, about what they do and say and the things they leave undone or unsaid. Moreover, 'sectarian' is usually a negative judgement that people make about someone else's behaviour and rarely a label that they apply to themselves, their own sectarianism always being the hardest to see. In this chapter we are inviting the reader to keep asking the question: do I recognise these dynamics in any form in my own life, in my family life, in the groups to which I belong, or in society in general?

We have approached the task of defining sectarianism with the intention of making the definition a tool that can assist people in analysing the phenomenon in order to help them to move beyond it. In our work with groups we have found that better understanding has indeed facilitated movement. This approach has meant, however, that our definition is longer, more complex, and more detailed than those proposed by others.[1] Below we give the full text of our definition, and, after some preliminary comments on intentions and consequences, we take each phrase in turn and tease out some of the major aspects or implications.

Sectarianism ...

... is a system of attitudes, actions, beliefs, and structures
   – at personal, communal, and institutional levels
   – which always involves religion, and typically involves a negative mixing of religion and politics

... which arises as a distorted expression of positive, human needs especially for belonging, identity, and the free expression of difference

... and is expressed in destructive patterns of relating:
- hardening the boundaries between groups
- overlooking others
- belittling, dehumanising, or demonising others
- justifying or collaborating in the domination of others
- physically or verbally intimidating or attacking others.

This definition is a generic one, i.e. it has elements that could equally well be applied to other types of 'isms' such as racism, of which sectarianism is a close relative. It is an attempt, which some may regard as unwieldy, to focus attention on the different layers of the system, without allowing anyone the luxury of imagining that they are not somehow implicated in it. It is also an analytical tool, which can be used by individuals and groups to help them make judgments about the sectarian nature of actions or events, their own or other people's. One of the keys to making judgments about whether actions or events are sectarian is the relationship between intentions and consequences.

Intentions and consequences
One way to gauge whether or not speech, an event, an action, or a decision can be judged to be sectarian is to look not only at the intention of the person or group involved, but also at the outcome or potential outcome of the speech or action, in as far as this can be foreseen. If the outcome entails the development of, or the augmenting of, one or more destructive patterns of relating, then the speech or action can be judged to be sectarian. The most potent destructive patterns of relating which we have identified are: hardening the boundaries between groups; overlooking others; belittling, dehumanising, or demonising others; justifying or collaborating in the domination of others; and physically intimidating or attacking others. We will examine these in detail below. The importance of the distinction that we are making between intentions and consequences is that it allows people to expose the operation of the sectarian system at a point where it is most subtle. This point is the distortion of the good intentions of any person or group.

When challenged, people reflexively appeal to their intentions to absolve themselves from guilt: I was defending the truth, upholding my tradition, standing up for my community. But a claim of purity of intent does not protect anyone from being judged to be speaking or acting in a sectarian way. There can be sectarian outcomes – of speech, actions, omissions, or decisions – which were not intended. People can say, do, or decide things with one set of intentions in mind, which are, in their terms, wholly good, justifiable, and possibly even necessary. Yet their speech, action, or decision can have a sectarian outcome. The Roman Catholic church's stance on integrated education, for example, is not intended to be sectarian, it is about identity, ethos, and community building. But in a society where the dividing lines are so substantial that in places they are built in brick and metal, the general refusal to engage in the conversation about integrated education at best tends to harden the boundaries between Roman Catholics and Protestants through suspicion of the Catholic Church's motives, and at worst lends itself to belittling Protestant or State education. It is important to notice in this example that it is not a question of whether or not integrated education is seen as a good thing in and of itself. That is a wholly other discussion. Rather it is the destructive patterns of relating engendered by refusing to enter into discussion which attract the judgment of being sectarian.

Equally the relationship of Protestant churches with Loyal Order church parades is not intended to be sectarian. It is an historical link with a group which aspires to the ideals of upholding the Protestant faith and doing charitable works, and which also acts as a certain force for social cohesion, especially in rural areas. In a society, however, where the right to respect and parity of esteem is so contested that it has had to be enshrined in a constitutional settlement, some of the activities associated with some Loyal Order church parades lend themselves at best to the interpretation of overlooking Catholic/nationalists and at worst to belittling or dominating them. Such activities would include insistence on parading in Catholic/nationalist areas without prior dialogue with the residents; playing provocative music; making provocative or offensive gestures; carrying offensive or threatening banners; and including paramilitary colour parties in the procession. The Protestant churches are implicated by association, since it is they who continue to provide facilities for such services to which the parades are geared.

Conerning this example, it is important to note that we are not suggesting that parading is sectarian, nor that all Loyal Order church parades are sectarian. Rather it is the destructive patterns of relating (overlooking, belittling, or demonising) involved in some of the activities associated with some parades which make them sectarian. In these cases, Protestant churches can also be judged to be sectarian, by association, if they do not actively try to ensure that there is no destructive behaviour associated with services in their churches. In mid-1998, Robin Eames, the Church of Ireland Archbishop of Armagh, decided to require those attending services in previously contentious situations, such as at Drumcree,[2] to agree to three affirmations aimed both at stopping the destructive behaviour before and after the service and in some measure at dissociating the Church of Ireland from the event. These affirmations were:

• the avoidance of any action before or after the service which diminishes the sanctity of that worship;

• obedience to the law of the land before and after the service;

• respect for the integrity of the Church of Ireland by word and action and the avoidance of the use of all church property or its environs in any civil protest following the service.[3]

This represents an attempt to take positive action to prevent sectarian consequences of church parades. It also raises, however, a very thorny problem for the Church of Ireland or indeed any church in a similar situation. The problem is whether or not this represents unacceptable limitations on ministry to church members who are also Orangemen.

Obviously, the particular context of contested public space and sharply divided groups in Northern Ireland increases the possibility of sectarian implications. Actions which in one context take on sectarian overtones, in another context might be deemed more or less benign or at least irrelevant. To continue the parading example, the large Orange parade at Rossnowlagh, County Donegal, passes off virtually without incident each year, because the Catholic/nationalist population, who are the majority in their jurisdiction, feel no threat from the parade. The context in Donegal allows a degree of toleration not possible in the contested atmosphere of Northern Ireland without some measure of dialogue and negotiation.

One danger with this type of distinction between intentions and consequences is that people could use it negatively, by claiming destructive outcomes in order to prevent others from taking actions. It is the type of logic that claims: you can't do that because it will have sectarian consequences, and I will make sure that it does. When organising a socio-political panel discussion, for example, a third level college found that if they invited Sinn Féin representatives, the Democratic Unionist Party (DUP) would refuse to take part. They were then faced with choices. They could decide not to invite Sinn Féin; in this case they could rightly be accused of being sectarian by overlooking them. Alternatively, they could invite them anyway and accept that the DUP would absent themselves and that therefore their voice would not be heard. In this latter case, someone might be tempted to say that this was the DUP's choice, they opted to exclude themselves. It is also true, however, that the college would be setting up the situation in a way that overlooked their concerns. The issue of whether or not a person agrees with their concerns is secondary. Here we are dealing primarily with the implications of destructive patterns of relating, and in this instance it appears that there is no way to avoid a sectarian outcome other than to cancel the event or to hold two separate panels.

We are arguing that the assessment of outcome is key to judging whether or not an action is sectarian. We also want to affirm that in the short term it may sometimes be necessary to make decisions or to take actions that have explicitly sectarian outcomes in order, or in the hope that, in the longer term, other choices may become possible. An example occurred when we were talking with a group about the sectarian effects of the nationalist boycotts of Protestant businesses that took place after Drumcree Two, 1996. One of the participants was looking at us with a pained expression. When asked what was wrong he replied that 'bad and all' as the boycotts were, the alternative was massive street violence. What is important here is for people to know that they are choosing a sectarian option, to know why they deem it to be so important that it is not to be avoided, and to know what they hope will be the movement that will make this type of choice redundant in the long term.

Understanding the complex relationship between intentions and consequences is, in our opinion, crucial to understanding how to judge whether speech, actions, or decisions are potentially or actually sectarian. A claim that a person had no intention of being sectarian cannot immunise anyone from responsibility for sectarian outcomes of their speech, actions, or decisions. Moreover, to claim purity of intent, whilst persisting in behaviour that has sectarian outcomes, is to strengthen and lend legitimation to the sectarian system.

A system of attitudes, actions, beliefs, and structures

When people think of sectarianism, most tend to think of its raw or violent expressions in murders, stand-offs, blockades, boycotts, bombings, and beatings, along with state implication in areas such as policing and the unequal distribution of resources. Indeed these actions are some of the most potent expressions of the system. But alongside this type of bold action is an array of smaller, perhaps everyday or semi-conscious attitudes, actions, and beliefs, which contribute subtly to keeping the sectarian system in place. We could give many examples. In terms of attitudes to institutions, people's response to the police service illustrates the false choices that people can make under the influence of sectarian logic. Many republicans and nationalists, having had no direct experience of discrimination from the police, will have nothing to do with them, even in situations where police help is needed. Similarly, many loyalists and unionists will uphold the police as beyond reproach even when faced with evidence of their wrongdoing. Both groups are applying pre-decided logic and allowing themselves to be trapped into a false choice of either totally writing off the police or wholeheartedly supporting them.

In terms of inter-personal attitudes, there is the almost unconscious series of questions or checks people go through when they meet a stranger in order to ascertain to which 'side' they belong and therefore how they should treat them: name, accent, school, place they live, how they pronounce the letter 'h' etc. Then there are the areas people instinctively avoid, the street they do not walk down, or the pubs they do not drink in. For most, these are nearly unconscious reflexes. People also make more conscious choices: where they live, only accepting housing in an area which is predominantly 'their' people; the type of colours or emblems that they choose to wear or to display. All of these smaller actions have a rational basis in either helping people to stay 'safe' or at least to minimise their possible exposure to danger, or in helping them to experience and express their sense of belonging in a more immediate way. All of them can also be read as maintaining or in some cases hardening the boundaries between 'them and us'. It is here that their contribution to sustaining the sectarian system begins to appear.

The examples above could be termed in some way as defensive actions. There are also other types of action which, although not directly attacking the 'other', open the way for or tend towards dehumanising others. Taken to their logical conclusion, such actions will eventually lead to actively or passively sanctioning attack. The way people think about others, and the language they use about them, is a case in point. To routinely think of and refer to others as Taigs, Huns, Black or Orange or Fenian bastards, typical Prods or typical Taigs has the effect of distancing people from the humanity of those named and maintaining the other always in a negative and destructive framework. From there it is but a step to saying that these people are not entitled to the same rights as everyone else. The further step is to say that these people are less than human. The consequence of this can be to treat them as less than human and to regard their lives as of less value than any other human life.[4]

There can be a similar effect with the use of humour. In saying this, we want to acknowledge that the sense of humour in both the loyalist/unionist and republican/nationalist communities, the ability to laugh in spite of terrible suffering, has been vital in helping people to retain their sanity and sense of balance and in enabling them to deal on a day to day basis with awful situations. Oftentimes this humour is self-deprecating. However, when people use humour against or at the expense of another individual or group, they need to recognise that they are subtly opening the way to dehumanising or demonising them.

The actions described above also have passive counterparts, which are equally destructive. These appear in one version when people listen to someone using sectarian language or telling sectarian jokes and do not object or challenge them. The tacit acceptance of such behaviour is usually read as assent or concurrence. Often such instances will occur during social moments and come and go in a few seconds. Sometimes the people who need to be challenged are family members or friends who are guests at table and in these situations the most polite and easiest thing to do is to let it go. The second version is expressed in the unspoken signals and norms that exist in families and groups. These norms, which at least underline and at worst positively harden the boundary between groups, can be revealed by asking fairly simple questions, such as, whom do parents accept the children bringing home? With whom would family, friends, or colleagues not accept someone associating?

At this point the reader may want to object that, in the scale of things in Northern Ireland, these are trivial matters and that we are nitpicking. We would not in any way wish to equate what we have described as small actions or omissions with more violent manifestations; there is a clear and demonstrable difference of order between them. One of the most difficult aspects to grasp about sectarianism, however, is that it is a system and that therefore everyone's actions are interdependent. Most of what is required for the system to continue to flourish is for the majority of ordinary, decent citizens to keep colluding in low level sectarianism and subtly re-inforcing the divisions between groups. The silence and inaction of the majority can be, and has been, taken as a mandate by the tiny minority who espouse violence.

What we have described as small actions or omissions are polite or acceptable forms of sectarianism which are alive and well not only in the leafy middle-class areas of this land, but also in church congregations. These stand in sharp contrast to the more raw and open expressions sometimes associated with inner city or largely working class areas. But we would contend that to demonise the raw expressions and working class manifestations of sectarianism without acknowledging the significant destructive contribution made by what one Protestant minister called 'the good suits' in his congregation is to miss a crucial point about how sectarianism functions here. If this society is to be able to move beyond sectarianism, it will require active and sustained effort at all levels and in all areas where the system operates, whether it is violent and overt or polite and more 'acceptable'.

Moreover, underpinning all these actions, whether gross or small, is a myriad of attitudes, beliefs, myths, and rumours, which thrive no matter what the social status of the groups involved. Some attitudes are common to the two main traditions, for example, mistrust and superiority. Many Protestant/unionists believe that Catholic/nationalists never tell the truth, or they distort the truth, and therefore are to be treated with scepticism and suspicion. Many Catholic/nationalists believe that Protestant/unionists will not keep their word and are not to be trusted. In both cases people can point to examples from various periods of history which support the rationality of their view. There are also negative stereotypes such as Roman Catholics being dirty, lazy, and breeding like rabbits and Protestants being arrogant, moralising, and workaholic. In terms of myths we have examples of Protestants thinking that all Catholics believe and obey everything that the Pope and the priests say and that all want a united Ireland. On the other hand, there are Roman Catholics who believe that all Protestants are monarchists, ardently support the union, and want power at all costs. The intensity and openness with which these attitudes, beliefs, and myths are held varies enormously, but they can be found, if only in residual form, in most strata of society.

Acknowledging the pervasiveness of the system and the profound way it has shaped everyone means accepting that, no matter how far people travel on the road of peace and reconciliation, sectarianism is only ever one step away. It is not something that most people will finally put behind them, but rather, like alcoholics for whom relapse is an ever-present danger, it would be most helpful to regard themselves as 'recovering sectarians'[5] and to behave accordingly.

At personal, communal, and institutional levels

One of the premises on which we approach the whole subject of sectarianism is that no individual or group is irredeemably sectarian. All people and all of the structures of society are inevitably shaped and influenced by the sectarian system. In terms of people that disorder is patchy and can be transformed. This is so because people are made in the image of God and therefore their identities are ultimately open to redemption. In terms of structures and institutions the potential for, and limits of, transformation will vary according to their founding identities and their ideologies. The transformation of institutions is discussed below in the section dealing with the path beyond sectarianism. In order to begin to move towards transformation, people have to appreciate that sectarianism works at all sorts of different levels, which are inter-connected. Such interconnectedness means that changes at one level can have an impact at other levels. If a lot of individuals, for example, are sensitised to sectarian issues and belong to a particular club or neighbourhood, they can, if they act together, positively influence their group. The reverse is also true.

At the personal level, sectarianism can involve anything from making a sectarian joke or comment, through not challenging such comments, or consciously/unconsciously avoiding contact with the 'other side,' to giving people beatings, torching houses, and killing people. Obviously, as we have said before, these actions do not all carry the same weight. Nevertheless they do all contribute in different ways to feeding the sectarian system.

The way the system works at communal level varies according to the groups and situations involved. A group can feel that it has a grievance against others or can wish to react to others in a manner that can be expressed corporately. Examples would be some of the activities of concerned residents groups or participation in boycotts or blockades. Here the group comes together to express a commonly shared position or reaction. A second and more sinister dynamic happens when people find themselves constrained to support boycotts, blockades, etc., under threat from paramilitary groupings in their area. In this example there is a real issue about how and why the 'silent' majority in a local area cede power to paramilitary groups. A third type of communal operation of sectarianism is that which happens in oppositional situations and especially in competitive events. One example is the type of sectarian chanting and violence which takes place at some sports events and oftentimes allows people to express extraordinary levels of negative emotions, particularly hatred. Another example is the sometimes violent emotions which rage when resources are deemed to be being unfairly or unevenly distributed in areas of need. Clearly, in areas outside the island of Ireland such oppositional or competitive situations also lend themselves to a divisive 'them and us' mentality and the expression of violent emotions. We have only to think of soccer hooliganism in England. What is key and most damaging in this situation is that sectarian elements get expressed in what should be non-sectarian events. So the Linfield and Cliftonville football teams had to wait more than twenty years to play at the Solitude ground, and then only early on a Saturday morning, with severely limited, all-ticket attendance and a heavy police presence. And this because a football event has taken on the symbolic significance of a clash between the two largest and apparently opposing traditions here.

In the light of the pervasiveness of sectarianism as a system, we are arguing that all institutions suffer from either the presence of, or at least the risk of, expressions of sectarianism within their structures or procedures. For example, in mid-1998 the Gaelic Athletic Association (GAA), the all-Ireland governing body for Irish sports such as hurling and football, voted not to drop Rule Twenty-One, which excludes members of the security forces from belonging to GAA clubs. Maintaining the rule means that in its very structure the GAA is sectarian, because it discriminates against, overlooks, and demonises people for political reasons. That the GAA has suffered sectarian treatment at the hands of the state, for example when part of its pitch in Crossmaglen was taken in order to establish a security post, may make its stance more understandable but it does not make it less sectarian. This is the clear influence of the sectarian system distorting the management of sport, which should be a pluralist and non-political activity.

Another example of institutional sectarianism is the way in which the Orange Order, from its foundation, has mixed the defence of the Protestant religion with the upholding of a particular political loyalty.[6] In this century, the order has been explicitly involved in defending unionism and has mixed this political stance with active anti-Catholicism. In December 1910, for example, faced with the possibility of home rule becoming law, the Grand Orange Lodge wrote to every Lodge in Ireland, encouraging members 'to set the example to other unionists by volunteering their service'.[7] The service in question was to take up arms in the Ulster Volunteer Force (UVF) to resist 'Dublin rule'.[8]

The Order's tendency towards anti-Catholicism is often given as the principal reason for condemning the Order as sectarian. In fact, while it is a significant, inherent risk built into their structure, it may or may not be acted out in a sectarian way. The Orange Order, as any institution, is entitled to make its truth claims about Roman Catholicism even in offensive terms such as 'popish'. Such claims, however, are not sectarian in themselves, but they open the door to sectarianism. We make this judgment on the basis that the intention of the truth claim is to condemn what is seen as the error and danger of Roman Catholicism. Depending on how the claim is made it may, but need not necessarily, lead to destructive patterns of relating between members of the Orange Order and Roman Catholics. In this sense it may open the way to sectarian attitudes and actions. We discuss these dynamics more fully in chapter four.

Which always involves religion,
and typically involves a negative mixing of religion and politics
The intersection of the realms of politics and religion is the main feature which we regard as distinguishing sectarianism from closely related 'isms,' such as racism, ageism, and sexism. Sectarianism always involves religion. The involvement may be an historic one that has been long forgotten, but it is this origin that distinguishes it from purely political discrimination. The potent and negative mixing of religion with politics gives sectarianism its key characteristics.

Some of our sympathetic critics have suggested that we should include 'power', the seeking of it and the abuse of it, as a significant factor. While we accept their basic point, we believe it is more helpful to use the term 'politics' with a small 'p', indicating the whole range of political interaction in society, not simply party political activity, as a way of including power relationships without problematising them. The issue of how imbalances of power may distort relationships is addressed below in the section on destructive patterns of relationship.

Religion, as it is used here, indicates the complete spectrum of religious expression and not simply doctrine. It includes attitudes, values, forms of worship, language, community structure, and outreach. In the case of the relationships between Northern Ireland, the Republic of Ireland, and Britain, religion refers primarily to the conflict between Christian denominations and only secondarily to conflicts between Christians and other faiths. It is a limitation of this study that we have focused exclusively on the intra-Christian expressions of sectarianism. It must be left to others to pursue the inter-faith manifestations of sectarianism on the island of Ireland.

We want to be very clear about what we are not saying about religion and politics. We are not saying that all mixes of religion and politics are unhelpful or downright bad. Clearly they are not. We have only to think of people like Martin Luther King, Jr, and more recently of Desmond Tutu, to see ways in which the bonding of religion and politics has become a major force for positive change in different but related situations. In these cases it has been a mixing that is good for politics, good for religion, and good for politics and religion. When we argue that sectarianism typically involves a negative mixing of religion and politics, we have in mind situations in which religious and political factors, overtly or subtly interwoven, become the primary basis on which people react destructively towards other groups or individuals.

Sectarianism cannot be equated with political or religious bigotry. Certainly bigotry can and often does play a role in sectarianism, but it is entirely possible to be sectarian without being bigoted. Most forms of overlooking the other, simply ignoring their existence, pretending that they do not have stories, claims, and concerns which need to be taken into account, are forms of non-bigoted sectarianism. A history teacher, for example, who chooses to leave out or gloss over important sections of the story, which would explain some of the possible reasons behind the actions or reactions of the 'other side', is acting in a sectarian way. This would not, however, represent what people usually understand by bigotry.

It may be appropriate at this point to explore one of the key differences between sectarianism and other 'isms' and to reflect on why sectarianism presents a different challenge to the churches than do issues of racism, ageism, or sexism. The difference we want to focus on is the fact that both religion and politics, in the sense of party politics, are personal choices in a way not ture of the significant factors in the other 'isms' – sex, race and age. People cannot choose their sex, race, or age in the way that they can choose their religion and political allegiance. We acknowledge, however, that in changing political, and especially religious allegiance, people often remain influenced to some degree by the background out of which they have moved. When we make this point in presentations or workshops, someone, and often it is a Roman Catholic, usually objects that this is not so. They go on to explain that in Northern Ireland people do not choose their religion or their politics, they are born into them. However seductive a line of reasoning this may appear, it is not true. We accept that there is often immense, and usually unspoken, pressure from within families and communities to conform to whatever the prevailing political or religious choice of the group may be, even if the allegiance is minimal or token. Such pressure can feel like no choice. We accept also that some people have more freedom to choose than others, because this choice is always situated in a particular social and cultural context. But people always have a choice, even if it is not readily apparent to them or may be costly to them.

It is also true, however, that one of the most potent dynamics of the sectarian system is to try to convince people that they have no or very limited choices, or to present them with false choices. The attempt to distance themselves from their choices, instead of taking personal responsibility for them, blinds people to and disempowers them from dealing with some of the out-workings of the sectarian system. To believe or to say that people have no choice prevents them from acknowledging that they are participants, actively or passively, in what is happening in this society, even if they have never lifted a gun, a petrol bomb, a stone, or even raised their voice. At the same time it allows them to imagine or to pretend that they have no power to change the situation, when in fact, as actively participating religious and political people, they do have power to influence the actions and policies of their political and religious leaders and communities. It suits the sectarian system that the majority should feel them-selves to be powerless and locked into 'opposing camps' with-out choice. As long as they continue to perceive themselves in this way, the system can absorb their best positive efforts, for ex-ample at neighbourliness, without losing momentum, because their vision, and therefore what is possible, will be stunted by the narrow confines of the sectarian system.

The element of choice in both religion and politics means that it is possible for each side to impute to the other a dangerous wrong-headedness in persisting with a bad choice which they could change. It allows the introduction of an aspect of chosen culpability, which is different from the culpability imputed in sexism, racism, and ageism, where no such choice exists. In sex-ism, for example, women may be blamed for the way they are and respond, or men may be similarly blamed, but there is no sense in the claim of culpability that they can stop being women or men. In sectarianism, however, the claim of culpability can include the fact that the person could change from Roman Catholicism to Protestantism or vice versa, or that the church concerned could alter its beliefs and doctrines to become more Christian, or that the person could change from loyalist to nationalist or vice versa. The charge of chosen culpability then is intrinsically related to belittling, and possibly with dehumanising and demonising the other, in a way that the charge of culpability in the other 'isms' may not necessarily be. This becomes particu-larly tricky in matters of religious belief, where the claim of dangerous and culpable wrong-headedness is made about matters which are sacred to the person or group.

One of the hard edges of sectarianism for the churches is that the element of choice can introduce a new dimension to an already existing, if unacknowledged, competition for members between churches. This pressure in churches is deepened and complicated by the increasing secularisation of society on the island of Ireland. Competition for votes is also an important factor for political parties, who must, therefore, keep an eye on their electorate. So people and institutions get sucked into a numbers game. This is potentially more damaging for the churches than for political parties, because the churches are governed by gospel imperatives that call them beyond such antics. One of the more far-reaching implications of this situation in the churches is that all church members, but particularly ministers, end up keeping an eye on other members and tailoring their actions or ministry to what others will 'allow'. In the course of our work, this theme – fear of their own side being greater than fear of the others – has been repeated to us often enough, and by a wide enough spectrum of people, for us to believe that it is a significant sectarian dynamic. Such a scenario makes brave and prophetic outreach to the 'other side' at least a costly, and potentially a disastrous, course of action. Whilst this is more true for some Protestant ministers, who are employed by local congregations and who can have their employment terminated if the congregation do not like their actions, it holds good in general.

The sectarian system therefore successfully turns what should be positive, self-regulatory impulses within the churches to its own ends as an internally sanctioned mechanism to limit action for reconciliation and peace. It is a neatly closed circle broken, at least in some small measure, only by the courage of those who refuse to be bound by internal sanction. Even then their efforts to break it require them to engage in such complex balancing acts that a good deal of their creative energy, which could be directed towards reconciliation, is absorbed in surviving and remaining 'just acceptable enough' in their church to continue to be heard and heeded. So the sectarian system wins a second time by effectively diffusing creative energy.

Arises as a distorted expression of positive human needs
for belonging, identity, and free expression of difference
This assertion is the most distinctive contribution that our definition makes to the understanding of sectarianism. We view sectarianism as a distorted expression of aspects of humanness that
are essentially positive. We want, however, to be very clear
about the import of the notion of 'distorted expression'. It may
seem at best weak and at worst grotesque to describe sectarianism in Northern Ireland as a distorted expression of positive needs when it is accompanied by the violence that has been
experienced in the last three decades. Other words, such as 'evil'
and 'sinful', may more readily come to mind. Few people need
to be reminded of the images of hatred, violence, and incon-
solable grief that have dominated the news about the island of
Ireland and about Britain on a regular basis. 'Distorted expression' is not a polite, academic term, designed to sanitise, still less
to minimise, the viciousness of sectarianism. Rather it is an attempt to acknowledge three inter-connected factors, which are
part of the psychosocial origin of sectarianism: that positive
needs for belonging, identity, and the free expression of difference are basic to humanness; that people distort identity by
expressing it negatively over against the other; and that a path
beyond sectarianism must be one of transforming or redeeming
it, not smashing it. The power of the sectarian distortion lies precisely in the fact that it is a 'fallen' version of something strong
and positive, namely basic human needs.

Positive needs for belonging, identity, and the free expression
of difference are basic to humanness – as such they carry with
them the full force of human instinctual life drive.[9] Human beings all need to have a sense that they belong to someone and
somewhere. Each person has multiple layers of belonging and
multiple expressions of belonging, such as family, neighbourhood, school, college, sports team, club, and church. These levels
of belonging are socially constructed expressions of the need. In
a wide-ranging survey of research, social psychologists Roy
Baumeister and Mark Leary argue that the need to belong as a
fundamental human motivation has been underappreciated by
psychologists. They suggest that it may be 'one of the most far-
reaching and integrative constructs currently available to understand human nature'.[10]

Similarly, every person has a need for identity and the freedom to be different from others. In the current understanding of how identity functions, it is assumed that each person experiences and deploys multiple and overlapping identities.[11] So, for example, a person who is a Roman Catholic, Scot, teacher of English, and a recreational musician experiences herself as having all these identities, which interact and overlap. But she brings different aspects to the fore when she is teaching English than when she is playing music, when she is supporting the Scottish rugby team than when she is leading a prayer group. These identities are not necessarily ranked in an order of priority, but chosen as a response to varying situations.

Karen Trew, a psychologist from Queen's University, Belfast, who has studied issues of identity in the conflict in Northern Ireland, recognises the deep division around issues of national and religious identity. In the light of research showing that human beings have a multiple identity structure, however, she regards it as conceivable that in Northern Ireland, which is variously seen as part of Britain and / or Ireland, individuals could

identify themselves as Irish (e.g. when visiting Britain); British (e.g. when visiting France); Northern Irish (e.g. when in Dublin) and European (e.g. when in America).[12]

There is also evidence that 'Northern Irish' is becoming a more popular identity with both Roman Catholics and Protestants. This suggests that a new and more unified, less oppositional identity may be slowly emerging.[13] Whichever of her or his identities a person may be expressing at any given moment, it is clear that everyone has a fundamental need to be accepted and respected for who she or he is.

As with other basic needs, such as the need for food and shelter, when they are not met, or when the threat of them not being met is present, people fight, literally or metaphorically, to get what they need. The relative violence of the struggle will depend upon a number of factors, not least the strength of the perceived threat. The term 'distorted expression' therefore can cover all behaviours on a spectrum from the mildest antipathy to murderous rage. The form of the distortion is that energy is directed against another because people perceive their existence to be threatened by them. Such a distortion stands in contrast to a positive expression of needs in which the life force is directed, more or less, in concert with the other to the creation of a 'world' where belonging and identity can be negotiated and respected, or at least tolerated non-violently. Billy Wright, the leader of the Loyalist Volunteer Force, who was murdered in the Maze prison in late December 1997, believed that he was involved in an apocalyptic struggle to save his British identity from extinction.[14] For him it was literally a case of succeed or be annihilated. Sadly his was a self-fulfilling prophecy, and he did not live to see another way emerging through the Belfast Agreement of April 1998, a way that may offer the possibility of belonging and respect for all.

The dynamic we are describing here is not unique to sectarianism. It flourishes in any situation where groups are competing for scarce resources, whether recognition, space, power, or material goods. In that sense the sectarian system is grounded in and harnesses what are essential human survival mechanisms, turning their energy to destructive relating, which will lead to a deepening sense of threat from the other and to further resistance. And so the cycle continues.

People distort identity by expressing it negatively over against the other. The distortion of the expression of identity at the heart of sectarianism is the tendency to create identity negatively over against the 'other' instead of in positive relationship in difference with the 'other'. In a certain sense all identity is created 'over against' the other, because this is the heart of any process of differentiation by which individuals understand themselves to be separate from others. In sectarianism, however, people create what Marc Gopin, Jewish theologian and specialist in conflict resolution, calls a 'negative identity' and what Alan Falconer, a leading figure in the World Council of Churches, has called 'identity in opposition'.[15] The import of negative identity is to create a situation where people require a threatening 'other', or need to keep repeating oppositional antagonism, in order to maintain a sense of who they are. In this dynamic they find themselves constrained, consciously or unconsciously, to interpret the actions and words of the other mostly in the worst light in order to maintain this identity. Any move to change the status of the other from threatening to friendly, or even to neutral, precipitates some form of identity crisis for them. Thus it becomes a very difficult and painful cycle for people to break.

The picture becomes more complex when we take into account the fact that people experience multiple identities. The complexity raises interesting possibilities and questions. We are suggesting that it must be possible to have negative identity in one area that co-exists with positive identity in other areas. In the case of the sectarian dynamic, negative national or political and religious identities could then co-exist with positive identities, such as gender, employment, education, socio-economic status, or class. This might explain why many people find themselves able to work happily alongside colleagues of different political or religious groupings, because their focus in this situation is a shared positive identity as cleaners, managers, or whatever. Such positive relationships will come under strain or break down when an issue arises in the workplace that touches into areas where identity is negative, for example disputes over displays of emblems such as poppies or flags. The dynamic here is complex, because it may be as much a case of being seen to 'stand with' rather than being seen not to 'stand against' the other. For example, a Methodist minister described being verbally attacked because he failed to wear a poppy when conducting a Remembrance Day service. The inference was that he was supporting the no-poppy lobby, therefore the nationalist stance, and not standing with his own people. In fact he was trying to stand in the middle, supporting neither one side nor the other.

It may be the existence of positive identities which makes possible certain types of unlikely or distinctive between-group alliances in Northern Ireland. An obvious and creative example would be the Northern Ireland Women's Coalition, where shared gender identity seems to move towards transcending political and religious differences. Other examples might include alliances between community development organisations in which socio-economic or class identity have become similar bridges. Perhaps strong positive identity in one or more shared areas may allow people to transcend negative, over-against identity and to form creative alliances.

The question then arises, are some types of positive identity more resilient in the face of negative, over-against identity than others? Shared employment identity is functional and contingent in the sense that people can change jobs or re-train for other employment more easily than they can change social status. Unless a group of people has a very strong love of their work, or a deep sense of 'vocation', this shared identity appears to be particularly vulnerable to the intrusion of issues which resonate with areas of negative identity, as in the example about wearing poppies already cited. Gender, socio-economic status, and class, on the other hand, are deeply embedded social and cultural issues in which some groups both feel and are disadvantaged, and other groups both feel and fear that they have a lot to lose. There are therefore other dynamics in society, including solidarity in adversity and struggle for achievement of improved place, or maintenance of a place, which are integral to these shared identities and may make them more resilient. The question we are raising here is whether an overarching issue in terms of gender or class equality can be of such importance, and require the investment of such amounts of energy and commitment, that it can withstand more easily the potential disturbances caused by negative religious or political identities? This remains, however, an open question. Of course, the struggle for betterment in societal terms is a two-edged sword since, unless carefully managed, it can easily slide into competition or opposition again, especially if one group feels that another is gaining disproportionately or unfairly. It is surely significant that a number of the more innovative between-group alliances are happening around gender or community development issues.

A path beyond sectarianism must be one of transforming and redeeming sectarianism, not of smashing it. Sectarian behaviour is always negative and destructive, and it can lead to the appalling evil that people have witnessed in various atrocities over the years. But essentially sectarianism is the distorted expression of basic human needs that are positive. Therefore a path beyond sectarianism cannot be one of trying to destroy it, smash it, or stamp it out, because this risks damaging the good along with the evil. Such an approach also risks augmenting the sense of threat to identity and belonging in those who are behaving in a sectarian way and is likely to drive them deeper into the distortion. We are proposing that the task of moving beyond sectarianism requires an approach of redeeming, transforming, and converting people's understanding, attitudes, and ultimately the heart of each person as well as societal institutions, where possible.

In light of that, we would take issue with some aspects of the anti-sectarianism lobby, which variously approaches sectarianism from the point of view of 'stamping it out' or 'smashing' it.[16] We see this as problematic in two ways. Firstly, such slogans focus too exclusively on the immediate practical manifestations of sectarianism at the expense of addressing the more long-term question of tackling its roots. Secondly, the approach risks demonising those who are seen to be acting in an overtly sectarian manner, while at the same time allowing the majority to pretend that they are not implicated in the dynamic. The paramilitary boot on the 1999 Students Union anti-sectarianism campaign literature, for example, was eye catching, but it also subtly conveyed three unhelpful impressions at once. Firstly, that sectarianism is the preserve of those who engage in or support paramilitary activity. This too easily allowed the majority of students and the rest of the population to dump the blame, and therefore the responsibility for action, at someone else's door. Secondly, that it should be stamped on with a heavy boot, but this, as we have said, risks smashing what is good as well as what needs redeeming. Thirdly, that using violent methods is the best way to tackle sectarianism. This risks encouraging an already apparent tendency to respond to violence with violence, a pattern that perpetuates the cycle and drives society into a steadily downward spiral. Similarly their more recent 'bigots beer' campaign images suggest either that sectarianism necessarily involves bigotry or that the worst forms of sectarianism involve bigotry. Again this risks allowing people who practice more polite and acceptable forms of sectarianism to avoid their responsibility.

Obviously, organisations like the Students Union are dealing daily with raw and difficult situations and they require a hard hitting and effective strategy. We acknowledge that they are working very effectively in difficult and complex scenarios and in no way want to undermine their work. Rather we have chosen to address their approach precisely because we want to see their already good work extended to implicate all people and to require all to change fundamentally, and not to demonise some while allowing others to feel complacent.

Similarly, we would take issue with the non-sectarian approach, which operates on the principle that groups or organisations can be sectarianism-free zones simply by being inclusive and putting a non-sectarian policy in place. Such an approach ignores both the pervasiveness of sectarianism as a system and the need to challenge even those who think that they are inclusive and non-sectarian to positively name and face their responsibility for contributing to the system. It caters for the overt expressions of sectarianism but does not deal with the more extensive and more subtle expressions, which if unchecked will continue to feed the system. A non-sectarian approach can only cope with 'life as usual', and develops no resources for dealing with crises when they arise.

Both the non-sectarian and the anti-sectarian approaches are based on the belief that sectarianism is bad or evil and therefore to be either avoided or smashed. In this understanding, to say to someone, 'you are being sectarian,' is to say to them that they need to become other than they are, because what they are is wrong or bad. The truth of this position is that sectarianism leads to and is expressed in evil actions. The difficulty and limitation of the position is that it risks creating resistance by reinforcing people's sense of threat to their identity by communicating that they have to become something other than they are.

On the other hand, we are proposing a twin strategy, which proceeds by seeking what is good and then using it to redeem or transform the expression of identity of the person or group. This approach is based in the Christian belief that all individuals and groups have the potential to be redeemed. The first strategy starts from the premise that sectarianism is a distorted expression of positive needs; therefore people need to reclaim the positive in their identity and tradition and to recover a deeper sense of, and pride in, who they are. The second strategy entails learning to express identity positively and to be able to give others the space to do the same. What we are proposing may appear to be a too easy and pain free process. There will, however, undoubtedly be deep and cherished aspects of people's identities and traditions that are, in terms of sectarianism, negative and undesirable and which they need to leave behind. For example for Catholic/nationalists it may well be the identity of 'victims', which has to be transformed into an identity of equal and co-responsible citizens. For Protestant/ unionists it may well be the identity of 'political power holders', which has to be transformed into an identity of equal and co-responsible citizens. We are talking here of change that will take generations and which will require a massive and unrelenting re-imaging of people and their relationships to one another and to the state. The necessary drive for such a change can only come from helping people to first get in touch with the positive and constructive energies and resources in their identity and tradition.

Our approach, therefore, is effectively to say that people, individuals and groups, need to become more positively who and what they are, and not something other than they are. We turn now to the question of whether the same can be true also for institutions, structures, and their ideologies, and if so under what conditions. We are trying to encourage people to undertake the task of transforming and redeeming institutions and structures rather than condemning or writing them off. But clearly there are limitations to a transformative model. It would be naïve not to take seriously the potential for radical evil in human beings and especially in their institutions and ideologies. The Jewish Holocaust and the episodes of ethnic cleansing of the last century are sobering reminders that this is necessary.

Institutions, in their structure and in their formal statements, represent the ethos and ideology of a group in its most unambiguous form. They provide as it were one particular template of identity, which may be multi-faceted, and which is incarnated by individuals and local cells of the organisation. The nature of that incarnation will vary from person to person and group to group within the overall framework of the institution. So, for example, parishes of the institutional Roman Catholic Church express their identities differently according to the composition and needs of their local membership and their geographical location; they are nonetheless discernibly local assemblies of the Roman Catholic Church, following basically the same church law and rubrics. An institution, therefore, presents a definite expression of identity and values to which individuals and groups may subscribe, if they wish to be considered members of that institution. There cannot be within institutional identity the same fluidity and multiplicity of identities that we recognise as a capacity in individual human beings.

This has certain consequences for any model of change that is based on transformation. It requires that there be at least a core of the institution's foundational identity that is positive and has the potential to be developed when undesirable elements are left behind. It raises the question of whether transformation maintains sufficient continuity with the old institution to be regarded as transformation, or whether in some cases it would have to be so wide-ranging that it is in fact an act of founding a different institution. Finally, it raises the question of whether some institutions, their structure and ideology, are so much an expression of the worship of false gods and of destructive relationship that they simply have to be resisted.

One example of institutional transformation is the ongoing change from the Royal Ulster Constabulary to the Northern Ireland Police Service. The current process, with all its attendant difficulties, is essentially the transformation of an institution whose core identity should be an impartial law enforcement agency. In the transformation, the old expression of core identity is being re-framed, free from the taint of sectarianism, the imbalance of political / religious representation, and with a new emphasis on upholding the human rights of all citizens. Arguments about the name, symbols, and uniform evidence the struggle to retain elements of continuity versus the drive to radical discontinuity. This is a courageous attempt to set the positive core identity of policing in a new, more inclusive, institutional framework.

A second institution that has the potential for transformation is that of the paramilitaries. Such transformation would have to be wide-ranging and might have at least two aspects. Firstly, it could focus on the development of the positive core of their identity: the political ideas integral to their position, and their capacity for strategic thinking. This process is already underway with the flourishing of political parties who admit association with paramilitary groups, such as the Progressive Unionist Party (PUP) and the Ulster Democratic Party (UDP), or who admit to having influence with them, as is the case with Sinn Féin. These parties are even now making a difference to political life in Northern Ireland. Their further development could help the process of finding political pathways towards lasting peace.

But the achievement of peace will mean, at least, that paramilitaries give up violence and the threat of violence, whether it be defensive or offensive, as a method of political expression. This is a core element of their identity, which will have to be left behind. They are militarily based units formed for defensive and offensive roles in a situation of violent struggle. For most paramilitaries it would not make sense for their organisation to continue to function in the same manner in a peaceful society. Effectively, then, such a transformation would mean paramilitary groups becoming purely political parties or movements, pursuing their agendas by use of democratic and non-violent strategies. It is not clear whether paramilitaries would recognise this as a transformation of their organisations, or whether it would appear to them to be the establishment of different but related organisations.

Many people on the island of Ireland and in Britain regard the Orange Order as an irredeemably sectarian institution. They point to the founding inspirations at the Battle of the Diamond in 1795, which included virulent anti-Catholicism, the seeking of economic advantage, the desire to secure socio-political power for Protestant people, and the furtherance of the Protestant religion. They note also that the Orange Order was linked with the old UVF in the battle over home rule early in the last century and the manner in which the Order to this day remains vehemently anti-Catholic and formally linked with Ulster unionism. We have argued elsewhere in this chapter that it is the negative mixing of religion and party politics in the Order, rather than its anti-Catholic stance per se, which attracts the judgment that it is sectarian. With this in mind we would argue that there are some sufficiently strong positive elements in the founding identity of the Orange Order that have the potential to be redeemed.

These elements are focused around its religious identity. The Order could have a role, like any other religious group, in propagating and upholding the Protestant religion, in particular the place of the Bible. There could be scope to extend its religious educational activity, both with its members and with the wider society. It already engages in Christian charitable work and is a force for social cohesion, especially in rural areas. Its cultural expressions in music, symbols, and parading to church, especially those associated with 12 July, if stripped of their political baggage and treated as a celebration of common history, have the potential, given time and if managed with care, to take on the air of community festivals.

Such transformation would require both effort and imagination on the part of the Orange leadership and members. It would require the Order to sever its formal links with political unionism and become a religious, cultural society devoid of overt political affiliation and activity. It would require also a willingness to actively mitigate their anti-Catholicism so that it no longer fuels antagonised division within the community. It is not a matter of having to relinquish the truth claim that the Roman Catholic Church is radically in error, but rather, on the one hand, it is a question of separating that claim from issues of political sovereignty and party political considerations and, on the other hand, of building relationships with and acting co-operatively with the Catholic/nationalist community, where possible, to further the development of peaceful, civic society in Northern Ireland. We believe that, just as the foundational identity of the Order was in keeping with the socio-political reality of the land in 1795, which was a ferment of socio-economic and religious-political competition, the vision we outline here is in keeping with the socio-political reality of Northern Ireland today, a community struggling slowly and painfully towards a peaceful, inclusive society in which difference is respected. The obvious question that this vision of possible transformation poses is whether or not members of the Orange Order would recognise their institution in this incarnation. Would the de-emphasising of political elements and the emphasising of religious, cultural, social, and civic elements so change the nature of the institution that it would cease to be recognisably the Orange Order?

We are arguing that there are sufficient positive elements in the identity of the institutional Orange Order for transformation to be attempted. This would not, in our opinion, be true of all similar organisations that began as secret societies. We certainly do not assume, however, that every institution or ideology is redeemable. To waste no time on subtle or ambiguous cases, we go directly to one of the twentieth century's defining horrors, Naziism. Apart from the most vague and general categories, we see nothing redeemable in the ideology or the institutions it inspired. So 'irredeemable' may be a just judgment of institutions or ideologies. We need to qualify this statement in two ways, however. First, the people involved in those institutions and marked by those ideologies are always redeemable. Naziism will suffice as an example of this as well. Millions of people involved to varying degrees in the Nazi system were, in varying degrees, subsequently transformed and redeemed. Admittedly, in the most extreme cases an individual can seem to have embraced an evil so firmly and been shaped by it so profoundly that it is all but impossible to imagine that their redemption is possible. In such cases, the affirmation that these people are redeemable is more a statement of faith in the ultimate power of God over evil than it is an immediate, concrete human possibility. Our second qualification is that the judgment 'irredeemable' should come reluctantly at the end of a process that has had a generous bias toward seeking the redemption of the institution. This is necessary to counter both the general human tendency to demonise and scapegoat and also the specific tendency of the sectarian system to foster judgments that are too often harsh, quick, and even casual.

Expressed in destructive patterns of relating
Sectarianism shares with all other 'isms' certain destructive patterns of relating. This element of our definition is generic and therefore readers need to keep in mind, as they explore the patterns of relating, that the key variables in sectarianism are religious and political differences.

We acknowledged earlier in this chapter that power is a significant factor in sectarianism, and nowhere is this more apparent than in reflecting on destructive patterns of relating. Primarily this is so because imbalances of power can enable poisonous ideologies to flourish. For evidence we need only to look to areas such as former Yugoslavia, in particular Serbia, or to Rwanda, to see how superior power enabled policies of ethnic cleansing to be pursued. It is also the case because power differentials, even in the most positive situations, tend towards distortions and make open and balanced relationships difficult to maintain. While reading this section, therefore, we invite the reader to consider how imbalances of power in the Northern Irish situation can amplify, and have amplified, the distorted patterns that we describe.

The list moves in ascending order of destructiveness but it is not clear to us in which order 'hardening the boundaries between groups' and 'overlooking others' should come. Much of the strength and import of these two patterns depends upon the situation concerned. We have opted to begin with hardening the boundaries between groups.

Hardening the boundaries between groups. There is a variety of ways to do this: conceptual, physical, and emotional. Moreover it can take place both between traditions, involving for example Roman Catholic and Protestant, or loyalist and republican relationships, and within traditions, involving two or more factions within a certain tradition, e.g. hard-line and more moderate republicans or loyalists. The effect of the hardening of boundaries is manifold. Most obviously it pushes the different groups apart and sets up further or deeper tensions between them. It acts to impede, if not prevent, those who wish to do so from reaching out across the divide. Perhaps most damagingly, it cuts off groups from one another, with the result that there is little or no chance of a group being able to test their understandings, myths, or concepts about the other against the reality of the other. This creates a vacuum of knowledge within which further and usually more distorted ideas, half-truths, and untruths can flourish. We will give one small but powerful conceptual example of the possible depths of absurdity that such distortions can reach and the extent of suspension of normal, rational thought which they can induce. A Catholic teacher, who is involved in promoting Education for Mutual Understanding (EMU), told us of working with a group of intelligent, Protestant secondary school pupils who genuinely believed that what Roman Catholics call 'holy water' (ordinary water which has been blessed by a priest and is available in the fonts at the church doors) would burn them if they put their hands into it. These young people were all familiar to some degree with the basic laws of science, and yet they were prepared to believe that water over which a priest had said some prayers could burn them. The example in itself is trivial. It betokens, however, a frightening level of ignorance and superstition in young people, which could be dispelled by a short period of contact with young Catholics and (after a suitable period of preparation) with holy water! The cycle of hardening boundaries is one way in which the sectarian system becomes self reinforcing: hardened boundaries give rise to distorted ideas which lead to more fear, separation, ignorance and so to further hardening of the boundaries.

Language plays a significant role in conceptual ways of hardening the boundaries between groups, because language conveys conscious and unconscious attitudes, beliefs, and values. Two examples may make this clear. Roman Catholics often refer to Protestants as 'black Protestants'. The use of the adjective 'black' in this context resonates psychologically with what is dark, evil, frightening, bad, or to be despised. It is the opposite of white and light and evokes what is other and undesirably other. The term has, of course, profoundly racist overtones and underlines the close relationship between sectarianism and other 'isms'. It functions to harden the boundary between one group and the other which is considered undesirably other. Here the evocation, which was once conscious, has become for the most part unconscious. Some Roman Catholics, for example, even those working for peace and reconciliation, will use the term 'black Protestants' in a half joking kind of way and think that they mean no harm by it. Language, however, can also be used consciously for the same purpose. It happens for example in the conscious marrying of 'Sinn Féin' and 'IRA'. Such a conjunction is intended not only to meld Sinn Féin, the political party, to the IRA in the minds of hearers, but by association to suggest that anyone who supports Sinn Féin must also be sympathetic to the IRA. Thus it not only hardens the boundaries between Catholic/nationalists and Protestant/unionists, it can also, by falsely appearing to distinguish those who are sympathetic to the IRA, harden boundaries between groups within the broader sweep of Catholic Nationalism.

Physical manifestations of hardening the boundaries more often happen between tradition groups than within a tradition, which would tend to share symbols, emblems, and memories. There are obvious exceptions to this in the sharp differences between some paramilitary groupings: INLA with the IRA or the UDA with the UVF. These groups might share the republican or loyalist tradition but would emphasise different heroes or remember different events.

Physical manifestations include painting kerbstones, producing murals or slogans on gable walls, or asking for barriers to be erected between areas of Protestant and Catholic housing. The latter is usually an expression of a need for security in situations where people feel very vulnerable and under threat. The remaining manifestations are more directly linked with what we have termed negative identity, i.e. identity formed negatively over against the other instead of in positive, negotiated relationship with the other. The painted kerbstones seem to evidence a certain primitive need to mark out territory over against the 'other side'. The murals, on the other hand, have a more definite and significant political role to play. In his book, *Politics and Painting: Murals and Conflict in Northern Ireland,* Bill Rolston traces the development of mural painting traditions in Northern Ireland, the oldest being the loyalist tradition, and argues that the murals reflect both the state and concerns of the movements that produce them. He goes on to argue that murals are

> part of the process of political definition; their function is mobilisation. That mobilisation takes place at the local level but is no less important for that. ... [I]t is at the local level that the battle for state legitimacy is waged daily. In the midst of

that battle, murals are not just folk artifacts but a crucial factor in the politicisation of the community. Politically articulate murals simultaneously become expressions of and creators of community solidarity.[17]

It is not the fact of the murals which is a problem in terms of destructive patterns of relating, it is their content. When positive community solidarity becomes distorted into 'us' over against 'them', and murals carry evidence of threat, the desire for domination, or inappropriately quoted biblical texts, they become potent means for hardening the boundaries between groups. Simultaneously, they can act to raise both fear in the other and inflamed passions in their own community.

Emotional ways of hardening the boundaries can function effectively at both within- and between-tradition levels. They are most evident in myths and rumours about 'them' and what 'they' have done, are doing, or want to do to 'us' or 'ours'. One between-tradition example dates back to the 1970s and concerns what appears to have started as random acts of vandalism on the houses of Protestant families in an area already in transition from being a predominantly Protestant part of Belfast to a predominantly Roman Catholic one. Rumours spread, and were fuelled by some Protestant politicians, that the nationalists wanted the 'Prods' out. This provoked immense fear in the already shrinking Protestant community. The fear caused the Protestant people in general to become less open, more reticent, more suspicious, to start moving out of the area, to stay quietly or to aggressively display their allegiance. It also gave licence to elements both within that community and from other areas to organise themselves to 'defend' the Protestant people, now perceived as under siege. As one woman from the community put it: 'We ended up reacting to fear of the fear, without knowing whether or not the Catholics did want our people out.' The rumours and the fear combined to seal off the two communities from one another more effectively than any number of physical barriers. This in turn made checking the facts – i.e. how the Roman Catholic community actually felt about the vandalism – require such courage and delicacy that it became virtually impossible. Physical barriers soon had to be erected to try to give a sense of security in the area. The physical barriers remain, and the area continues today to be a flashpoint for serious street violence between the two groups.

The most obvious within-tradition example of emotional ways of hardening the boundaries between groups is the often negative reaction of families and groups to members who wish to marry 'across the divide', or to members who accept their children marrying someone from the other tradition. The subtle, and at times not so subtle, emotional pressure on young people to look within their own group for a partner can act as a very effective boundary maintenance mechanism. At the same time it powerfully re-inforces the sense of 'us' negatively over against 'them', which is the heart of negative identity. The problem for Catholic-Protestant, inter-church couples is that their very existence threatens those who are living out of negative identity, and so they can become targets of abuse for people from both traditions. Pressure on young people often comes, in the first instance, from their parents or close family members. It can come from positive motivations such as wanting the children to maintain the community. This would be especially true where numbers are few. Perhaps it is a concern for ease of understanding or relationship between the couple; a feeling that marriage is difficult enough without adding another layer of fundamental difference to be negotiated. It can take the form of low-key expressions of anxiety about the future of a couple proposing to marry, unease about how the relationship will be viewed in the larger community, or disappointment about the implied rejection of their tradition. Equally, it can involve much more direct and open confrontation, condemnation, or attack. In a very real way the family members are acting as immediate channels for a pressure which is being exerted by the larger tradition group. The cost to couples who choose to marry a partner from the other tradition can be, though not necessarily, high: loss of friends or family, moving out of their area to a more neutral or mixed area, and constant background anxiety about safety. The cost to parents too may be high. One Presbyterian minister told Cecelia that an elder, a friend of many years, was so unhappy at the minister's failure to confide in him in advance that one of his children was marrying a Roman Catholic that he severed his connection with the congregation.

Over the centuries the Christian churches, as institutions, have been involved in all the destructive patterns of relating described in this chapter. Today, however, their active contribution to sectarianism is mostly in the form of hardening the boundaries between groups and in 'overlooking', to which we turn next. Once a group begins to separate from another and to deepen the divide between them, it opens up a way to ignoring or overlooking their concerns. This is true not only because they are regarded as in some sense in opposition to one another, but also simply because group members get out of touch with the truth of who others are and what they think.

Overlooking others. This could be termed a polite or acceptable form of sectarianism. To overlook is simply to ignore the existence, needs, rights, or aspirations of the other. It is to speak, write, or act as if the other person, group, or tradition either does not exist, is of no consequence, or is not who they claim to be. Its subtlety and seduction lie in the fact that it does not require a person or group to be actively hostile or offensive toward others, simply to behave as if they do not matter. Thus it involves no great passion, confrontation, courage, or aggression, but rather depends upon a mix of social conventions, amnesia, and shared blind spots. The politeness and acceptability of overlooking, however, mask its enormous potential for destroying personal, communal, and group relationships.

This destructive potential is expressed not only in the pervasiveness of overlooking, but also in the fact that it is very hard both to grasp and to challenge. If someone is actively offensive towards another, others have something to point to and challenge, and by social convention it is acceptable to challenge actively offensive behaviour. If someone simply ignores another and their concerns, however, others may first of all be left in confusion, wondering is this deliberate, is it malicious, is it a genuine oversight or area of ignorance about which the person will be embarrassed or uneasy later? Then they are faced with the task of drawing attention to the overlooking. The problem here is a murky area of social convention, which in latter days would have suggested that people did not whinge about being ignored or try to draw attention to themselves, but simply accepted the behaviour gracefully and in silence. With the advent of 'political correctness' this conventional response is being challenged and changed. Not withstanding this, and depending upon the circumstances of the overlooking, the task of challenging such behaviour is still tricky, because it can appear as petty, self-centred griping. In terms of sectarianism as a system, then, overlooking is an important dynamic, especially in British-Irish culture, which tends to be formal, reserved, and to some degree, if only unconsciously, bound by social convention. The importance of the dynamic consists in the way it subtly uses the power of convention and the veneer of acceptability and politeness to mask its destructive potential.

Overlooking can take a number of forms. We find it buried in a common use of language. Unionist politicians, for example, often talk of 'the people of Ulster', by which they usually mean the Protestant/unionist people. The use of one phrase, which is consciously or unconsciously exclusive, allows them simply to ignore the aspirations of the Catholic/nationalist people of the six counties or to subsume them into their own agenda. Similarly, republicans argue that the Troubles are really a British-Irish conflict and that northern Protestants are just the 'dupes' of the British. This not only ignores the aspirations of most northern Protestants, but it does so derisively. Moreover, such a line of argument often goes hand in hand with the assertion, which may be either blatant or hidden, that northern Protestants, who claim to be British, are not what they say they are – they are really Irish but just do not know it! The scope and offensiveness of this type of overlooking is just breathtaking in its capacity to see others only through one frame of reference and not to allow place for, or legitimacy to, their chosen frame of reference.

If overlooking is present in language, it is alive and well also in people's actions. How many turn off the sound, or the television/radio, or get up to make a cup of tea when someone with whom they disagree, religiously or politically, is speaking? We are not suggesting that people should listen to everyone all the time, but rather that this is a way of shutting out or ignoring others and their points of view. If people do this consistently, how will they be able to understand the concerns of the group represented by the people they ignore? It is not a question of agreeing with the viewpoint, but rather of allowing themselves to hear and give consideration to their concerns rather than summarily dismissing them.

Another way in which overlooking creeps into people's actions can be in the use of quite unconscious reflexes which come out of the background of their tradition. Around the time of the death of the Anglican Bishop McAdoo, for example, who had been the co-chair of ARCIC (Anglican-Roman Catholic dialogue process), a Roman Catholic priest, whom we know to be a committed ecumenist, was addressing a group of Catholic and Protestant students. The Roman Catholics were the majority in the group. The priest suggested that they might like to pray for the repose of the soul of the bishop and then immediately launched into a version of Catholic prayers for the dead. Naturally, all the Roman Catholics joined in and all the Protestants were left silent and stranded. The Protestant woman who recounted the story to us said that she had no problem with the priest praying out of his own tradition. She would, however, have liked him to acknowledge what he was going to do, rather than behaving as if the whole group was Catholic and ignoring the rest.

At this point, the reader may want to object that these examples show how trivial the issue of overlooking is compared to more active and violent expressions of sectarianism. But that is to miss the point. People's everyday language and reflexive actions are part of the dynamics which give rise to the ethos of this society. If sectarianism is a distorted expression of human needs for belonging, identity, and the free expression of difference, then a society which is moving beyond sectarianism will strive to ensure that the positive accommodation of difference becomes a dominant thread in that fabric. This can best come about when people learn to respond reflexively in an inclusive and open manner to those whom they perceive to be 'other'. The combination of overlooking with hardening of the boundaries between groups makes such inclusive responses nearly impossible.

Overlooking is also present in the way churches describe what they believe. We are going to use as an example the document on Eucharist, *One Bread, One Body: A Teaching Document on the Eucharist in the Life of the Church, and the Establishment of General Norms on Sacramental Sharing,* issued by the Catholic Bishops' Conferences of Ireland, Scotland, England, and Wales in late 1998.[18] The document focuses on questions concerning inter-communion, contains a lot of positive teaching about Eucharist, and is an attempt to frame that teaching for an ecumenically aware church membership. We want to acknowledge, too, that the intention of the document does not appear to be sectarian, nor do we think it was intended to damage ecumenical relationships. Indeed, it appears to be more about internal church discipline than about theological or even educational concerns.

Some might argue that *One Bread, One Body* is not primarily an example of overlooking but is rather a consequence of holding a particular set of beliefs. They would see this as analogous to, for example, Protestant beliefs that preclude them from worshipping with Roman Catholics. This argument is based on the sense that it is the exclusion from communion or separation that is the content of the overlooking. This is not so. The Roman Catholic Church is entitled to maintain a closed communion table if they so wish and they must recognise that to do so risks hardening, but need not necessarily harden, the boundaries between traditions. We would encourage them to consider ways of mitigating the possible divisive effects of that truth claim.

We regard *One Bread, One Body* as an example of overlooking because within the text it overlooks the faith commitment and concerns of Protestant ministers, whose ordination it refuses to acknowledge.[19] It also overlooks the faith commitment and concerns of the Protestant partner in Catholic-Protestant interchurch marriages.[20] The message to them is that the Roman Catholic Church does not accept you as who you say you are, that is, faithful ministers and followers of the gospel of Jesus, who broke bread with his disciples. It is as if the faith commitment that they live daily does not exist or is of no account.

This is further underlined by the fact that Protestants are referred to in one place as 'non-Catholic', which suggests that their faith commitment has no positive content in and of itself but is to be defined only negatively in relation to Roman Catholicism.[21] The incipient sectarian danger of this type of position is that it suggests that Protestant faith is somehow less than Roman Catholicism. This can, then, open the door to a form of belittling of the Protestant tradition. Whilst one reference may not be significant in itself, the attitude that it betrays appears more extensively elsewhere, for example in the use of the term 'church'. Throughout the document the word 'church' most often means the Roman Catholic Church (it is used this way in the sub-title), sometimes means the whole Christian communion, and only when it is stylistically necessary to distinguish it from other Christian churches is the term 'Catholic' juxtaposed to it. Indeed, the document makes clear that the Roman Catholic Church's capacity to make 'space' for the other in the Eucharist, which it acknowledges to be the heart of its life and tradition, is severely limited.

It would seem, from the whole tenor of the document, that the bishops regard the distinctive identity of Roman Catholic Christians as being eroded in some way by the popular practice of inter-communion. They are writing, therefore, precisely to re-emphasise the distinction. This need not be a problem. Every person and group is entitled to make truth claims and, as with all forms of truth claim, these can be made in a manner which ranges on a spectrum from humble to bigoted. There is no sense in which *One Bread, One Body* is bigoted. The problem in terms of sectarianism arises because the truth claims in *One Bread, One Body*, which overlook Protestants and lead to a hardening of boundaries between Roman Catholics and Protestants, feed into a well established system of antagonised division in Northern Ireland. The sectarian system involves such a complex inter-weaving of religion and politics that descriptive terms from each sphere (Catholic, Protestant, nationalist, and unionist) are often used synonymously. Therefore the sectarian implications of *One Bread One Body* have to be assessed in this context of antagonised division and may not be the same as in England, Wales, or Scotland.

A subtle variation on the theme of overlooking is expressed in the spoken or unspoken expectation or demand that others 'fit in' with a particular way of being or doing. It is a common dynamic between large groups and small minorities and has been largely the case, for example, for Protestants in the Republic of Ireland. They have been expected to fit in with the prevailing Roman Catholic culture. This type of expectation or demand, like overlooking itself, fails to respect people and to take them seriously for who they are in their distinctive identity. Like overlooking, the demand to 'fit in' is based on a collective sense of superiority.

Overlooking, then, can be expressed in a variety of forms: through language, in deliberate actions, in reflexive actions, in formal writings, and in the demand to 'fit in'. Its destructive power lies in the framing of people's lives as if the other, with his, her, or their concerns, does not exist, or is of no account. It is doubly dangerous because of its subtlety; no one needs to notice and there is no direct offence. Its overall effect, however, is to demean the other which, in its turn, opens the way to actually belittling, dehumanising, or demonising others.

Belittling, dehumanising, or demonising others. It is a short step from separation, hardening the boundaries, or overlooking to belittling, dehumanising, or demonising another. In its least aggressive form, belittling can entail the mere suggestion that the other, or the other's tradition, is somehow 'less' than one's own. This is one of the incipient forms of sectarianism in the *One Bread, One Body* document, which was discussed at length in the last section. In its most aggressive form belittling involves caricaturing and making fun of, or mocking, another, another's tradition, or what the other has experienced. Two striking, and at the same time sickening, examples come to mind. Firstly, in 1995 an Orange Order parade down the Ormeau Road in Belfast paused outside Sean Graham's bookmakers shop, where earlier in the year five Roman Catholics had been shot dead. The crowds then chanted 'five nil, five nil'. Secondly, in 1997 after the death of Billy Wright, graffiti appeared in Andersonstown, West Belfast that read, 'What is the difference between Billy Wright and a black taxi? Billy Wright can't take five in the back.' We need to be clear that no matter how unequal in terms of emotional impact the least and most aggressive forms of belittling are, they both contribute to the augmenting of the sectarian system. While the aggressive forms might inflame passions and evoke rage and disgust, and the less aggressive suggestion that the other tradition is less than one's own might appear understandable, and even acceptable, they do in different ways maintain and underline the sectarian divide here. Indeed the more gross the expression of sectarianism, the easier it is to identify and to attract support for tackling it. It is much more difficult to garner sufficient understanding and energy in the general public to tackle the more acceptable forms. There is no debate about the nature of the chanting outside Sean Graham's shop that day. There is often debate and rational defence of the type of incipient sectarianism present in the *One Bread, One Body* text. Such defence is usually made on the grounds either that it is someone's faithfully held beliefs, which people do not have a right to challenge, or that if someone attacks the beliefs of others they may be challenged to relinquish some parts of their cherished tradition too. Nevertheless, if people are going to move beyond sectarianism these types of belittling, and all forms in between these two extremes, will have to be challenged and changed.

Buried in the examples from Ormeau Road and Andersonstown is the outworking of a whole process of dehumanisation of others. The taunts and the cheap joke were about the deaths of six human beings, with families still grieving over their loss. In the taunts and the joke the dead have been stripped of all humanity and have become objects to be used for provoking others or for evoking laughter or at least surreptitious smirks. Whereas belittling is damaging, dehumanising moves the destructiveness of the pattern of relating to a new level, because it opens the way ultimately for justifying all forms of physical violence towards other people, even to the extent of annihilation. They are no longer seen as human beings who are loved by fathers, mothers, partners, daughters, sons, etc., but are rather objects to be manipulated in someone's cause; their suffering or death is of no real consequence to those who oppose them. The step that moves the process of dehumanisation towards actual physical attack is that of demonisation, literally portraying other people as demonic or as symbols of the demonic.

Demonising overlaps with belittling and dehumanising in the process of caricaturing the other. In belittling, the caricature is aimed primarily at mockery, derision, or suggesting that the other is less than one's own group, and in dehumanising it is aimed at portraying others as not worthy of human consideration and respect. In demonising, on the other hand, it is aimed primarily at inducing fear and hatred of, or shock at, the tradition, practices, representatives, or beliefs of the other. So, for example, people regularly caricature the leader of the Democratic Unionist Party (DUP), Dr Ian Paisley, as a raging anti-Catholic, anti-Irish, Bible-thumping unionist, capable of inciting a rabble to violently enforce his wishes. The demonising of Ian Paisley, Sr, encourages people, many of whom have no more knowledge of him than his media profile, to project on to him all that they most fear and hate about what he stands for. It is also calculated to induce a sense of fear, or at least foreboding, when they see his image, even before he opens his mouth. As with all demonisations, it contains elements that are true, but they are not the whole truth. Ian Paisley is implacably opposed to the Roman Catholic Church and is vehemently anti-Catholic. But anyone who knows him as a constituency MP, knows that he works as diligently for his Roman Catholic constituents as he does for his Protestant ones.

Demonisation makes the 'us' and 'them' reality poisonous

and increases the hardening of boundaries between groups. Instances from the realm of church life exist in the way that groups within churches or traditions vilify and demonise others for their beliefs or their interpretation of beliefs, for example the vilification of evangelicals in Evangelical Contribution on Northern Ireland (ECONI) by other evangelical groups such as the Caleb Foundation. Demonisation also allows people to project their fears and hatred on to another person or group, whilst pretending that they are somehow blameless. Often when we are working with mixed and church-going groups of Protestants and Roman Catholics, at some moment, some one will say, 'Isn't it wonderful how well we get on? It's those bad boys out there that you should be talking to, they're the ones doing the bombing and the beating.' It is too easy, even for people who are willing to acknowledge some personal responsibility, to look and find someone who is more overtly sectarian than they are and to point their fingers at them. But such demonisation masks the truth that all are implicated, and therefore all are responsible for acting to transform sectarianism.

Sometimes we are asked what is the worst form of sectarianism. We have two responses: firstly, that which involves violence, and secondly people's own sectarianism, because it is the one that they can do something about. Demonising other people without working to move beyond one's own sectarianism is to make both active and passive contributions to the sectarian system. It is too comfortable for people to point a finger at apparently blatant sectarianism, without looking into their own hearts. In the Drumcree situation, for example, the Orange Order, the residents' coalition, the RUC, and the Church of Ireland have all been demonised for their part in the conflict. It is true that each group has a responsibility for their decisions and actions in relation to Drumcree. It is also true, however, that these groups are acting out, in a dramatic, high-profile way, the struggle which is raging in small and large ways throughout Northern Ireland. Their struggle is everyone's struggle, and the best way that most people can contribute to a resolution is by working on their own sectarian issues, thereby not only modeling a different way but also beginning to change the overall context within which Drumcree is taking place.

Justifying or collaborating in the domination of others. This includes any behaviour, which supports or actively has a hand in suppressing, dominating, or discriminating against the other or their tradition, on the basis of their political or religious allegiance. It is a basic and classical abuse of power and is a risk anywhere that power is held predominantly by one group. Therefore, at a national level, it is as much a risk for Catholic nationalism in the Republic of Ireland as it is for Protestant unionism in Northern Ireland. One of the sad truths about the way the sectarian system operates on the island of Ireland is that it has encouraged within-tradition, as well as between-tradition forms of domination.

In its between-tradition form, domination can be expressed in many ways, for example through discrimination and harassment, through the denial of rights to individuals or groups, and through the suppression of aspects of the other's life and culture. There have been numerous instances of discrimination in the workplace, in the allocation of housing, and in the distribution of resources. The Catholic nationalist population of Northern Ireland, until after the Civil Rights marches in the late 1960s and the violence which followed them, disproportionately experienced such discrimination. The existence and work of the Fair Employment Commission, and now the Equality Commission, have formalised state attempts to overcome discrimination towards members of any community. Notwithstanding this, discrimination against all kinds of groups is still practised.

Elements of the denial of rights and the suppression of the culture of others are exemplified in any dispute over parading. Competing rights are pitted against one another. The right to assembly and to peaceful demonstration, for example, confronts the right to live peacefully in a neighbourhood without being subjected to 'walks' deemed by the local population to be offensive and threatening, or which are undertaken without prior consultation. In another sense, the right to assembly and peaceful demonstration can also conflict with the right to express culture by walking in an area which, because it is disputed, has become an area of threat and therefore requires a heavy police and army presence. The paramount dynamic here is to enforce 'our' will over against 'their' will. This is domination by another name. In the example of parading, the interplay of needs for identity, belonging, and the freedom to be different can be seen most clearly to be expressed in distorted 'over against' forms characteristic of sectarianism. On one hand, Orange Order members think that unless they can walk exactly the same route as usual, their identity and culture are being undermined, and their belonging as traditional power-holders is being challenged. They must stand against this. On the other hand, residents think that unless they can have a say in the routing of a procession through their area, their newly emerging identity as co-equal citizens, no longer second class, and their emerging sense of belonging and having the space to be different, are being trampled. They must stand against this.

In a very real way, the sense of threat to identity and belonging in both groups is accurate. The Orange Order needs to make the transition from their image of themselves as traditional power-holders to that of equal and co-responsible citizens. Undoubtedly, this will feel like loss and diminution. It may even feel distasteful to be sharing society on an equal basis with those whom they have regarded as inferior and untrustworthy. One of the positive aspects, apart from securing lasting peace, is that equality and diversity has the potential to bring a different type of creativity and development in Northern Irish society. Similarly, the residents need to make the transition from their image of themselves as second-class citizens and agitators against an unjust state to equal and co-responsible citizens. Whilst this looks like, and is, a big gain, it comes with a measure of responsibility which will undoubtedly feel uncomfortable and possibly even restrictive. It will no longer be possible to blame the 'others' for their woes in quite the same way, and there will be the harsh reality of making hard and unpopular choices which are part and parcel of a task of governance. In both cases, the movement needed must transform the sense of identity, belonging, and difference from a negative, over-against pattern into one characterised by co-existence and equality. It is a transformation which denies to the sectarian system the power to separate and set groups over against other groups on the basis of religion or politics.

The role and power of some paramilitary groups in local areas is perhaps the best example of the type of within-tradition domination spawned by this conflict. In no peaceful civic situation would the vast majority of citizens of an area countenance submitting to such an exercise of power by a small group of violent individuals without recourse to help from the police service and local government. It is a tragedy of the conflict that groups have imitated the violent strategies of the inter-group war in their dealings with their own. Intimidation of people to make them give money to the cause, fly flags at certain times of the year, or support the painting of kerbstones is commonplace. Displeasure, behind which stands the implied threat of violent response, towards anyone who takes an initiative in a local area without their approval, even a community-developing and positive initiative such as setting up much needed training for co-counselling, is a powerful tool of control. The paramilitaries can determine who receives help and who does not, how the community will develop and how it will not. In some areas, people have to ask permission to buy and sell houses or to set up businesses. Whilst it is true that paramilitaries have acted in some way as protectors of their communities, the price exacted on the local population in terms of stifling domination is high. We recall one community worker in a group we were working with sitting back in amazement when she recognised the extent to which they had ceded power to a small group of paramilitaries in their area. In her view this seems to have been a process which happened gradually and almost unnoticed. It is accepted as part of how things are, with an air of resignation which allows the paramilitaries to continue unchallenged, even where the majority of people do not like or agree with their actions. A complicating factor is the truth that what began as simple and necessary protection has developed an economic aspect through the acquisition of businesses or extortion of protection money from businesses. The task of wresting power from these groups is going to be difficult and complex, because they have much to lose not only in terms of power, but financially also.

The distorted expression of identity, belonging, and the freedom to be different in the within-group pattern of domination functions in two different ways. Firstly, it operates to inculcate into the group a falsely homogeneous image of what it means to be republican or loyalist, nationalist or unionist. The message is, 'We say how you will express who you are, and everyone will toe the line.' In this process there is little space for acknowledging all the natural differences which exist within a community. To acknowledge differences of opinion or outlook is seen as weakening the group. Whatever may be said privately, there is a strong feeling that 'we have to put up a united front' for fear that the others will take advantage of us. Such an approach tends to re-emphasise the dividing line between groups and to deepen division. Secondly, it operates to project this falsely homogenous image over against the other group. The message is that our strength is in our unity and that we are different from you. This, of course, crudely ignores or masks the myriad ways in which some republicans and loyalists, nationalists and unionists, Protestants and Roman Catholics can have more in common with the other group than with their own.

The extent to which the untruths about homogeneity over against the others and the deep seated fear and mistrust of the other play a role in keeping the paramilitaries in their dominant position became clear to us in January 1998. It was the period of sustained reprisal killings of Catholics which followed the murder of Billy Wright in the Maze prison in late December 1997, and to which republicans responded by killing two loyalists. Cecelia was working with a mixed group in North Belfast who had spent months getting to know one another and beginning to discuss some hard questions about sectarianism and what was going on in their area. The group had gelled well, worked hard, and developed reasonably warm personal relationships. Shortly after two Catholic men had been murdered in the area, Cecelia asked the group how they were feeling about the situation. One of the Roman Catholic women, a late-middle-aged regular church-goer, who was a faithful and active member of the group replied, 'Sure they are never going to change, we need "the Ra" back on the streets. Them's the only ones who'll protect us.' Most of the Catholics nodded in silent agreement, and those who did not nod gave no sign of unease about the comment. The Protestants in the group, for the most part, looked stunned but said nothing; one or two nodded silently. The shockingness of this scene lies partly in the fact that the statement came from an educated woman who believes in dialogue, who, in principle, has no time for the IRA and its violence, and who is a calm, sensible, well-loved, and respected member of her community. This was no young hothead! It lies partly also in the tacit acceptance of her comment by both the other Roman Catholics and some of the Protestants present. Cecelia asked, did they think that was wise? Was there not another way? The response was uniformly summed up in, 'Well, what do you expect?' The level of fear, resignation, and depression in both the Catholic and Protestant members was palpable.

It is evident that the stronger the destructive pattern of relating, the more obvious the systemic nature of sectarianism becomes. Domination is not only a mindset and series of discrete events, it has assumed the proportions of an entire culture or worldview, both internally to groups and between them. This culture is kept in place by the willingness of ordinary decent citizens to remain inert, to resign themselves to the situation, and to allow or advocate violent methods of seeking security.

Physically or verbally intimidating or attacking others. Whatever the struggle for power and domination, and however damaging it may be, the bottom line in destructive relationships is the total breakdown of trust and respect which is evidenced in physical violence or the threat of physical violence. Any act of violence shatters the web of relating not only at the physical but also at the psychological level. It shatters it in a way that makes trusting very difficult and the way back very long, because the perpetrator and/or their group can become an unconscious symbol of threat and hurt for those traumatised. Then, no matter how much someone wishes to forgive the person or group and to restore the relationship, conscious efforts are likely to be consistently undermined by unconscious reactions. It usually requires sustained psychological help to undo unconscious damage and to open the way for positive relationship. Organisations like Women Against Violence Empower (WAVE) and other counselling and support agencies for those who have been traumatised are essential to the process of recovery, not only of individuals and families, but also of society in general.

It is a measure of the damage caused by thirty years of conflict, that actions such as frightening or intimidating people in their homes, burning them out, burning schools, churches, and Orange halls, paramilitary beatings, planting bombs and shooting people, no longer surprise and rarely shock. Natural sensitivities and reactions have become dulled through saturation with violence, shock, fear, and grief. The Omagh bombing in August 1998 was an exception because it happened after the Belfast Agreement had been signed and because of the scale and callousness of the carnage. Even in this period of supposed ceasefire, people tolerate the continuation of many violent activities, albeit at a reduced frequency. It is as if they are part of the fabric of life here, and their absence would cause many to become uneasy and disorientated. This is in part because people have, of necessity, become adept at managing their lives around the violence and the threat of violence.

So children learn, almost by osmosis, when to speak and when to keep quiet, which areas are safe and which are not, and what to do in the event of trouble. A young mother, who lives in an inner city interface area, explained that she has two names for her four-year-old son, Seamus and Billy. The child knows that if they are in the park and she calls him 'Billy' there is some danger and he should come to her immediately and keep quiet. A man in his twenties described how as a school child he knew that if he heard loud noises he should 'hit the deck and stay there.' He believes that it saved his life on a day when he was passing an Army patrol and he heard sharp cracks. As he dived face down onto the pavement, a young soldier fell dead beside him with a bullet hole in his head. Many people listen almost addictively to news and current affairs programmes, especially at times of heightened tension. They need to know what is happening where, when, and why, not just out of interest, but because people need to know which places to avoid, or because they want to be prepared for what they might meet along the way and to have viable alternatives in mind.

Most people do not think about the ramifications of understandable and rational protective reactions that have, by now, become reflexive. The slow accretion of these protective strategies, however, has fundamentally distorted the way people relate here. The extent, and lack of awareness, of the distortion became apparent during an 'analysis for action' group meeting programme when we asked people to work in small groups to tease out in detail aspects of sectarianism in their area. In the plenary sharing, when we had the floor littered with flipchart sheets detailing the different dynamics and activities, one man, in his forties, sat back perplexed and said that it had never occurred to him just how abnormal was what he considered to be normal life! Indeed when we looked closely at the sheets, they revealed a picture of everyday avoidance, separation, mistrust, belittling, demonising, and violence. Nearly his whole life has been lived in the shadow of the conflict, and until that night it had not occurred to him to stand back and survey the way he had been constrained to relate to others. Perhaps only the relative luxury of the ceasefires has allowed space for such reflection. The need to organise their lives around violence and the threat of violence, however, has meant that people have developed patterns of behaviour and organisation that actually contribute actively and passively to maintaining the sectarian system. Any move beyond sectarianism will require that everyone exposes and changes these patterns.

The blatant disregard for human life entailed in acts of violence is the grotesque end result of a process that usually runs through the prior stages of separation, dehumanisation, and demonisation. It is a final movement which allows others no space even for the unsatisfactory co-existence of what Miroslav Volf calls 'assimilation', that is, being allowed to go on living with 'our' group as long as you give up 'your' identity and become totally like us.[22] Violence, in its various forms, is essentially the attempt to 'annihilate' the other, either metaphorically by driving them out of the area, or literally by blotting them out from the earth. In terms of the sectarian system, violence is the ultimate triumph in two very concrete ways. Firstly, violence destroys and damages relationships and engenders fear and mistrust to such an extent that people willingly, and understandably, move apart, stay apart and are reluctant to come together again. Secondly, violence means that people have to use energy just 'staying safe', energy that in other circumstances could be directed to building positive relationships.

Conclusion
Understanding sectarianism, what it is and how it functions, is a crucial element of any movement beyond it. Only when people can identify, name, and expose the ways in which the sectarian system has distorted, and continues to distort, their relationships will there be any possibility of taking effective steps to move beyond it. It is vital that the majority of people in Northern Ireland, especially the decent, church-going people, recognise that there are subtle and polite forms of sectarianism, that there are attitudes and beliefs which they take for granted, which actually significantly underpin this phenomenon. The raw and obvious expressions of sectarianism are only the visible tip of a large iceberg. Only when people realise that, however benign they consider themselves and their communities to be, they are all tainted and shaped by sectarianism, and only when they start taking active responsibility for this, will there be sufficient communal energy generated to dismantle the sectarian system. It will require sustained effort over generations. It will require strategies of transformation and mitigation. Perhaps it will require most of all a willingness and openness to be changed in the process.

CHAPTER 4

Dynamics and Varieties of Sectarianism

The working definition we have presented is comprehensive and therefore also general. In fact it could work, at least in a rough way, as a definition of nearly all negative 'isms'. Only the line about religion gives the definition clear specificity – if we were to substitute a line about gender or race, for example, we might have a reasonable definition of sexism or racism. In addition to refining this general definition, therefore, we have worked at identifying and analysing the dynamics and varieties of sectarianism, the different ways that sectarianism is expressed in particular instances.

The organisation of this chapter follows the shifting flow of our developing ways of thinking about sectarianism. Having been confronted with the need to name varieties of sectarianism, we began to build up a list of types, based on the group in which we encountered this type. This approach was useful, but not sufficient, and in some ways it could be misleading. Increasingly, then, we organised our conception of various expressions of sectarianism around their internal dynamics, which has proved more satisfactory. In this chapter, we combine the two approaches. While we continue to use the old types (liberal Protestant, conservative Catholic, etc.), they now function largely as illustrative material, subsumed under and subordinate to the broader framework of dynamics. One other alteration of our initial thinking about varieties of sectarianism soon presented itself. We discovered that any attempt to work on sectarianism between groups – which is the way sectarianism is typically perceived to work – was likely to uncover sectarian tension within groups. We conclude the chapter with a look at the distinctive dynamics and implications of this intra-group sectarianism.

Whose problem is sectarianism?
The need to think about varieties of sectarianism was one of the

first themes to emerge from our research. Early in the consultation phase, the name Moving Beyond Sectarianism prompted one wise and experienced friend to remark, 'That name will make Catholics feel smug and Protestants feel got at.' His remark has proved prophetic and could even be taken one step further. We find a widespread sentiment that sectarianism is not merely a largely Protestant problem but specifically a problem of conservative Protestantism, whether identified as fundamentalism or evangelicalism. All others, far from needing to consider their own responsibilities, can safely sneer dismissively in that direction and be done with the matter. We have heard in some ecumenical circles, for example, the opinion that to be ecumenical is by definition not to be sectarian, that the idea of ecumenical sectarianism is an oxymoron, an impossible contradiction. Introducing the idea of Catholic sectarianism has sometimes met with denial, amazement, or anger, even the occasional walkout. On the contrary, we see sectarianism in all quarters of church and society, even though expressed in different forms and with varying degrees of intensity.

Types of sectarianism

As these reflections suggest, our initial approach to varieties of sectarianism was to identify them in terms of where we first or most often encountered them. If a particular form of sectarianism seemed to emanate most often from liberal Catholics, we identified that as liberal Catholic sectarianism, if it came from fundamentalist Protestants, that was fundamentalist Protestant sectarianism, and so on. Our list has varied, but at the moment we are working with ten varieties: fundamentalist and evangelical Protestant, liberal Protestant and ecumenical, conservative Catholic, liberal Catholic, nationalist, republican, loyalist, unionist, state, and secular liberal.

Several points about these categories require comment. None of these groups is constantly or inherently sectarian – sectarianism is a temptation to which they occasionally succumb. Many of them do have core convictions that leave them open to the possibility of sectarianism, but they can choose to express these in ways that are not sectarian. And when a particular expression of sectarianism is related to a group's ideals – as many are – it is often a distortion of an ideal, not a direct expression of it. In practice, then, we have identified the forms of sectarianism pre-

sented in this chapter, not in the realm of ideals and formal convictions, but in our observation of the type of attitudes, behaviour, and practices that sometimes emerge among self-perceived
and self-identified members of that group. In particular, our
findings sometimes originated in observations of the groups
into which such people coalesce and which are therefore identifiable as evangelical, conservative Catholic, ecumenical, etc. The
activities and stances of such groups can provide an opportunity
to observe their relationship to outsiders of different types. Thus
the varieties of sectarianism we identify – although sometimes
expressions (albeit distorted) of a group's core convictions – are
drawn primarily from the world of lived experience.

The varieties that may require some particular preliminary
explanation are the two that combine two groups, fundamentalist and evangelical Protestant, and liberal Protestant and ecumenical. For each combination, we observed temptations toward
sectarianism in both groups that were so similar in essential
form that they did not warrant separate categories. Thus fundamentalism and evangelicalism are distinct, though connected,
religious groupings, and their characteristic expressions of sectarianism are of a similar type. Liberal Protestantism and ecumenism, for their part, are intersecting categories, the intersection
taking the form that most liberal Protestants, in our experience,
are inclined to view themselves as broadly ecumenical, in general
sympathies if not in active commitment. In this case, the kind of
sectarianism we began to observe in some ecumenical circles included, by definition, some liberal Protestants. As we did not
encounter any other form of sectarianism that was peculiar to
liberal Protestants, we chose to identify liberal Protestant and
ecumenical sectarianism as a single type.

This approach, naming varieties of sectarianism according to
the groups associated with them, has had real strengths. Not
least, it has allowed some people, unaccustomed even to considering the possibility that their group or convictions might be
capable of generating sectarianism, to think afresh about their
own situations, where before they might have been inclined to
bewilderment or to put the entire responsibility on others. If this
challenge has occasionally elicited hostile responses, it has met
far more often with brave and generous responses from people
who chose not to be affronted but to make these new insights an
opportunity to re-think their situations and responsibilities. A

second merit of this approach to varieties is that the categories involved fall into useful groupings. As a first step, they may be divided broadly into predominantly religious and predominantly political forms of sectarianism.

Religious	Political & Religious	Political
fundamentalist and evangelical Protestant	secular liberal	loyalist
liberal Protestant and ecumenical		unionist
conservative Catholic		republican
liberal Catholic		nationalist
		state

The exception here is secular liberalism, which has both political and religious implications. In one sense, of course, religion and politics are not neatly separable categories, as we have argued earlier: these forms of religion can have political implications, and these political orientations can have religious, or quasi-religious, significance. But secular liberalism straddles the intersection of religion and politics in a particular way by virtue of its concern for a certain ordering of the relationship between the state and organised religion. In Ireland, where the Christian churches are powerful in both political jurisdictions, this concern also involves secular liberalism in a relationship, often antagonistic, with the churches. Secular liberalism aside, a particularly revealing way of using these groupings is to match categories into pairs within a single tradition – e.g. conservative Catholic and liberal Catholic, or loyalist and unionist. This we will turn to at the end of the chapter, having first worked through the dynamics of sectarianism.

Identifying varieties of sectarianism by association with groups also has some weaknesses, however. First, some people have misunderstood us to be saying not that these groups are subject to the possibility of sectarian distortions, but that they are inherently sectarian. Despite increasingly strong and frequent disclaimers, of the kind already mentioned in this chapter, we have not always been able to dispel the misunderstanding. Had that been the only problem, we might have done no more than to work harder at more effective disclaimers. A greater problem, however, is that the more we worked with varieties, the more often we saw the dynamics we were associating principally with one group working in others as well, although perhaps less often or in weaker forms. Still, if other groups seem to be subject to some form of the dynamics we have associated with fundamentalist Protestant sectarianism, for example, it then raises questions about continuing with that particular designation.

Dynamics of sectarianism

At this point, we have not chosen to abandon identifying sectarianism with groups, but to make this approach secondary to identifying varieties by their core dynamic, how they characteristically work. We are currently working with nine themes and subthemes. All sectarianism can be understood as *a destructive way of dealing with difference*, and this works in two main ways, by *magnifying difference* and by *minimising difference*. Magnifying difference often takes the form of a *search for truth and purity*, which typically results in *separation*. Minimising difference, on the other hand, has two main variants, *failing to recognise that every new inclusion creates a new opportunity for exclusion* and *failing to recognise and respect difference*, the latter having *patronising* and *assimilating* variants.

Sectarianism as a destructive way of dealing with difference			
Sectarianism as the magnifying of difference	Sectarianism as the minimising of difference		
Sectarianism as an outcome of the search for truth and purity	Sectarianism as a failure to recognise that every new inclusion creates a new opportunity for exclusion	Sectarianism as a failure to recognise and respect difference	
Separation		Patronising	Assimilating

For our current purposes, we are going to focus our explication of the varieties and dynamics of sectarianism primarily on their religious expressions. The dynamics apply much more widely, of course, and the churches are not necessarily any more responsible than the other groupings we list. In fact some brief comment on secular liberal sectarianism will fit naturally into this chapter, and political forms of sectarianism have already been touched on, directly or indirectly, in the earlier history chapter. Because our work has been with a largely church-based constituency, however, that is where we find ourselves best qualified to comment. We have less experience working with the dynamics of sectarianism as expressed by the main political orientations in Northern Ireland, and still less working with state and secular liberal sectarianism.

Sectarianism as a destructive way of dealing with difference
The essential dynamics of overt, hard sectarianism in dealing with difference might be described as:
1. encounter
2. judge
3. condemn
4. reject.
These steps always have an aftermath of:
5. separation and
6. antagonism, although this antagonism may be intermittent or latent,
and the whole usually, but not necessarily, results in some level of
7. demonising.

To start where too many people reflexively start, this is the dynamic of the Orange Order's relationship with Catholicism. So far so familiar to readers of liberal perspectives. We begin here, however, not to reinforce prejudices but to take a reading of a contentious, polarising situation that we hope might challenge the ordinary assumptions of the Order's friends and critics alike.

Along with many positive religious exhortations, the document known as 'The Qualifications of an Orangeman' calls on members, as committed defenders of Protestantism, to

strenuously oppose the fatal errors and doctrines of the Church of Rome, and scrupulously avoid countenancing (by his presence or otherwise) any act of Popish worship; he should, by all lawful means, resist the ascendancy of that church, its encroachments, and the extension of its power, ever abstaining from all uncharitable words, actions, or sentiments, towards his Roman Catholic brethren.[1]

Presumably based on some sort of encounter with Catholicism, the stages of judging, condemning, and rejecting are clearly and concisely present here: Catholicism is marked by 'fatal errors and doctrines' which Orangemen must 'strenuously oppose'. This is foundational to the Orange Order, and on the basis of this principled anti-Catholicism, the Order is often judged or assumed to be sectarian.

Note, however, that while encountering, judging, condemning, and rejecting are necessary elements in the dynamics of sectarianism, they are not, on their own, necessarily sectarian. Though these four steps do not make up the whole of discernment, they are necessary steps or options in the discernment process. The person who has never encountered a person, idea, doctrine, movement, or institution she felt she must 'strenuously oppose' is probably not adequately engaged with the world.

We might go further and say that this passage presents one possible nonsectarian model for those who find themselves in strenuous opposition. Having called on the Orangeman to oppose and resist the Catholic Church, the Qualifications go on to require him to '[abstain] from all uncharitable words, actions, or sentiments, towards his Roman Catholic brethren.' For a Christian organisation, this call to abstention is a very weak version of Jesus' commands to 'love your neighbour as yourself' and to 'love your enemy', but it is a recognisable version or at least a step in that direction.

Taken as a whole, then, this passage from the Qualifications effectively calls the Orangeman to hate the sin and love the sinner. But this is a widely and, to a degree, justifiably derided notion. After all, those who imagine themselves to be hating the sin and loving the sinner generally do much better at the former than the latter. 'Hate the sin and hold the sinner in contempt' would seem to be a more honest formulation of what usually happens, and few enough rise above 'hate the sin and patronise the sinner.' On the other hand, the 'sinner' on the receiving end of such love is not likely to be impressed, especially when he in no way accepts that the conviction or behaviour in question is wrong or 'sinful'.

Imperfect as this 'hate the sin, love the sinner' formulation may be, anyone with strong convictions is likely to require some version of it if he is to steer clear of sectarianism, because no adequate alternative exists. 'Hate the sin and hate the sinner' is obviously flawed, loving the sin is silly, and judging it as other than sin – or in some way deeply flawed – is not always a serious option. The best that can be accomplished in circumstances like this is constraints and modifiers on judgment: the person who would judge may be exhorted to take the beam out of her own eye before removing the mote from another's; to be slow to judge; to remember that 'with the judgment you make you will be judged, and the measure you give will be the measure you get' (Mt 7:2); to keep the judgment proportionate, i.e. to judge people and ideas in the context of all that they are, not to focus solely on the negative or the point of contention.

After every constraint has been recognised, however, most people will still find some occasions in which they judge someone or something as so wrong that they feel compelled not only to disagree but to 'strenuously oppose' and 'resist'. All that will keep a person from outright demonising is finding ways to oppose and resist that still allow him to 'love the sinner', which must involve, at minimum, maintaining a sense of the humanity and rights of those he opposes and keeping open the possibility of communication. The Orange Order's commitment to '[abstain] from all uncharitable words, action, or sentiments' towards Roman Catholics, tied to accepting them as in some sense 'brethren', is recognisably a version of what is required from the holders of strong judgments if they are not to rush straight into sectarianism.

With a framework in place for restraining judgment – and therefore for restraining sectarianism – everything depends on how the framework is acted upon. Does the Orange Order, do individual members, live up to the standard of behaving charitably, or at least not uncharitably, toward Roman Catholic brothers and sisters? However that question is answered, it is a standard of accountability they have set and accepted for themselves.

Having dealt with the dynamics of encountering, judging, condemning, and rejecting, we now move on to separation, antagonism, and demonising. Separation, as is often the case, is the crucial pivot here. The Order does have a degree of separation built into its Qualifications in requiring that the Orangeman

'scrupulously avoid countenancing (by his presence or otherwise) any act of Popish worship', but this is not what we have in
mind. This kind of separation is narrowly confined to acts of religious worship and does not extend to a general, comprehensive social separation. While any separation can pose difficulties, separation is most likely to be problematic when it becomes
so broad and comprehensive that it prevents honest communication.

People are too self-serving ever to trust their own evalu-
ations of their behaviour, so judging the charity of particular
actions must involve hearing from others, especially the ones toward whom that charitable behaviour is directed. In other
words, if the Orange Order wants to know whether it is living
up to its standard of abstaining from all uncharitable behaviour
towards Catholics, it needs clear and honest communication
with significant numbers of representative Catholics. This is one
place, we believe, where the Order falls far short of its ideals and
into sectarianism. To take a high profile and contentious issue,
one hears from Orangemen stories of places and times in which
Orange parades were or are well received by Catholics, and this
is genuinely the case. At the same time, we have heard many
stories from diverse Catholics of situations where Orange parades
represented fear, humiliation, and subjugation. Until these stories
are taken seriously, the Order has not been honest in assessing
whether it is living up to its own standards. Likewise, the Order
has often refused to talk to Catholic residents' groups objecting
to Orange parades, dismissing the groups and their complaints
as stage managed by Sinn Féin. We accept that Sinn Féin may at
times have had undue and distorting influence on some groups,
but this is no valid reason to dismiss everything those groups
are saying – we have watched mild, moderate, and middle-class
Catholics shake with silent rage as they try to talk about what
Drumcree II, in the summer of 1996, meant to them. If the
Orange Order had sufficient relationships with Catholics, they
would know the same.

Separation then, with a consequent absence of adequate communication, is the pivot that turns negative but not necessarily
sectarian judgment in the direction of sectarian consequences. In
the terms of our definition, then, the question becomes, do
Orange Order parades sometimes result in hardened boundaries between communities, demonising, and violence? Surely

they do. It is true that these effects are never unilaterally imposed by the actions of one party. They depend on a particular response from other parties. But in the absence of genuine communication with antagonistic parties, the Orange Order cannot absolve itself from responsibility for the consequences to which it contributes.

The general principle here is that strongly negative judgment of a group, combined with separation, leads almost inevitably to sectarianism. For those who wish both to make strong judgments and to resist sectarianism, some kind of honest relationship with the other group is crucial. Relationship and communication will not necessarily be enough to prevent sectarian outcomes – antagonism and demonising might still follow. But some kind of effective communication is likely to improve the chances of a positive outcome. In the absence of such a relationship, verbal commitments to nonsectarianism, however sincere, may well be meaningless.

The sectarianism of Orangeism's liberal opponents

Applying this standard to the Orange Order has obvious consequences: opposition to Catholicism combined with separation from Catholics leads to sectarianism. But the same standard applies to many people who in one form or another combine opposition to and separation from some group. The consequences of antagonism and demonising may not be manifest, and people may mistake this situation for peace, but the ingredients are primed and ready for circumstances to set off an open conflict. When this happens, many will be shocked and wonder how this could be, but in fact the mechanism for conflict had been well prepared.

This standard is also revealing when applied to liberals who understand themselves to be opponents of sectarianism in general and the Orange Order in particular. Much of what passes for anti-sectarianism is in reality a mirror image response that feeds the sectarian system – even as it imagines itself to be fighting sectarianism – by copying sectarian dynamics: encounter, judge, condemn, reject; separation, antagonism, demonising. We have in mind a particular journalist who has been a vigorous critic of the Orange Order for its sectarianism, and yet if one considers the structure of his critique, it duplicates this sectarian sequence precisely, even though the content of his arguments opposes sectarianism. As such, his work cannot be an effective counter to sectarianism, because in its structure it pays homage to sectarianism and reinforces it by employing its logic. In our judgment, this journalist, far from being unusual, represents much of liberal opposition to sectarianism. By mimicking sectarian dynamics even while making different judgments about content, such supposed opposition to sectarianism becomes itself a form of liberal sectarianism.

Regardless of the specific content of judgment, then, the conjunction of negative judgment of another party with separation from it is likely to yield a sectarian outcome. This is true even of secular liberalism, which we mention here partly because we deal with it nowhere else in this book and partly because it is inclined even more than other forms of liberalism to regard itself as inherently, by definition, non- or anti-sectarian. But moving beyond religion does not mean moving beyond sectarianism. Religion is only one element of sectarianism, after all, so removing religion from the equation may do no more than create a secularised sectarianism rather than eliminate it. In any case, secular liberalism does not so much remove religion from the equation – in a place like Northern Ireland, secular liberalism may wish to do so, but it has no such power – as take a different stance toward it, and that stance will not necessarily do anything more than provide a different spin on the old sectarian problem, breeding new forms of exclusion and discrimination.

Nor will secular liberalism's admirable commitment to tolerance necessarily combat sectarianism. Every conception of tolerance has its limits, and it is the ground beyond those limits where any group finds its main temptations to sectarian attitudes, judgments, and actions. Tolerance is a useful tool for resisting sectarianism, but not sufficient on its own. Another problem, with implications for sectarianism, is that too many adherents to secular liberalism, perhaps because it arose as a product of the enlightenment long after the various Christian traditions, assume that contentious, problematic truth claims are a distinctively religious problem from which secular liberalism has broken free. But there is no identifiable place 'beyond' truth claims from which one position may sit in judgment on others. Every grouping makes truth claims, at least implicitly if not explicitly, and every group will face temptations to make them in destructive, even sectarian, ways. The first step toward making them well is to recognise that one is making them. Finally, secular liberalism is a stance around which coalesce movements, institutions, and therefore loose forms of community. Every form of community, of corporate identity, creates boundaries. From these boundaries follow insiders and outsiders and the possibility of forms of exclusion which, if not dealt with creatively and conscientiously, can feed the sectarian system.

Sectarianism as the magnifying of difference

If all sectarianism can be understood as a destructive way of dealing with difference, some forms work by magnifying difference and others by minimising it. Many of the expressions most typically associated with sectarianism, however, work by magnifying, and we begin here. In our experience, sectarianism as magnification of difference works in a straight line through *the search for truth and purity* to *separation,* taking both conservative Protestant and conservative Catholic forms.

Conservative Protestant sectarianism

For our immediate purposes, conservative Protestantism includes both fundamentalists and evangelicals. Although the kind of sectarianism we describe here may be a greater temptation for fundamentalists than for evangelicals, evangelicals are subject to it as well, and every evangelical will recognise the logic of such sectarianism in a way that Christians from other traditions may not. Nonetheless, in this section we will use the phrase 'fundamentalist sectarianism' as shorthand for this type of sectarianism. We do so for two main reasons. First, the problem takes its sharpest form among fundamentalists, and second, the story on which we base this section involves a self-defined fundamentalist. The essential dynamics, however, are likely to apply to any conservative Protestant group.

Fundamentalists' sectarianism is often rooted, we believe, in their extreme anxiety to maintain the pure, orthodox truth by being separate from all with whom they disagree – compromise is the ultimate fundamentalist obscenity, and to avoid it they must stay scrupulously separate, especially in religious matters. Thus the frequent repetition of phrases from 2 Cor 6:17, typically in the King James Version: 'Wherefore come out from among them, and be ye separate, saith the Lord, and touch not the unclean thing; and I will receive you.' So inspired, fundamentalists often develop a comprehensive separateness that easily insulates them from any meaningful contact with those outside their own circles, especially but not exclusively Catholics.

A story drawn from one of Joe's interviews will illustrate why we find this radical doctrine of separation problematic and prone to sectarianism. During an interview with a self-described Protestant fundamentalist minister, Joe was probing the issue of separation, trying to understand what are the limits, what are all the reasons for it. He asked in particular if there were 'common denominator' experiences in which contact between Catholics and fundamentalist Protestants would not be threatening or problematic. The minister gave several examples, including the following.

> Take our position, for example, on the Brook Advisory Centre[2] in Belfast. We would go down there, and we would have our protest outside, and we would be joined every time by Roman Catholic people. We would talk to them – they would phone up and come visit us here at home, which we don't have any difficulty doing, even if I'd have to say on the other side were paramilitary people who would come and visit us. I mean that to me is life, that is the way it should be. ... There are so many areas [where] we don't have to get into a theological compromise in order to at least accommodate a person's friendship and to reciprocate their friendship as well – no difficulty at all.

Joe asked, 'That [Brook example] doesn't feel compromising to you in any way? It's cooperation of Catholics and Protestants, but it's on a very particular kind of issue.'

'It's not even cooperation,' he responded.

> I know some people have made gain out of that, and across America they published photographs ... and defined it as an ecumenical protest. You can imagine [that] couldn't have been further from the truth. ... [Roman Catholics] probably have a different emphasis, and they do have a different emphasis, [about] why they're there. I mean they would clearly be there because of their very strong anti-abortionist position, mainly because the removing of the child, the aborting of the child, diminishes the whole numerical strength of church involvement and that would be the over-riding influence that they would have. We wouldn't see it from that point of view, obviously. We see it much more as a moral,

scriptural position, not church orientated, so we wouldn't say there was cooperation, but there was understanding.[3]

The riddle here is to understand how this minister could judge Catholic opposition to abortion, which is based on core Catholic moral commitments, to be based not on moral considerations, but on a crude numerical power play, an 'over-riding influence' that abortion 'diminishes the whole numerical strength of church involvement'. He is clearly an intelligent man, so that is not the issue, and if more people were to take on his consistently courteous manner of dealing with opponents, Northern Ireland would be a better place. Furthermore, the kind of separation he advocates is hardly objectionable. It is confined to the religious sphere, and it not only allows for social interaction and even friendship with those from whom he differs, he himself practises what he preaches, opening his home to his religious opponents. Many people of theoretically more tolerant convictions have in practice done less. 'I mean that to me is life, that is the way it should be. ... There are so many areas [where] we don't have to get into a theological compromise in order to at least accommodate a person's friendship and to reciprocate their friendship as well.' So how did he come to misunderstand Catholic anti-abortionist activists so badly?

Several possible answers, complementary and overlapping, present themselves. His judgment may represent a kind of psychological transference: the big Protestant political fear of being overcome by Catholic numbers applied to the specific issue of abortion. It may also represent a need to magnify difference when similarity looms. After all, what he described looked a good deal like cooperation, but since cooperation stands as a step on the slippery slope to compromise, he chose to describe the situation as 'understanding' rather than 'cooperation'. In a situation where Catholic and fundamentalist motivations for opposing abortion look remarkably similar to an outsider, right down to the kind of language they characteristically use, the need to steer well clear of compromise may have inclined him to magnify differences in motivation.

This also seems to us, however, to be an example of how a subtle but effective separation can distort perceptions despite a degree of social interaction, even friendship. Sectarianism does not require absolute separation, only a certain level of superficiality where contact exists. In this case, interaction did not extend to a level where motivations could be honestly shared, and the result was a harsh, demeaning, and false characterisation of Catholic anti-abortion activists.

We see this situation as an application of separation resulting in sectarianism, but we want to be clear about why we make this judgment. We do not base our judgment on whether the doctrine of separation is bad theology or good theology, although we believe it is severely limited theology; we are not commenting on whether this doctrine is biblical or unbiblical, although we believe it ignores huge and central aspects of the biblical witness. Rather, we are saying this doctrine of separation too easily leads to sectarianism by causing, in the terms of our definition, destructive patterns of relating, a spiral driven by the hardening of boundaries and demonising. Separation, when systematically applied, forces people to operate on the basis of stereotypes about those from whom they are separate. These stereotypes are often half truths or less, and yet separation means that people have no means of correction – in fact, stereotypes are likely to take on a life of their own and develop unchecked. Thus in this story, five minutes of substantial conversation with Catholic anti-abortion activists about their real motivations would have revealed to the minister that their motivations are precisely the same as his.

'We wouldn't say there was cooperation, but there was understanding,' he concluded. In fact there was not understanding, because his application of separation, while it welcomed a basic civility and allowed for a degree of shared activity, prevented an openness of sharing that would have quickly corrected his misconception. This kind of separation borders on being inherently sectarian, because the very fact of separation means it is hard for people to get the kind of accurate information they need to correct false stereotypes; and if they try to take the steps necessary to correct their stereotypes, they may stand accused by their own party of sullying the purity of the group's separation. If this doctrine of separation is so important to some people that they wish to maintain it despite its demonstrable tendency to divide and demonise, this is their privilege, but they must recognise that they may well be choosing sectarianism along with separation.

While we see the doctrine and practice of radical separation as frequently prone to sectarianism, we have carefully refrained from calling it inherently sectarian. We believe instead that Christians require a varied repertoire of strategies for dealing with the world around them, and that in some circumstances evil is so rampant that the best thing, perhaps the only thing, for Christians to do is to withdraw, to survive, to endure, to wait, to hope – in other words to be radically separate. This is a way of responding to cataclysm and crisis. We think, for example, that such a strategy might have been one faithful Christian response to the Nazi regime; it is still more likely to arise as a credible and legitimate response by Christians subject to intense persecution. The point of connection here is that it is typical of fundamental-ism – formed in the twentieth century as a response to modernity and so keenly aware of 'the toxicity of twentieth century Western culture'[4] – to make precisely this judgment: that the world is in such a mess, that evil is so flourishing, that Christians have no faithful choice but radical separation. We strongly dis-agree that this a correct reading of the times as concerns Northern Ireland. But our reason for making this point is to sug-gest a perspective: when other Christians are disagreeing with a fundamentalist about radical separation, they are not dealing with someone who is holding an absolutely wrong, fund-amentally anti-Christian position; they are disagreeing with a brother or sister who reads the signs of the times differently than they do.

Regrettably few of the settings in which we work have in-cluded fundamentalists, and one typical reaction in groups to this story about the Brook protests is spontaneous, incredulous laughter that the minister should have misunderstood the moti-vations of Catholic anti-abortionists so badly. Sometimes we have laughed, too. But having had years to reflect on the story, we are left uneasy – our laughter and incredulity now seem too easy and self-satisfied. Is there really no shock of self-recogni-tion for us in this story? Are there perhaps those with whom we are so out of sympathy and contact that we believe dangerous nonsense about them? In this story, the separation and its conse-quence are the results of an ideology, specifically an approach to faith that we do not share, but it is the *fact* of separation as much as the reasons for it that allows the flourishing of rampant, unchecked, distorting stereotypes. Might those of us who re-spond incredulously to this particular story be tainted by our own, differently motivated versions of the same dynamics? An attitude appropriately suspicious for the task of dealing with sectarianism requires that we at least be alert to the possibility.

Conservative Catholic sectarianism
The Catholic tendency to regard sectarianism as a solely or at least mainly Protestant problem derives, we believe, from the fact that Northern Protestant sectarianism during the Stormont regime, 1921-1972, was accompanied by political power to give effect to that sectarianism. Having suffered this potent sectarianism, one's own, which is always the hardest to see, would seem comparatively minor.

In fact traditional, conservative Catholic sectarianism is largely a mirror image of fundamentalist sectarianism: ours is the one true church, the guardian of all truth, and without the greatest care, such truth claims lead easily to those foundational sectarian stances, hardening of boundaries and demonising. Although Second Vatican Council teachings have made serious inroads into such thinking, it is far from extinct. Conservative Catholic sectarianism is, in its own way, as concerned about separation and boundaries as is Protestant fundamentalism, although the rhetoric is less strident. Some of the key defining, separating issues are mixed marriage, mixed communion, and mixed schooling.

Our first point about separation and sectarianism applies particularly to both conservative Catholics and fundamentalist Protestants, but few groups escape it entirely. Confronted with the possibility that some practice, belief, or institution might be sectarian, people reflexively respond to the effect that 'we have no such intent; we are not being sectarian, these are deeply, sincerely held beliefs.' Many Catholics, for example, especially conservative ones, will respond in exactly this manner when questioned about Catholic belief and practice regarding mixed marriage, communion, and schooling. The question of sectarianism cannot be entertained, many feel, because these are practices arising not from sectarian motives, but from respect for authoritative church teaching, which reflects fundamental beliefs and is designed to strengthen the Catholic community.

Although we are occasionally inclined to question some protestations of pure intent, we try to resist the temptation, because few exercises could be more fruitless or even counter-productive. Such exchanges rarely rise above the level of 'Yes, you are,' 'No, we're not.' But neither can these matters be dropped at the first cry of innocence, for if such issues could be settled by assertions of innocent intent, one would find that sectarianism had magically disappeared even though nothing had changed, because what others identify as sectarian in a group, they see as loyalty to truth, justice, and community. As discussed in chapter three, we have been led, therefore, to distinguish between sectarian *intent* and sectarian *consequences:* is it possible that an innocently, positively held conviction can at the same time have sectarian consequences? This is one of the uses to which we put the five modes of sectarian operation in our definition: does the belief or action in question have any of these outcomes? If so, it may be said to have sectarian consequences, which a person or group must deal with, regardless of their innocent intentions. In the case of conservative Catholics one needs to ask, do segregated marriage, communion, and schooling practices have sectarian implications in Northern Ireland? Surely they do. In the first instance, they will be inclined to harden boundaries between communities, and where this occurs, overlooking or belittling too easily follow. Confronting sectarianism requires people to look beyond their intentions to consider the consequences of their beliefs and actions.

We would stress that recognising possible sectarian outcomes does not dictate, does not necessarily even hint at, what to do about any of the issues involved. To take one highly contentious example, recognising that segregated education can have unintended sectarian consequences may well raise the issue of integrated education, but it does not necessarily mean that society must cast out denominational education and install integrated education. Our approach to confronting sectarianism does require, however, that people consider more than intentions, dealing with the consequences of their beliefs and actions as well.

Sectarianism as the minimising of difference
Much of what people immediately think of as sectarianism operates by the mechanisms described above: magnifying difference, divisive truth claims, separation. But several more subtle, but no less destructive, varieties of sectarianism operate in a nearly opposite way. If the preceding varieties have represented characteristically conservative temptations, the sectarianism of

minimising difference is most often practised by liberals who, ironically, are likely to understand themselves as opposing sectarianism. Measured by consequences rather than intentions, however, minimising difference is marked as sectarian by potential outcomes of hardening boundaries, overlooking, and belittling, even demonising.

Sectarianism as a failure to recognise that every new inclusion creates a new opportunity for exclusion

Dynamics of human relationship do not come much more basic than this. Two states enter a political pact, making a third feel threatened; the prodigal son is re-united and reconciled with his father, and the elder, obedient son is resentful; on schoolyards everywhere, the cosy circle of friends is oblivious to those excluded. We have observed this dynamic particularly among ecumenical groups.

Ecumenical sectarianism

By being a pioneer in dealing creatively and bravely with difference, especially religious difference, the ecumenical movement may justly regard itself as an example for all those seeking to move beyond sectarianism. This does not mean, however, that ecumenism has removed itself from the realm of sectarianism. In fact the illusion that it has done so means that ecumenical sectarianism can sometimes be marked by a double unawareness, which makes it doubly insidious: because many who regard themselves as ecumenical define what it means to be ecumenical as not-sectarian, they are easily left unaware of even the possibility of their own sectarianism.

Ecumenical sectarianism arises precisely through failure to recognise that every new inclusion creates an opportunity for new exclusion. Those who are conscious of a new and hard-won unity with former antagonists, while also remaining keenly aware that the new unity retains ample difference requiring careful attention, may then give less attention to how the newly united parties are regarding those outside their circle. In fact the bond that now unites them can serve as a barrier to those outside. Furthermore, a negative regard for outsiders can be an easy, though spurious, way of nurturing unity within any relationship, perhaps especially a new and tentative one.

The effects are illustrated by the experience of one of Joe's interviewees, a man with a particularly varied and colourful spiritual pilgrimage. In the 1980s, wearied by what he was finding to be a harsh and judgmental spirit in the charismatic circles that were then his home, he went to an annual conference sponsored by the Irish School of Ecumenics and the Corrymeela community. He was in part looking to stretch himself, but even more he sought respite and healing in a more inclusive Christian setting. He was bitterly disappointed then to find that some participants treated him with contempt as a charismatic; he did not find the acceptance he sought. This is a tale we have heard versions of far too often to dismiss: charismatics, evangelicals, and house church members who, venturing tentatively into ecumenical circles, have felt disdainfully, derisively treated by groups that understand themselves as tolerant and inclusive. In reality such groups can have as much difficulty as any community with dealing constructively with the stranger.

A similar dynamic can arise in a more structural, less personal way when local clergy groups are established in Northern Ireland. Such groups have been an important growth area in recent years. The potential benefits are tragically apparent in the experience of the Omagh bombing in August 1998, when pastoral response to the situation was greatly enhanced by relationships formed through the Omagh Churches Forum, then only a couple years old. Laudable as this development undoubtedly is, the churches represented are almost always confined – not deliberately, but in practice – to the four largest, Catholic, Presbyterian, Church of Ireland, and Methodist. As a result, the already substantial gap between those churches and the numerous smaller, and usually more conservative, churches grows wider and deeper. No one is acting in a deliberately exclusive way in such a situation, and yet this deepened division does not need to be deliberate to be lamented. In this and any similar cases, participants entering new cooperation or reconciliation need to develop the habit of thinking through the implications for other relationships. What will be the new stress points? Will anyone feel excluded? Are there ways of anticipating and dealing with possible bad feeling? Who among the new group has contacts and relationships that might be useful in fostering constructive relationships between the new group and other parties? While the problem we identify here is an inherent danger in reconciliation, at least the worst effects can be mitigated by thoughtful, creative anticipation and response.

Sectarianism as a failure to recognise and respect difference
Another form of minimising difference is simply failing or refusing to recognise it. In 1996 we organised a conference attended
by an unusually diverse group of Northern Ireland Christians.
At several points, however, we noticed that some of the more
liberal participants, who were more experienced and at ease in
mixed gatherings, were overlooking or failing to appreciate the
extent of the diversity represented. At the end of the conference,
one such participant expressed regret that the group had been
too similar – people held all the same beliefs, she thought. At the
same time, we were aware of one evangelical participant who
felt that her perspectives had been consistently ignored or marginalised by others working from largely unspoken assumptions that all right-thinking people agreed on certain things. The
effect of such overlooking is to deepen division and belittle. We
have noticed two main variants, patronising and assimilating.

Patronising
Ecumenical, Evangelical, and Catholic sectarianism
We first noticed patronising, albeit kindly and well-meant, as an
ecumenical temptation in regard to conservatives. A progressive
model of truth, coupled with the consciousness among ecumenists that they themselves have been dealing with sectarianism
for many years, too easily yields the assumption that conservatives more recently addressing sectarianism are simply toddlers
along the same path. The result can be intimidating or infuriat-
ing or both for conservatives, some of whom might admit to
being toddlers, but all of whom, given their different starting
point, resent the assumption that they will necessarily be taking
the same path ecumenists have trod. Those long experienced in
dealing with sectarianism may be of real benefit to relative newcomers, but only if they carefully avoid 'been there, done that'
assumptions and work consciously at teasing out and respecting
differences in starting point, context, and guiding beliefs.

We have come to recognise, however, that our identification
of patronising with ecumenism was based on the mistake of
highlighting that which was novel and unexpected to us and
downplaying the familiar. At least two other forms of patronising
are endemic and debilitating. One is the breathtaking evangelical
confidence in pronouncing on who and what is or is not
'Christian'. We are certainly not calling for an uncritical acceptance

of anything and everything as somehow Christian, including some of the things that sometimes pass for it, and some critical judgments may not be easy for all to hear. But we are calling for generosity and humility. Too often 'Christian' turns out to mean 'that with which I am familiar and comfortable' or even 'just like us' while 'non-Christian' means 'different', or just 'unfamiliar'. Many Catholics also fall for the patronising temptation. One of the classic forms is the common expression 'non-Catholics', as all those Presbyterians, Baptists, Pentecostals, etc., not to mention other religions, are dissolved into the single category of 'not us'. Failures to recognise and respect difference do not come much more transparent. Another form, blending into the assimilation category, is the assumption – prevalent before the Second Vatican Council and far from vanished today – that church unity will mean the return of others into the Catholic Church. This is rarely transparent, but from time to time we see it as the internal, unspoken, and perhaps not fully realised logic of statements that would not otherwise make sense.

Readers will note that the examples of patronising presented here are not exactly equivalent, and in chapter six we will discuss more precisely what it is that makes a religious statement sectarian. For now, suffice it to say that all patronising statements are potentially divisive, they represent a degree of overlooking, and they fall somewhere between belittling and dehumanising.

Assimilating
Liberal sectarianism, especially liberal Catholic
In our experience, liberals are inclined to emphasise the value of unity. Among liberal Catholics in particular, we encounter a consistent, powerful, and faith-based vision of the things that unite humanity, which we admire and regard as one of their important contributions to other Christians. But this admirable trait can also have a down side: it can minimise difference, failing to respect difference adequately. In its presence, anyone already feeling overwhelmed or on edge is likely to reject or even flee what will seem like a smothering embrace. Sometimes when we are participating in a mixed gathering in Northern Ireland, especially if we have helped to organise it, we will be acutely aware of the tensions in the room: who does not get along with whom; who is only just getting involved in this sort of

thing and is not at all sure of its integrity or value; who is here only furtively, because his parishioners would savage him if they knew he was here; who is torn between hope that things learned here may release her from an oppressive situation and fear that she may be compromising old and valued traditions; and so on. As we make our way through the session, with more or fewer stumbles but at least some measure of success, near the end someone, in our experience often a liberal Catholic, is likely to say something like this: 'Isn't it wonderful how much we all have in common, how alike we are?' At times such a statement derives, we have sometimes heard later, from an anxiety that in fact the supposed commonality is not the case – the spoken wish is an attempt to create the desired reality. Many times, however, the statement is made in full sincerity, and the sense of common-ality may be real, even if exaggerated beyond its tentative stand-ing. But saying so at this point in the group's experience is super-ficial and therefore destructively premature. Knowing how such statements are heard by the hesitant, we cringe as we feel the in-ward retreat of those who are so keenly aware of all that divides the group. Those who are reluctant about or fearful of such gath-erings will need to make sure that everyone understands and re-spects all the ways people in the group differ before they can se-riously consider what they share. The rush to inclusion can feel presumptuous and imperialistic, and the intention to include can have the effect of repelling.

Intra-tradition sectarianism
Most of what is commonly understood as sectarianism is directed by one group against another, Catholics against Protestants or vice versa. We have discovered, however, that serious work on sectarianism almost always uncovers significant tension and conflict within groups as well. Although sectarianism as an inter-group problem seems so basic that some may object to classifying intra-group conflicts under the same heading, we have found it useful to think of some intra-group conflict as sect-arian. The dynamics of these internal conflicts, after all, typically reproduce aspects of the dynamics of sectarianism between groups. Furthermore, the antagonisms within and between groups reinforce one another and work as a kind of system, so that distinguishing sharply between them would seem rather artificial. One central dynamic of this relationship, for example, is that tension between groups makes groups feel the need for

internal solidarity, and the search for solidarity exposes the absence of it. As a result, rival parties within a group, fearing that their differences cannot be resolved or dealt with fruitfully, sometimes suppress their differences for the sake of the all-important appearance of group unity in the face of external threat from the other group. When differences do become public, parties within a group are particularly bitter against one another for letting down the side, which would never have been so important if it were not for the conflict between groups.

These tensions are exacerbated when, as in Northern Ireland, the groups in question are also traditions. The significance is that conflicting parties within a tradition contest not only current issues and interests, they also both share and contest a common historical heritage. To illustrate some of the dynamics involved in intra-tradition sectarianism, we have organised matching pairs occupying opposite ends of a continuum, with the poles relating to their shared legacy in different ways. For thinking in terms of intra-tradition sectarianism, our categories have required some recasting. Creating pairs works best for the religious and political groupings that clearly share a historical tradition and yet differ sharply as to how that tradition is best interpreted and lived. We have therefore removed the ecumenical, state, and secular liberal categories. We do not observe within the ecumenical movement the dynamics characteristic of the other continua, perhaps because ecumenism is a comparatively recent phenomenon and so has had less time to develop such patterns. Ecumenism may also be different, however, by virtue of its principled, central commitment to unity, which correlates in practice with a fluid and informal notion of membership, based on drawing participants from various traditions without removing them from those traditions. State sectarianism simply does not fit the categories we develop here, because the state does not have a comparable internal dynamic. Secular liberalism might be paired with a category like 'religious' or 'traditional' to yield at least a weak version of the dynamics we describe, but the pairing would not constitute a tradition in anything like the sense of the other four we use. Fundamentalism and evangelicalism have not disappeared from the scheme as we present it here, they have been subsumed under the general category conservative Protestantism, of which they are different expressions. We are left with four pairings: conservative Protestant-liberal

Protestant; conservative Catholic-liberal Catholic; loyalist-unionist; and republican-nationalist. Described inclusively, these are Protestant, Roman Catholic, unionist, and nationalist traditions.

Religious		Political	
Conservative Protestant ↕ Liberal Protestant	Conservative Catholic ↕ Liberal Catholic	Loyalist ↕ Unionist	Republican ↕ Nationalist

Attempting to name the two poles reveals some of what is at stake in these relationships. Evaluating the continua from the outside, 'conservative' and 'liberal' would be obvious labels – and possibly acceptable to both parties – if we were talking about the religious varieties only, but these do not say much that is useful about the two political continua. If the word 'fundamentalist' could be purged of its negative connotations and used descriptively it might say something useful about the top end of the continua, but the term has probably come to be too exclusively pejorative to be used generally. From the inside, categories present themselves more obviously. Those situated at the bottom of the continua are likely to regard their end as 'moderate' and to criticise the other end as 'extreme'; alternatively, they might identify themselves as 'progressive' and the others as 're-actionary' or 'fundamentalist'. Those located at the top, however, are likely to regard themselves, whether or not they use the exact words, as 'traditional' or 'pure', while the other end is 'compromised' or 'sold-out'.

For our immediate purposes, and without really resolving the issues at stake, we are going to describe the upper end of the two religious continua – which are our main concern here – as 'traditional' and the lower end as 'moderate' on the grounds that these terms would be agreeable to those being described. Moderates are not necessarily any less committed to the tradition than are people at the traditional end; they simply disagree with the way that traditionalists relate to the tradition and therefore advocate another way. Even so, moderates are unlikely to de-scribe themselves as traditional, whereas those at traditional end would readily accept this description of themselves. While this is more true of the two religious than the two political con-tinua, many republicans have in reality been every bit as com-mitted to a fundamentalist interpretation of their tradition – commitment to the authority of the Second Dáil is a stark exam-ple – as Free Presbyterians are to a fundamentalist interpretation of Protestantism.

These conflicting ways of describing the continua and the parties within them suggest one significant difference between the opposite poles. These continua represent traditions – shared experience, shared history, shared beliefs – and the two poles contest which of their differing approaches to the tradition more adequately represents and embodies it. For people at the top end, a consciousness of tradition always shapes their descrip-tions of the two ends: they locate themselves and others with reference to the tradition in an immediate and direct way. Moderates at the bottom of the continua may be every bit as committed to their traditions, but the way the commitment is conceived of, expressed, and lived is markedly, qualitatively dif-ferent. A 'progressive/reactionary' distinction stigmatises con-servative attachment to tradition as narrow and limiting, and contrasts it with the forward- and outward-looking alternative represented by liberals. 'Moderate/extreme' conveys a similarly negative judgment – the approach to tradition characteristic of the conservative pole is excessive and stunted – while one of the dynamics that moderates the moderate pole must surely be an openness to forces outside the tradition. While the differing approaches to the tradition cannot be neatly, exclusively charac-terised, we risk this generalisation: even though both poles in-terpret and appropriate the tradition, those at the upper pole are more likely to be conscious custodians of tradition, while those at the lower end operate out of a looser sense of tradition as more a starting point and general context, less a direct obliga-tion. An important implication is that because these genuinely are traditions, statements or actions that appeal directly to the tradition, as the top end characteristically does, will always have a kind of inherent plausibility, even authority. This is true especially if bottom-end actions, and the logic behind them, can plausibly be portrayed as having abdicated the field of tradition in favour of alternative frameworks, leaving top-end formulations of tradition as the sole contestants.

Concerning the contest for the soul of the tradition, the four continua share several features. First they are magnetised at both extreme and moderate poles. At the two ends, the pull of the other is little felt and may even be closer to repulsion, but those who live in between feel the pull, and there is considerable movement in both directions. Thus many Presbyterian congregations will have significant numbers of members drawn from fundamentalist or conservative backgrounds, while the largest single grouping in the early years of the Free Presbyterian Church – even though it has no organic connection with Presbyterianism – was former Presbyterians who left because they felt that the Presbyterian Church was becoming too liberal.[5] Second, as this example suggests, the various continua are largely self-contained. A republican, for example, could jump continua and become a unionist, or vice versa, and such things do happen, but for the most part, disgruntled republicans will become nationalists rather than unionists. Third, and paradoxically, communication across continua can sometimes be easier than between the poles of a continuum, because when one deals with outsiders, that contest for the soul of the tradition is not at stake. Some of Joe's interviews were with people who might be classified as progressive evangelical, for want of a better term. Many of them told moving, powerful stories about how contact with Catholics had changed their attitudes, about what they were learning through conversations with Sinn Féin, and so on. After they had talked in this way for a while, Joe would ask them if they had ever had similarly transformative contact with liberal or ecumenical Protestants. One respondent was representative of them all: he visibly started at the notion, then smiled and said, 'Now that would be asking too much!'

As regards sectarianism, a particularly important issue is the nature of the magnetism at the traditional pole, operating in its manifestation as extreme. At this pole, each tradition is haunted by a ghost, either a characteristic, constant sectarian temptation, or one that usually lingers in the background but leaps to the fore in times of crisis, appearing dangerously plausible, even necessary. For the Protestant tradition, that ghost is anti-

Catholicism, enshrined in foundational statements of faith such as the Thirty-Nine Articles (1563) for the Church of Ireland and the Westminster Confession of Faith (1646) for Presbyterians, and taking a range of forms ever since. The ghost of the Catholic tradition is anti-Protestantism, launched by Tridentine (1545-1563) anathemas and characterised by a comprehensive sense of superiority and the judgment that Protestant churches are not actually authentic churches at all. The ghost of the nationalist tradition is violence. When is it legitimate to pursue political ends by violent means, and when is it not? Having justified violence in one case, it is not always clear to some why it cannot be justified in others. The ghost of the unionist tradition is threatened violence, specifically what Frank Wright calls 'defiance actions', which he defines as 'actions which obliged the metropolitan power to recognise that its own sovereignty rested upon the tolerance of the citizen population'.[6] Massive Protestant resistance to home rule for Ireland, as expressed in the 1912 Solemn League of Covenant, is both a crucial step on the road to partition and a classic defiance action – threatening to resist Home Rule 'by all means which may be found necessary' – that successfully forced the British government to back down. The 1974 Ulster Workers' Council Strike, which brought down the short-lived power-sharing executive in Northern Ireland, is another successful Protestant defiance action directed against the will of the British government, and similar dynamics can be observed since 1995 in the tensions surrounding the annual Orange Order parade commencing from Drumcree church outside Portadown.

Insights drawn from an apparently unlikely conjunction of books, Walter Wink's *Engaging the Powers* and Conor Cruise O'Brien's *Ancestral Voices*, are helpful in understanding these dynamics. In a remarkable trilogy on the biblical concept of the principalities and powers, Wink reveals how institutions, groups, and movements have both

> an outer, visible structure and an inner, spiritual reality. The Powers, properly speaking, are not just the spirituality of institutions, but their outer manifestations as well. ... It is the spiritual aspect, however, that is so hard for people inured to materialism to grasp.[7]

All institutions, all sets of relationships – families, political parties, nations, businesses, parishes, clubs, etc. – have a spiritual aspect. Since people are generally unaccustomed to thinking in these terms, reflecting on an institution's characteristic mood or ethos or atmosphere can provide a good way to begin appropriating such concepts.

O'Brien's *Ancestral Voices* amounts to a case study of how a malign 'spiritual aspect' has driven physical force republicanism in Irish history. The phrase 'ancestral voices' he borrows from Samuel Taylor Coleridge's epic poem, *Kubla Khan:*

And mid that tumult Kubla heard from far
Ancestral voices prophesying war.[8]

By way of introduction, O'Brien links these war-prophesying ancestral voices to three quotes, culminating in words from Patrick Pearse, written on Christmas day, 1915, just a few months before the 1916 Easter Rising.

Here be ghosts that I have raised this Christmastide, ghosts of dead men that have bequeathed a trust to us living men. Ghosts are troublesome things, in a house or in a family, as we knew even before Ibsen taught us. There is only one way to appease a ghost. You must do the things it asks you. The ghosts of a nation sometimes ask very big things and they must be appeased, whatever the cost.[9]

These are the themes O'Brien pursues, principally from the 1790s into the 1990s: what the ancestral voices, the ghosts of Irish history, have asked of Irish republicans, and what has been the cost of appeasing them. At key points in Irish history, O'Brien reveals a harsh and bloodthirsty spirituality driving a movement that its adherents would prefer to think of as secular and political.

These ancestral voices reside at the traditional pole of our four continua, calling out for a harsh, extreme, and sometimes violent sectarianism. Even as a person moves away from this pole, the ancestral voices can at times sound dangerously plausible, attractive, and authoritative. An acquaintance raised in a working class, republican, Catholic home became, as an adult, a Protestant, a socialist, and a pacifist. He once ruefully said, however, 'Get me into a pub, get a few jars in me, get the band playing rebel ballads, and pretty soon my gut will be churning. I'll pump my fist like everyone else, and I'll be thinking, "Sure isn't it the only way we ever got anything at all ?"' Protestants raised with the sound of a Lambeg drum may recognise a parallel power of evocation. The ancestral voices sound most powerfully in times of crisis, of course, when even those who thought they had long since shut out the ancestral voices can be drawn to them again. This has been one of the dynamics of confrontations around the Drumcree parade in recent times, perhaps especially since the summer of 1996, as Protestants and Catholics around Northern Ireland have found themselves caught up emotionally in the issues at stake, and ancestral voices got a hearing that may have surprised both others and themselves.

People who want to resist the ancestral voices do so in several ways. Some flee to the opposite pole and then ignore or oppose the ancestral voices. This option can have real integrity, but it is potentially deceptive and definitely limited. Deception takes the form of the illusion that leaving behind the most extreme forms of sectarianism means leaving them all, so that sectarianism becomes exclusively someone else's problem. But there is no place to stand that is not capable of sectarian distortion. The limitation is that dealing with the ancestral voices by fleeing, however necessary this may be, is a personal solution to a problem that is both personal and corporate. The person who flees separates himself from the community that continues to be subject to those voices, and in fact he probably renders himself an object of suspicion and contempt, a Lundy. Anything he has to say can be dismissed by reason of his departure, and the ancestral voices continue calling, undiminished, even though one person has left them behind.

There are alternative ways of resisting the ancestral voices, however. The bewitching effect of the destructive ancestral voices is such that people hear them calling for nothing but hatred, maybe blood, separation at very least, and they persuade some people, as they did Pearse, that the ghosts have to be obeyed at any cost if they are to be appeased. Pearse is right at least this far: the destructive voices cannot finally, completely be extinguished, nor can they simply be ignored, on the pretense that they are extinguished or on the assumption that the mere passage of time or changes in circumstance have left them irrelevant and powerless. By one means or another, for one reason or another, deliberately or unintentionally, foreseeing the consequences or not, a group's ancestors called forth these destructive ghosts. They will always be there to be called upon, and at times they may call on a community, demanding to be appeased. They will finally disappear only with the extinction of that community.

But people do grant the destructive ancestral voices too much power. If they cannot be extinguished, they can be countered, contained, diminished, and finally left all but powerless. What is required is to re-tune one's ears to alternative voices. Some of these are likely to be, and almost certainly need to be, voices coming from outside one's own tradition. Outside voices are unlikely to be enough, however, because accepting them whole and in place of major elements of a community's tradition is a form of communal suicide, which is something communities do not do. Efforts at wholesale appropriation of outside voices are likely to provoke a backlash in at least part of the community. What is far more constructive is for a community to learn to hear its own ancestral voices anew, with or without the aid of outside voices. To a re-tuned ear, the ancestral voices are by no means limited to those calling for a deadly sectarianism. Other ancestral voices, emanating from the very same source, offer healthier alternatives, sometimes the antidote to their poisonous counterparts. And because this particular antidote takes the form of another ancestral voice, it speaks to the community with an authority that an outside voice cannot match. When destructive ancestral voices are countered from within the tradition, they are weakened and silenced as effectively as they ever can be.

Joe's Mennonite tradition, descendants of the reformation-era Anabaptists, offers a useful example of countering destructive ancestral voices with other ancestral voices. We offer this story here as an outside perspective that may help to explain examples we take later from the peace process in Northern Ireland. Although Anabaptists were always a small minority in the Reformation, some of their radical teachings made them the object of close and suspicious attention. Based on their reading of the New Testament, Anabaptists baptised adults rather than infants, refused to take oaths (then regarded as a foundation of the state), granted a much greater than usual role in church life to lay members, and denied the state any role at all in the life of the churches. Furthermore, most Anabaptists also rejected all violence, whether personal violence or participation in state violence. Taken as a whole, Anabaptism represented a comprehensive challenge to conventional ways of organising the church and to established patterns of church-state relationship. As a result, they suffered much persecution, including martyrdom.

In the 1530s, a time of tumultuous change, uncertainty, and

anxiety in parts of Europe, one centre of Reformation ferment was the German city of Münster. In February 1534 increasing controversy and power struggles resulted in Anabaptists taking over the city and expelling adults who refused to be baptised. In these millenarian times, the Münster Anabaptists conceived of their new situation as the New Jerusalem, the first manifestation of God's coming kingdom on earth, and persecuted Anabaptists from around the area began to make their way to Münster. The new Anabaptist regime in Münster, which was immediately under continuous siege and occasional attack by state authorities, eventually took three controversial stances: armed resistance patterned on an understanding of godly violence as practised in the Old Testament; community of goods, probably based on the practice of the earliest Christian church in Jerusalem; and polygamy, probably another New Jerusalem practice derived from the Old Testament. The Münster Anabaptists held out for more than a year, but in June 1535 they were overwhelmed. The Anabaptist leaders were tortured and paraded from town to town around the area as an example. Half a year later they were finally executed, but they continued to be an example, as their corpses were hung in cages from the front of a Münster church. Replica cages remain to this day.

Münster also made a useful example for Protestant and Catholic historians and theologians. For centuries, even into this century, the terms 'Münster' and 'Anabaptist' were all but inseparable, and the former was all one needed to know about the latter: Anabaptist principles would lead inevitably to sordid and fanatical practices. The influential Reformed theologian Guy de Brez (1522-67), an early and vehement critic of the Mennonites, was typical of those who followed, arguing that while Mennonites might appear to be peaceable, law-abiding lambs, governments must be vigilant, lest their wolf-like nature, revealed at Münster, should assert itself again.[10]

The Mennonite experience of Münster and its implications bore little relationship to the reflections of others on it. Polygamy in Münster had been a straightforward aberration among Anabaptists, without precedent or antecedent. Anabaptists had previous practised community of goods in varying degrees in some places, and it would be a recurrent though relatively minor theme ever after.

The practice of violence, however, potentially an ancestral

voice in the making after the Münster experience, would provide Anabaptists with their greatest test. Although an ethic of
nonviolence was normative for a large majority of Anabaptists
already before Münster, some significant voices justified violence for some reasons in some situations. Would appeals to
holy violence now become a recurring theme, an ancestral
voice? To a significant extent, the violence of the Münster
Anabaptists had been patterned on a reading of God-led holy
war in the Old Testament: the few against the many, the weak
against the strong, victorious only by God's miraculous intervention. But God had not given them victory. Would they now
develop a more pragmatic view of violence, something more in
line with the mainstream just war tradition? Could the movement survive at all? Would Anabaptists view the Münster
experience as indicating an inherent flaw in their movement,
though previously hidden from them, and melt in shame into
the mainstream?

In fact within a few years Mennonites had firmly rejected
everything that Münster stood for in terms of violence. The descendants of the one-time holy warriors became what the
theologian Miroslav Volf calls 'consistently the most pacifist
tradition in the history of the Christian church'.[11] The violence of
Münster seems to have been an ancestral voice silenced not long
after its conception. On the few occasions when Mennonites
have been tempted by millenarian movements, they have been
entirely nonviolent; when they have been tempted by violence,
whether participation in the state's violence or communal self-
defence (as in Russia in the early twentieth century), that temptation has arisen from immediate causes without even a trace of
influence from the ghosts of Münster. Why and how they rejected
violence is as important as the fact that they did. Mennonites accomplished this by an appeal to and readjustment of what was
already perhaps their strongest characteristic, a radical bibli-
cism. In response to Münster, the dominant Anabaptist biblical
hermeneutic became close to universal: what Anabaptists read
as the clearly nonviolent thrust of the New Testament message
would have hermeneutical priority over doubtful interpretations
of Old Testament violence and New Testament apocalyptic literature alike. The Bible was the foremost of the Mennonites' ancestral voices, and the Bible reaffirmed and reinterpreted was
the force that contained the ghosts of Münster. The constructive
ancestral voices silenced the destructive ones.

Through the centuries, Mennonites responded to the equating of Anabaptists with Münster in at least two main ways. One way was to deny that the Münsterites were Anabaptists at all. After all, most Anabaptists always had been nonviolent, and the subsequent movement was almost entirely nonviolent, so the Münsterites were just pseudo-Anabaptists significant only in the eyes of Mennonites' detractors. This stance has some plausibility and some merit, especially since Reformation-era Anabaptism was as much a category imposed by enemies who lumped all religious radicals together as it was a self-defined, cohesive movement. From our point of view, however, the better approach is to accept that Münster did indeed represent a strand of Anabaptism, but a strand now and long since rejected. Acknowledged ghosts are more safely contained than are ghosts denied.

If the Mennonite experience in this case represents a clear and settled historical case of ghost management, we recognise the same dynamic, although in a more fluid state, at work in the current peace process in Northern Ireland. We see it most strikingly in examples like Sinn Féin and ECONI (Evangelical Contribution on Northern Ireland), groups we mean to equate only in terms of the structure of change they are currently engaged in.

The destructive ancestral voices Sinn Féin must address are those depicted so clearly by Conor Cruise O'Brien: the ones demanding the absolutist pursuit of a united Ireland by violent means. That Sinn Féin could sign up to the Good Friday Agreement is an astonishing change in republican thinking, apparently the fruit of at least ten years of political evolution. What we might refer to as mainstream republicanism now accepts that a united Ireland can only come about by consent, not by violence, which means that a united Ireland may never come into being, and if it does, no one can say when. Although ambivalently at times, and with fits and starts in the process, many republicans are facing down the ancestral voices. Because of it, authentic and positive elements of the republican vision, long enfeebled by the association with violence, can emerge as never before and contribute much to teaching different groups how to share a political enterprise. And crucially, this is not a matter of a few individuals or a small group saying no to the destructive ancestral voices, it is the larger part of physical force republicanism.

The appeal to violence in the uncompromising pursuit of un-negotiable goals still has potentially dangerous adherents in the broader republican community, and certain actions by the state or by the unionist community could give the ancestral voices new appeal. Nonetheless, it is important to recognise that Sinn Féin, in moving from advocating physical force to constitutional poli-tics, has probably brought with it a higher percentage of republi-cans than in any parallel situation in Irish history.

The ancestral voices that challenge ECONI and conservative Protestantism as a whole are both hard and soft, immediately obvious and known principally by an absence. The hard and ob-vious is a virulent anti-Catholicism. The more elusive voice, but destructive enough in its own way, is one that calls evangelicals to stay away from the concerns of the world and say little about them, leading lives, individually and collectively, of negligible public impact. Since the late 1980s, ECONI has confronted these voices, speaking out most directly and forcefully on the immedi-ate concerns and responsibilities of evangelicals, but also ad-dressing all the things that make for peace where evangelicals might reasonably have a contribution to make. In one sense, their discontent with their own tradition represents a continual dynamic of the fundamentalist/liberal Protestant continuum: conservatives who grow dissatisfied with fundamentalism or evangelicalism. Typically, however, disgruntled conservative Protestants have become liberal Protestants and their critique of fundamentalism is then the liberal critique, easily dismissed by conservatives. ECONI's significance is that they are challenging the sectarianism of conservative Protestantism while remaining evangelicals and by employing evangelical logic. They are, in ef-fect, challenging the bigoted ancestral voices by calling forth the best of the ancestral voices. Part of that appeal is to aspects of evangelicalism's historical tradition, but far more their appeal is to evangelicalism's core document and final court, the Bible. The sectarianism of conservative Protestantism cannot be effectively addressed in any other way.

It should be noted that ECONI has fought the sectarian im-plications of Protestant anti-Catholicism without demanding from evangelicals a single stance toward the Catholic Church. What might be called ECONI's left wing accepts the Catholic Church as a Christian church which one disagrees with in vari-ous ways while also accepting that one can learn from

Catholicism. The right wing does not differ doctrinally from traditional anti-Catholicism: the Catholic Church is so radically flawed that cannot be considered Christian, and Catholics who become Christians should leave it. On a kind of middle ground, some evangelicals do not accept the Catholic Church as Christian, but readily accept individual Catholics as Christians. What unites the three stances within ECONI is a firm commitment that, however one evaluates Catholicism, this must not lead to destructive patterns of relating. At very least, positive, respectful relationships in civil society and civil rights and fair treatment for all are a necessary standard, regardless of one's stance toward the Catholic Church.

For our purposes, what Sinn Féin and ECONI share is simply this: from within their own traditions and speaking with the authentic voice of their traditions, they challenge the destructive, sectarian ancestral voices that haunt their traditions. In doing so, they have put all of us in their debt, because their effective and largely unprecedented work is one reason to be hopeful about the possibility of a lasting peace for Ireland. They have also given us an example. In our judgment, every tendency, party, or grouping within Irish religion and politics requires an equivalent renewal movement similarly designed and orientated.

CHAPTER 5

Tools, Models, and Reflections:
Getting to Grips with Sectarianism

Introduction

Working with a wide variety of groups since 1995, we developed several tools, models, and exercises for thinking about sectarianism and how to counter it. One of these models, 'The Pyramid of Sectarianism in Northern Ireland', we brought with us from previous work. The remainder we developed in response to issues raised by groups, and we then tested them with groups as the basis for further modification and refinement. The sections of this chapter are based, therefore, on some of the main exercises and models that groups and individuals have consistently found helpful in addressing sectarianism. However, in the process of being translated from orally presented material to written material, each section has been significantly expanded and, to varying degrees, modified.

'The Pyramid of Sectarianism in Northern Ireland' works first to illustrate how it is that all are implicated in sectarianism, even as degrees of responsibility vary dramatically. It also indicates the way in which religion contributes, even when it does not mean to do so, to maintaining the structure of sectarianism. 'The False Allure of Benign Apartheid' explores the seductiveness of living as separate, segregated communities in the absence of violence – as opposed to reconciled communities – and asks how far this is a desirable or possible model. 'The Level' is a tool for exposing and analysing the ways and means of sectarianism as it operates in a particular setting. 'Approaches to Dealing with Difference' addresses the problem of sectarianism's tendency to operate in accept/reject mode when encountering others. From that starting point, we propose a range of alternative ways of dealing with difference. 'Mitigation' is a strategy for dealing constructively with non-negotiable truth claims and other situations in which compromise is unlikely or impossible. Finally, 'Bifocal Vision' provides an image for the characteristic mindset necessary, we believe, to respond fruitfully to the stunted logic of sectarianism.

In *Sectarianism: A Discussion Document*, a 1993 report to the Irish Inter-Church Meeting, the Working Party on Sectarianism (WPS) described the structure of sectarian attitudes in Northern Ireland as resembling a pyramid.[1] As well as sectarian attitudes, however, the pyramid is a model of sectarian complicity. All acts of sectarianism, from the obvious to the subtle, are related, the WPS argued, and they further suggested that many who regard themselves as innocent of sectarianism are in fact implicated. Opting out of the pyramid is not really possible.

Working with groups as part of MBS, we found that the first merits of the pyramid model exactly followed the WPS intention. The pyramid gave people an image that revealed how one could be complicit in sectarianism even without intending to be and how all sectarianism is connected within a single framework. Beyond this, we extended and altered the pyramid model in order to say more about why this complicity arises and to highlight the role of segregation, especially religiously-rooted segregation, in fostering sectarianism.

'Mad dogs'
At the peak of the pyramid lies a thin layer of extreme violence. It is occupied by people sometimes called 'mad dogs', because their violence seems to have little rationale beyond creating sectarian terror, and they often act as individuals, or at least outside any main structure, paramilitary or otherwise. Typical of this layer were the killers, still unknown, who on a Sunday morning in November 1983 walked into Darkley Pentecostal Church in south Armagh and opened fire with automatic weapons, killing three worshippers and wounding seven. Another example was Michael Stone, the loyalist who in March 1988 killed three Catholics and injured more than fifty at a burial service in Milltown Cemetery, Belfast, by peppering them with gun shot and grenades.[2]

Paramilitaries
Beneath the 'mad dogs' is the paramilitary layer. Here the violence is more structured and even those who despise the paramilitary

notion of 'legitimate targets' will recognise that some adherence
to a conception of rules of war does limit paramilitary violence.
Paramilitaries will not necessarily admit to sectarianism, and
some will indignantly deny it, on the grounds that their purposes
are political, not sectarian. Judged on the basis of consequences,
however, paramilitary violence is exposed as one of the most
effective purveyors of sectarianism. No force contributes more to
hardening boundaries, dehumanising and demonising enemies,
and collaborating in the domination of others.

The commitment to and practice of violence makes the top
two levels, 'mad dogs' and paramilitaries, inherently sectarian.
Their motivations may be positive, no different, in most cases,
from the communities they come from, and they did not create
the sectarian system. But paramilitary violence, their defining
feature, demonstrably extends and deepens sectarianism. For
individuals and for organisations, transformation necessarily
means giving up violence and embracing politics.

Leaders

The next layer down is more ambiguous. Here we find society's
leaders, political, religious, and other. Virtually all will condemn
illegitimate violence, and yet a few, in the words of the WPS,
'use platform, pulpit or the pages of the press to express bigoted
and inflammatory sentiments',[3] thus inciting the violence they
condemn. Some loyalist paramilitaries have made this accusation against some Protestant preachers and politicians, saying
that they felt they had been encouraged to commit violence for a
righteous cause and then condemned or ignored when they
were jailed for doing so. A stark example of this dynamic occurred at a conference held on the Shankill Road in October
1994. In an angry exchange with one of the speakers, DUP councillor Iris Robinson, an 'obviously agitated' participant said to
Mrs Robinson: 'You and your husband [DUP deputy leader
Peter Robinson] and your party has cried for the people out
there to get out onto the streets and fight Republicanism! You
can't deny them now, you have to stand by them!'[4] A parallel
ambiguity haunts Sinn Féin as they seek to become a solely constitutional political party. The desire may be genuine, but they
will not be allowed easily to forget the day in 1981 when Danny
Morrison put chilling and cynical rhetorical questions to a Sinn
Féin Ard Fheis: 'Who here really believes we can win the war

through the ballot box? But will anyone here object if, with a ballot paper in one hand and the Armalite in the other, we take power in Ireland?'[5]

The ambiguities of violence and condemnation can take a more subtle form. Even when leaders genuinely and consistently deplore violence, violence from within their community, whether spontaneous outbreaks of violence or tactical violence by paramilitaries, forms part of the political crisis that gives strength and authority to the proposals of the nonviolent politicians. If we achieve certain political goals, the constitutional politicians effectively argue, then the violence will end; if these goals are not achieved, then, they at least imply, the violence will continue.

This ambiguous relationship between violence and constitutional politics in Northern Ireland is not an accident. It is a dynamic inherent in what the political scientist Frank Wright calls an ethnic frontier conflict, of which Northern Ireland is one example. The structure of an ethnic frontier society, Wright explains in his outstanding work *Northern Ireland: A Comparative Analysis*,[6] dictates that moderate, constitutional politicians will be responding to a situation substantially shaped by the violence of those sharing their general political goals. Some of the strength of constitutional politicians' proposals comes, therefore, from demonstrating that their policies provide the best way of eliminating paramilitary violence and other sectarian violence. The most significant people 'in a vortex of antagonism', says Wright, 'are those who can both threaten violence and control the threat simultaneously.'[7] This applies directly to paramilitaries, of course, but indirectly to constitutional politicians as well. They can despise violence and seek to end it, but at least in the short-term their power, within their community and outside it, depends in part on their ability to control violence by offering an alternative, and their proposed alternative carries the implicit warning that if it is not enacted, then the violence will continue, which may well be the case. This ambiguous relationship between power, violence, and the control of violence can be desired, nurtured, manipulated, and exploited – hence the ballot box and the armalite – or it can be deplored and worked against. In either case, however, the initial ambiguity is not consciously created by any individual or group. It arises almost inevitably as part of the inherent, structural logic of an ethnic frontier conflict.

Understanding the ambiguous relationship between violence and constitutional politics in an ethnic frontier society helps to explain how unionist accusations of a 'pan-nationalist front' arise. Viewed from within the nationalist community, the idea of a pan-nationalist front is nonsense. Every nationalist knows, for example, the intense, passionate rivalry, sometimes passing into mutual contempt and even hatred, between the SDLP and Sinn Féin. Viewing nationalism from outside, however, some will inevitably observe the shared political goal and therefore see the SDLP and Sinn Féin not as rivals, but as complementary parties pursuing different strategies addressed to the same end, i.e. as a pan-nationalist front. Such a perception will not finally disappear until political violence, and the threat of it, are ended and constitutional politics prevails, freed now to operate in a changed political context that has shed the ambiguities of an ethnic frontier society.

Citizens

At the base of the pyramid is a broad band of citizens, those whom the WPS called 'ordinary, decent people'. Their report had particularly in mind people who 'do not want to appear bigoted, but they are ambivalent about the use of force; they encourage by vote, religious view and private opinion the layer above them.'[8] Complicity takes other forms as well, sometimes quite independent of personal attitudes. Some people are rendered complicit, with varying degrees of directness, by participation in organisations that have taken sectarian stances or acted in sectarian ways. There is also a complicity of doing nothing, thereby allowing the sectarian system to carry on unhindered. Others find themselves implicated because their employment is in some way dependent on dealing with or responding to sectarian violence or other sectarian actions. A significant proportion of work for builders and lawyers, for example, has resulted from sectarian violence. Even those whose work is directed against sectarianism find themselves ironically dependent on sectarianism. This is one of the ways we find ourselves implicated as the Moving Beyond Sectarianism project, because much of the community relations sector, what sometimes gets called the reconciliation industry, exists because of sectarianism. The end of violence will not mean the end of sectarianism, but it is likely to mean diminishing funding for programmes dealing in some way with sectarianism. For some, the process of moving beyond sectarianism will mean the end of employment. In a society long shaped by sectarianism, claims to stand outside, innocent, pure, and detached, are always likely to be found wanting. The sectarian system extends its distorting influence everywhere.

Implications

The WPS drew out two main defining features of the pyramid:

(1) *'[P]eople at each level, when it comes to the crunch, disclaim responsibility for the words and actions of the layer above.'*[9] The dynamics of condemnation are so obvious as to hardly need commenting on. Paramilitaries condemn the undisciplined violence of the 'mad dogs'; political and social leaders condemn paramilitary violence; ordinary citizens condemn inflammatory statements or actions by leaders.

Obvious or not, behind all this condemnation lies a hard question: if each level in the pyramid of sectarianism condemns the levels above, why doesn't the whole structure of sectarianism simply collapse for lack of support? The WPS moved part of the way to an answer with a second observation.

(2) *Each level grows out of the one below and could not exist without support or permission from below.* Starting from the top, the 'mad dog' is likely to have learned his trade in one of the main paramilitary groups and may belong to a splinter group. And while they may be generally denounced, they can also have their supporters. Michael Stone, for example, became something of a folk hero for some loyalists. Furthermore, the division between levels is often blurred. While failure to adhere to disciplined limits of violence may distinguish the most extreme actions at the top level from the typical action at the paramilitary level, the distinction is far from absolute. At points, the loyalist paramilitary conception of legitimate targets has seemed to be 'any available Catholic', and the IRA's notion of legitimate targets has included the likes of milkmen delivering to RUC stations and construction workers on security force sites. Even if one accepted the idea of legitimate targets, many paramilitary killings would fall well outside any likely definition. If an apparent rationale of creating sectarian terror is the mark of the 'mad dog' level, then some paramilitary violence belongs to the same category. The sometimes arbitrary nature of the 'mad dog'/paramilitary distinction is further indicated by those occasions when the killer

denounced by paramilitaries is later integrated quietly into paramilitary command structures in prison.

Paramilitary support and permission from below comes in several forms. We have already mentioned how certain kinds of statements from community leaders can contribute to an atmosphere in which violence is seen as acceptable. But the more important support and permission comes from the citizen level. The revolutionary fish, said Chairman Mao, does not require direct support, only water to swim in, i.e. an acquiescent general population. The same logic applies to paramilitaries. In fact they do get some direct support, in a general way from those who see paramilitary violence as justified, and particularly from people who provide safe houses, store weapons, and otherwise assist the paramilitaries. Almost as important, however, are those people who may not give any direct support, moral or practical, but who turn a blind eye, say nothing, and gradually cede control of their communities to paramilitaries. This is not support for paramilitaries, and it may be coerced rather than willingly given, but it is a form of permission, and arguably the paramilitaries could not exist without it. While active paramilitaries may number only a few hundred, the systems that allow them to function spread much further.

Political leaders grow out of the layer below in the most direct way possible: they are elected by citizens. People may not always like the choice they are given, but these candidates have been chosen by their parties as the people most likely to be elected. Other leaders, religious leaders, for example, may not always be chosen as directly as are politicians, but their power and influence is largely dependent on their ability to elicit a response from the public. In a study of nineteenth-century elections in Ireland, political scientist John Whyte concluded that the Catholic clergy, sometimes believed to have all but absolute control of the laity, 'on the whole … could lead their people only in the direction they wanted to go'.[10] Some version of the same dynamic always applies to leaders and their followers. Citizens simply cannot wash their hands of their leaders.

When the pyramid is examined from this perspective, the dynamics running between levels are shown to be as important as the boundaries separating them. And if one layer is tied to the next, it follows that the top layer of sectarian terror grows out of the bottom layer of ordinary citizenry, even if indirectly. Most people 'would be horrified to be told they are connected with the extreme violence at the top of the pyramid,' wrote the WPS. 'Yet it is not hard to see how each individual stone supports the total structure.'[11] After all, those who choose violence have not immigrated from some alien society; they have grown up in Northern Ireland's churches, attended Northern Ireland's schools, and generally been formed by Northern Ireland's institutions and social ethos. None of this diminishes their individual responsibility for their actions, because other people have been shaped by the same environment and made radically different choices. But it does mean that the rest of the society would be most unwise to pretend that they have no shared responsibility for the ugliest expressions of the sectarianism that runs through the whole.

Part of the reason, therefore, that the pyramid does not collapse from lack of support is communal ambivalence about the layers above. People disown the layers above them at times, yet they also provide support and permission.

Roots of ambivalence

But why this ambivalence? Why this contradictory behaviour? To answer that question requires altering the WPS model of a pyramid, with its implication that the structure stands because one stone rests on another. A more suitable model for these purposes might be a tent held up by a centre pole, that centre pole representing the division between Catholic nationalist and Protestant unionist communities in Northern Ireland. That division is not absolute, of course – there are unionist Catholics and nationalist Protestants, along with some people who simply do not fit the categories. Nor is it the only division. Some other divisions tend to run along the same axis, but others – gender, class, and some interest groups, for example – cut across the Protestant-Catholic divide. When such useful and necessary qualifications have been made, however, the division between Catholic nationalists and Protestant unionists remains the one that dominates political and social life in Northern Ireland.

Without this centre pole of Catholic-Protestant division, cross-community abhorrence of some sectarian actions just might collapse the sectarian tent. As it is, the division helps to explain one of the key forces that keeps the tent standing. For example, much as many people may dislike some of their politicians at times, a sense of threat sometimes comes from the opposite side of the divide, and therefore people cannot disown their politicians, who may function at times as a defence against that threat. With still greater degrees of ambivalence, the same argument applies to the paramilitaries who claim to act in defence of their community. Most people did not ask for it, they may hate what paramilitaries do, their own community is often victimised by 'their' paramilitaries, and yet people cannot, as a whole community, ignore the fear that these detested paramilitaries are functioning, or might in some dreaded crisis function, as a deterrent against a greater threat from the other side of the divide. This fear of a threat emanating from the other side is one key to explaining the ambivalent attitudes that help to maintain sectarianism.

The place of the RUC
The centre pole also helps to fill an absence that some readers may have wondered about: where does the RUC fit in this model? Perhaps more than any other institution in Northern Ireland society, the place of the RUC depends on the standpoint of the person doing the placing, especially whether she is nationalist or unionist. The different ways of placing the RUC were well summed up in sessions Joe led for RUC recruits from June 1995 through September 1996. During that period, Joe spent one hour-and-a-half session working with all new RUC recruits, as part of their community relations training, on understanding sectarianism and how it would influence their work. A standard exercise with those groups was to introduce this pyramid/tent model and to ask them two questions: Where does the RUC fit in this scheme? And where would you like it to fit ideally? A composite of the reflections and discussions in those sessions says much about the place of the RUC.

The ideal was the easier issue to address. Someone was sure to suggest that the RUC should be, and perhaps is, above it all, effectively outside the model. Sectarianism is a problem the RUC must address and the context in which they must operate, but not their problem. To join the RUC is to leave communal identity behind and replace it with a new identity as an RUC officer, equidistant from nationalist and unionist communities and standing impartially between them. Sometimes the recruits expressed it through a formulation said to run back to John Hermon, chief constable of the RUC from 1980 to 1989: there are three kinds of people in Northern Ireland – Protestants, Catholics, and RUC officers. While this point of view has obvious attractions for the RUC, not least for bonding new recruits, some recruit was sure to point out that part of the integrity of the pyramid/tent model is its representation of the impossibility of being entirely separate from sectarianism. On reflection, groups were likely to conclude that they would inevitably bring with them into the RUC the assumptions of their communities. Their effectiveness as RUC officers would not depend on denying this or on pretending that joining the RUC had made them rootless, it would depend on understanding how they had been shaped and finding appropriate ways of relating to their own community and others. Such thinking suggested various images of an ideal fit into the pyramid/tent model, but a common one was a layer running across the pyramid/tent between the paramilitaries above and the politicians and citizens below, effectively between the illegal and the legal. This image recognised that officers would remain part of their communities, while holding out the ideal of serving both nationalist and unionist communities.

Such an ideal, recruits realised, was distant from the perceptions of many in Northern Ireland. For some people, predominantly middle-class Protestants, the RUC at least approximates the ideal: an impartial body serving the whole community in almost impossible circumstances. But sober reflection on a growing list of other perspectives led recruits to conclude that this is almost certainly a minority viewpoint. Few Catholics would share it. To most Catholics, the recruits thought, the RUC is a sectarian force. Catholics might differ as to whether this sectarianism is constant or occasional, whether it is policy or convention, but few would see the RUC as in any way impartial. For many Catholics, in fact, the RUC amounts to a Protestant paramilitary force, even to the extent, some recruits noted, of harbouring, nurturing, or encouraging 'mad dogs'. Recruits were also aware that since the 1985 Anglo-Irish Agreement traditional Protestant support, especially among working class loyalists, had eroded badly. Two of the key indicators cited were the number of police families intimidated out of their homes in some Protestant areas, and politically tense situations in which the RUC met taunts along the lines of 'you're Sinn Féin's police'. At least one recruit noted that even support could sometimes be a problem if beneath it lay an assumption that 'you're our police'. Taken together, these recruits' observations give a fair impression of the radically different ways different sectors of society would place the RUC in the pyramid/tent model.

The role of religion

The modified image of a tent with a centre pole dividing Northern Ireland into Protestant unionists and Catholic nationalists also helps to explain how religion contributes to nurturing and maintaining sectarianism. Already in the WPS's pyramid model, with its stacked layers of ever more concentrated and ferocious hatred, some expressions of religion are understood to be a source of hatred. The image of a tent and centre pole, however, expresses religion's primary contribution to sectarianism today: not to direct and active hatred, although that cannot be neglected, but to separation. While the separation indicated by that dividing centre pole is propagated and maintained by a variety of forces, none is more important than religion. Marriage and family, church and worship, education, and residence, four crucial spheres of socialisation, are all strongly segregated on the basis of religion. In the first three cases, separation results from deliberate policy. The fourth case, religiously segregated neighbourhoods, results from thirty years of violence, not from church policy, but the separation is no less significant because of it. Taken together and in conjunction with the still substantial religious commitment of people in Northern Ireland, these four areas give the churches an unrivalled impact on the socialisation process. Much of this socialisation is positive, and the result is strong communities and healthy individuals. In a divided and sectarian society, however, it is inevitably socialisation into division as well, and with division come conflict and sectarianism. While the separation is deliberate policy, the sectarian outcome is not. It is not possible, however, to ignore the unintended consequences of well-meant actions. In Northern Ireland that means taking responsibility for the ways in which separation sustains sectarianism.

The 1994 Ministry Conference, an annual inter-church event jointly sponsored by the Irish School of Ecumenics and the Corrymeela Community, was one of the first times Joe presented this pyramid/tent model to a group. Responding to it, Brian Lennon, a Jesuit priest then working in Portadown, said that this model made him consider a sad paradox: the more successful I am in my ministry, the more I contribute to the problem. As I build up more and more activities in my parish, he explained, this is counted as success, and in community-building terms, it is success. But as long as this labour is exclusively directed to my people and done with my people and for my people, I am strengthening not only community but separation and therefore sectarianism. What we need, he added, is to redefine what we mean by success. Strong communities are more likely to be reconciled than weak ones, so community-building will continue to be necessary. But the balance will need to shift. In some circumstances, perhaps developing one initiative across the sectarian divide should count as success as much as ten intra-parish initiatives. Both Brian's diagnosis and his prescription have become part of our own thinking about the churches and the problem of sectarianism.

THE FALSE ALLURE OF BENIGN APARTHEID

The second 'tool' is no more than a simple concept intended to help people in Northern Ireland stay alert to how they are answering a crucial question: what kind of peace are they seeking? The question is important because what is finally achieved, by what means it is sought, and what people are willing to settle for in the interim, will all be shaped by the vision of peace they are pursuing. Our purpose here is to warn against understandings of peace that fall short of reconciliation, settling instead for what we call benign apartheid: simple coexistence of communities, as separate as ever, but living without violence. While we have only seen one reference (which we will discuss later) to the term 'benign apartheid', it expresses the logic behind some approaches to conflict and peace. In our own work and in conversation with others doing similarly work, we consistently see evidence that some people, impossible to quantify but too many to ignore and representing diverse communities, do not remember, imagine, or even desire more for Northern Ireland than separate development in the absence of violence.

Benign apartheid might look attractive for a variety of reasons. An obvious and understandable reason is the simple desire for safety. Northern Ireland has always been substantially segregated, and even where communities and individuals have lived side by side, mixing has usually been subject to unspoken but definite limits. During the course of the Troubles, however,

residential segregation increased sharply, much of it for reasons
of safety: living in mixed areas was dangerous, safety meant living among one's own people. Given this experience, benign
apartheid, separate development in the absence of violence, has
obvious attractions. A second reason to desire benign apartheid
might be disdain, distaste, or just a lack of interest in the other
community. Such people long for the violence to end, but they
never cared much for the other community, and nothing about
the Troubles has made them think differently. Benign apartheid
expresses the full extent of their vision for peace. A third rationale involves not so much a desire for benign apartheid as a willingness to settle for it. Derived from conflict-weariness in many
cases and likely to be presented as hard-headed, unblinking political realism, this is the conviction that no more than peaceful
coexistence is possible in Northern Ireland and therefore the
pursuit of something more is a waste of time and possibly
counter-productive.

A fourth reason to desire benign apartheid requires particular
notice, because it is common among church people. We recall,
for example, speaking with a Methodist minister who regretfully
observed that many of the most faithful, active members in his
congregation could not be bothered with any kind of cross-community activity. This was no mark of bigotry, he said, they simply found themselves fully and happily occupied with life in
their own church community, and their vision extended no further. One of the people Joe interviewed was a gentle, devout,
older Catholic man, troubled and bewildered by the violence of
the last three decades, who had lived most of his life in a sharply
divided border town. When asked what he hoped for, he wanted
an end to violence, but he did not look forward to any new social
arrangements. Instead he looked back to a time when Protestant
and Catholic communities largely left each other alone, people
were generally polite when paths unavoidably crossed, and he
and the rest of his community could get on with the satisfying
business of being Catholics. Could such a state be restored, he
would be content. A similar logic of separate but peaceful co-
existence seems to be shared by some people within many, perhaps all, denominations and groupings.

We can readily sympathise with some of these reasons, and
all are understandable. Benign apartheid would be vastly
preferable to what the Troubles have brought, and thirty years

of violence, much of it inter-communal, is more likely to breed a desire to be separate than to be together. Besides, in formulating a vision for what peace means, people in Northern Ireland have little historical experience of anything better than benign apartheid. Commenting on those who recall a golden age of nonsectarian community relations, the historian K. Theodore Hoppen dismisses the evidence typically adduced as 'molehill peaks of togetherness [that] stand out merely because of the flatness of the surrounding countryside'.[12] Nor are all the reasons to desire benign apartheid solely negative, a matter of limitations and absences. Communities in Northern Ireland are strong and stable, and if some people find them oppressive, many others will experience them as warm and secure. A life that hardly extends beyond community boundaries can be richly fulfilling.

While a desire for benign apartheid may be understandable, it needs to be tested against the merits of reconciliation. In our judgment, considerations of both pragmatism and principle weigh against benign apartheid and for reconciliation.

Pragmatic political judgment needs to proceed from the answers to two basic questions. Is benign apartheid a sustainable arrangement? Is reconciliation a realistic political goal? In 1994 Kevin Boyle and Tom Hadden, influential political scientists who frequently collaborate as a writing team on Northern Ireland issues, published *Northern Ireland: The Choice*. The stark choice in question, which they put before the Northern Ireland public and policy makers, was 'between policies based on the acceptance of separation and policies based on the objective of sharing',[13] 'separation' and 'sharing' corresponding broadly with our understandings of benign apartheid and reconciliation. The bulk of their book is given over to a careful, balanced consideration of the different analyses supporting separation and sharing and the policies necessary to implement these opposed outcomes. While their treatment of separation and sharing mostly takes the form of an even-handed, fair-minded presentation of pros and cons, they do seem to prefer sharing, and at least once they say so directly.

> If it proves impossible to secure sufficient agreement on workable structures for sharing, the best alternative may be separation. This can scarcely be regarded as a particularly satisfactory outcome. But it may be preferable to indefinite communal conflict.[14]

Hadden and Boyle do not say clearly whether they prefer shar-
ing-based structures for reasons of principle, pragmatism, or
both. Their preference is almost certainly shaped, however, by a
factor they stress at key points in the book: the patchwork communal geography of Northern Ireland.[15] While there are greater
and lesser concentrations of Protestants and Catholics in different areas, there are minority pockets everywhere and no clean
dividing lines. This simple geographical reality renders every
plan based on separation much more difficult. Whatever their
reasoning, not only do Hadden and Boyle prefer sharing, even
the separation options they advance are for agreed, negotiated
separation, the political equivalent of a civil, amicable divorce.[16]
They finally conclude, however, that '[a]lmost any of the alternatives outlined above for communal sharing or separation in
Northern Ireland would in principle be workable.'[17] If this is
something less than a rallying cry to the cause of reconciliation,
they have certainly demolished any idea that political forms of
reconciliation fall short of the demands of political realism. In
their analysis, a political settlement based on sharing is both desirable and realistic.

Frank Wright's work stresses the necessity of reconciliation
more sharply. On the one hand, his long study of ethnic and
national conflicts left him pessimistic about the possibility of
reconciliation. Reflecting in 1986 on 'reconciling possibilities in
the North of Ireland', he wrote in a crucial passage,

national conflicts do not, by and large, end up with reconciliation of antagonists. More commonly they are concluded
only by victories or mutual separation. For reasons I cannot
go into at length here, I am convinced that neither of these
outcomes will generate a "peace". Victories would not be
final and the intensified separation would not dispel the
antagonism.[18]

Here Wright begins with pessimism about reconciliation and
moves on to still greater pessimism about the possibility of
anything worthy to be called 'peace' coming out of victory or
separation. The reasons he does not go into in this passage are
presumably those he discusses at great length and in depth in
his 1987 masterwork, *Northern Ireland: A Comparative Analysis*.
Analysing Northern Ireland as one of five examples of an ethnic
frontier society conflict, Wright concluded that the 'force field'
generated by the absence of 'sacred order', i.e. what all parties

accept as an agreed legitimate authority, 'breaks up nearly all the mechanisms that might cancel it'.[19] One of those possible mechanisms for cancelling a force field, however rough and crude, could be the victory of one party over the other. In an ethnic frontier society conflict, however, what might appear to be victory would only nurture the loser's righteous cause, thereby creating the conditions for a future round in 'a circular pattern of violence and response',[20] thus 'victories would not be final.' Mutual separation, a mechanism almost as crude as victory, would equally fail to bring peace. Separation would not address any of the issues underlying the conflict, and given that patchwork communal geography highlighted by Boyle and Hadden, even 'intensified separation' could never be comprehensive enough to prevent the resurgence of antagonism.

Such reasoning leaves Wright presenting a choice, but a different one than Hadden and Boyle's choice between sharing and separation. For Wright, the choice is between reconciliation, however difficult and unlikely, and more of the same, an inherently unstable situation endlessly capable of generating more violence. Wright chose reconciliation. In formal political terms, this made him an advocate, albeit a cautious one, of the 1985 Anglo-Irish Agreement, which he judged to be 'the context in which the least illegitimate secular authority can take root'.[21] But in Wright's view, reconciliation was not in the gift of political agreements or even of 'the least illegitimate secular authority' that he hoped would develop, although these things are part of reconciliation and necessary for reconciliation. Their main reconciling function, however, would be to create a situation in which 'the reconciling forces in this society will flourish.'[22] Here he undoubtedly had in mind people pursuing an agenda similar or complementary to that of his beloved Corrymeela Community, from which he had learned so much. He explicitly dedicated *Northern Ireland: A Comparative Analysis* to Corrymeela[23] and in effect to all those living out of a similar logic. Near the end, he wrote,

> I couldn't have written these lines from any other experience than that of meeting many who in their lives refused the siren call of effectiveness, did not embrace reasons for violence with which they were amply provoked, and who practise their faith by living risks in order that that part of humanity they come into communication with shall be one. ... Politics can teach little that this light does not already teach.[24]

Wright's commitment to reconciliation is all the more significant because it arises not out of a naïve optimism, but out of a well-grounded pessimism pursued to its depths. He found there that if people in Northern Ireland, and places like it, wish to break out of a situation endlessly capable of generating violence, they must choose reconciliation.

For many people, the contrasting visions of benign apartheid and reconciliation will raise issues of principle as well as issues of pragmatic political judgment. For the purposes of this book, we need specifically to address issues of religious principle for Christians.

While no responsible reading of the New Testament could deny that reconciliation is a key biblical concept, it is possible to interpret reconciliation in a way that renders it politically irrelevant and impotent. Such a reading requires just two simple movements. First, reconciliation is interpreted as having to do with the relationship of God and humanity and with relationships between people within the Christian church, but not with relationships in society generally. Second, churches other than one's own, or at least some other churches, are regarded as less than Christian. From this perspective, held most noticeably today by some conservative Protestants in relationship to the Catholic Church, reconciliation can be viewed as a theme important for spiritual life and within the church, but with little or no relevance for the Christian approach and contribution to public life.

We strongly disagree, believing instead that a biblical concept of reconciliation necessarily involves social, public applications.[25] It is possible, however, to hold the two basic positions about reconciliation and other churches described above and still pursue a religiously-rooted vision of a reconciled society. The key to this vision is not a direct pursuit of explicit reconciliation, it is in following a strand of biblical teaching on how to relate to neighbours, even when those neighbours are pagans, and perhaps oppressors or enemies. An important text in this regard is the prophet Jeremiah's letter to those people of Jerusalem who have been taken into exile in Babylon by King Nebuchadnezzar.

> Thus says the Lord of hosts, the God of Israel, to all the exiles whom I have sent into exile from Jerusalem to Babylon: build houses and live in them; plant gardens and eat what they

produce. Take wives and have sons and daughters; take wives for your sons, and give your daughters in marriage, that they may bear sons and daughters; multiply there, and do not decrease. But seek the welfare of the city where I have sent you into exile, and pray to the Lord on its behalf, for in its welfare you will find your welfare. (Jer 29:4-7)

Such a prophecy is full of import for people living in political circumstances they despise and among people of radically different, even detested, religious convictions. Not only are they called to settle down and live an ordinary, peaceable life within their own community, they are to look outward and actively 'seek the welfare of the city' that holds them captive, and to 'pray to the Lord on its behalf'. The logic behind this is not a test of obedience to God's arbitrary decree, it is an essentially reconciling logic, although the term is not used. The idea that 'in its welfare you will find your welfare' says that these two groups, radically different as they are, somehow belong together, that their well-being is mutual. This is not reconciliation premised on the discovery or creation of unity, nor on the dissolution of boundaries between groups, nor on any hint of the compromise or watering down of convictions feared by some of reconciliation's critics, both conservative and radical. It is a minimalist reconciliation, but reconciliation nonetheless, based on recognising that a people's welfare is bound up with the welfare of others and depends on seeking what is good for all those they live among, even when they may remain estranged, or at least separate.

A similar strand continues into the life and teachings of Jesus and the life of the early Christian church. A passage from Paul's letter to the Christians in Rome, a plausible Babylon equivalent, is instructive in this regard. 'If it is possible,' he writes, 'so far as it depends on you, live peaceably with all.' (Rom 12:18) On its own, this verse might sound banal, but it comes squarely in the middle of a passage clearly telling the Roman Christians how to live in a hostile environment: 'bless those who persecute you'; 'do not repay anyone evil for evil'; 'never avenge yourselves', but leave any vengeance to God; serve your enemies; 'overcome evil with good.' (Rom 12:14, 17, 19-21) Paul's teaching here points to the source of such ideas, as he mostly quotes or paraphrases the teachings of Jesus. The most directly pertinent of those teachings concern the love of neighbours and enemies. A Jewish lawyer asks Jesus, 'What must I do to inherit eternal life?'

Love God and love your neighbour, Jesus tells him, but the lawyer wants to know, 'And who is my neighbour?' Jesus responds with the well-known parable of the good Samaritan. A Jew is attacked, robbed, and badly beaten while travelling. Two fellow Jews pass by without helping him. The third person to arrive is a Samaritan, a group held in contempt by the Jews, but he rescues and generously cares for the Jew who has been beaten. The circle of your neighbours extends even to those from whom you are most alienated, Jesus suggests; to be a good neighbour, 'Go and do likewise.' (Lk 10:25-37) Here the enemy is presented as neighbour. Elsewhere Jesus directly commands, 'Love your enemies,' the context making it clear that this includes practical service even to those who have treated you badly. (Mt 5:38-48, Lk 6:27-36)

For any Christian, but especially for conservative Protestants likely to turn to the Bible as authority and to be suspicious of ideas that seem to minimise or dissolve difference, the reconciling implications of such teaching are enormous. To call someone a neighbour is essentially reconciling logic, because a neighbour is someone whose well-being, present and future, is tied to ours. When the circle of neighbours embraces not just those who are different, but enemies as well, a person's welfare is effectively tied to everyone he lives among. Difference remains, but how they deal with difference and how they live with those from whom they are separate are now subject to the standards of unsentimental, practical love. Followed through with any consistency at all, such teaching will have reconciling impact on personal, social, and political relationships.

The relevance of the reconciliation theme for public life is a simpler, more direct matter for those who believe, as we do, that the various churches are part of the one Christian church. The teaching outlined above about neighbours and enemies applies here as well, but another set of teachings, about unity and reconciliation, also comes into play. A key passage is Paul's reflection in Ephesians on the meaning and effect of Jesus' death and resurrection. To Jewish and Gentile Christians he wrote,

But now in Christ Jesus you who once were far off have been brought near by the blood of Christ. For he is our peace; in his flesh he has made both groups into one and has broken down the dividing wall, that is, hostility between us. He has abolished the law with its commandments and ordinances,

> that he might create in himself one new humanity in place of
> the two, thus making peace, and might reconcile both groups
> to God in one body through the cross, thus putting to death
> that hostility through it. (Eph 2:13-16)

The logic is inescapable. If an enmity as deep as that between
Jews and Gentiles is to be replaced by one new humanity in the
church, the effect of the cross will be the same for all hostility
based on national, ethnic, or religious difference. From this
point of view, the call for former enemies to be reconciled in
Christ and in the church is fundamentally incompatible with
any form of apartheid, benign or otherwise. This is one of those
cases where a simple religious affirmation has direct consequences for the organisation of public life: those who are called
to be reconciled in the church can hardly accept apartheid in the
public sphere. In any case, in Paul's vision of the implications of
Jesus' life and death, that in Jesus 'all the fullness of God was
pleased to dwell, and through him God was pleased to reconcile
to himself all things, whether on earth or in heaven, by making
peace through the blood of his cross,' (Col 1:19-20) the scope of
reconciliation is limitless. Any Christian community formed by
such a vision could never accept benign apartheid as anything
more than a temporary arrangement – limited and regrettable,
but preferable to active antagonism – on the way to a more authentic, reconciled peace.

If the biblical logic of reconciliation is inescapable, practical
expressions of it are easily and widely avoided. Benign
apartheid is frequently accepted by those who know they are
called to live as neighbours, by those who know they are called
to be reconciled in the church, and in general by those who, out
of varied reasoning and motivations, know that their circumstances require reconciliation. Frequently, we suspect, acceptance of benign apartheid is a matter of even the best and most
committed being worn down by the hard work and often meagre
results of pursuing reconciliation. Such a feeling comes through
the words of an experienced nationalist community worker interviewed by Fionnuala O Connor in her outstanding book, *In
Search of a State: Catholics in Northern Ireland*, published in 1993.
We thought we had coined the term benign apartheid, but at
least this community worker was there first. The worker described the feelings of local Catholics and Protestants.

> [O]n both sides they just want to be left alone. I'm working

towards acceptance of two traditions of equal validity, living apart if necessary. No patsy notions of reconciliation. I'll settle for that for the time being, because I think people reconcile from strength. If you're feeling vulnerable about your own identity and culture and status, you're not going to hold hands. So you have to build people up first. Even though that's a very narrow goal, I'm actually working towards benign apartheid.[26]

Tensions, and perhaps contradictions, run through this passage. People 'want to be left alone', thus the community worker is 'working towards benign apartheid'; and yet, other phrases suggest that this is only 'if necessary', 'for the time being', a tactical manoeuvre. The worker rejects 'patsy notions of reconciliation' and yet sees a short-term settling for benign apartheid as part of a larger, if circuitous, strategy for nurturing authentic reconciliation.

The problem is that in a society in which many forces push in the direction of separation, even a well-intended acceptance of benign apartheid as a temporary strategy may succeed only in making separation deeper and more comprehensive. What begins as a strategic manoeuvre can result in hardened boundaries and diminished vision. A lowering of standards seems to be what O'Connor sees in the community worker's comments. '[Benign apartheid] was not a phrase I had heard from any Catholic previously: when last I'd heard a Northern nationalist reference to apartheid, it was as one of the swear words used to draw damaging parallels between the social vision of unionists and the whites of South Africa.'[27]

From our point of view, then, the allure of benign apartheid is false and deceiving. It is called into question by the tests of both pragmatism and principle. Some political form of reconciliation, accompanied and undergirded by a broader religious, cultural, and social reconciliation, offers the best hope, perhaps the only hope, of sustainable peace. In fact it is the only alternative to more of the same or something worse. In Northern Ireland apartheid cannot ultimately be benign, reconciliation is realpolitik, and political pragmatism and Christian principle press in the same direction.

THE LEVEL

The level is a tool for exposing and mapping the ways of the sectarian system. Simple as it is, few concepts we introduce to groups in Northern Ireland get heads nodding in recognition so immediately, and few prove so useful to groups for grappling with the patterns and structures of sectarianism in local settings.

Joe did one set of interviews around a town in the Glens of Antrim. One of the men he interviewed there referred constantly to 'the level' in the town.* As he spoke, his meaning became clear: the level refers to a certain community equilibrium that sets limits people rarely talk about and that are not consciously taught, but that everyone knows and most people usually accept and observe. The level sets the point one does not go beyond in sectarian terms. The level might in any given situation tell people things like: where they *may* shop and where they *ought* to shop; what they can talk about with their own and what they may talk about with others; what happens to mixed marriage couples; what it means to join a different church; which sports are mixed, which are separate; where they should live; to whom they may sell land. The level may speak to many other areas as well, and the level will include some understanding of what are the costs or penalties incurred by violating it.

Characteristics of the level
The level is an intensely local phenomenon. Every community is likely to have an identifiable level, of course, and some features are characteristic almost everywhere. To name some of the most obvious: few Catholics join the RUC, fewer Protestants join the GAA, and shared worship remains infrequent and attended by few. Despite some common features, however, no single version of the level applies to all communities in Northern Ireland. One man, for example, a Catholic undertaker, told Joe how in his town undertakers were selected on a strictly denominational basis. In his long career, the exceptions were few and memorable.**

* We must set aside our usual policy of anonymity for interviewees and group work participants to thank Mr William Cunning for introducing us to the concept of the level. Of course we do not hold him responsible for the ways in which we have interpreted and developed it.
** A community leader informs us that in recent years the level has shifted, so that both undertakers get some business from both communities. Both undertakers however, still get by far the largest part of their work from their own community.

Fifteen miles away in another town, however, he was regularly hired for Protestant funerals as well as Catholic. Different towns, different levels.

As this story suggests, another mark of the localism of the level is arbitrary standards. Sometimes the standards imposed by the level do have a clear, rational explanation, especially where those standards are widespread. Catholic reluctance to join the RUC is an obvious example. Catholic RUC members are few because many Catholics have political objections, others fear harassment and discrimination within the RUC, and some who might be interested are intimidated by community and paramilitary pressure. And sometimes variations in the way the level works between one place and another can also be rationally explained. We observe, for example, that in some locations Catholic and Protestant children hardly play together at all, where in other settings cross-community friendship is common up to a certain age. Much of the difference can be explained in terms of recreational facilities, residential patterns, and the location of schools. But other variations in the level defy explanation. In the story above about undertakers, if there was any coherent reason why the one town should choose undertakers on a denominational basis and the other town should have no such practice, this man did not know it. Many of the local variations in the level seem to have no rationale beyond arbitrary custom, nor do they need any further rationale in order to serve the purpose of maintaining an equilibrium of separation. And arbitrary standards imposed by the level can be evident not only between locations, but within one place. The same undertaker who told of the arbitrary differences in funeral customs between two towns, identified a similar arbitrariness within his own town. Here undertakers double as florists for weddings, and despite the rigorous sectarian separation around undertaking, in the flower trade market capitalism prevails, sectarian standards disappear, and value for money is the only criterion of selection.

The local nature of the level is further indicated by the way it resists outsiders. We heard several stories, often told as comic, in which passing outsiders attempted to intervene in petty, local, sectarian disputes, thinking they were taking the side of the party from their own community, only to have both locals turn on them. Outsiders coming to settle can pose a more difficult problem. While long-established local people, either Protestant or Catholic, might most obviously be threatened by significant numbers of new people from the other community coming into a town, we found that longstanding residents belonging to the same community as the newcomers could be equally apprehensive. Newcomers arrive ignorant of the subtleties of the local level, of course, and they bring with them understandings and ways of living that are the product of another level from another location. They are likely, therefore, to violate the local level, disturbing the comparative tranquillity and equilibrium produced by its observance. While within any location the level serves most clearly to establish a line of limitation and separation, the same line sometimes functions, relative to the outside, as a bond of shared experiences and understandings, even if they are largely negative.

While the level most obviously operates by setting limits *beyond* which people may not go, it can also set limits *beneath* which they should not fall. In this Antrim community, for example, during the course of the Troubles, the most blatant violation of the level was by the somewhat eccentric son of a leading local Protestant gentry family who became a nationalist councillor. The price he paid was assassination by loyalists. Although there were convictions, local nationalists were never entirely satisfied that all involved were convicted, and suspicions of security force collusion lingered. But even in such traumatic circumstances, the level came into play, in a manner, in restoring the situation, as local nationalists resisted outside nationalists who wanted to come in and seek revenge. This was a local problem and would be sorted out within the bounds of the local level, which in this case helped to prevent a descent into retaliatory violence.

Another story illustrates both the way the level can resist efforts to lower it, as well as to raise it, and the way the level resists what are perceived to be outside pressures. This town has had reasonably cordial relationships between the churches, and one mark of that cordiality was a pre-Christmas carol service that rotated between churches, drawing participants from the Catholic Church and most Protestant Churches. This was a well-established custom. One year, however, a new minister had moved into one of the Protestant Churches from another Northern Ireland town; he was, therefore, the product and the purveyor of a different level. One of the innovations he attempted was to withdraw his congregation from the annual carol service. When this became known, several local lay leaders from the different churches involved met informally and agreed that this was a step backward, an unwanted lowering of the level. Consequently, leaders from the new minister's congregation had a discreet word with him about how things are done locally, and the level was restored.

If the level can sometimes help to maintain a local equilibrium, it does have great problems and limitations. First, the level depends on stable communities that intuitively know the limits and boundaries. But this necessary stability cannot always and in the future be counted upon. As mentioned above, more established folk in a town sometimes talk rather regretfully about new people moving in numbers into the area, and it is clear that part of the regret (class difference can be another part) is that they will not understand or live by the local level of equilibrium. In the story about the carol service, for example, the restoration of the level in that one case has proved to be a significant exception to what some community members see as a gradual lowering of the level, due at least in part to a succession of new and relatively hard-line Protestant ministers. More dramatically, in the case of at least some of the parades that have proved contentious in recent years – Orange parades running through Garvaghy Road in Portadown and the Lower Ormeau Road in Belfast head the list of obvious examples – one dynamic among the many at work is that a certain unspoken, working level used to exist, but shifting populations over the years now mean that the old local level no longer works. A second and much greater difficulty is that if the level maintains an equilibrium that sometimes prevents problems or maintains standards, it also hinders increased contact and cooperation, and because the community equilibrium is too often at a fairly low level, it will not necessarily be able to cope with all the pressures put upon it. Thus when the level that works in some way adequately on a day-to-day basis meets a crisis, the level is likely to fail, leaving people with few or no resources for dealing with the crisis. The level has a third problem that is too often the case with forces for good and for bad: in general, the level is more easily lowered than raised, and while people can with perseverance and hard work slowly raise the level, one crisis can bring their good work crashing down in an instant. Since 1995, the ripple effects around Northern

Ireland of a series of difficult, polarising marches in Drumcree have in some cases exposed local levels for the limited and inadequate structures that they are, as crisis brought levels low. Some individuals and communities, believing that local attitudes and community relations were at least stable if not necessarily positive, were shocked by what the Drumcree crisis revealed.

The fourth and greatest difficulty is that the level typically serves no better purpose than to ensure that apartheid is benign in its effects. As discussed in the previous section, we see evidence that many people in Northern Ireland are willing to settle for benign apartheid, and in fact some actually prefer it. People of many traditions find it a good thing to be absorbed in the life of their particular community, whether it be Presbyterian, Roman Catholic, evangelical, or whatever, and one can lead a satisfying existence that does not extend meaningfully beyond the limits of that community. If this is the limit of a group's vision, then they will need nothing more than a smoothly functioning level to maintain minimal but cordial relationships with other communities. There are many reasons, however, to doubt that apartheid can be benign or that a low level can function well for any significant length of time. If people aspire to something more, whether for reasons of pragmatism or principle, then the level will need to be dramatically raised and radically transformed, for Northern Ireland as a whole and for communities, groups, and institutions within it.

The level is good, the level is fallen, the level will be redeemed
In the context of discussing the level, we want to introduce an interpretative scheme taken from Walter Wink's *Engaging the Powers,* a book on the biblical concept of the principalities and powers.[28] The powers, says Wink, are the various systems, institutions, structures, and customs by which society operates. Each of the powers has an outer, visible, and material aspect and an inner, spiritual aspect. A police service, for example, will have an outward reality made up of officers, buildings, vehicles, patterns of deployment, characteristic operations, and so on. At the same time, a police service will have an inner, spiritual aspect that is no less real. This will include characteristic relationships between people within the service and between the service and the public and, in general, all those elements that go to make up the ethos of an institution. Inner and outer aspects of a power

are linked, but not in a strictly determinative way. A particular way of structuring a police service, for example, might nurture a particular ethos, whether positive or negative, but at the same time one can imagine two similarly structured police services that nonetheless differ significantly because of the different ethos that animate them.

According to Wink, the powers are part of God's good creation; but the powers have often been turned from their good original use and have become fallen and destructive; even so, God wills that the powers should be redeemed, which God is accomplishing in part now and will ultimately accomplish fully. So Wink's scheme is: the powers are good, the powers are fallen, the powers will be redeemed. Government, for example is good and necessary for human well-being. Yet a particular government can become a monster, abusing, destroying, and generally running against everything God desires for human society. But the answer cannot be to destroy government or to attempt to do without it, because that is not possible. No, the fallen power that is government must be redeemed, perhaps only partially now, but fully in God's time. The family might be another example: good and necessary, but sometimes it turns against what family is meant to be, and instead of nurturing it abuses, instead of caring it neglects. Yet the Christian response to this fallen power surely cannot be to destroy or neglect it, but to redeem it for God's purposes. The family is good, the family is fallen, the family will be redeemed.

We introduce this good/fallen/redeemed triad in order to suggest that the level is such a power, good but fallen, fallen but redeemable. At its best the level is a kind of social lubricant, a set of institutions and customs that structure community life. Probably every community or church or family or nation – every grouping of human beings – has some kind of a level. These are the folkways that at first seem peculiar or at least distinctive to an outsider, but that insiders hardly notice or, if they do notice, that seem natural and right; when the outsider no longer notices them, it is a major marker on the road to integration into that community. When tainted by sectarianism, however, the level becomes a fallen power that stifles growth, nurtures sectarianism, and persuades people that a low level is a tolerable level, maybe even the best they can achieve, or even the best they ought to desire.

Transforming the level, this fallen power, requires broadly the same steps involved in transforming any element of the sectarian system. First the level must be exposed, named, identified, and understood, because the fallen powers operate by deceiving people into believing that they are simply natural and normal, that they cannot be changed, that there is no other way. If those undertaking the exposure of the level are doing so as an academic exercise, then this first step will not necessarily have any positive effect. In fact, it is possible to imagine that the ways of the level, once exposed, could be acted out more virulently. If, however, those exposing and identifying the level are local people doing so out of a commitment to a healthier community, then the very act of exposing and identifying already serves to deprive the level of much of its negative power over them. The level will have lost its fundamental power to persuade people that it is just the way things naturally are. What remains is to consider further the kind of community people want and the kind of structures, values, and customs that will support it. This is, in effect, to replace the unspoken level with a consciously chosen and affirmed alternative which will serve the community rather than rule it. When, in time, some aspects of the new arrangement settle into a framework of unspoken assumptions, i.e. into a new level, it will be the benign product of a healthy community, no longer an expression of sectarianism.

APPROACHES TO DEALING WITH DIFFERENCE

Introduction

We initially developed the model for dealing with difference, presented in this section, in order to help people to explore a variety of ways of circumventing a false choice between agreeing with or rejecting those who are different. Subsequent developments were designed to help people to grasp a variety of ways of relating positively with those whose difference they find difficult or obnoxious. We have worked with the model in a large number of groups from different backgrounds and in different settings, adjusting and teasing out its complexities in response to their questions. The generous and enthusiastic welcome they have given the model suggests that whilst we are not describing anything that people do not already know, we are putting it into a framework which helps them to understand better their relationship with various types of difference. It also provides a

Dealing with difference

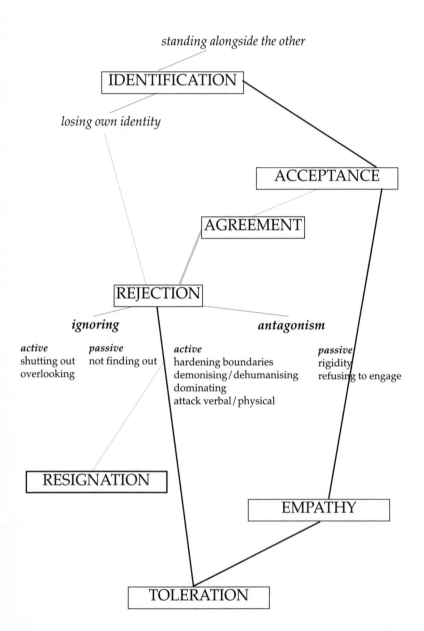

stimulus to begin to imagine more creative ways of dealing with difference which they find troubling.

The false choice between agreeing with and rejecting a person or group arises from two inter-dependent factors. One relates to inter-group conflict in general, and the other relates specifically to the way the sectarian system operates to reinforce itself. Conflict between groups, because it involves a hardening of group boundaries and issues of safety, tends to generate fertile ground where suspicion and magnification of differences can flourish. One such magnification is a lie, central to the sectarian system, that difference cuts all the way down through every level of possible relationship between one's own group and those who are different. Early in our work we noted that a significant effect of this lie is to create a false choice between agreeing with an individual or a group who are different and rejecting them. In other words, sectarianism breeds a type of binary logic, which suggests that if I cannot agree with you then I must reject you. In this case, agreement means to hold broadly similar attitudes, views, or beliefs and to subscribe to roughly the same worldview. Such an understanding of agreement comes closer to conformity than to simple agreement. Rejection, on the other hand, means not simply to disagree but to dismiss, ignore, be antagonistic towards, dehumanise, demonise, or attack.

A compounding factor in this cycle is that because sectarianism proffers an inclusive, conformity model of agreement, it tends to operate as if agreement and acceptance are the same. Similarly, because the model of rejection is so all-embracing there is a danger of equating disagreement with outright and total rejection. We would argue, however, that a true relationship of acceptance involves welcoming and being able to sustain both the differences and the disagreements between parties within a framework of mutual respect and esteem. Conversely, we would argue that disagreement about one or more issues, no matter how significant, does not necessarily entail a negative relationship of rejection, but could be sustained within any level of positive relationship from toleration to identification, terms we will develop later in this section.

Central to our model is the notion that the ways of relating, which we describe as toleration, empathy, acceptance, and identification, do not depend upon agreement. It is possible for people to develop a deep acceptance of others even though they fundamentally disagree on certain important issues. One obvious example of this is the positive relationships which have developed between some ex-paramilitaries, who, whilst retaining their different political allegiances, have become friends and fellow campaigners against violence as a means of settling differences. Another is the formation, in 1996, of the Northern Ireland Women's Coalition (NIWC), a political party which brings together women of very mixed social, economic, political, and religious backgrounds. NIWC is a brave attempt to do politics in a different way in Northern Ireland. This type of nuanced differentiation between agreement and acceptance is made possible because the people concerned have developed personal relationships, and they have learned that the 'other' is more than just his or her politics and that there are common goals or bonds which unite them beyond their political or religious differences. Most people probably have a friend with whom they radically disagree over some issues, but the friendship can carry the weight of the disagreement, even if the differences remain irreconcilable.

Sectarianism typically works through stages from being suspicious or afraid of difference, to magnifying difference, and then finally to rejecting difference. The liberal counter to such a process is to seek to cherish diversity. This point of view has integrity, especially in two very positive aspects. Firstly, there is a case to be made for cherishing difference in general, because being able to view an issue or question from more than one point of view helps one to see more clearly what is at stake. Secondly, since no person or group is infinitely gifted, there are varieties of otherness or types of difference, which bring richness into, and serve to expand, people's limited worlds. Learning to cherish difference as a richness and not a threat is a pre-requisite for building a truly inclusive and plural society.

The process of seeking to cherish diversity also has limits, however, because people have limits to their capacity to tolerate difference. A question then arises about how people respond when they come across a variety of difference that they find really difficult or obnoxious. How do they deal with the types of difference or otherness that exist at the very outer limit of their tolerance, the types of difference that they find hard to live with? How do they prevent themselves falling into rejection of the person or group, even while radically disagreeing with them?

For Christians there is an added complication, because they are called by Christ to love all people, even their enemies. This can be interpreted as meaning that unless a person can accept others totally and unconditionally, she is not fulfilling God's word. When this is taken together with the sectarian tendency to confuse acceptance and agreement, people end up thinking that unless they can agree almost totally with the person or group, they cannot accept them, and then they are failing to be Christian. But people need to recognise, firstly that acceptance is not necessarily about agreement and secondly that Christ's call to love unconditionally is an ideal to which one aspires. Often unconditional love and acceptance are not yet possible. With some individuals or groups it may never be possible this side of the grave. While some people do live love in important and sur-prising ways, many live it as no more than a moderately positive level of relationship with most people, apart from those to whom they are closest. When it comes to those whose differ-ence we experience as obnoxious, this moderately positive rela-tionship may diminish to no more than the barely positive strat-egy of doing them no harm. These realisations do not relieve Christians of the imperative to seek to love and accept others un-conditionally, but they can help people to be honest about how they respond to others, even where that falls far short of Christian loving. Only when people can be very honest with themselves about where they are in the process of dealing with difference that they find troubling are they in a position to recognise the need to change their attitudes and approach.

Dealing with difference in our 'own' group
An insight emerging from the group work that Cecelia and Malcolm conducted is that learning to deal positively with dif-ference within single tradition groups can be almost more diffi-cult than between tradition groups. There is, as we noted previ-ously, a tendency to want to pretend that differences of view do not exist in one's own group and to present an agreed line on everything. As one group put it: 'now we can't be behaving like this when we meet the others, we must present a united front.'

There seem to be at least two major elements at work here. Firstly, facing diversity opens up a process of questioning the 'certainties' that many people thought they had about their own tradition, and it raises a fundamental worry about what is the 'truth' as one's own group or tradition would describe it. This is an uncomfortable and confusing place to find ourselves, and it is a situation that most people resist strenuously. Secondly, there is a concern about the unity of one's own group, a concern that has aspects relating to both internal group issues and to how the group will be perceived externally. Internally, the unity of the group is one of the chief sources of security for members in a situation of threat. The existence of significant differences not only threatens that security, but also seems to generate a fear that externally these differences will be read as a weakening of one's own 'side' against their 'side', which, in a conflict situation, is to be avoided at all costs. There is a sense in which it is nearly easier to deal with the other 'side', whom you expect to be different, than to face family, neighbours, friends, and people with whom you have worked or worshipped for years and to realise that actually you disagree significantly about important areas.

We are convinced that finding ways of helping people to face positively the diversity that exists in their own groupings is a crucial means of helping them to be more receptive towards difference in other groups or traditions.

A model for dealing with difference

There are two keys in the process of helping people to deal with difference which is difficult or obnoxious. They are firstly, to help them grasp that agreement and acceptance are not the same, and secondly, to help them to identify other positive ways of relating, such as toleration and empathy, which stop short of acceptance. We are not suggesting that toleration or empathy are adequate ways of dealing with difference, but they are at least better than rejection. Moreover, distinguishing different levels of positive relationship with difference can provide people with language for describing where they stand at present, and with indicators of where they need to direct their energy and focus in order to learn to deal better with a particular type of difference. The model for dealing with difference that is offered here schematises a number of possible ways of relating. What follows is a description of the different levels of the model; these are illustrated (in italics) by two true stories. The first is of a Catholic woman who learned to move from rejection to empathy in relation to Protestants who think that she is not Christian because she is Catholic.

Rejection
Rejection is a negative and destructive relationship with a person or group such that people continuously, consciously or unconsciously, cast the other party as different from, distinct from, or unlike themselves in ways that they wish to dissociate themselves from, disparage, change, or annihilate. Contrary to popular perception, rejection is not a state of no relationship. Furthermore, it is possible to agree with some of the attitudes or positions of those one rejects, within the framework of an overall destructive and oppositional relationship. The apparently simple position of rejecting another can take many forms, both active and passive. The destructive patterns of relating that are identified in the definition of sectarianism in chapter three are all present in some form in rejection: hardening boundaries, overlooking, belittling, dehumanising, demonising, dominating, and physically or verbally attacking. Rejection expresses itself in patterns that can broadly be described as either 'ignoring' or as 'antagonism'.

Rejection as ignoring
Rejection as ignoring has both active and passive forms. In its active form, ignoring involves shutting out the person or group from one's own world or deliberately overlooking their needs and concerns. In this mode, people behave as if the other does not exist or impinge on their world. They do not offer the other party even ordinary human discourse or politeness. In its passive form, ignoring is a lack of interest in or curiosity about the other, simply not bothering to find out who or what they are. Both of these forms are attractive to educated, middle class people and to church people, because they do not usually involve confrontation, they do not require any great effort, and it is possible to relate in this way and still be seen as someone who is nice, reasonable, and does no harm. If one looks more closely at this behaviour, however, it becomes apparent that it is an insidiously destructive pattern of relating, and it is difficult to challenge because the person appears to be 'doing nothing harmful'.

At first the woman dismissed the position of Protestants who think that she, as a Catholic, is not Christian, as intransigent bigotry, which she believed is contrary to the gospel. She had never had a conversation with any of them and did not want to waste her time and energy talking with these people. She almost totally dismissed them at every level. She shut them out of her sphere of life even in terms of ordinary human exchange, not seeking contact with them and actively avoiding them when necessary. She felt so angry and offended by their behaviour that had she spoken with them, she would have berated them about their lack of Christian charity and challenged them about failing to live the gospel.

It is important to note here the bigotry and intransigence of the woman's position. Her behaviour was nearly a mirror image of theirs and for similar reasons: she believed their position to be wrong and un-Christian.

Rejection as antagonism
Rejection as antagonism also has both active and passive forms. In its active form antagonism is most readily recognised in all forms of attack, whether physical or verbal. The destructive patterns of relating – such as hardening the boundaries between groups, belittling, dehumanising, or demonising others, and all forms of dominating others – fall clearly into this category. In its passive form, it has characteristics of passive-aggressive behaviour, expressed in rigidity of view and a refusal to engage even when the other seeks or offers engagement.

Resignation
Resignation is a siding and dead end in the movement towards dealing positively with difference. It is the mode in which one views the present state of difference, leading to conflict and division, as the way the world is. This is accompanied by a belief that the situation cannot be changed, that to try to change it is a waste of energy, and that one has to learn to live with it. It is characterised by a phrase which was repeated to Cecelia and Joe several times in the early stages of their work: 'sure when you have been here a bit longer, you'll realise that that is just the way things are here.' Such a view is profoundly depressed and depressing, and it lends itself easily to a justification for adopting benign apartheid as a means of resolving the situation. Resignation is a downward spiral, trapping people within ever decreasing horizons and tending to accentuate the need for unity and conformity within their own group, however that group is defined. It is a very difficult position for people to break out of, because it saps the creative energy and hope needed for envisaging another way forward. It is also difficult for others to

help people out of resignation, because it requires those who feel resigned to risk engagement with the 'other' and an exploration of their own attitudes and actions, all of which can be at least threatening to their sense of identity and at most a totally life-changing experience. In general, human beings resist vigorously having to undertake such in-depth work on identity, so there is a lot of resistance to be overcome in order to help them to begin to move.

Conditions that encourage people
to move out of rejection and resignation modes
Possibly the most tricky transition in any approach to dealing with difference is to move away from outright rejection of the other or from resignation towards some less negative position. As with all significant journeys in life, the first step is the one that requires most courage and energy, because one does not know where the path will lead nor who one will be at the end of it. High levels of stress and anxiety ordinarily accompany the uncertainty about identity raised by such a transition. In a sectarian situation this anxiety can be further heightened because a movement towards positive relationship with 'the other' could mean being criticised, ostracised, or even attacked by one's own family, friends, community, or church congregation. In the light of this, it is not difficult to imagine why the level of inertia at this point is high. A person can be greatly assisted in making this transition by particular conditions, which can include:
    1. changes in the overall context, e.g. changes brought about by significant political accommodation such as the Belfast Agreement, or by changes in personal circumstances;
    2. recognising negative consequences in terms of continuing loss or harm;
    3. seeing positive gain;
    4. support that minimises the risks involved in encountering the other, in exploring one's own attitudes and actions, and in being penalised by one's own people.

The woman changed employment and found herself working close-ly with Protestant colleagues who were open and supportive. She was touched by both conservative and more liberal Protestants, who, like herself, were impatient with anti-Catholicism and viewed it as unbiblical. Their empathy for her position moved and challenged her. In the light of her colleagues' support, she began to wonder how she should be responding to them and to their attitudes to those who thought that she was not Christian. This led her inevitably to examining her own attitudes. Gradually, it began to dawn on the woman that she was doing to those who thought her not Christian what she experienced them doing to her. She describes herself as able to contemplate moving towards toleration if only because she did not like what she saw in the mirror and could not bear knowing that she was behaving exactly like them.

What helped the woman to make the transition was a combination of change in context by changing her job, support from sympathetic Protestant colleagues, and the realisation of continuing negative consequences in terms of how she viewed herself.

Toleration
Toleration is the state in which a person or group can just about stomach the other's views as a possible way of looking at world. It implies no agreement with them or acceptance of them. In this model, then, toleration is a barely positive concept. It is quite distinct from the strongly positive concept of toleration as an open and inclusive attitude to difference associated with the notion of being a tolerant person. It does mean, however, that people can begin to let the other into their sphere, to listen to them, to seek to know about them, and to accord them respect in ordinary human ways, whilst still rejecting their position.

At this point, the woman began to try to listen to those who thought her not Christian, and to understand their logic. It was a struggle. She found their views deeply offensive, and very often their sure and almost arrogant manner of delivery compounded the offence. The woman describes herself as drifting along in this struggling, semi-listening mode for a couple of years.

Empathy
Empathy is the ability to put ourselves into the shoes of another, to see the world from their standpoint, to understand their feelings and the logic of their way of being or acting, and to be able to communicate that understanding to them. It does not necessarily imply any agreement with them. It is not about sympathising with them, or excusing or condoning their behaviour. It does, however, require people to be able to be in touch with the way they feel and to be able to reflect it accurately. For most peo-

ple this is an uncomfortable place to be, especially when they are trying to empathise with people who have hurt or offended them. Throughout this study, we have found that those who have made significant journeys from bigotry to understanding of the other are those who have routinely put themselves in situations where they are not comfortable, those who have actively sought to understand and to relate with the other.

In the course of her work, the woman had occasion to address a clergy group in which one cleric, a chaplain to the Orange Order, told her that he thought that she was not Christian because she was a Catholic. Throughout the meeting his demeanour towards her was critical and argumentative. By chance she happened to find herself alone with the cleric at the end of the meeting. It was autumn 1997 and the Orange Order had cancelled some parades over the previous summer in order to decrease tensions, which were threatening to erupt into widespread violence and civil disorder. The woman told the cleric that she admired the courage of the Orange Order in taking those decisions. The woman described the effect of her comment as 'like throwing a switch'. The cleric began to talk openly about what that decision had meant and how much abuse those who made the decision had taken from their own members. He described spending the summer preaching in Protestant churches about charity to their Catholic neighbours.

Then, without prompting, he alluded to his comments about her not being Christian. He explained that if, as he does, he believes that she is in gross error, and if he loves both her and God, then it is his duty before God to point out the error to her and to try to bring her back to God. The woman said that suddenly she began to realise that he, and probably many others, are actually sincere and genuine people who like herself are struggling to be faithful to God as they understand God. Their attitude cannot be dismissed as blind bigotry. She still does not agree with their understanding of God or their biblical interpretation, but recognises that she shares some common ground with many of these people whom she formerly thought of as enemies. Subsequently, she has felt more able and more inclined to try to engage with them and has where possible tried to establish relationships with them.

It is important to note here the intricate choreography of this conversation. Initially it was the woman's openness to the cleric which made room for the encounter that ensued. He then made a movement of trust in confiding to her the personal and emotional toll of the parades decision, and followed this with a further disclosure about his desire to promote charity to Catholics. Given his attitude to her during the working session, accepting that he had preached about charity to Catholic neighbours required of the woman a stretch of both imagination and empathy. Then, sensing that she was neither going to argue with nor attack him, the cleric felt able and willing to try to explain the positive stance behind his judgment that she is not Christian. This opened the way for her beginning to enter fully into empathy with him. She did not at this point choose to either question or challenge him. It is, however, only when people can empathise with someone that they can really challenge him or her in a positive and constructive, rather than destructive, way. If they try to challenge even at the level of toleration, it will likely be experienced as attack or at best as destructive criticism, because there is not sufficient sense of positive relationship to sustain the elements of disagreement.

It is clear that significant progress on the journey to the level of empathy can be made without being in ongoing relationship with the person or group that one finds difficult. Periodic encounters, openness, generosity in listening, and some consistent seeking to know the other can carry a person into empathy. The development and deepening of empathy, however, does require more sustained relationship.

Acceptance
Acceptance is a positive relationship between individuals or groups such that they can acknowledge differences and disagreements, even serious divergences, yet sustain them within a continuing state of mutual respect and esteem. Acceptance is not agreement, but requires a sufficient level of agreement on some issues in order to be able to maintain a conversation with the other. Such a dialogue may be uncomfortable for some, or even most, of the time. The notion of being able to really accept another outside the context of an ongoing positive relationship is empty and meaningless. The development of acceptance demands ongoing relationship, generosity of interpretation, and a deepening empathy for the other. Above all, it requires a willingness to accept the other's story of 'how things are' as genuine and coherent within itself, even when it differs substantially from one's own version of 'how things are'. This does not, however, imply

agreement, only a willingness to let the other be radically other and to accept them in their otherness. One then faces the task of learning, slowly and painfully, how to accommodate, to work with, and eventually to value that otherness and difference.

> *The woman concerned has not yet reached this level of relationship with those who believe that she is not Christian. She is not sure that she and they will ever be able to attain acceptance because it requires a two-way relationship of generosity and openness. She recognises that both she and they hold positions that entail an implicit or explicit demand that the other change their view in order to be able to relate equally. The woman, however, is now able to enter into more open and cordial relationships with those who think that she is not Christian and hopes that through these relationships some may come to recognise the spirit of Christ at work in her life.*

We would tend to agree with the woman's pessimism about reaching acceptance in this case, because the type of difference at issue here is one in which one party is making the pernicious claim: 'you are not who you say you are.' This is a fundamental rejection of the other's story of 'how things are' and leaves little or no basis for establishing more than empathy. Moreover this stance is profoundly dehumanising in that it takes from the person the right to say who and what they are, while at the same time claiming, 'I am what you say you are.' It may be possible to mitigate or ameliorate this stance to some degree by, for example, developing other aspects of the relationship such as common work or social interests. If, however, the party making the claim continues to keep this claim to the fore in the relationship, mitigation will be to little avail.

Agreement

Agreement is common understanding of and assent to a particular approach or approaches to a specific issue or issues. It may, but need not, imply acceptance of the other or the other's position as a whole. Agreement can subsist at a number of levels. It may be tacit or articulated recognition of a common mind on a subject or a similar approach to an issue. On the other hand, it may involve negotiation of a common approach to or resolution of an issue. In this case it would imply significant expectation and trust that the other will honour whatever conditions the agreement entails.

Identification

The level of identification has two poles one of which is positive, i.e. 'standing alongside the other', and the other negative, i.e. 'losing one's own identity'. Standing alongside the other is the ability to get inside the thoughts, values, and way of being of the other, without sharing them and without losing one's own identity. This is usually combined with a capacity to describe and explain the position of the other in a way that the other can readily recognise and own. It is the maturing of empathy, through sustained positive relationship, into an 'organic' feel for who and what the other believes themselves to be. It may, but need not, include significant areas of agreement. An example may help to illustrate what we mean.

> *It is a true story recounted to Joe and Cecelia by a relatively liberal Catholic priest and an evangelical Presbyterian minister, who were long time colleagues in a chaplaincy situation. The two had become close friends and had worked hard, over a number of years, at understanding the integrity of one another's beliefs and points of view. The priest found himself in the situation of being challenged about the theology of the Mass by a young, male Catholic student. The student had been influenced by a conservative Protestant group through whom he had picked up some very distorted notions about what constituted Catholic theology concerning the Mass. No matter which way the Catholic priest tried to explain the actual teaching of the Catholic Church, the student refused to accept or believe it. The Presbyterian minister then joined in the conversation. He was able not only to recount accurately what his Catholic colleague believed he was doing when he celebrated Mass, but also to do it in a way that the young man could understand and accept. When telling the story, the two chaplains pointed out that at least part of the reason that the young man could accept the explanation from the Presbyterian minister was because he was identifiably conservative and evangelical in his theology.*

One of the striking features about this story is how different the Catholic priest and the Presbyterian minister are in their theology, their churchmanship, and their patterns of socialising and yet how deeply they have been able to develop a sense of who the other is and what he believes and intends by his actions and words. The openness, trust, and humour between them is obvious. Their way of living identification should dispel a fear harboured by many people: that to identify closely is, perhaps unconsciously or even unintentionally, to become similar – the fear of losing distinct identity. Yet in this story it is precisely because the Presbyterian minister is identifiably evangelical that he can help the student understand and accept the Catholic theology of the Mass. Their exploration of difference within a context of growing friendship has helped them to become more them-selves and more true to their tradition, not less. This is because, while they do not agree about many things, they experience their difference as a richness and a strength, especially in their team ministry.

The negative pole, to lose one's own identity, is the process by which a person or group becomes so immersed in the other and the other's tradition that they begin to lose touch with and possibly to repudiate their own tradition. It usually involves sig-nificant agreement with, and even adoption of, the other's atti-tudes and views. Indeed, the twin tendencies to demonise their own tradition and to unrealistically glorify the other tradition is the sectarian dynamic applied in reverse. Usually people glorify their own and demonise the other. This then becomes a form of rejecting both self and the other by over identification, hence the reconnection of this level to the rejection level on the model.

Conclusion

The purpose and importance of this model is to debunk the lie purveyed by the sectarian system that to accept is to agree and that to disagree is to reject. At the same time the model offers a number of options for positive relationship with kinds of differ-ence that people find obnoxious. In working with groups, we have found that the model has helped people to assess and to understand where they are in relationship to difference that they find troubling, and then to think about strategies for beginning to move towards other levels of relationship. Above all, it has helped people to recognise that it is okay to be at a low level of valuing and dealing with difference, if this is all that one can manage. To be able to barely tolerate a particular expression of difference, whilst not adequate, is already better than being in a mode of rejection or resignation about it. It is already one crucial and courageous step on the journey beyond sectarianism.

MITIGATION

In any conflict situation, a capacity to compromise is a vital skill. The points where groups clash can be negotiated by giving a little here, taking a little there. People accept, however grudgingly, a degree of disappointment, perhaps even bitter disappointment, as the price of a degree of satisfaction. They give up things they desire and value as the necessary cost of peace. In the absence of some ability to compromise, conflict can be intractable.

Some ideas and commitments, however, may be effectively non-negotiable, beyond the reach of compromise. These beliefs are so fundamental, an individual or a group believes, that they cannot be abandoned or even modified without damaging something essential to personal or communal integrity. Although many ideas can be held as non-negotiable, religious ideas in particular have a tendency to become non-negotiable, because people not only value them highly, they believe that these ideas are in some way, perhaps quite directly, God-given. Because of this, at least in Christianity and Judaism and undoubtedly in some other religions as well, principled, radical unwillingness to negotiate has a high and honoured place. Already in the late second or early third century, Tertullian famously observed what had been true from the beginning, that the blood of the martyrs, the ultimate in non-negotiators, is the seed of the church, and so it has remained through the centuries. This is one impulse Christianity inherited directly from Judaism, which from the beginning extolled uncompromising faithfulness. From this perspective, some beliefs may be accepted or rejected, but they are not really up for negotiation.

While some people seem to treat every detail of their beliefs as non-negotiable, even people with good compromising, negotiating skills may hold some beliefs or commitments that are non-negotiable. In fact, most people probably have some non-negotiable beliefs. They may never become aware of it, because circumstances never expose the beliefs as non-negotiable, and in any case, most non-negotiable beliefs never become a source of conflict. When non-negotiables do clash, however, they make a conflict vastly more difficult.

Conflicting non-negotiables might be resolved in several ways. One possibility is that the non-negotiability was only apparent; when pressed hard on the matter, a group discovers that it had falsely elevated this particular stance to the realm of the non-negotiable, and compromise is in fact possible, whether willingly or grudgingly. Or perhaps the stark clash of non-negotiables takes both parties well past bitter compromise and allows them to see issues in a different light, where a new and superior synthesis or alternative emerges, to their mutual benefit. Another possibility is that a non-negotiable core remains, but the process of negotiation reveals that certain accretions to that core can be stripped away without loss, and the reconfigured core no longer poses the difficulties it once did.

Another possibility, however, is that the apparently non-negotiable will prove to be actually non-negotiable. The group cannot alter or abandon this particular commitment without doing grave and unacceptable damage to their identity. Imagine, for example, a situation in which group A, a Christian group, is in conflict with group B, which adheres to another religion. A mediator between them identifies a crucial clash of core beliefs. 'Group A,' she says, 'you have your ten commandments, group B happens to have seven commandments. In fact you share five of these commandments, and it is the ones you do not share that aggravate the conflict. Therefore, if you could both agree to keep the five commandments you share and abandon the remainder, this could be the shift that would make peace between you possible.' From outside those groups, retaining most of one's beliefs and giving up a few for the sake of peace might seem like an honourable solution. But from inside, the issue is likely to look entirely different. These are not just any beliefs, people might think, and we did not make them up to suit ourselves so that we might now abandon them to suit ourselves; they were given to us by God, and we conform our lives to them. Abandoning these beliefs is too high a price for peace, because it is at the cost of our integrity, identity, and allegiance. Either there is another way to peace or there is no peace.

An actual and very difficult example of non-negotiability concerns the claims of the Abrahamic faiths, Islam, Judaism, and Christianity, each to be the exclusive way to salvation. In fact, some adherents of these faiths do negotiate the difficulties posed by exclusivity, principally by ignoring or rejecting it. Effectively they are saying, we are committed Moslems, Jews, or Christians, but we do not accept these particular exclusive tenets of our faith, we believe there are other ways to salvation. Some such capacity to negotiate might seem essential to create lasting peaceable relations between these three religions. Without a recognition by adherents of any faith that people from other faiths can not only be saved, but can be saved through the observance of their own faith, it might appear, there cannot be peace between the religions and therefore there cannot be peace.

Certainly one approach to non-negotiables that can have real integrity and good effect is to make them negotiable. No doubt much of what people regard as non-negotiable should not be, and the best way of dealing with it is to demote it to the ranks of the negotiable. That strategy will not always work, however, and a good example is the exclusive claims of the monotheistic faiths. While Joe and Cecelia take different approaches to the issue of exclusivity, we agree that making acceptance that believers from other faiths will be saved in and through their faiths a necessary condition of peace is likely to be a counsel of despair, because it will never be adhered to sufficiently to make peace. The problem is not that people hang on to exclusivity out of some bigoted, perverse desire to feel superior to others or even to sustain conflict, the problem is that these exclusive claims are deeply embedded in scriptures held to be of inestimable, God-given value. Therefore, attempts to neglect, deny, or overturn, or in any other way negotiate, what is plausibly held to be non-negotiable cannot form a stable basis for peace, because such efforts will always inspire protest and reaction. The protest may be by a majority against an elite, a minority against a majority, one generation against the previous, but it will surely be made, and in every case the protesters will make a persuasive, powerful case that they are being faithful to the sacred tradition. Attempts to negotiate what faithful adherents reasonably believe to be non-negotiable are likely to lead to the kind of split in the tradition, whether formal or informal, that will undercut the peacemaking benefits meant to follow from the negotiation.

Arguing that some beliefs with potentially damaging consequences simply cannot be negotiated successfully may sound like our own counsel of despair. We do not mean it to be, although we recognise the gravity of the problem. Mitigation is the scheme we want to propose for dealing constructively with situations where conflicting non-negotiables lead to sectarian consequences and yet cannot be compromised. By mitigation we mean the capacity to lessen or eliminate possible negative outcomes of a belief, commitment, or action. What cannot be negotiated can sometimes be mitigated.

One fundamental distinction between negotiating and mitigating applies consistently: negotiation works by rejecting, neglecting, or substantially changing the perceived obstacle to peace, while mitigation maintains the problematic belief or practice, but seeks to nullify destructive consequences. The line between negotiation and mitigation is not always entirely clear, however. This is not surprising, because they are different means to the common end of peace. Both are likely, therefore, to be driven by a common desire for peace, and one person or group may practice both, in tandem or at different times.

The boundary between negotiating and mitigating is also blurred at times by the type of strategies employed. A consistent, if not quite constant, feature of mitigation is that it seeks to lessen destructive consequences arising from within a tradition by appealing to resources from that same tradition. The tradition works to heal the tradition. If mitigation does occasionally employ strategies not directly drawn from the tradition, such strategies will, at very least, never contradict the tradition. Furthermore, the externally-derived strategy is likely to be rephrased in terms compatible with the tradition or to be downplayed in favour of strategies clearly drawn from the tradition and therefore more easily embraced by adherents.

Negotiation, too, can work by means either external or internal to the tradition. The balance is different, however, as negotiation is much more likely to operate by external means. In fact, negotiation by external means is negotiation in its sharpest and most characteristic form. It works by applying, whether explicitly or implicitly, some principle of judgment that is external to and effectively higher than the tradition. Often times, beliefs or practices are rendered problematic by the intellectual and spiritual tension and contradictions arising from a clash of value systems. More precisely, the belief in question typically arises from a faith tradition thousands of years old and collides with the powerful and persuasive beliefs and assumptions of secular modernity. Caught in these circumstances, many will be inclined to negotiate, rejecting the problematic belief or practice because it seems somewhere between faintly ridiculous and simply outrageous. The negotiators will usually justify that rejection on grounds ranging from a clear articulation of an alter-

native principle to, more typically, some appeal based on com-
mon-sense modernity and built around phrases like 'outdated',
'outmoded', and 'in this day and age ...'. Concerning the particular issue in question, the tradition has been trumped by an
alternative. This is external negotiation.

But negotiation can also employ strategies and logic internal
to the tradition. It is this kind of internal negotiation that more
closely resembles mitigation. Internal negotiation is clearly negotiation, because a problematic belief, practice, or institution is
being rejected, ignored, or substantially altered rather than
maintained. And yet the means to achieve this, as with mitigation, is by an appeal to the tradition. Internal negotiation too is
the tradition working to heal the tradition.

Differing strategies for dealing with the issue of women in
Christian ministry illustrate the difference between external negotiation and internal negotiation. Despite significant exceptions, women have been excluded from formal Christian ministry in most times and places. It is a stance that clashes sharply
with modernity's great tradition of equality and human rights,
but it is also a stance easily justified by biblical practice and
teaching. The alternatives appear stark – either modernity or tradition – and many have made their choice, for or against women
in ministry, on that basis. Some Christians could not make that
choice, however. They were clearly negotiating, not mitigating,
because their goal was to abolish the practice of preventing
women from being ministers. Even as they valued the prospect
of women in ministry, however, they could not violate the tradition, so the two needed to be reconciled, which could only be accomplished by making the case for women in ministry in terms
of the logic of the tradition, i.e. by means of internal negotiation.
Such internal negotiation has been accomplished to the satisfaction of many in a variety of ways. Some point to a biblical trajec-
tory: if, as Walter Wink argues so compellingly, 'in every single
encounter with women in the four Gospels, Jesus violated the
mores of his time,'[29] living out a vision of unprecedented respect
and equality, does this not point to a radical equality of which
women in ministry is just one logical expression? Others highlight various biblical texts pointing to an equal and mutual relationship between women and men, or evidence of women in
leadership in the New Testament church which has been suppressed because translators assumed this could not be the case.

For these people, if negotiation was to be possible, it could only be internal negotiation.

Further practical examples may clarify how mitigation works and the difference between external negotiation, internal negotiation, and mitigation.

The Jewish people and the death of Jesus

An example of great historical relevance for the Christian tradition as a whole concerns those biblical statements that make the Jews responsible for the death of Jesus. A stark example might be Matthew's account of Pilate trying to release Jesus after his arrest, but the Jewish crowd, stirred up by the chief priests and elders, demanded that Jesus be crucified.

> So when Pilate saw that he could do nothing, but rather that a riot was beginning, he took some water and washed his hands before the crowd, saying, "I am innocent of this man's blood; see to it yourselves." Then the people as a whole answered, "His blood be on us and on our children!" (Mt 27:24-25)

Taken as an eternally relevant self-condemnation by the Jewish people as a whole, the effect of this text and others reinforcing it, rattling down through history, has been horrific. Over the centuries, Christians have seen to it that the answer of the people has been literally fulfilled, making it the justification for numerous pogroms against Jewish communities and even a plausible root of one of the twentieth century's defining horrors, the Holocaust. Faced with this legacy, Christians concerned to repent of it can take several approaches, including at least the trio of external negotiation, internal negotiation, and mitigation.

Negotiation is likely to involve recognising within the New Testament an anti-Semitic strand, deriving from conflict between Judaism and the early Christian community. The negotiating stance will respond by rejecting any texts suggesting anti-Semitism, effectively removing them from the canon, or by concentrating on positive texts while downplaying negative ones. This may well be internal negotiation, taking from scripture a more positive approach to Judaism.

But some people will not be able to proceed with an approach that effectively eliminates part of the canon. This is God's word, they will reason, so it must be of profit for us, read properly. Mitigation is the only course available to them. A miti-

gating reading of a text like the one from Matthew quoted above
might proceed by interpreting it as both more particularly historical and more universal in meaning than does the destructive
reading. As a historical statement, one might argue, this text is
about what a particular mob did on a particular day, and despite
their words, they have no power or right to call down wrath on
future generations. As for extracting a meaning beyond the immediate historical situation, confining the relevance of this passage to the Jewish people is far too narrow. In this view, the
proper way of reading the text is not to assign blame to a particular group, it is to recognise that the mob in question, those religious leaders, even that Roman ruler, could have been oneself.
This is not a story about a particular group of Jews, it is a story
about everyone. Read in this way, the text will not allow any triumphalist blame and scapegoating of others, it will draw a nearly opposite response of humbly recognising and appropriating a
story about universal human failure and responsibility.

One Bread, One Body and Dominus Iesus

For our immediate purposes, these recent documents are useful
in showing how the Catholic Church evaluates Protestantism
and some of the tensions arising, although this is a minor aspect
of both documents. We have earlier discussed *One Bread, One
Body*, a teaching document on the eucharist issued by the British
and Irish Catholic bishops in 1998. In the way it handled exclud-
ing Protestants from sharing communion with Catholics in all
but a handful of instances, the document had, we argued, the
sectarian consequences of hardening boundaries and overlooking. We discuss *Dominus Iesus*, issued in August 2000 by the
Vatican's Congregation for the Doctrine of the Faith, in the next
chapter, 'When Is a Religious Idea Sectarian?' Only the Catholic
church is a fully Christian church, according to this document.
While the merits of the Protestant churches are recognised, they
are not actually 'Churches in the proper sense', but rather
'ecclesial communities'. The potential sectarian implications in
such a judgment are obvious.

   Some Catholics who disagree with these stances on sharing
communion and the status of the Protestant churches take a
negotiating approach to one or both issues. In both cases, negotiation will involve rejecting or ignoring the formal Catholic
teaching involved. In the case of the eucharist, negotiation may

further involve the practical step of offering communion to Protestants. Negotiation in these cases is likely to straddle the line between external and internal. If the frame of reference is the Catholic Church, this is apparently external negotiation, drawing on outside values and convictions, although some negotiators will want to insist that these values are in fact internal to the Catholic tradition, although not applied in these instances. If the frame of reference is the broader Christian tradition, however, then negotiation is likely to appear internal, based on other strands of Christian and biblical teaching.

But many Catholics who share with negotiators a regret about sectarian consequences will not wish or be able to deal with the problem by means of negotiation. Catholic teaching is a whole, they may reason, so Catholics are not free to pick and choose as they please. *One Bread, One Body* is a reiteration of traditional Catholic teaching on the eucharist, and no doctrine and practice is more central to the life of the Catholic community. *Dominus Iesus* too simply reiterates traditional Catholic teaching on the ecclesial status of Protestantism, although some Catholics find in the document a less irenic approach to this problem than has been characteristic of the Catholic Church since the Second Vatican Council. Given the precedent for the teachings of *One Bread, One Body* and *Dominus Iesus*, some Catholics, probably many, will see no room for negotiation. They do not wish to give offence, but if sectarian consequences can only be dealt with by rejecting or ignoring these doctrines, then they cannot be dealt with.

In these circumstances, mitigation might take several forms. Concerning communion, one is simply to be sensitive in anticipating and avoiding circumstances in which the practice of exclusive communion might give offence. Another approach might seek positive relationships with Protestants, including sharing worship in ways that are approved by Catholic teaching and that work around and do not draw attention the problem of communion. A third, in this case drawing explicitly on the standards of the Catholic Church and all but indistinguishable from internal negotiation, is to consider the varieties of accepted practice concerning shared communion within the worldwide Catholic Church. In the same vein, mitigators might think through the content of various agreements the Catholic Church has reached with others on the subject of communion and test

whether the implications of those agreements has been sufficiently put into practice. A mitigating spirit at least considers the
question, does the existing and accepted practice and teaching
of the Catholic Church allow a degree of latitude concerning
shared eucharist that is not sufficiently explored in Ireland
today? Concerning how Catholics should regard Protestant
Churches, mitigation will involve a question of proportion. The
negative judgment of Protestant churches as merely ecclesial
communities rather than full and proper churches will be maintained only in the full awareness of the genuine merit of
Protestant expression of faith, of the way God has used
Protestant churches as instruments of salvation, and of all that
Catholics have to learn from Protestants. Since the Second
Vatican Council, such mitigating stances have characterised formal Catholic teaching on Protestantism. How far Catholics have
lived it out in relation to Protestants has varied, of course, from
time to time and place to place.

Anti-Catholicism
A third issue is the anti-Catholicism of the Protestant tradition.
The traditional stance of the Protestant mainstream, enshrined
in doctrinal statements by the Church of Ireland (the Thirty-Nine
Articles) and Presbyterianism (the Westminster Confession) and
in much rhetoric and practice by Methodism, might be characterised as believing that the teachings and practice of the
Catholic Church are so radically in error that it cannot be accepted
as a Christian Church, or at least that the Catholic Church is a
deficient and lesser church. It is essentially the mirror image of
the traditional Catholic judgment of Protestantism. The potential for sectarianism in this judgment is great. The likelihood of
hardening boundaries is most obvious, but perhaps more dangerous is the possibility of imposition. The logic behind saying
that a group claiming to be Christian is not actually Christian is,
essentially, that 'you are not what you say you are.' We will
argue in the next chapter, 'When Is a Religious Idea Sectarian?',
that this risks encroaching on a group's right to define itself.

Historically, the Protestant mainstream churches embraced
some version of this judgment of the Catholic Church. In the
current teaching and practice of most Protestant Churches,
however, such traditional judgments have been significantly re-
defined in much more positive terms in light of new experience

and insight. These churches altered their former views by re-thinking the teaching of scripture and their doctrinal traditions, not by abandoning those authorities and replacing them with another. While some individuals and sub-groups within the mainstream churches have refused to accept this internal negoti-ation, and some have left the churches in part over this issue, the change has been accomplished without actually splitting tradi-tions. To take the three largest Protestant Churches in Northern Ireland as examples, no cohesive group within them decided that refusing to accept the Catholic Church as authentically Christian was a non-negotiable aspect of church identity so that today we have rival Catholic, Church of Ireland, Methodist, or Presbyterian Churches defined in significant part by their re-fusal to negotiate on this issue.

Concerning anti-Catholicism, internal negotiation remains a potent dynamic. Over the last two decades, significant numbers of evangelical Protestants in Northern Ireland, whether individ-uals or parachurch organisations or congregations, have con-cluded on biblical grounds that they can and should accept the Catholic Church as Christian, and the Christian landscape looks noticeably different for it. The same approach will continue to be an option for conservative Protestants concerned to re-think their approach to the Catholic Church.

Negotiating anti-Catholicism will not be an acceptable op-tion for everyone, however. For these people, the old Protestant critique of Catholicism continues to maintain its integrity and authority. What has seemed to other conservative Protestants a legitimate and necessary internal negotiation – i.e. changing atti-tudes to Catholicism for reasons of faithfulness to the gospel message – will seem to non-negotiators to be straightforward ex-ternal negotiation and as such contemptible – abandoning the gospel in order to embrace a position in step with modernity. Negotiation of any sort is least likely to be an option for the Orange Order. For a denomination, congregation, or individual, no matter how vehemently anti-Catholic, this position is still only a negative corollary of a particular understanding of their basic Christian commitment. Anti-Catholicism is stitched into the Orange Order's basic commitments and documents in a far more direct way, so negotiation would call into question the Order's reason to exist, or at least require a radical reconstitution of identity.

For those who cannot negotiate, the only way to meet the moral imperative to address the sectarian implications of anti-Catholicism will be mitigation. Of the mitigating resources available within conservative Protestantism, we will mention just two. The first is a distinction between religious separation and social separation. As several fundamentalists told us, what their critique of Catholicism requires of them is religious separation, expressed chiefly in objecting to and avoiding shared worship. But social separation need not follow. The distinction allows at least positive neighbourly relations and, potentially, cooperation in various enterprises without a religious element. We observed above the importance over the past twenty years of those evangelicals who have rejected anti-Catholicism. In fact another aspect of the same general movement has involved evangelicals who have retained essentially the old Protestant critique of Catholicism, but, acting on their freedom to relate to and work with Catholics outside the explicitly religious sphere, have been involved in some important cross-community initiatives with Catholics. It is a stance that puts those who take it in awkward and difficult circumstances at times, but it also opens up creative opportunities for mitigating the sectarian implications of anti-Catholicism, and therefore for peace in Northern Ireland, through positive relationships and shared work.

While the Orange Order will have available to it this mitigating principle of distinguishing between religious and social separation, we want to mention another that is particular to one of the Order's core documents, *The Qualifications of an Orangeman*. *Qualifications* begins with an exhortation to Christian commitment and practice and then moves on to detail the Orangeman's stance toward Catholicism.

> [H]e should strenuously oppose the fatal errors of the Church of Rome, and scrupulously avoid countenancing (by his presence or otherwise) any act or ceremony of Popish Worship; he should by all lawful means resist the ascendancy of that church, its encroachments and the extension of its power.[30]

Anti-Catholicism, then, is a non-negotiable woven into the very fabric of Orangeism, along with the potential for destructive and sectarian consequences that follows from it. *Qualifications* proceeds without a break, however, to put forward a mitigating principle: the Orangeman is to maintain this stance toward

Catholicism while at the same time 'ever abstaining from all un-charitable words, actions or sentiments towards his Roman Catholic brethren'.[31] Abstaining from uncharity may be a weak version of the command for Christians to love their neighbours, but it is a recognisable version. It is also a potential mitigating principle to apply to words and actions with sectarian implic-ations or consequences. The very possibility may strain the credulity of many outside the Order, but we know that it does serve a mitigating function at times. An Orange chaplain known to us was surely acting in this spirit when, having participated in the decision to cancel an Orange march down the Lower Ormeau Road in Belfast in order to defuse tensions in the sum-mer of 1997, he spent the rest of the summer in Protestant churches preaching charity to Catholic neighbours. And William Bingham, Presbyterian minister and Orange chaplain, must have been similarly motivated when he advised the Orangemen to pull out of a very tense Drumcree parade situa-tion in the aftermath of the murder of the Quinn boys in the summer of 1998.

* * *

In many cases then, as in the three we have briefly described here, what cannot be negotiated can in some way be mitigated. Indeed, read by any Christian with a mitigating desire and spirit, the bible, and especially the teaching and example of Jesus, re-veals itself as a treasury of mitigating principles. If we were to choose a bottom line from among the many mitigating princi-ples to be drawn from the bible, we would probably cite Jesus' command to 'love your enemies and pray for those who persec-ute you.' (Mt 5:44) As a mitigating principle, this is as tough-minded as it is idealistic. It simply assumes that Christians will have enemies, and the idea that enemies might be dealt with by negotiating the points of contention is not entertained. It is framed in clear and simple terms, and positioned in the centre of faith; Jesus' followers are to live like this, he says, 'so that you may be children of your Father in heaven', (Mt 5:45) who loves in just this way. It is set in a context that makes it clear that lov-ing enemies is about behaviour as much as attitude. As a miti-gating principle, it is entirely incompatible with doing harm to opponents and calls for much more.

For any reader of even a slightly sceptical bent, however,

citing the resources in Christianity for mitigating may be significant chiefly for exposing the too common and sometimes spectacular failure of Christians to use these resources. Walter Wink
summarises 2000 years of Christian thought and practice concerning a biblical text on love of enemies by saying, 'Christians
have, on the whole, simply ignored this teaching.'[32] Without a
mitigating spirit, mitigating principles are a dead letter.
Unpractised, they are more a chastisement and embarrassment
than a resource.

The existence of that mitigating spirit in Northern Ireland
can seem tenuous. At times, an exacerbating spirit is much more
noticeable. We do want to recognise and honour, however, the
presence of a mitigating spirit, which operates in a way that provides a welcome exception to Wink's judgment that Christians
have largely ignored biblical teaching on loving enemies.
Forgiveness is always a form of love, and practiced in hard cases
it is specifically the love of enemies. Forgiveness is also a gospel
value that seems to have penetrated Irish Christianity in its
many forms, and to profound effect. While the public significance of forgiving those who have wronged one's own people
has been most apparent in a few high profile cases during the
Troubles, it is surely the widespread practice of forgiveness, by
Christians and others, in its most basic form – renouncing retaliation – that has been of inestimable value in keeping the death
rate relatively low and maintaining a relatively intact society.
Keeping conflict in Northern Ireland in a proper perspective
must include recognising how much worse it could have been.
The practice of forgiveness has been an important form of mitigation.

Whatever the state of past and present practice, mitigation is
a mix of skills, habits, and mindset that is accessible to everyone.
In every situation, but especially a situation of endemic conflict,
mitigation is also, we believe, an obligation on everyone who
has any pretensions to being a person of good will. From radical
and conservative perspectives alike, reconciliation is sometimes
criticised as the compromising, negotiating enemy of justice and
truth. The criticism is that fear of giving offence will prevent the
rightly and necessarily offensive truth being spoken, that reconciliation operates in the spirit of crying peace where there is no
peace. The practice of mitigation, by recognising the integrity
and necessity of making truth claims and setting some bound-

aries on how it is done, simultaneously answers the criticism and returns the scrutiny on to those who make truth claims. If those pursuing truth claims are genuinely concerned with the truth, then they may not fear to give offence, but they will take no pleasure in it, and they will certainly fear giving needless offence, which can only harm the cause of truth. Where truth is pursued without regard for destructive consequences, it calls into question whether the pursuers' commitment is really to the truth or to some other cause, in which truth claims are merely weapons. Mitigation is both a tool for making truth claims in a constructive way and a standard of judgment for assessing the integrity of those making truth claims.

BIFOCAL VISION

One reason for the efficiency of the sectarian system in propagating itself is the simplicity of the reasoning it requires. Every question has one answer, a 'yes' or 'no' answer; black and white are the only shades of opinion allowed; every decision is either/or. In sectarianism, 'maybe', grey, and both/and hardly exist. The sectarian system demands to know, 'whose side are you on?', and no hesitation, equivocation, or complication is allowed.

If sectarianism attempts to dictate a single answer, a single way of doing things, one obvious response from those seeking to move beyond sectarianism, is to do the opposite. If sectarianism excludes, its opponents will include. If sectarianism despises diversity, then they will cherish diversity. If sectarianism in its crudest forms operates by magnifying difference, then those who oppose sectarianism will minimise difference.

Merely contradicting sectarianism with an opposite approach is rarely a sufficient response, however. Inclusion is definitely part of the answer to exclusion. But what will be included? On what terms? According to what standards? As for those who seek to respond to sectarianism's fear of diversity by cherishing diversity, they will inevitably encounter that expression of diversity which they cannot cherish, and then they are left without another response, except perhaps to despise it, thus mimicking the sectarianism they oppose. Ironically, responding to sectarianism by taking an opposite stance can sometimes become a form of sectarianism in itself. No example makes the point more clearly than the effort by sectarianism's opponents to minimise difference where the most obvious forms of sectarianism magnify difference. In fact minimising difference becomes a distinct strand of the dynamics of sectarianism, as discussed in chapter four.

In the preface to this book, we mentioned the concept of comparative sectarianism. People are inclined to approach sectarianism by drawing lines between 'them' and 'us', and since a person or group can always find a 'them' out there whose actions can be plausibly construed as worse than their own, 'the real sectarian problem' can, with apparent integrity, be identified as 'them'. Working with a variety of illustrations, we introduced this idea of comparative sectarianism early on in most groups we worked with, and it always connected with participants' experience. The antidote to the problem of comparative sectarianism, we proposed, was to develop the habit of bifocal vision: a capacity to focus on and work with two (or more) ideas simultaneously, sometimes ideas in tension with each other.

In fact bifocal vision, not contradiction, is the characteristic mental framework required for an appropriate, effective response to sectarianism. The examples cited above illustrate the point. Where sectarianism excludes, those who would move beyond sectarianism will focus on inclusion, but at the same time, bifocal vision requires that they also focus on the principles of discernment and judgment necessary for acts of inclusion to be meaningful.[33] For those who wish to challenge sectarianism's destructive fear of diversity, bifocal vision requires that they complement cherishing diversity with a second strategy for dealing with expressions of diversity that they find beyond cherishing. Those who recognise the sectarian implications of magnifying difference will not make the mirror image mistake of minimising difference; they will develop a bifocal strategy built on the conviction that both what people share and where they differ need to be appropriately recognised if we are to move beyond sectarianism. And comparative sectarianism, with its tendency to draw lines between 'us' and 'them', between the innocent and the guilty, will not be dealt with by abolishing the distinction between innocence and guilt. In this case, a bifocal strategy will begin by recognising that the line between the guilty and innocent has a certain integrity, not everyone is equally guilty, the distinction between degrees of guilt matters. In fact any approach that suggests that degrees of guilt do not matter will rightly be scoffed at and dismissed. In this case, then, a bifocal approach will recognise the line between 'us' and 'them', but relativise it by insisting on drawing a second line, underneath which all people are implicated in sectarianism. Beneath this second line, to borrow from Tim Winton's novel *Cloudstreet*, '[I]t's not us and them anymore. It's us and us and us. It's always us.'[34] The first line recognises the importance of the distinction between guilt and innocence. The second line recognises that, at least in a society marked by endemic sectarian conflict, absolute innocence is not available; to some degree, all are stained by and complicit in sectarianism. Bifocal vision insists that both lines must be kept in focus if society is to move beyond sectarianism.

Perhaps the most fundamental characteristic of sectarian reasoning is its insistence on either/or choices. One is either British or Irish, Catholic or Protestant, in or out, with us or against us. In response, moving beyond sectarianism requires the opposite approach, both/and reasoning. A both/and approach begins by querying every demand for an either/or choice: why am I being asked to make this choice? Are there other options that are not presented? Is it properly a choice, or might both options be true and compatible, at least to a degree? Necessary and liberating as both/and reasoning is, however, it is not a sufficient response to sectarianism, at least if conceived of as merely the opposite of either/or reasoning. Practised exclusively, both/and reasoning might spin out into endless options, leaving its practitioner without a capacity to make the decisive choices, characteristic of either/or reasoning, that situations sometimes require. That either/or reasoning is characteristic of sectarianism does not mean that it is always false or useless. Bifocal vision comes to the rescue, then, by allowing that even though both/and reasoning will be the main stance of those concerned to move beyond sectarianism, either/or reasoning retains a subordinate but necessary role. Looked at through the lens of bifocal vision, an adequate conception of both/and reasoning is seen to require both both/and and either/or reasoning.

While we frequently introduced the idea of bifocal vision to groups, we did little to make it an exercise for them to work with. Looking back, that seems a mistake, because the concept lends itself to application by groups. Bifocal vision might be applied as an exercise with a structure as simple as: naming elements and dynamics of sectarianism; testing whether simple contradiction can be a sufficient response; then, as an application of bifocal vision, identifying what combination of actions and ideas might be necessary for a more adequate response. By way of illustration, the chart below works with various dynamics of sectarianism identified in the course of this book. The left column names a stance, strategy, or aspect of sectarianism, while the right column indicates what elements might constitute an appropriate bifocal response. We are confident that the groups we worked with would have made good use of such an exercise.

Sectarianism	Bifocal Vision
sectarianism is out there, it is someone else's responsibility	<u>sectarianism is out there</u> sectarianism is our responsibility
sectarianism is a matter of intentions	<u>sectarianism is a matter of intentions</u> sectarianism is a matter of consequences
diversity is a threat to be rejected	<u>diversity is potentially enriching</u> we have a range of strategies for dealing constructively with expressions of diversity that we cannot accept as enriching
difference cuts all the way down – we are 'opposite religions', we share nothing	<u>difference is real</u> there are always shared qualities beneath difference
maximise difference	<u>difference is real</u> sharing is real
minimise difference	<u>sharing is real</u> difference is real
exclusion	<u>inclusion</u> discerning standards of judgment for inclusion
false either/or choices	<u>both/and reasoning</u> either/or reasoning
our enemy is a demon	<u>we have enemies</u> our enemy is a human being, made in the image of God
truth claims are to be hammered home, they are weapons	<u>truth claims are good and necessary</u> some truth claims are dangerous and must be mitigated

CHAPTER 6

When is a Religious Idea Sectarian?

As with the material in the previous chapter, the ideas presented here originated as one of the tools developed in the course of the Moving Beyond Sectarianism project for helping groups to think about and respond to sectarianism. However, while the basic model was in our repertoire for several years, we worked less with it than with the ones in the previous chapter, so when we came to write it out, we did not have as clear a sense of how groups characteristically responded. Furthermore, as we began to open up the issues involved, their inherent complexity became apparent, and the resulting text expanded far beyond the comparatively simple model with which we had begun. The importance of these issues also became increasing apparent, so it has seemed right to make them the subject of a separate chapter.

The issues we address in this chapter arise commonly in a group that has worked hard to understand how sectarianism begins and develops. Observing that sectarianism can have roots in actions, ideas, and structures that appear benign and are certainly innocently intended, people are inclined to ask questions like these: Can I make any truth claim without being sectarian? Is the mere fact of belonging to different churches somehow sectarian? What makes a religious idea sectarian?[1] Glancing at our chapter title and graphic scale of sectarian danger, a Protestant friend asked Cecelia,'Does that mean I can't say the Pope is the Antichrist anymore?' Our answer is: maybe yes, maybe no. It depends on exactly what he means and intends in saying it, how he says it, and in what context he says it. The purpose of this chapter is to explore in depth what it is that makes a religious idea sectarian.

If issues about the integrity of religious truth claims arise naturally when thinking about how sectarianism works, many people will also have been predisposed to ask such questions by prevalent aspects of contemporary popular thought that regard religion as inherently or commonly dangerous. To cite just two well-known examples, one consistent strand of the career of the prominent Irish journalist Eamonn McCann has been to expose and attack religion as fundamentally ridiculous and frequently damaging,[2] while the eminent biologist Richard Dawkins has stated that Christianity causes wars and generally causes 'people to do ill to one another because they are so convinced that they know what is right'.[3] At the beginning of *Does Christianity Cause War?*, an extended and elegant rebuttal of Dawkins's assertion, the sociologist David Martin observes that 'the proposition [Dawkins] advances is embedded in an Enlightenment narrative which is very widely disseminated and tends to be accepted uncritically.'[4] Suspicion of religious truth claims is a consistent feature of western culture, and sectarianism in Northern Ireland is understood to be prime evidence for the prosecution case.

The issue at stake here is momentous. Our response takes in two poles and the tension between them. On the one hand, we are arguing that attempts to dismiss all religious truth claims as inherently sectarian are misguided and false. Religious truth claims arise as particular expressions of basic human needs and tendencies, and they can be made with integrity. On the other hand, we recognise that religious ideas can and do contribute to sectarianism – which is, after all, one of the main themes of this book. Attempting to do justice to the truth of both poles requires distinguishing the kinds of religious ideas that are inherently sectarian from those that are not, while also setting out the conditions necessary for making religious truth claims in a way that does not contribute to sectarianism, or at least in a way that minimises sectarian consequences.

We also mean to be responding to a popular perception in Northern Ireland, common especially among conservative Christians, that ecumenism and reconciliation are concepts hostile to and incompatible with truth claims. As one Orange Order chaplain said to us, 'If I accept what you are saying, then I'll have to dilute the truth, and I won't any longer be able to preach the truth.' While some people committed to ecumenism or reconciliation may have contributed to such an impression, we like to think that we are not among them. In any case, attributing such convictions to these movements generally is false. We intend, by developing our argument in an ecumenical and reconciling context, to show the compatibility of religious truth claims with ecumenical and reconciling perspectives. It is certainly well that this should be so, since ecumenism and reconciliation are grounded in a particular set of truth claims, but setting those out goes beyond our immediate task.

To open up this issue with groups, we developed an eleven-point scale of increasing sectarian danger.

A SCALE OF SECTARIAN DANGER

1. We are different, we believe differently.
2. We are right.
3. We are right and you are wrong.
4. You are a less adequate version of what we are.
5. You are not what you say you are.
6. We are in fact what you say you are.
7. What you are doing is evil.
8. You are so wrong that you forfeit ordinary rights.
9. You are less than human.
10. You are evil.
11. You are demonic.

The eleven points all represent approaches to marking or evaluating difference. Each statement is a distillation of the logic behind statements we have heard or seen in the context of religious proclamation or controversy. Each point might also find expression in some other settings where difference becomes contentious, especially if that difference involves making truth claims and moral judgments. Conflict between competing political ideologies, for example, could involve most or all of these points. For our purposes, however, we do not mean to go beyond the sphere of religion in Northern Ireland.

Before we discuss the individual statements, however, we need to develop several ideas necessary for thinking about whether or not a religious idea is sectarian. We need also to issue a kind of health warning to readers at this point: what follows is complex and difficult – necessarily, we believe – and it will not be of interest to everyone. Put simply, our case concerning truth claims can be framed as a plea for another application of bifocal vision, in this case on a green light and an amber light. The green light is in recognition that making truth claims is an ordinary and necessary part of being human. As such, most truth claims have nothing inherently sectarian about them, so people should relax and be confident about what they are undertaking. The amber light, however, is an acknowledgment that a few types of religious ideas have sectarianism built into them and, in a situation marked by long-established sectarianism, many kinds of statements can have sectarian implications – unintended, but still potentially damaging. Therefore, making truth claims in a positive way, so they are not undermined or tainted by sectarianism, requires real care. In the matter of making religious truth claims, bifocal vision requires a stance of caution and confidence.

CATEGORIES OF DISCERNMENT:
HARDENING BOUNDARIES, DEHUMANISING, AND IMPOSING

Our definition, as developed in chapter three, identifies sectarianism in terms of five destructive patterns of relating: hardening boundaries; overlooking; belittling, dehumanising, or demonising; dominating; and physically or verbally intimidating or attacking. For the sake of relative simplicity, however, we are not going to apply these categories directly to religious ideas. Instead we will use one of the five as it stands and subsume the remaining four into two broader categories. Thus the consequence or implication that makes a religious idea sectarian is likely to fall under one of three headings: it hardens boundaries between groups, it dehumanises another group, or it imposes on another group.

The three headings can be understood as running on a continuum from least to most destructive. It is possible, after all, to harden boundaries without dehumanising or imposing, and it is even possible to dehumanise without imposing. In fact, however, the three are easily linked: when boundaries are hardened, it is easier to dehumanise others; when others are dehumanised, it is easier to justify imposing on them.

While recognising the clear continuity between these three categories, we are also concerned to emphasise the stark difference between them. These are not just three different markers of sectarianism, each denotes a significantly, even exponentially, more destructive type of sectarianism than the last.

Hardening boundaries
Hardening boundaries is genuinely a problem. Preventing people from dealing imaginatively and constructively with difference,

hardened boundaries are fundamental to allowing and nurturing all other forms of sectarianism. At the same time, hardening boundaries is not only less damaging than dehumanising and imposing, it is sectarian in a different way. The very same idea or activity that sometimes serves to harden boundaries can also be in other circumstances a legitimate and necessary means of building, nurturing, or maintaining identity. Quite subtle variations in application, perspective, and motivation, but above all in context, make the difference. In fact a practice that serves the positive function of strengthening boundaries can simultaneously harden boundaries in a damaging way. Education segregated on a religious basis is an example we have used before and will use again. Practised in a society not marked by sectarianism, church-based education serves the faith community running it and need have no negative repercussions. But practised in a sectarian society, in exactly the same way, for the same reasons, and even with the same community-building benefits, it will inevitably have sectarian implications that need attending to – i.e. it can easily harden boundaries and therefore reinforce the sectarian system.

Hardening boundaries, then, is the softest and most subtle of our three categories. Given the efficiency of the sectarian system in employing positive, well-intended ideas and activities to nurture sectarianism, hardening boundaries is so close to inevitable that even the diligently aware are unlikely to avoid it entirely. In fact overly scrupulous efforts at purity on this matter are likely to lead sequentially to paralysis, revulsion, reaction, and apathy. What can reasonably be expected of people, we believe, is to be alert to unintended sectarian consequences and to mitigate them as far as possible.

Dehumanising
No such subtlety applies to dehumanising. Dehumanising takes in all those ways of thinking and acting that lead people to regard others as wholly wrong or wholly evil and, even more, as incapable of change and therefore beyond any practical redemption – which clears the way for varieties of degrading treatment outside the ordinary framework of rights. 'Incapable of change' is the key element here, because growth and change are essential to human being. Therefore, when a group has been judged incapable of change, they have been dehumanised in a fundamental

way. If one group applies to another the rhetoric of 'wholly evil' or 'wholly wrong' but still allows that the other is capable of positive change, then they have not fully dehumanised the other group; if, on the other hand, a group eschews the rhetoric of 'wholly evil' or 'wholly wrong' but nonetheless effectively believes and acts as if the other is incapable of change, then they have actually dehumanised the other group. If dehumanising, like hardening boundaries, arises as a distortion of positive human needs, the distortion is more grotesque and destructive, and the distance from the positive human need much greater. Where hardening boundaries can sometimes coexist with the positive function of strengthening boundaries, dehumanising has no such counterpart. Dehumanising has no positive purpose and therefore needs to be eliminated from moral practice, not merely mitigated.

Imposing

Imposing combines sectarian intent and will with the power to do something about it. Imposing is about bringing into practical effect the destructive ideas and attitudes of sectarianism. In its strongest, hardest forms, imposition involves the power of the state or the power of violence. Because no person or group is ever entirely without power, however, imposition can also take less dramatic forms.

Like dehumanising, imposing has no positive function and must therefore be eliminated, not mitigated. But just as dehumanising is a sharply different kind of sectarianism than is hardening boundaries, so imposing is another leap beyond dehumanising. Imposing is sectarianism in its most acute form. After all, if one group constructed rigid boundaries to guard against contact with another, or even if the first group believed insulting, dehumanising things about the other, the second group might be regretful, concerned, and perhaps angry, but the offensive beliefs would not necessarily have any great effect them. It's their problem, not ours, the offended party might say. When the first group imposes on the other, however, what could previously be dismissed as 'their problem' can no longer be so easily distanced. The difference between dehumanising and imposing is the difference between having racist attitudes on the one hand and subjecting others to racist legislation or attack on the other.

Because imposition is the sharp edge of sectarianism, at once its consummation and the aspect that does the greatest and most lasting damage, an especially important aspect of the context in which religious truth claims are made is the relationship between the Christian churches and imposition. Two historical counter-truths need to be borne in mind when considering this issue. The first truth is that for much of their history, the Christian churches have been only too happy to employ coercive imposition in its strongest, crudest form: state imposition. Hence the legacy of crusades, inquisitions, forced conversions and baptisms, and a range of advantages given by the state to established churches, including state-imposed tithes and legal sanctions against dissenters. This is a sad story with what appears to be a happy ending, because little of the practice of imposition remains, nor would it any longer be justified in theory. The taint will linger for a time, however, and while it does, it must be one consideration whenever Christians think strategically about how they make truth claims and how they will be received.

The counter-truth is that imposition has no basis in Christianity's original teachings and early development, as recorded in the Bible. Not only do the teachings of Jesus and of New Testament writers not justify imposition, the strong and consistent tendency of Jesus' life, witness, and death, and of New Testament teaching generally, is a powerful refutation of imposition. If Christianity has had a primary, principled justification of its embrace of imposition, it comes not from the Bible, but from Augustine's doctrine that error has no right. Attempting to make a biblical case for state compulsion in religious matters, Augustine resorted to a twisted interpretation of one of Jesus' parables. Illustrating how the kingdom of God is open to all, Jesus told a story about a person of some standing in his community who held a great banquet. He first invited his equally privileged friends, but they all excused themselves for a variety of reasons, economic and social. Now the host changed his tack. Instead of throwing a party for the privileged, he told his slave to go out into the surrounding countryside and bring the people of no account. When this had been done, there were still places at the banquet, so the master said, 'Go out into the roads and lanes, and compel people to come in, so that my house may be filled.' (Lk 14:23) The intent of the parable and the larger context of Jesus' ministry make an absurdity of Augustine's effort to use the word 'compel' here as justification for state coercion for religious purposes. That so great a genius and profound a Christian should be reduced to so shoddy an argument demonstrates the essential poverty of his case. Christians need go no further than their own origins to find the remedy for their shameful and destructive historical dalliance with imposition.

Without attempting to go into the problem in depth, we need also to recognise more subtle, although not necessarily less difficult, potential for imposition where a particular church is in a majority situation. The overwhelming Catholic majority in the Republic of Ireland provides some stark examples, perhaps none more difficult than the debate over abortion. Were Catholics to say, 'This is a Catholic country, so Catholic social teaching should be enshrined in our law and constitution', this would clearly be imposition and therefore sectarian. The argument of the Catholic Church, however, is not based on sectarian considerations but on the conviction that a ban on abortion serves the common good. But for those who advocate a more liberal regime, a restrictive one is likely to look like imposition and therefore sectarian; they will see only that a majority has had its way and care little about the majority's rationale. No easy answer to the problem presents itself. Where is the line between sectarian imposition and the appropriate rights of majorities?

A spirit of imposition
We need to outline one particular variation on the theme of imposition. Not crude, explicit imposition in this case, but a spirit of imposition, which will be received by others as arrogance and presumption and can taint beliefs and practices that do not inherently impose.

A spirit of imposition is closely linked to a stunted and distorted expression of two basic and complementary human needs: the need to belong and the need for freedom to be different. Healthy expressions of these needs require groups to engage in a process of observing, constructing, and negotiating difference. While this process might be defined in various ways, we want to note at least three stages that we regard as essential.

(1) The first stage involves the linked activities of observation, discernment, evaluation, and judgment, applied both externally to other groups and internally to one's own group. Thus a group forms its identity by a cyclical process of looking out-

ward to note and evaluate what others are and are not, then turning inward to note and evaluate – and to compare – what one's own group is and is not, then looking outward again. What is crucial is that identity is necessarily formed in relationship, however minimal, to others. In distorted forms, this is the 'negative identity' referred to by Marc Gopin or the 'identity-in-opposition' analysed by Alan Falconer. Of necessity, however, the formation of positive identity entails understanding *that* we are not you, *how* we are not you, and *why* we are not you.

(2) As this outward / inward cycle develops, it leads to a second stage of informal negotiation with others and, out of that negotiation, reconstructing or refining one's understanding of one's own identity, others' difference, and the relation between them.

(3) A third stage involves agreement – probably informal and even unspoken – with others about where the boundaries of difference and similarity between groups lie.

We need to stress what we mean and do not mean by three key terms in this process: relationship, negotiation, and agreement. Each term might reasonably be taken to mean something more formal and comprehensive than we intend for our immediate purposes. 'Relationship' can suggest something explicitly agreed and mutually understood between two parties, while both 'negotiation' and 'agreement' carry overtones suggesting formal, long, detailed, and exhaustive processes. For any reader thinking of these issues in respect of another group that is despised for understandable reasons, such meanings of relationship, negotiation, and agreement might seem like an intolerable and unbearable burden. For our current purposes, however, relationship, negotiation, and agreement can be informal, implicit, and minimal practices. Relationship with another group can mean as little as recognising that it exists, accompanied by some willingness and capacity to take it into account in an honest way. As for negotiation and agreement, they are likely to be informal and unspoken practices, done indirectly and implicitly rather than through face-to-face contact.

This three-stage process does not yield fixed and final results. Context shifts, others shift, parties shift, their perceptions of each other shift, meaning that this whole process of establishing a sense of belonging and of difference is a fluid one. Stages one, two, and three may well overlap and recur. What it means to be Protestant or Catholic in Northern Ireland, for example, may include elements that are stable over a long period of time, but both will also change significantly. Research summarised by John Whyte in *Interpreting Northern Ireland* makes the point graphically. In 1968, on the eve of the Troubles, 76% of Catholics identified their national identity as Irish, with 15% calling themselves British and 5% identifying with Ulster. Protestants were spread more evenly over three national identities: 20% Irish, 39% British, and 32% Ulster, while 6% (along with 3% of Catholics) labelled themselves as 'sometimes British; sometimes Irish'. Just ten years later, after a decade of conflict and violence, the numbers had changed dramatically. The number of Catholics identifying themselves actually fell to 69%, and those calling themselves British stayed at 15%, while Ulster and British/Irish categories rose to 6% and 8% respectively. Protestant change was more dramatic. The number of Protestants willing to call themselves Irish shrunk to 8% and Ulster fell to 20%, while the British category shot up to 67%. A 1986 survey introduced a new category, Northern Irish, which proved immediately attractive. A full 20% of Catholics opted to identify themselves as Northern Irish (along with 1% Ulster); 11% of Protestants chose Northern Irish, in addition to 14% who identified themselves as Ulster. This 1986 survey also saw a further erosion of the Irish percentage – to just 3% among Protestants and down to 61% for Catholics.[5] While the specific causes of these shifts are not easily identified, the mere fact of the shifts graphically illustrates the impact of changes in context, priorities, and perceptions on what a particular identity means at any particular point.

What matters most for our immediate purposes is that the fluid nature of identity arises as a consequence of the inherent element of relationship in identity formation. No identity at all can be formed entirely in isolation from others, even if this does not go beyond the rudimentary sense that 'we are not you.' Beyond this, the element of relationship in stages two and three means that healthy identity continues to rely on relationship at every stage.

We want to suggest here that a spirit of imposition arises when a person or group attempts to cut out the necessary element of relationship in identity formation and attempts to make it an entirely internal process. In other words, it is a process that is essentially stuck in one part of the first stage, entirely ignoring the elements of negotiation and agreement in the second and third stages and substituting a unilateral declaration of what constitutes the difference between parties and its significance.

A spirit of imposition is effectively the opposite of a spirit of mitigation. Where mitigation lessens the damage of a sectarian or potentially sectarian situation, a spirit of imposition is likely to increase the danger or damage. It is always hard, for example, to be on the receiving end of the judgment 'we are right and you are wrong,' the third of the eleven statements we will examine below. But if the group making that judgment has entered into a relationship with the judged party, sufficient for the judged to accept at least that those judging really do understand them, and the differences and similarities between them, then the judgment at least feels sufficiently based on reality that the group judged to be wrong can understand how the judgment was arrived at, even though they cannot accept it. The focus of disagreement is on the content of the judgment, because the process seems to have a basic integrity. If, however, a group hears 'we are right and you are wrong' from another group with which they have no relationship, their anger is as likely to focus on a sense of arrogance and imposition – how do you know? on what basis do you make that judgment? what right do you have? – as on the actual content of the disagreement.

A spirit of imposition not only does an injustice to the party being judged, it fundamentally distorts the judgment involved and therefore damages the group doing the judging. The judgment is distorted because judgments made unilaterally are most unlikely to be accurate. In fact, when the process of judgment, as a part of identity formation and affirmation, continues outside the context of relationship over a long period, the judgment is likely to become increasingly unrelated to reality, taking on a life of its own without any checking mechanism. Joe recalls being part of a conversation with two evangelicals, one an older man from Northern Ireland, the other a young man from the Republic. The Northern Protestant had an image of the Republic, derived from a fairly detailed knowledge of incidents like the Mother and Child Scheme and Fethard-on-Sea controversies of the 1950s, as a country dominated by triumphalist and oppressive Catholicism and hostile to and dangerous for Protestants. When the younger man, Dublin-born and based, protested that the Republic had changed a great deal and that young Protestants were entirely at home there and happy to identify themselves as Irish, it was as if the older man heard nothing, merely repeating the same set of stories that buttressed his perception of the Republic. Those stories had a fixed and necessary role in his construction of identity, and the absence of relationships that might provide evidence against which to test them had left him with perceptions impervious to changing reality.

The integrity of truth claims depends on relationship. Extending this, we can also say that developing and nurturing a healthy identity depends on truth claims made in the context of relationship. When truth claims are made outside that context, they are increasingly likely to take on an element of self-serving fantasy, and consequently the related aspects of identity are distorted and stunted.

A standard of discernment: three questions

Using the headings of hardening boundaries, dehumanising, and imposing, we have formulated three questions to provide a basis for assessing whether a religious idea or its expression is sectarian.

* Does an idea contain within it a logic that inherently hardens boundaries, dehumanises, or imposes?
* Does an idea contain within it a logic that *can* or *does* contribute – though not necessarily – to hardening boundaries, dehumanising, or imposing?
* Was an idea expressed in a way that hardens boundaries, dehumanises, or imposes?

If the answer to all three questions is 'no,' then no sectarianism is involved. If the answer to one or more questions is 'yes,' then the process has identified a problem that must be addressed. In the case of each question, however, a 'yes' answer requires slightly different responses.

Returning to the theme of relationship, as developed above, we must emphasise that meaningful answers to the three questions cannot be obtained by means exclusively internal to the group answering them; they require some kind of relationship to the parties potentially affected. In its most minimal form – and in a society marked by the pain and trauma of endemic conflict, the minimal form will, at times, be asking a lot – the necessary relationship would at least involve observing the consequences for that group. If possible, a more adequate alternative might involve indirect access to that group through an intermediary, and ideally the questions will be answered on the basis of direct contact. In general, the greater the extent and quality of the relationship, the greater the integrity of the answer.

Does an idea contain within it a logic that inherently hardens boundaries, dehumanises, or imposes? If the idea is shown somehow to have inherently destructive consequences, three basic questions must be considered.

* Can the idea be discarded?
* If it cannot be discarded, can it be altered in a way that removes those consequences?
* If it cannot be discarded or altered, can the negative consequences be mitigated in any way?

The process of mitigation, as developed in the last chapter, will be crucial throughout the rest of this one, and it is the bottom line in answering this question. If a group cannot or will not discard, alter, or mitigate, then their intention to deal with sectarianism is at least called into question. The possibility arises that the group is willingly and consciously embracing sectarian attitudes and behaviour.

Does an idea contain within it a logic that can *or* does *contribute – though not necessarily – to hardening boundaries, dehumanising, or imposing?* In the case of a 'yes' answer here, exactly the same issues of discarding, altering, or mitigating arise. Because in this case the idea involved is only potentially sectarian, not inherently sectarian, a positive response, especially a mitigating response, ought to be easier. A problem arises, however. As discussed above, in a divided society suffering long-term conflict, ideas and practices that might be benign elsewhere can have negative consequences.

In particular, a whole range of positive identity-forming and affirming activities can have the consequence, probably unintended, of hardening boundaries. We used the example of church-based education, but a host of church and pastoral activities might serve as well. Because ideas and activities like these are positively intended, because they are not inherently sectarian, and because they contribute 'only' to hardening boundaries – which is not as immediately or obviously damaging as dehumanising or imposing – the need to address the issues they raise will be

less obvious. Because this dynamic – positive intentions sub-
verted by a sectarian context – shapes the meaning of so many
well-intended ideas and activities, the will to address their sectarian implications may flag. Nonetheless, dealing with such
issues goes to the heart of what it will mean for the churches to
make their most important contribution to dealing with
sectarianism. First and foremost, theirs will not be the relatively
immediate, public, and exciting work of challenging flamboyant
sectarianism, negotiating with paramilitaries, or lobbying politicians. Their fundamental work will involve the much more low-
key and long-term tasks of making sure that building community
means building bridges as well as walls. There will be little
drama in it, and the required virtues will be not so much
courage in the face of danger as a vision of peace and the perseverance and patience to pursue it.

*Was an idea expressed in a way that hardens boundaries, dehuman-
ises, or imposes?* A 'yes' answer to this third question requires a
different kind of response. This is a problem of communication,
and the content of the idea goes to the background. What comes
to the fore, even more than with the second question, is the context of a divided society in long-term conflict and the way this
shapes how those hearing a truth claim actually receive it. If
some kind of relationship is necessary to answer any of these
three questions with integrity, it is absolutely paramount in this
case.

With any form of communication, the intent of the speaker
matters, of course. In the case of sectarianism, we need to ask,
did the speaker intend to harden boundaries, dehumanise, or
impose? On the surface, the question is fairly easily answered,
and the answer is almost certain to be no, the speaker had no
negative intent. But a fuller understanding of intent needs to
take in underlying motivations as well, and judging intent in
this sense is a most difficult task, simply because of the near impossibility of knowing the motivations of another person or
group, apart from what they state, and the problem of self-
deception when thinking about one's own motivations. Although
these problems are inescapable, they do not absolve a group
from thinking as honestly as possible about whether imposition
is any part of its intentions. Two possible structural aids to improve the quality of such reflection take us back to the importance of relationship: reflect in groups rather than as individuals,

and seek to know how others, including opponents, see one's intentions.

In theory if not in practice, knowing how a truth claim is received is simpler than knowing intentions. It involves hearing from recipients whether they perceive any sectarianism in the truth claim being made and understanding the context in which the claim is made and received. The recipient's perception on its own does not determine whether a truth claim is sectarian. But no factor is more important. What can be said with certainty is that if the recipient of a truth claim feels that sectarianism has been involved, then it has to some extent become a sectarian problem – the content of that problem may be no more than that the long-term presence of sectarianism predisposes people to see everything through a sectarian filter, but that still leaves a problem that it would not be wise to avoid.

With sectarianism, as in many areas of life, certain kinds of experiences make it all but impossible for some people to hear certain ideas from certain other people. This general truth has no more direct and potent instance than that people who have been abused, or perceive themselves to have been abused, will have difficulty hearing the abuser, and endemic conflict involving a sectarian component leaves many with just claims to having been abused. In such circumstances, hearing words coming from across the boundaries of conflict is rendered at least complicated and difficult, and sometimes impossible. A historical example of this problem, which has ongoing resonances and parallels, is the nineteenth-century Protestant campaign in Ireland to convert Catholics, as discussed in chapter two. No doubt many Protestant evangelists understood their work as freely offering a gift, not as any kind of imposition. It is equally beyond doubt, however, that the characteristic thought of the time in British and Irish Protestantism about the close relationship between good religion and a good state meant that many evangelicals had mixed political and religious motives. Vigorously asserted in a context of political and religious struggle, evangelical activity would inevitably be received by many Catholics as imposition and therefore sectarian. Hence the statement by a Catholic apologist that the Bible, for Protestants the standard of truth and freedom, offered to Catholics 'without note or comment, is not less a means of Protestant dominion than the Orange Yeoman's military array'.

That example comes from a time when sectarianism was written large and bold across Irish society. Much of today's sectarianism, and especially the more subtle varieties we are focussing on in this book, may turn up more often in the fine print. But the same principle applies: a context of sectarian conflict shapes how people hear and receive every communication – including religious truth claims – especially when it comes from those with whom a group is in conflict. An exchange in a cross-community group we were working with illustrates the problem. During intense work on fine-tuning a working document, a hard to define tension settled around a phrase involving the word 'solidarity'. Finally one Protestant member said that to him 'solidarity' is a Catholic word, putting a polite face on essentially tribal dynamics and reflecting a Catholic-skewed equality agenda. Catholics were dumbfounded, as it meant no such thing to them, but, at least for this thoughtful Protestant, a sectarian context had turned 'solidarity' into a sectarian word. In the ensuing conversation, a Catholic member admitted that he finds himself bridling at the phrase 'political and religious liberty' as used by Orangemen. Although he would regard himself as an advocate of political and religious liberty, a sectarian context had disposed him to hear instead a sectarian slogan. This issue could only surface because this group had a long history of friendship and working together. More typically, we suspect, such tensions sabotage communication while remaining undefined or at least unspoken. In these circumstances, anyone who genuinely wishes to communicate in a way free of sectarianism, or sensitive to sectarian implications, must pay steady and careful attention to how a sectarian context shapes what various parties hear. Without such attention, words uttered are unlikely to communicate effectively, and they may not be communication at all, amounting to little more than speaking to oneself or one's own. Every expression of a religious truth claim in a sectarian society needs to take these dynamics into account.

With these background factors in mind, we are equipped to analyse our list of eleven statements expressing different kinds of religious ideas and truth claims. The basic framework of what follows is a three-fold distinction between the first six statements, statements seven and eight, and the final three. The first six are legitimate expressions of intellectual and moral judgment and need not reflect or lead to sectarianism, although they might do so. The next two statements pose a most difficult problem:

each will have a sectarian outcome, and yet in different ways each can be, appropriately expressed and in limited circumstances, a valid expression of discernment and judgment. The last three are always and inherently sectarian.

1. We are different, we believe differently
Some versions of this statement can be nothing more than a statement of fact, an observation rather than a judgment. This is the simple, literal sense of the statement and, as such, it is anything but sectarian. The ability to recognise difference is a foundational capacity necessary for thinking creatively about living with difference, indeed for any attempt at intellectual and moral discernment about a society. What we are saying here may sound so self-evident that it will seem strange that we should bother saying it at all. Two aspects of the Northern Ireland situation make it necessary and important to affirm, however, that difference, especially religious difference, is not inherently sectarian.

The first problem is the characteristic usage of the term sectarian. For the most part, describing something as sectarian is a harsh, negative judgment. Another kind of occasional usage is more neutral and descriptive, however, making 'sectarian' more or less synonymous with 'religious'. This would not be a problem if patterns of usage allowed people to distinguish, clearly and obviously, whether the negative or the descriptive meaning was intended, but in fact we have discovered no such pattern. Instead, confusion reigns. Take for example a statement like, 'The school system in Northern Ireland is organised on a sectarian basis.' Is this a simple statement of fact, with no moral judgment intended, i.e., 'The school system in Northern Ireland is organised on a religiously-differentiated basis'? Or is it a negative judgment, i.e., 'The school system in Northern Ireland is organised on a basis that promotes destructive patterns of relating'? In fact it might mean either, or, if the speaker is someone who sees both sectarianism and religious difference as destructive, then the two statements might be understood as synonymous: to organise schools on a religiously-differentiated basis is inherently to promote destructive patterns of relating. Such ambiguous use of 'sectarian' can turn up in ordinary conversation, the media, and political discourse. It obscures and distorts the issues at hand, which is why we recommend that 'sectarian' and 'sectarianism' should be used as exclusively negative terms.

A second problem revisits the issue of context. In settings where difference is handled constructively, a statement that 'we are different, we believe differently' is easily accepted as no more than a simple, factual observation. Sectarianism, however, characteristically approaches difference, especially religious and political difference, with suspicion and in judgment. In Northern Ireland, therefore, an effect of the sectarian system can be that statements that are a version of 'we are different' sometimes carry resonances of statements further down our eleven-point list, loading them with overtones of negative judgment and triumphalist superiority, whether the hearer imposes this meaning or the speaker actively intends it or surreptitiously or unconsciously implies it. In a sectarian society, handling difference well can mean that the simplest observations about difference need to be made sensitively and perhaps accompanied by disclaimers. They need also to be received with a generous spirit, slow to take offence.

Approaches to the significance of religious difference need to be bounded by two considerations. First, those who are suspicious of religious difference need to recognise that it does not always produce destructive patterns of relating; therefore religious difference is not inherently sectarian. The need for the freedom to be different is the necessary complement of the human need to belong. In bewildering varieties, people construct social difference, define identity in terms of those differences, set boundaries around them, and negotiate relations between them. Religious difference is, in one sense, simply one among many variations on the themes of belonging and difference. Critics of religious difference and its manifestations need to demonstrate specific destructive outcomes to make their point; merely observing the fact of religious difference is not sufficient. A common practical example concerns evaluating the significance of religiously segregated education in Northern Ireland. People offended by segregated education need to show how this is problematic rather than assuming that it is inherently problematic simply by virtue of being based on religious difference.

A second consideration requires equal emphasis. Those who find themselves defending religious difference need to recognise that it does sometimes lead to destructive patterns of relating; therefore religious difference is potentially sectarian. This potential

sectarianism requires defenders of religious difference to address at least two basic issues. First, it is not enough simply to assert that religious difference is not inherently sectarian.
Defenders must recognise that it does sometimes have destructive outcomes, and when it does they need to demonstrate
rather than assume that this sectarianism is not necessary or inherent. Such a demonstration must involve showing how the
sectarian outcome can be or could have been different – perhaps
positive and at least not destructive. Second, it is not enough to
note that religious difference is one among many varieties, defenders must also recognise that religious difference is a special
variety. What makes religious difference distinct from other
kinds of difference is that it often involves factors that are non-
negotiable because they are linked to understandings of divinity
and ultimate reality. This non-negotiability factor is so basic that
there is a case for defining a person's actual, practical religion as
that which one cannot or will not negotiate, as we noted in
chapter one. Non-negotiability is one reason why strongly held
commitments that are not overtly religious – perhaps political,
ecological, or social – can take on a quasi-religious cast and dynamic. Non-negotiables create special problems, and defenders
of religious difference must face up to those problems.

2. We are right
3. We are right and you are wrong
While the first statement grows out of and reflects the categories
of identity, belonging, and difference, these second and third
statements express the human need to understand what is true
and right, intellectually and morally. Again we need to assert
what ought to be blindingly obvious: making religious truth
claims, intellectual or moral, is not inherently sectarian.
However, because so much of sectarianism has roots in truth
claims badly and destructively made, what ought to be obvious
is far from obvious, and making truth claims – especially religious truth claims – is widely regarded as an inherently sectarian
activity. In fact, making truth claims, and judgments based on
them, is a normal, necessary, and constant part of life for every
intellectually and morally conscious person.

In its most basic form, the need to know 'what is true' is the
need to know 'what is', the way things are. Consistent, workable
answers to this question are essential to helping people negotiate

their way through life, indeed to maintaining sanity. A need to
know 'how' and 'why' follow immediately in the train of the
need to know 'what is', and taken together answers to these
questions concerning what is, how, and why form essential aspects of the framework that mediates experience of life. Beyond
these questions, human existence as social beings brings with it
a need to know what is right in a moral sense if any set of relationships – interpersonal, social, or political – is to flourish. Thus
moral truth claims are concerned overwhelmingly with the
structure of relationships, welding moral aspects to that mediat-
ing framework. The connected needs to know what is true and
what is right are inescapable aspects of being human.

In some people or for a period of time, the desire and need to
understand what is true may, at least in part, atrophy or be suppressed by external forces, but it will always reassert itself. The
desire and need to understand what is right may be embodied in
moral values varying widely over time and from place to place,
but every set of relationships – informal or formal, small or large
– will include moral standards as part of its structure, usually in
a conscious, formal way, but at least informally. Whether it is
claims about washing powders, political candidates, social behaviour, or religious beliefs, assessing the truthfulness and the
relative merits of these claims is a regular part of human life.
Certainly anyone reading this passage is likely to be motivated,
at least in part if not wholly, by a desire to understand the truth
about sectarianism, and evaluating the truthfulness of what we
are saying will be part of the process of reading. Furthermore,
the desire to understand is likely to be linked to a moral concern
about what sectarianism does to individuals and groups. In
matters great and small, the processes of discerning truth and
making moral judgments are embedded as a regular part of day-
to-day lives.

'We are right' and 'we are right and you are wrong,' the two
statements under consideration in this section, are expressions
of these fundamental human needs to understand what is true
and to make moral judgments. As such, they are not inherently
sectarian – nothing in them necessarily involves or leads to
hardening of boundaries, dehumanising, or imposing. At the
same time, these statements, and statements built on the same
logic, can have many shades of meaning, more or less open to
the possibility of sectarian implications.

The second statement, 'we are right,' is more open-ended and ambiguous than the third, 'we are right and you are wrong.' When a group asserts that what it believes or does is right, this may or may not imply a judgment about what others believe or do. 'We are right' can have at least the following meanings.

1. Our way is right, but other ways are, or at least may be, equally valid.

2. Our way is right, and we are not really interested in other ways of doing things – we make no judgment about them, one way or the other.

3. Our way is right, and it is better than yours, although yours is not without some merit.

4. Our way is right, your way is wrong.

Of course the statement 'we are right' leaves unarticulated the negative judgment of others in the last two meanings. Different reasons as to why the judgment has been left unspoken give further possible shades of meaning, as in the following examples.

5. We are right and you are wrong – but in this one particular area, so we do not emphasise this, because you and we have a great deal in common in other areas.

6. We are right and you are wrong – but out of concern and respect for the relationship between us, and in hope of living in harmony, we have no wish to stress this.

7. We are right and you are wrong – contemptibly, dangerously wrong, but we cannot say so, perhaps because it would be dangerous, or at least politically incorrect or socially unacceptable, if we did.

The third statement, 'we are right and you are wrong,' may seem to leave a narrower range of interpretations than the second, because it makes negative judgment of others explicit. Even so, why that judgment has been articulated in this case rather than left unspoken does open up quite different possible shades of meaning.

8. We have chosen to say that you are wrong because it puts the relationship between us on a more honest basis.

9. We have chosen to say that you are wrong because we are so enthused about what we believe and do that we hope you will accept it, too.

10. We have chosen to say that you are wrong because it is our duty to denounce error or expose injustice.

11. We need to stress that you are wrong because we would

	Hardening boundaries			Dehumanising			Imposing		
	does	could	mitigates or could mitigate	does	could (or * = could allow)	mitigates or could mitigate	does	could (or * = could allow)	mitigates or could mitigate
1.			✓		✓	✓			✓
2.		✓			✓			*	
3.		✓	✓		*	✓		*	
4.		✓	✓					*	✓
5.		✓	✓			✓			✓
6.	✓	✓	✓		✓	✓		✓	✓
7.		✓						✓	
8.		✓	✓			✓			
9.		✓						*	✓
10.	✓				*			*	
11.	✓				✓			*	
12.	✓				✓		✓		

be uncertain about our rightness if we were not certain of your wrongness.

12. We need to stress that you are wrong because we are in a struggle with you, and the conviction of not only our rightness but your wrongness strengthens us in that struggle.

Clearly these two statements can carry many shades of meaning, depending on the speaker's intent, the hearer's disposition, the way they are made, and the context in which they are uttered.

In a way exactly parallel to approaches to the significance of religious difference, critics and defenders of religious truth claims need to justify rather than merely assert their convictions. The necessary starting point is to recognise the two poles between which this debate is properly conducted: because truth claims do not always produce destructive patterns of relating, they are not inherently sectarian; because truth claims sometimes do have this negative consequence, they are potentially sectarian. From this stance, particular statements and instances can be analysed. Sweeping generalisations will not do. Critics need to show how certain truth claims, either inherently or in the way they are made, cause, nurture, or allow destructive patterns of relating, i.e. sectarianism. Defenders need to recognise cases in which truth claims have been made in a sectarian way or yielded sectarian consequences and then think through whether that claim can be made in a benign way, whether sectarian consequences can be avoided or mitigated, and, if so, how they can be avoided or mitigated.

We have identified twelve possible meanings of the statements 'we are right' and 'we are right and you are wrong.' Applying the standards of hardening boundaries, dehumanising, and imposing to these meanings yields a mix of results (see table). We have asked of each meaning: does it harden boundaries, dehumanise, or impose? Could it harden boundaries, dehumanise, or impose? Does it or could it mitigate the possibility of hardening boundaries, dehumanising, or imposing? From our own answers to these questions, we draw the following observations about different meanings of truth claims. While we recognise that others might answer these questions differently than we do, we hope that our answers will correspond sufficiently for our observations to be useful.

a. Of the twelve meanings, only the first one – our way is right, but other ways are, or at least may be, equally valid – both does not and could not have sectarian consequences. In fact, this statement could have a mitigating effect, lessening the sectarian dynamics of a situation by relativising the differences between parties. This does not mean that we imagine some perfect world in which all truth claims are framed in this way. No such world is possible, because it is in the nature of truth claims that some of them will be exclusive, or at least that not all can be equally valid. It is useful, however, if some truth claims take this form, as they can have a mitigating effect on negative consequences that could follow from other, more definite claims. If none of a person's truth claims take this form, it suggests an incapacity to make nuanced distinctions of judgment and an unhealthy tendency to absolutise everything he believes.

b. Of the twelve meanings, numbers seven, ten, eleven, and twelve do inherently have sectarian consequences:

7. We are right and you are wrong – contemptibly, dangerously wrong, but we cannot say so, perhaps because it would be dangerous, or at least politically incorrect or socially unacceptable if we did;

10. We have chosen to say that you are wrong because it is our duty to denounce error or expose injustice;

11. We need to stress that you are wrong because we would be uncertain about our rightness if we were not certain of your wrongness;

12. We need to stress that you are wrong because we are in a struggle with you, and the conviction of not only our rightness but your wrongness strengthens us in that struggle.

Each of the four has within it an inherent effect of hardening boundaries. Number twelve is also inherently imposing, because it does explicitly what some other meanings might imply or allow: it takes the truth claim out of the arena of different and competing truth claims, subordinates it to a broader power struggle, and makes it a weapon in that struggle.

Of these four meanings, seven, eleven, and twelve seem to us neither to have any positive function nor to be redeemable. But number ten – *we have chosen to say that you are wrong because it is our duty to denounce error or expose injustice* – is quite different. It belongs with the other three, because it does have an inherently sectarian consequence: denounce the errors of others or expose their injustice, and it will harden boundaries. At the same time, there are errors that need denouncing and injustices that must be exposed, so truth claims with this meaning, unlike the other three, will be necessary. If the denouncer or exposer is really committed to truth and justice, therefore, she must be prepared to take steps that will mitigate the inevitable hardening of boundaries. This mitigation might take various forms, but one obvious possibility is to make sure that the denouncing and exposing take place in the context of some form of positive relationship with the group in question. This allows the possibility of focussing on the particular error or injustice instead of effectively denouncing the group as comprehensively in error or unjust. Other forms of mitigation might be effective as well. In the absence of any efforts to mitigate, however, the truth and justice in question are likely to be reduced to merely tribal truth and justice and, as such, simply one more weapon in the struggle between contesting groups.

c. Working with this table, we decided that the 'could' categories required a possible second kind of meaning. An ordinary tick ($\sqrt{}$) means that this statement has within it a logic that could, but need not necessarily, harden boundaries, dehumanise or impose. With some of the statements, however, while they do not explicitly contain such a logic, they seemed to us, in the way they are framed, to leave open the possibility of hardening boundaries, dehumanising, or imposing, or even to point in that direction, i.e. they 'could allow' these consequences. This 'could allow' judgment is indicated by an asterisk (*). Six meanings – two, three, four, nine, ten, eleven – fall in this 'could allow' category. All could allow imposing, and two of them could also allow dehumanising, we judged.

d. Concerning four meanings –

3. Our way is right, and it is better than yours, although yours is not without some merit;

5. We are right and you are wrong – but in this one particular area, so we do not emphasise this, because you and we have a great deal in common in other areas;

6. We are right and you are wrong – but out of concern and respect for the relationship between us, and in hope of living in harmony, we have no wish to stress this;

8. We have chosen to say that you are wrong because it puts the relationship between us on a more honest basis

– we judged that while they could harden boundaries or dehumanise, they were also framed in such a way that they mitigate or could mitigate the effects of hardening boundaries, dehumanising, and imposing. Three features seem to supply this potentially mitigating effect. First, what each meaning shares is an intrinsic respect for the other group, even though some aspect of its life is being judged comparatively and negatively. Second, they also share (though this is only implicit in number three) a concern for the relationship with the other group. Third, meanings three and four allow for two different ways of relativising the difference and disagreement between us. In the case of meaning three, the relativising follows from recognising that the difference between us is in this case the difference between good and better, not between good and bad. In meaning four, the difference in question may be very sharp, but it is contextualised as a particular area of difference amid important areas of agreement.

The implication of these four meanings, each involving both negative judgment and mitigation, is very important. If, as we noted earlier, some statements not inherently sectarian can be tainted with sectarian meanings by a spirit of imposition, other potentially sectarian statements can have a mitigating effect because they are made in a spirit of respect and of seeking a common good. In one sense this frees people making truth claims. Not only are such claims not inherently sectarian, they can be made, with the right attitude and skills, in a way that mitigates possible sectarian outcomes. At the same time, it puts a responsibility on those same people. If the possibility of making truth claims in a way that mitigates destructive outcomes is once recognised, then the absence of any mitigating aspects suggests that a group is unconcerned about sectarian consequences. It further suggests that the group may have put advocacy of truth at the service of a tribal cause, thus making it an instrument of imposition. Where the possibility of making truth claims in a spirit of respect or even reconciliation is known but not grasped, it nullifies cries of innocent intent and suggests that the offenders are operating out of a spirit of imposition.

4. *You are a less adequate version of what we are*
5. *You are not what you say you are*
6. *We are in fact what you say you are*
In discussing the first three statements, we have dealt with the basics. The first statement, 'we are different, we believe differently,' covers the categories of difference, identity, and belonging.

The second and third statements, 'we are right' and 'we are right and you are wrong,' cover the areas of intellectual and moral truth, and belief generally. Most religious ideas are likely to fall somewhere within these categories of belonging and belief, as do the final eight statements in our list of eleven. What these eight statements offer, then, is not new categories, but significant variations.

Statements four, five, and six fit together because they derive from the peculiar tensions arising when groups are in some way claiming a single legacy. Specifically, the three statements carry a particular sting because the shared but contested framework of Christian faith introduces the dynamics of sibling rivalry. In fact the statements are really only possible by virtue of a common and close framework. If, for example, the groups involved in a conflict were Marxist and Christian, these particular claims and counter-claims would not arise at all. Whatever the relationship between Marxism and Christianity, they are manifestly not versions of one another, less adequate or otherwise; the occasion or motivation to declare that 'you are not what you say are' is unlikely to arise; and 'we are in fact what you say you are' would be nonsense.

In Northern Ireland, however, the fact that the religious groups involved are all Christian churches shapes the characteristic tone of sectarian conflict. A shared religious framework is not intrinsically contentious. Churches could take the stance, for example, that the differences between them are of no great consequence, and so each stands in an equal relationship with the Christian faith. But some people will and do judge that the differences between churches are of real importance. Consequently, they believe that one church is a more faithful expression of the Christian faith than are others. Certainly for most of post-Reformation Irish history, this has been the typical stance of the churches toward one another, not only between Catholics and Protestants, but also between the various Protestant churches. In its sharpest expression, this has taken the form of saying that another church, or all other churches, cannot properly be considered Christian churches at all. Well into this century, this has been the dominant stance, hence statements five and six: 'You are not what you say you are,' 'We are in fact what you say you are.' It remains a significant stance, especially among conservative Protestants toward the Catholic church, and by the Catholic

Church toward all Protestant churches. The official Catholic stance was stated clearly in the document known as *Dominus Iesus*, issued by the Vatican's Congregation for the Doctrine of the Faith in August 2000. The Catholic Church has no difficulty accepting the Christian integrity of individual Protestants, or even of the Protestant Churches themselves, which 'have by no means been deprived of significance and importance in the mystery of salvation. For the spirit of Christ has not refrained from using them as means of salvation.'[6] Catholics are not, however, to view the Protestant churches as 'sister churches', as Cardinal Joseph Ratzinger made clear in a letter, issued a month before *Dominus Iesus*, to the presidents of conferences of bishops throughout the Catholic Church.[7] Despite their spiritual merits, Protestant Churches, according to *Dominus Iesus*, 'suffer from defects' and are therefore 'not churches in the proper sense', but 'ecclesial communities'. '[T]he Church of Christ, despite the divisions which exist among Christians, continues to exist fully only in the Catholic Church.'[8] From the Second Vatican Council onward, emphasis on the value of Protestant faith and churches has been meant to have a mitigating effect on the harshest effects of Catholic claims to superiority, and certainly the inter-church climate today is far more generous and less strident than it was prior to Vatican II. Nonetheless, the propositions 'you are not what you say you are' and 'we are in fact what you say you are' could not be more clearly articulated than they are in official Catholic teaching about the Protestant Churches.

Despite the ongoing significance of statements five and six, in recent times a softer form of judgment has come to the fore, in which other churches are regarded as genuine Christian churches although not necessarily equal or even fully adequate. Hence statement four: 'You are a less adequate version of what we are.' Although we are aware of no formal church statement expressing this reasoning, we suspect, without being able to quantify it, that some version of this judgment may well prevail among Christians in Northern Ireland today. Indeed, Cardinal Ratzinger's very concern to clarify official Catholic teaching on the relationship of the Catholic Church to Protestantism may be an indication of the extent to which a more casual approach, in which the Protestant Churches are recognised as true churches, if not fully equal, has taken hold among many Catholics.

If these three statements –

4. *you are a less adequate version of what we are*
5. *you are not what you say you are*
6. *we are in fact what you say you are*

– belong together by virtue of deriving from a shared but contested Christian framework, number four needs to be differentiated from five and six. The issue begins with the differing sectarian implications of the statements. *You are a less adequate version of what we are* is a potentially sectarian statement, i.e. it could cause hardening of boundaries and dehumanising and, less directly, it could allow or smooth the way for imposition. But is not inherently sectarian. Admittedly, being on the receiving end of this statement is always likely to hurt to some degree. And yet if the statement is made in the context of a relationship of genuine mutual respect, the mitigation of offence can take effect more or less simultaneously. After all, the statement *you are a less adequate version of what we are* can stand alongside a real appreciation of aspects of the community being judged, including a recognition that this community has something, perhaps even much, to teach the one making the negative comparison.

Statements five and six – *you are not what you say you are* and *we are in fact what you say you are* – are potentially much more damaging. In one sense, a relationship of mutual respect could provide the same mitigating effects for statements five and six that we mentioned for statement four. There is more to mitigate, however, because statements five and six, unlike statement four, will be received as imposition: attempting to take away and arrogate to one's own group another's basic right to define for themselves who they are. But the issue is not that simple, because the group making the judgment will understand itself not as imposing, but as exercising that same right of self-definition by naming boundaries. Commitment to a group can legitimately involve making judgments about where acceptable boundaries should be drawn, and that may well involve concluding that some group claiming to be Christian falls outside those boundaries – i.e. they are not what they say they are. Understood from the point of view of the one making the statements, five and six are necessary for their exercise of their own right of self-definition.

Statements five and six represent not only a clash of rights, it is the clash of two contradictory applications of the same right.

As such, we are inclined to see these statements as potentially rather than inherently sectarian – but the potential for hardening boundaries and imposition is especially close and great. If this potential is to be thwarted, a fundamental element of mitigating the possibility of imposition will be a fine but crucial distinction between claiming the right to say *you are not what you say you are* but nonetheless recognising the right of the other party to define themselves as they wish, even if the party making the judgment objects.

For our own part, aware of the dangers that accompany these statements, our basic stance is to accept that a Christian church is a group that understands itself to be a Christian church. That leaves ample room for disagreement, even radical disagreement, about what it means to be a Christian or a Christian church, but it puts that disagreement within a context of shared faith. While this is our basic and preferred stance, we do find, however, that we sometimes encounter a group whose core convictions push beyond the boundary of what we can accept as Christian, and we must reluctantly make, or at least allow the possibility of making, the judgment, *You are not what you say you are*. Because this is a judgment to be made only with great caution and we cannot enter into the topic in depth here, we will use a distant historical example that we hope is uncontentious, the Marcionites of the early church period. The Marcionites not only emphasised the priority of the New Testament, they entirely rejected the Old Testament as describing a different and evil god. In our judgment this decision to work to a radically different canon of scripture and source of authority, reflecting a complete rejection of Christianity's Jewish roots, crosses the line between a Christian group with which we radically disagree and a group that we could not accept as Christian.

7. *What you are doing is evil*

Our seventh statement, *what you are doing is evil*, is an extension of the moral dimension of statements two and three. We have included it as a separate statement, however, because it is a radical extension. Describe something as evil instead of bad, and the stakes are raised exponentially. In one sense the difference between bad and evil can be understood as running in a straight line, so that evil is distinct from bad by virtue of being a further point on the same continuum. Evil can suggest something more, however, something less reformable, if reformable at all. What is bad, most will agree, might be redeemed; what is evil may be bound for destruction instead of redemption. This sense puts evil off the end of the continuum. For Christians, there can be the further sense that to say something is evil may suggest some link with the devil, who is, after all, in the words of the Lord's Prayer, 'the evil one,' from whom all Christians pray that they may be delivered.[9] Again, this puts evil off the end of the continuum. What is bad is likely to be simply human – our wrong choices and their destructive consequences. To say that something is evil suggests the possibility of the influence of and alignment with transpersonal evil forces.

In our judgment, *what you are doing is evil* is an inherently sectarian statement, because given its radical nature it will, inevitably, harden boundaries. It could also dehumanise, and it could allow imposition, so this is a dangerous statement. At the same time, we believe that a capacity to identify and name evil is a necessary skill in the repertoire of moral discernment. Without an ability to identify evil, a person's or group's moral vision and practice will be impaired. Alone of our first seven statements, then, *what you are doing is evil* is in the paradoxical position of being both inherently sectarian and morally necessary. This hard combination suggests at least that this is a statement to be used cautiously and sparingly. It also suggests, even more than for previous statements, the crucial importance of mitigation if the moral benefits are to outweigh the sectarian consequences.

8. You are so wrong that you forfeit ordinary rights

In our judgment, the first six statements are not inherently sectarian. Each can have potentially sectarian applications and meanings, and some are dangerous enough that they should be made only with great caution, but made in appropriate ways they can be legitimate statements. The last four statements we judge to be inherently sectarian, and in a less complex way than the seventh statement, which we found both sectarian and necessary. Unlike the first six, the last four are not statements that can be turned in a sectarian direction or have sectarian application in certain contexts. These last four express, directly and without significant exception, hardening of boundaries, dehumanising, or imposing. When a religious idea contains within it the logic of one of these last four statements, then it can be said to be inherently sectarian.

The statement *you are so wrong that you forfeit ordinary rights*
corresponds both to the classical formulation 'error has no right'
and to imposition, so this is sectarianism in a strong form. At the
same time, of the final four statements, this one is in some ways
the least likely to find expression, theoretical or practical. Within
the churches, error has no right has been repudiated as a formal
doctrine, and a commitment to religious liberty generally prevails in the North Atlantic context relevant here. Within society
at large, the prevalence of a rights culture also helps to ensure
that ordinary rights of religious belief, expression, and practice
are upheld. This statement might seem of largely historical interest.

The idea that *you are so wrong that you forfeit ordinary rights*
can sometimes be a practical, contemporary issue, however, although in a softer form than its historical precursors. In fact, this
soft form can have legitimate as well as abusive applications.
For example, the commitment of a rights culture to maximise
liberty and to tolerate as much as possible will necessarily bring
with it the hard tasks of defining, generally and theoretically,
where the limits of toleration lie and, occasionally, making practical judgments about those limits. Applied too restrictively,
these concerns will effectively deprive people judged to be
wrong of their ordinary rights. Applied sparingly, however,
these are legitimate considerations in ordering society for the
common good. Making such judgments around issues of religious liberty would be relatively simple if religion could be defined as a private sphere entirely distinct from politics. As we
have argued earlier, however, religion is not solely a private
matter and it intersects to a degree with politics. When and how
the rights of the loyal orders to parade may be restricted because
they clash with the rights of residents groups is an obvious, immediate, and extremely difficult case in point. While we advocate the general principle that rights should be extended as far as
possible, even where the practice of that right may be odious to
others, whether minorities or majorities, we also recognise that
no general commitment will ever make it easy to define in practice what 'as far as possible' means or to adjudicate when rights
clash.

9. You are less than human
10. You are evil
11. You are demonic

Our final three statements are grouped together because they are all inherently sectarian in much the same way. Each hardens boundaries, each dehumanises, each could allow imposition and provide a rationale for it. Because all are comprehensive, radical, and unqualified damning judgments, they at least suggest that the group or person is not simply wrong but beyond redemption, which offends against basic Christian teaching. Unlike the eight previous statements, these three have not even a limited or qualified appropriate use, so they should be removed from the repertoire of truth claims.

The three err most fundamentally by judging the whole rather than particular attitudes, actions, or commitments. It is this sweeping quality that negates the possibility of even a limited use of these statements. To say that a particular action was evil, inhuman, or demonic might be warranted; to extend this judgment to the group or person as a whole is not. In terms of Christian convictions, the case against these statements seems simple and straightforward. Humanity is created in the image of God, and that is a gift that can be abused but not taken away. People may do evil, but they do not become evil, in the comprehensive sense that they are beyond redemption. People may be possessed by demons, but they do not become demons. Given human limitations of perspective, people will do best to confine themselves to judging the particular action or manifestation, not the group or person.

In their hardest forms, versions of these three statements have justified gross injustices. Obvious examples are the way that Christianity has in some times and places bolstered anti-Semitism, the slave trade, and the conquest of the Americas by arguing the inhumanity or inferior humanity of Jews, black Africans, and American natives. Probably the starkest example in Irish history is the way that Christian teaching sometimes justified and reinforced the 'barbarism of the Irish' theme discussed in chapter two.

In Northern Ireland today, although one is less likely to encounter the straight, hard versions of these statements, softer but recognisable variants continue to distort attitudes and relationships. All three statements, for example, carry an implication of comprehensively writing off the group in question as so fundamentally flawed that they cannot change and are therefore beyond redemption. The convictions that others cannot or will not change pervades life in Northern Ireland and stands as a barrier to movement that could prove to be a self-fulfilling prophecy. Two of the most obvious and difficult examples concern the attitude of many nationalists to the police in Northern Ireland and of many unionists to Sinn Féin. Although applied by communities in conflict to different organisations, the implicit logic – i.e. the organisation in question is incapable of change and therefore fit only for abolition or exclusion – is nonetheless virtually interchangeable.

Another variant concerns the stance of different groups in relation to one another and the state. The political scientist George Schöpflin, in an essay bristling with insights relevant to Northern Ireland, argues that one of the fundamental requirements of ethnic groups in a modern state is 'to be accepted as communities of moral worth, as coequal with other such groups.'[10] We want to suggest that refusing to accept others as communities of moral worth is a softer but still destructive version of statement nine, *you are less than human.* Furthermore, the need identified by Schöpflin for acceptance as a community of moral worth does much to explain issues at stake in Northern Ireland. This is probably most obvious in the pervasive sense in the Catholic community of having been treated as second-class citizens and the corresponding centrality for them of what is called 'the equality agenda'. Some version of this has been a constant since the foundation of the state, and since the 1960s, no dynamic has been more central to society and politics. Since at least the 1985 Anglo-Irish Agreement, a Protestant version of this dynamic has been developing, expressing itself as a sense of abandonment by the British government and a conviction that change consistently means Catholic gains and Protestant loss. In a presentation in the spring of 2000, Democratic Unionist Party Councillor Gregory Campbell noted that even though, at the time he spoke, well over half of the Protestant community clearly favoured scrapping the Good Friday Agreement of 1998, the British and Irish governments took no notice and persisted in pressing ahead with it. He doubted that they would have done the same in the face of opposition by more than half of Catholics. His case is plausible enough to help make sense of a growing sense of Protestant disadvantage.

In the week that we first drafted this chapter, the issue of communities of moral worth was in the news, although not in those words. On Saturday, 27 May 2000, the Ulster Unionist Council voted by a narrow margin to have the Ulster Unionist Party re-enter government with Sinn Féin on the basis of an IRA commitment to put their weapons permanently and verifiably beyond use. Speaking shortly after that vote, UUP leader David Trimble commented on Sinn Féin's performance during the first, brief period of devolved government in late 1999 and early 2000. As recorded in the *Irish Times* of 29 May 2000, he said,

> As far as democracy is concerned, these folk ain't house-trained yet. It may take some time before they do become house-trained and I think we do actually need to see the Assembly running so the checks and balances that are there eventually bring them to heel. ... We are dealing with a party that has not got accustomed to democratic procedures.[11]

While a negative evaluation of Sinn Féin was so predictable that it would have drawn little comment, the language of 'house-training' and 'bringing to heel' the Sinn Féin dog caused considerable anger and upset. These dehumanising metaphors tap into the ancient 'barbarism of the Irish' theme, and as such angered not only Sinn Féin supporters but other nationalists. But a reluctance to accept others as communities of moral worth is not a feature solely of unionism. In that same edition of the *Irish Times*, the journalist John Waters, who writes from a nationalist/republican perspective, headed his weekly column, 'Welcoming Unionists to the Family of Democracy'. In fact the welcome was qualified and provisional, but Waters was willing to explore the possibility that the UUC vote was a watershed acceptance of democracy by unionists. Prior to that vote, he wrote, 'what appeared to be breakthroughs were actually illusions'; unionism had not been 'capable of comprehending the rudiments of democracy'; it had been 'a supremacist, racist outlook, acquiring meaning and identity only by virtue of its desire to deny the humanity of people residing in the North of Ireland who happened to be Catholic and/or nationalist'. While Waters was concerned that 'one should never underestimate the unionist genius for negativity and inertia' nor forget the possibility that the UUC vote was a merely strategic ploy, he finally allowed that 'it may be time to welcome a sizeable section of Northern unionism to the family of democracy.'[12] Without using the house-training metaphor, Waters created much the same effect by his consistently condescending tone and by his assumption of being in a position and having the right to decide who qualifies for the family of democracy. While Trimble and Waters occupy entirely different positions in their communities, both articulated a strand of condescending superiority embedded in those communities. At times, the moral worth of other communities is only grudgingly recognised.

* * *

Religious ideas and truth claims, then, need not be sectarian. Framed correctly, many truth claims are entirely legitimate and necessary expressions of intellectual and moral discernment, neither hardening boundaries, dehumanising, nor imposing. Nevertheless, those engaged in such discernment need always to recognise that some truth claims are inherently sectarian and others can be turned in a sectarian direction. Making religious truth claims in a sectarian context is particularly difficult, because that context can put a sectarian spin and implication where none was intended and none need be. Taking reasonable care in how a group makes its truth claims is an important contribution to moving society beyond sectarianism.

CHAPTER 7

Redeeming Identity and Belonging:
Theological Reflections on Moving Beyond Sectarianism

Introduction
In dealing with theological issues entailed in a consideration of
sectarianism, we expected to take a systematic approach: examining sectarianism in relation to christology, soteriology, doctrines of God, etc. Indeed this has been the approach of others,
for example, the work begun by the Church of Ireland sub-committee on sectarianism.[1] Such an approach undoubtedly needs
to be continued and extended. Our central argument throughout this book, however, is that at the heart of sectarianism are
distorted expressions of positive human needs for identity and
belonging. A Christian's primary identity and belonging is in
and to Christ, and this is usually lived out through membership
of a church or faith community. This chapter, therefore, focuses
on ecclesiology. It reflects on what it means to be 'church' and on
how churches have lived their calling to be 'church' in a situation of antagonised religious and political division.

Because we are dealing here with sectarianism, and not one
of its close cousins such as racism or ageism, the distortions of
identity and belonging in question typically issue in and are created
by malign combinations of religion and politics. Specifically,
people are constructing their religious and political identity, and
therefore their belonging, as groups in opposition to other
groups in such a way that they require a threatening other in
order to maintain a stable sense of who they are.[2] This is not the
healthy boundary maintenance of distinct groups confident of
their religious and political identity, marking their difference in
a way in which diversity becomes at least tolerable and possibly
even a richness. This type of distorted identity and belonging is
focused on constructing and maintaining boundaries of what
people are not, over against the other group, making their sense
of themselves in some way dependent on the other. Northern
Ireland, of course, is not alone in evidencing these types of dis-

torted expression; areas such as Serbia, Croatia, and the Middle East suffer a similar phenomenon. Miroslav Volf, in his book *Exclusion and Embrace: A Theological Exploration of Identity, Otherness, and Reconciliation,* has produced a very fine reflection on these themes and related issues.[3]

The religious and political nature of the antagonised division characteristic of sectarianism raises fundamental and uncomfortable questions for the self-understanding of Christian churches on the island of Ireland. It raises questions, for example, about how churches are maintaining boundaries, religiously and politically; about how churches have stood, as they are called to do as church, as witnesses to the reconciling relationship of God in Christ to the world; and about how far they have been seduced into trading their unique being and mission in order to maintain internal cohesion, or attain social approbation and power.

Can we, as Christians, speak with any credibility about the destructive system of sectarianism in which some of our beliefs and practices are not only a contributory factor, but also a defining element? Some, perhaps many, people think that the Christian churches are so much part of the sectarian problem that they must simply be dismissed. In large part, the churches as institutions and many individual Christians in Northern Ireland still live their lives as if sectarianism is not an issue for them. The level of denial that persists among church people is worrying and presents one particular barrier to efforts to move beyond sectarianism in society.

The tragic events surrounding the contested parade to and from Drumcree church, County Armagh, have become for many, nationally and internationally, a sign that it is time to consign religion, if not to the dustbin of history then at least exclusively to the realm of the private – removing all traces of it, and rights regarding the expression of it, from the public sphere. The recent move to enforce a neutral environment in a home for the elderly in Portadown, by prohibiting the singing of hymns in the communal lounge, is but one manifestation of this process of public containment already underway.

This move to deny religion legitimacy in the public sphere is one of a number of pressures facing the churches at this time. A second, identified by David Stevens, the general secretary of the Irish Council of Churches, is that, as the peace process moves on and a certain 'civic amnesia about the past' takes hold, churches will be scapegoated.[4] This is not the 'necessary judgment,' alluded to by David Stevens, under which every civic institution must fall when people come to examine what has happened, but rather a mostly unconscious, ritualistic cleansing and disavowal of blame by the majority by naming a few culprits as being the 'real' problem. One irony of the situation is that there will be many within the churches who will indulge in scapegoating their own institutions.

Such stances, of course, mostly ignore the positive and courageous contribution of many churches and individual Christians to peacemaking, publicly and privately, in the last decades. Churches have played a role as agents of peacebuilding, transformation, and healing. It is a role that is becoming more, not less, important as society advances towards a working political accommodation. The scaling down of violence and the gradual stabilising of the political situation is creating the possibility for people to allow the hurts and the hatreds engendered by the conflict to surface, in order to be worked through. The pastoral challenge facing the churches in the wake of the conflict, therefore, is growing.

Churches have a choice. They can choose to play a role in the public and ongoing healing process in Northern Ireland or they can choose to be consigned to oblivion through denial, through privatisation, or through scapegoating. If they are to play a role then it is crucial that they lead the process of 'necessary judgment', starting with themselves. This will require not only courage and honesty, but also a process of sustained reflection around a number of issues, including sectarianism.

The contribution of the churches and theology
to transforming sectarianism
Some believe that the churches have little or nothing to offer to a process of moving beyond sectarianism. Not surprisingly, and whilst acknowledging the failures of churches, we wish to disagree. We do so for two reasons. Firstly, there are serious biblical and theological issues underpinning any discussion of sectarianism, not only because the phenomenon involves religious elements, but still more because sectarianism is about how people relate with one another as human beings in society. Lived imperfectly or not, Christian community can provide significant

insights into the moral and spiritual dimensions of communal life. Moreover, if the Christian churches were magically to disappear overnight, the problem of sectarianism would not necessarily go away; indeed it might even get worse as the restraining influence of churches were removed. The search for God and the drive to religious and spiritual expression are inherent in human beings even if, from time to time, people would like to pretend that this is not so. Differences over religious expression, however these are named and described, will remain part of any human community, and where such differences exist, there is the potential for sectarianism. As a locus for expressions of the religious and faith dimensions of human being, then, churches are still significant agents of social, moral, and ethical action in Northern Ireland. Rather than trying to marginalise them, people would do well to assist them in bringing their biblical and theological resources to bear on the task of transforming destructive ways of dealing with religious and political difference.

Secondly, despite its well-documented, negative contribution to many situations of religious conflict through the centuries, including in Ireland, Christianity has some powerful resources for helping communities, whether theistic or not, to deal constructively with antagonised division. Concepts such as love, justice, forgiveness, and healing, which have their roots in religious and quasi-religious settings, are as central to secular, political efforts towards peace as they are to religious ones. Indeed, the heart and thrust of the Christian message speaks directly to the development of loving, just, and wholesome human relationships and communities, a goal that can be shared by Christians and those who espouse different beliefs alike. Christianity – through its concepts of grace, sin, repentance, self-emptying, conversion, and redemption – also offers unique tools, and a vision of hope, for addressing the transformation of what has become perverted. This is crucial when we turn to sectarianism because, at its core, sectarianism involves distorted expressions of common human needs which are good in themselves.

Paramount in the contribution that Christian theology can make to reflection about the transformation of sectarianism, however, is the vision of Christian community, or *koinonia,* embodied in the church, and incarnated in the varied expressions of churches.[5] Alongside this vision of community, as a means of moving towards it, is the co-related vision of reconciliation. There can be no more effective critique of distorted identity and belonging than a vision of a community of love reconciled with God, itself, and the cosmos. That this vision is so poorly realised in the churches in Northern Ireland is a matter for sober consideration and repentance.

The scope of this chapter

In this chapter we have two clear but limited objectives. The first is to provide some thought-provoking, theological commentary on what we have found to be the case with regard to the underpinnings and dynamics of sectarianism. The second is to open up the process of helping the churches on the island of Ireland to reflect on what it means to be church in a society shaped by sectarianism and in need of reconciliation. In this way we hope to help churches to identify and to see possible ways of applying the resources in their tradition more directly to the transformation of sectarianism. Obviously, different churches and traditions will have different resources; some will be particular to that church or tradition and some will be shared with other traditions. Different churches will also apply resources in different ways according to their situations, e.g. the different structures of parishes and congregations will affect the way in which processes to transform sectarianism can be best be implemented and lived.

Clearly, this is not going to be an extensive or fully adequate theological treatment of sectarianism. Such a project would fill many volumes. What we aim to provide here is not a theological model for moving beyond sectarianism, but rather a series of reflections which we hope will both fire and in some small way better equip churches to develop their own models for moving beyond sectarianism, ones suited to their specific constituencies, structures, and situations.

The theme of what it means to be 'church' in a society riven with antagonised religious and political division will provide the overarching framework for our reflections. It is a framework that comprises issues of both identity and belonging. We are using the term 'church' here in its widest sense of the *ecclesia*, the Christian community 'gathered' for worship of God and service of the world. In this sense it encompasses not only the larger and smaller churches but also those Christian groupings, large or small, which do not necessarily regard themselves as formal churches. In order to stress this wider sense of the term 'church' we refer, from time to time, to church or churches and faith communities.

We will address the theme of what it means to be church through the inter-connected aspects of the church's being in terms of *koinonia* and its mission in terms of reconciliation. The realities of both 'communion' and 'reconciliation', which churches and faith communities are called to be and to live, speak directly to the processes necessary for the healing of ethnic-religious conflict. Next we will sketch out the nature and manifestations of some positive elements and some distortions of identity and belonging that we found in the course of our research in churches and faith communities. Finally, we will make some comments on implications for the role of churches and faith communities in any process of moving beyond sectarianism in Northern Ireland.

WHAT IT MEANS TO BE 'CHURCH'

We begin our reflection about how churches and faith communities have been 'church' in our context of antagonised division by exploring briefly what it means to be church in any situation. Again, this can be no more than an outline of key elements concerning the nature and purpose of the church and some models for understanding church in society. These will serve as a set of criteria against which to reflect about the reality of churches and faith communities in Northern Ireland.

The nature of the church

There are many dimensions to the nature of church, which have been explored in a recent study by the Faith and Order Commission of WCC. The study gives a picture of widely, though not universally, accepted elements of church and points to where areas of disagreement still lie.[6] The document issuing from the study, *The Nature and Purpose of the Church*, speaks of the church as called into being by the Word and Holy Spirit, a communion of those who have a personal relationship with God and a communion grounded in and centred on the gospel.[7] It describes the four traditional 'marks' of the church: that it is one, holy, catholic, and apostolic.

It is *one* because it is brought into being by and owes allegiance to the one God who is creator and redeemer.[8] The evident disunity portrayed by uneasy denominational divisions is a counter witness that the ecumenical movement is working hard to overcome. The challenge of unity, according to an independent, inter-denominational group of French theologians, the *Groupe des Dombes,* is a challenge to overcome both 'uniformity' and 'disparity' in a way that respects the integrity of all.[9] In an article on changing models of the church, Methodist theologian Johnston McMaster suggests that oneness is being re-visioned today as unity 'expressed in plurality'.[10]

The church is *holy* because God is holy and has sanctified the church through the Holy Spirit. The issue of whether or not the church can sin, or whether it is the human members of the church who sin, is still disputed. All agree that in the history of the church there is sin. Some hold that if the church is the gift of a holy God it cannot sin, it is the locus of salvation and healing. Others believe that if the church is a communion of sinful believers then the church does sin and that sin operates systemically and affects the institution of the church.[11] The *Groupe des Dombes* challenge the Roman Catholic Church to take seriously the sins of its ministers as sins of the church.[12] They also challenge the Protestant churches to shift the understanding of holiness away from emphasis on 'members' purity of doctrine or life' and back to Christ, its head.[13] They suggest that the challenge of holiness is about obedience and faithfulness to the gospel and to the promptings of the Spirit.[14] In a re-definition of this concept for our changing context, Johnston McMaster asserts that 'holiness' can be viewed as a 'commitment to the world and all creation [and is] embodied in an alternative lifestyle'.[15] Holiness, in this view, is expressed not only in piety, religious practice, and loving relationship with human beings, but also in living in a way that respects and does not dominate or abuse the created world.

The church is *catholic* because through the Word and the Holy Spirit, God makes the church the instrument whereby God offers the Word and salvation to all people whoever and wherever they are.[16] This stands in contrast to popular understandings, both Roman Catholic and Protestant, which tend to see universality largely in terms of denominational and territorial expansionism. The *Groupe des Dombes* note that the challenge of catholicity is precisely to make it possible for all people 'to venture towards the truth in its fullness'.[17] The fullness of truth is here understood as located in the person of Jesus Christ.

Similarly, Johnston McMaster argues that catholicity 'over-comes the privatistic, provincial and hierarchical and is radically universal'.[18]

The church is *apostolic* because the Word that calls the church into being is that Word to which the apostles were witness. The challenge of apostolicity, according to the *Groupe des Dombes,* is for the churches to live in accordance with the gospel and the preaching of the Word.[19] This too is being re-defined as a con-cept that is shaped by 'a Christ-centred mission in and to the world, involving both the personal and structural'.[20]

While this theoretical understanding of the nature of church is widely accepted, there are some differing emphases and de-marcations in the actual living of the reality of church that need to be acknowledged. We will indicate some of these briefly in the following section.

Some demarcations in understanding the nature of church
The description above is the general understanding of church to be found in Roman Catholicism and the confessional Protestant traditions. These denominations and faith communities main-tain a distinction between the visible and invisible aspects of church, the visible church being those who claim membership, and the invisible church being those who are judged by God to be faithful believers. They tend to be organised on a diocesan or regional basis and, after a period of induction, extend member-ship to anyone who asks. Practices concerning the rite of bap-tism vary, but tend predominantly to favour infant baptism. In keeping with their understanding of church as apostolic, it is and has been characteristic of these churches to have an ongoing commitment to social action and engagement. Social action is expressed in different ways at different levels from local to national and international. The existence of agencies such as Christian Aid, Oxfam, Trócaire, and the St Vincent De Paul Society are some of the most visible institutional embodiments of this commitment.

The understanding of church in evangelicalism has some dis-tinctive features. Evangelicals are found in the larger churches and in smaller churches and faith communities. In his recent study of evangelicalism in Northern Ireland, however, former ECONI research officer, Glenn Jordan, points out that '[f]or an evangelical the denomination that he or she belongs to is not the

Church.'[21] Church in this view tends to be a functional entity, which has more to do with tradition and upbringing than a coherent theology of church.

Nonetheless, traditional evangelical understanding recognises marks of an authentic church among which the correct preaching of God's Word and the fundamentals of Christian faith are central. What constitutes the 'fundamentals' of faith varies between groups, but most agree that it is not acceptable for them to be reduced to belief in the Trinity and the affirmation that Jesus is Lord. Other fundamentals are those given in the creeds, together with the authority of scripture, Christ's vicarious atonement, and justification by grace through faith.[22] There appears, however, to be a shift in emphasis emerging in recent decades, which suggests that for some evangelicals, worship style and a felt sense of being comfortable in a community are as much a determining factor for choice of church affiliation as preaching or theology.[23] This more recent movement stands alongside a longer religious separatist tradition within evangelicalism, represented by groups such as the exclusive Brethren, who wish to separate themselves as far as possible from the contamination of the world and who tend to regard anyone outside their fellowship as suspect.[24]

The sense of unity for evangelicals subsists largely in a shared commitment to a 'born-again' experience, whether instantaneous or more gradual, and a personal appropriation of the Bible. It is a community such as is envisaged in Jesus' prayer in the gospel of John, chapter seventeen.[25] Church then is a coming together of those who have come to personal faith in Jesus Christ, and are bound together by the Holy Spirit. In this visible church, there can be believers and unbelievers, a mixture of truth and error. Evangelicals often term those that they judge to be not living as Christians, or to be attending church for cultural or social reasons, as either 'non-Christians' or the 'unconverted'. Glenn Jordan comments, 'Non-evangelical Christians can sometimes be confused when they hear evangelicals speaking about non-Christians who regularly attend their local congregation or parish.'[26] While the evangelical tradition is undoubtedly missionary in the sense of wanting to share their faith and to bring people to faith in Christ, commitment to social engagement has waxed and waned under pressure from changes in social and especially theological trends.[27]

A further significant distinction in the understanding of the nature of church exists within evangelicalism between confessional and congregational models of church and is evident especially in the issue of baptism. Those who broadly subscribe to the confessional understanding of church espoused by their chosen denomination tend to practice infant baptism. Those who favour a congregational model of church, that is a gathering of those who have a living faith in Jesus Christ, whose lives should be marked by a commitment to both truth and holiness,[28] baptise only believers. This more congregational understanding of church is expressed for example in Baptist, Brethren, Elim Pentecostal, and many new churches. It entails a very particular sense of who can be counted among the Christian community.

Within the understandings of the nature of church described here, there are different levels of identity as church which are assumed but not examined. In the following section we explore briefly the interplay between individual, denominational, and cross-denominational aspects of identity.

Levels of identity in the church

The *Groupe des Dombes* tease out three categories of identity which they contend comprise church: individual Christian identity, ecclesial identity, and confessional identity.[29] These three interconnected understandings of identity are useful in that they allow us to think about being church from different perspectives: individual, collectively universal, and confessionally/socially conditioned. This will be important when we reflect on the distortions of identity and belonging as church that are part of the taint of sectarianism in Northern Ireland.

Individual identity is the most particular, ecclesial identity is the most universal, and confessional identity indicates the specificity of historical manifestations of ecclesial identity. They point out that Christian identity and ecclesial identity refer to the same reality but from two different and distinguishable, though not separable, perspectives, one individual and the other collective or institutional.[30] Christian identity is 'the relation which unites the believer to the person of Christ'.[31] This is the fundamental coming to faith of a believer. They characterise this identity as one of 'becoming' and argue that it is a radical and continuing openness to an 'eschatological beyond' and to others, and that, therefore, it is not compatible with a rigid need for secure identity.[32]

Ecclesial identity, they argue, is based on a vision that church is both communion *(societas)* and mystery, and comes about through the being and action of the Holy Spirit. It is an awareness of God's irreversible gift of presence through Jesus Christ.[33] The church, therefore, is called to be a visible sign of this presence and gift of God to the world. Like Christian identity, ecclesial identity is an eschatological gift, which creates a tension between now and the future. The implication is that no confessional church can be simply identified with the church of Jesus Christ.

The Roman Catholic and Orthodox churches do not accept this last point or the *Groupe's* third category of 'confessional identity'. These churches regard themselves, each in different ways, not as confessions but as the locus within which the church of Jesus Christ subsists.[34] It is important to acknowledge that this stance, adopted by the Roman Catholic Church during the Second Vatican Council, represented at the time a considerable self-relativising movement compared to its stance up to the early 1960s.

By confessional identity the *Groupe des Dombes* mean the historically situated, culturally and doctrinally specific way in which Christian and ecclesial identity is expressed in 'church' and in churches. Confessional identity is defined by aspects of church life such as theology, structure, liturgical life, devotional practices, and moral stances and is based on the particular gospel emphases of that church.[35] They speak of confessional identity as the 'profile' of a group of churches.[36] This third category of identity is important because 'church' is not a Platonic ideal that exists over and beyond the world. All religious identities are socially situated. They are incarnated in ways that are socially, culturally, politically, economically, and nationally specific, and this contributes to their meaning and their self-understanding. The context within which a church is located is a significant factor in identity.

The interplay of these different levels of identity coalesces in the concepts of community and communion. It is to these themes that we turn now through a consideration of the principle of *koinonia* or communion.

Koinonia

One unifying, biblical principle that draws together what we have said so far about the nature of the church is that of *koinonia*

or communion. This concept is being recovered in many denominations throughout the world in recent years, particularly by
way of the ecumenical movement. The ecumenical task of assessing and encouraging one another to move towards deeper
relationship is only one aspect of the usefulness of this rich concept. It can also provide a multi-layered, breath-taking, and demanding image of what church as a community of love in Christ
already is, and is called to be. The demands of *koinonia*, then,
constitute a biblical imperative for all Christians which can lead
them to rediscover a stronger concept of 'church'.

The term *koinonia* has a long history stretching back through
the Reformation and Patristic writings to the Christian scriptures.[37] The writers of the document *The Nature and Purpose of the
Church* link it also with two concepts from the Hebrew scriptures, covenant and *shalom*. They argue that the whole creation
has its integrity in communion with God and see this expressed
particularly through the concept of the 'covenant' established
between God and the chosen people (Ex 19:4-6; Hos 2:18-23).[38]
The depth and quality of the relationship between people and
God, and between human beings, intended in *koinonia* evokes
resonances of the relationship designated by the Hebrew concept *shalom*.[39] Together these concepts provide a first layer of the
image of *koinonia* as the whole cosmos called to be in peace-filled
relationship with one another and with God. The relationship
envisaged here is one of strong and deep connectedness in God,
and through shared belonging in God, deep connectedness with
one another, a connectedness which can transcend, though not
nullify, the tensions inherent in diversity. This vision of peace-
filled relationship integral to *koinonia* is dynamic and pre-sup-
poses an ongoing struggle to live the oneness, won for human
beings by God in Christ, which can only be fully realised at the
end of time. It is clearly not some utopic vision of peace-filled relationship as an absence of honest struggle and dissent, and still
less is it a vision of bland uniformity. Indeed, understanding the
imperative to change inherent in *koinonia*, the Fifth World
Conference on Faith and Order, which took place in Santiago de
Compostela in 1993, put forward the notion of *kenosis*, self-emptying, as a vision to help churches to find a biblical paradigm for
moving towards the radical demands of *koinonia*. 'Though he
was in the form of God ... he emptied himself taking the form of
a slave' – Jesus' readiness for and actual living of self-emptying

on the cross to which *kenosis* refers is the model churches are called to emulate in the search for *koinonia*.[40]

In the Christian scriptures *koinonia* is a term that Paul uses to express a number of qualities of participation, relationship, and sharing that should pertain in a community founded on and following Jesus Christ. The first is the source of communion, which he sees as flowing from fellowship with the Son and with the Holy Spirit and from participation in the body and blood of Christ.[41] *Koinonia*, then, is communion with God, freely offered to human beings, and this makes the Christian community 'one body' in Christ. The second quality is the depth and closeness of relationship demanded of members of the community and the willingness to be reconciled to one another, which is symbolised by extending 'the right hand of fellowship'.(Gal 2:7-9) The early Christian cummunity's deep love and acceptance of Paul, who had been a persecutor of the church, and of the validity of his ministry, is a call to overcome violence, suspicion, and division through faith in Jesus, and can be expressed as love and forgiveness of one another. Such love and forgiveness is lived out in a practical sense in the local community of faith. The third quality is the sense of *koinonia* as sharing resources so that all can live in dignity.[42] If communion does not issue in just relationships within and outside the community, then it is not communion based on and demanded by the love of God in Christ, who reached out to the poor, the marginalised, and the outcasts.

The concept of *koinonia*, then, fills out the understanding not only of interrelationship between the oneness, holiness, catholicity, and apostolicity of the church, but also of the continuous call to repentance, renewal, and conversion that God makes to the churches in their individual Christian, ecclesial, and confessional identities. The apostle Paul is very clear, and the churches can be also, that baptism into the death and resurrection of Christ means that as individuals and collectively human beings are called to be one, to be loving, to be forgiving, to be reconciling, to be sharing, and to be just in all their relationships. These are dimensions of being church before they are characteristics of our ministry as church. Insofar as people fail to live *koinonia* with one another, they are not true witnesses to the gospel, for they have not placed themselves fully under the demand and judgment of the Word who calls them into being as church.

The purpose of the church

Flowing directly from the being of church as *koinonia* is the purpose of the church as God's instrument to bring 'humanity and
all creation into communion'[43] under the Lordship of Christ as
envisaged in the epistle to the Ephesians.

> He has made known to us the mystery of his will, according
> to his good pleasure that he set forth in Christ, as a plan for
> the fullness of time, to gather up all things in him, things in
> heaven and things on earth.(Eph 1:9-10)

The plan that the writer of the letter to the Ephesians has in mind
here is not an imperialistic one. Rather it is a vision of entering
into the ministry of reconciliation exercised by Jesus, which Paul
asserts has been entrusted to the Christian community and
which will have its fulfillment only in the fullness of time.[44] The
concept of reconciliation is dense and complex and has a number of dimensions, sociological, philosophical, theological, etc.
We will concern ourselves here only with such dimensions as
are needed to provide an adequate account of Christian reconciliation and its implications for the church.

Christian reconciliation

We understand Christian reconciliation to mean the processes
and structures necessary to bring all the elements of the cosmos
into positive and life-giving relationship with God and with one
another. It is a vision of both an ongoing process to establish a
community of love in which conflict and injustice, though still
present, are actively being addressed, and the eschatological
goal of cosmic communion in love being definitively achieved.
Communities of love subsist already in partial and fragmented
ways at local, regional, national, and international level. All genuine efforts towards reconciliation participate in and contribute
to the wider process of cosmic reconciliation in Christ.

The global scope of our definition derives from two sources.
Firstly, the Pauline vision of reconciliation and of the whole
creation groaning as it waits to be set free from its bondage to
decay;[45] this has the potential to encompass both inter-personal
and ecological dimensions.[46] The second source is eco-feminist
insights that reconciliation must take seriously the relationship
between attitudes and actions of domination among human beings and abuse of the earth.[47] These are summed up beautifully
in the letter to the Colossians:

> [T]hrough him God was pleased to reconcile to himself *all things*, whether on earth or in heaven, by making peace through the blood of his cross.(Col 1:20; our emphasis)

In inter-personal terms, then, reconciliation means the movement from enmity or domination/subjugation to positive, life-giving relationship, both individually and collectively. In ecological terms, it means the movement from domination and abuse to care and conservation.

Our definition takes into account the traditional theological understanding of reconciliation as that which takes place between the individual and God and also the 'inherent social meaning of reconciliation' as described by Miroslav Volf.[48] Volf reflects on why committed Christians become perpetrators of violence and legitimators of ethnic conflict. Referring to the work of sociologist Ralph Premdas, Volf asserts that part of the problem is that many Christians engage in an 'idolatrous shift of loyalty' which is underpinned, at least in part, by a too individual and too 'justice first' theology of reconciliation. These Christians, whilst explicitly acknowledging allegiance to the gospel, act out of an overriding commitment to their culture, ethnic group, or nation.[49] He notes that the twin theological emphases on individual reconciliation with God and on liberation or justice as prior to reconciliation have divorced reconciliation from the social agenda of the church. He argues strongly that while individual reconciliation with God has the priority, reconciliation with other people is a constitutive dimension of a person's reconciliation with God. Reconciliation, therefore, has an inalienable social dimension and not just social implications that can be drawn from it.

This raises the question of the relationship between reconciliation and justice. Reconciliation is sometimes regarded as a 'soft option' as opposed to the hard task of realpolitik. It is seen as a religious version of 'forgive and forget' or 'kiss and make up' in which the causes of conflict or enmity, which are often issues of injustice or oppression, are not addressed. Indeed, calls for this type of reconciliation from church-based groups have sometimes amounted to no more than an exhortation to give up a struggle for justice and to support an oppressive status quo. Such a call in South Africa was exposed and opposed as 'cheap reconciliation' in the 1986 *Kairos Document: Challenge to the Church:*

> In our situation in South Africa today it would be totally

unChristian to plead for reconciliation and peace before the present injustices have been removed. Any such plea plays into the hands of the oppressor by trying to persuade those of us who are oppressed to accept our oppression and to become reconciled to the intolerable crimes that are committed against us. This is not Christian reconciliation; it is sin. ... No reconciliation is possible in South Africa without justice.[50]

Whilst sharing the judgement that cheap reconciliation is not Christian reconciliation, Volf argues that this approach counterposes 'peace' and 'justice'. Based on an exegesis of Paul's conversion experience on the Damascus Road, he argues that reconciliation must have priority over liberation and love over justice.[51] He does so on the basis firstly that it is not possible to achieve strict justice and secondly that God, while affirming justice has transcended it and has given priority to grace over justice.[52] This is the heart of the Christian message. This is not to imply that justice is not important, or that the demands of truth and justice need not be satisfied before reconciliation can come about. Rather he is arguing that the overarching framework and the initial movement is one of reconciliation, not justice.[53] Volf recognises that a liberation model, which may be appropriate where one party is clearly perpetrator and the other victim, carries a danger where the situation – and few situations of long term conflict are – is not so clear-cut. It runs the risk, where both parties see themselves as fighting for justice, of 'reducing the moral complexity of the situation and feeding into the self-righteousness of each party by assuring them that God is on their side'.[54]

With similar effect but in a different way, Gerry O'Hanlon, an Irish Jesuit theologian, in his paper 'Reconciliation and Justice', argues that justice is integral to reconciliation. He insists that reconciliation begins with the offer of forgiveness, which is, in fact, an expression of justice understood in terms of righting relationships. He identifies three biblically based aspects of reconciliation: a recognition of the offence; an unconditional offer of forgiveness; and a cost to forgiveness.[55] The cost to which he is referring is twofold. Firstly, the cost of the injured party being willing to 'absorb the offence to the relationship by his or her suffering,' just as Jesus Christ paid the ultimate cost which makes reconciliation possible for us.[56] Secondly, the cost to the injuring party in terms of conversion, repentance, reparation, and atonement. Justice is central to this conception of reconciliation in the clear naming of the offence and in the double movement of righting of relationships by the victim offering unconditional forgiveness, which frees the injuring party to repent and to make reparation. O'Hanlon argues that when the unconditional offer of forgiveness has become 'received forgiveness', through the sorrow and reparation shown by the injuring party, the full restoration of the relationship signified by the term reconciliation can come about.[57]

There are a number of paradoxes involved in any process of reconciliation. One, highlighted by Volf, O'Hanlon, and theologians Robert Schreiter and Donald Shriver, Jr, is that reconciliation is, typically, a movement initiated by the victim, which frees the perpetrator to repent, and not the other way round. Schreiter observes that if reconciliation is from God, the question is not how can I forgive but rather:

> How can I discover the mercy of God welling up in my own life, and where does that lead me?[58]

He argues that human beings do not make reconciliation. They discover it. For Christians, only the experience of being forgiven by and reconciled to God can open them to discovering reconciliation with others. A second paradox to which Schreiter points is the fact that the symbols of Christian reconciliation – death, blood and cross – are symbols that take people into the very heart of violence and injustice. He asserts that the task of reconciliation is so difficult and demanding that only strong, paradoxical symbols which can mediate both death and life are adequate. A third paradox is that reconciliation is not about restoring a previous relationship. The process and experience of reconciliation takes both the victim and the perpetrator into a new place. In Pauline terms, '[I]f anyone is in Christ there is a new creation: everything old has passed away.' (2 Cor 5:17)

The vision of Christian reconciliation that we are describing here pertains most obviously to individuals and small groups. Issues of forgiveness and repentance, however, become much less clear when people think in large group or societal terms. In moving beyond sectarianism in Northern Ireland, there will be a need for much individual and small group forgiveness, repentance, and justice. There will be a need also for reconciliation on a much wider scale.

In writing of forgiveness in society, theologian Donald

Shriver suggests that there are four signs of a society moving towards forgiveness: memory suffused with moral judgement; forbearance of vengeance; empathy with the humanity of the other; and the will to co-existence.[59] He reserves the concept of reconciliation to describe the end point of the process which forgiveness begins.[60] We agree with him in that his elucidation of the concept of forgiveness does not comprehend all the aspects that comprise reconciliation. We disagree, however, because, as we will argue below, we regard reconciliation as both the path and the goal of the journey. Shriver's work is important because he delineates well some key attitudes and actions that signify a movement towards reconciliation at societal level.

In presenting the concept of memory suffused with moral judgement, he argues that forgiveness begins not with forgetting but rather with 'a remembering and a moral judgement of wrong, injustice and injury'.[61] This remembering needs to be an agreed memory, as it were, a consensus about the rights and more especially the wrongs done by all sides. It is a setting down of a communal history of the conflict and the reasons for the conflict, in which as many voices as possible can be heard, not just those of the larger or stronger groupings.

Forbearance of vengeance, according to Shriver, does not mean abandoning all punishment of evildoers, but rather turning aside from the natural temptation to exact revenge, to make the enemy pay equally or even many times over. He warns that in the absence of forbearance of vengeance, memory suffused with moral judgement can simply fuel new enmity.

His third element, empathy for the humanity of the other, appeals to recognition of shared humanity as a basis for beginning to envisage the possibility of living as neighbours. Understanding reality as the other sees it is an important part of the process of moving towards forgiveness and ultimately reconciliation. Empathy, however, does not necessarily mean agreeing with the other, but is rather an acknowledgment that the other's story is as plausible and internally coherent as the story that we tell ourselves.

The final element is a will to co-existence with the other. What Shriver is looking towards is the will to establish a minimal relationship of civility, which can, in turn, facilitate a developing relationship of positive mutual affirmation in the political realm. In other words, if people cannot annihilate or exclude the other, then, at some moment they need to recognise that they have to live with them and they must actively choose this co-existence. Co-existence will be a more stable, sustainable, and beneficial state if it is at least civil.

Conclusion

The model of 'church' that we are developing here, with its vision of the nature of church as 'communion' *(koinonia)* and its mission as 'reconciliation', is one in which relationship is fundamental: relationship to self, relationship to God, relationship to others within our faith community and to those outside it. In the service of those relationships, the call to Christian discipleship, as individuals and as church, is radical in terms of the attitudes of openness and inclusivity that it demands and the boundary crossing that it entails. At the same time, this inclusivity and boundary crossing are not indiscriminate; they are to be exercised with discernment based on criteria drawn from the ministry of reconciliation of Jesus Christ, whose mission the church shares. Central to these criteria is the truth that in the life and death of Jesus, God has given priority to grace over justice, and this, therefore, must be a primary stance for all Christian faith communities.

In the section that follows we will examine how the churches in Northern Ireland have been, and are, meeting the demands of *koinonia* and reconciliation, the demands of openness, discernment, inclusivity, and boundary crossing, inherent in the call to be 'church'.

DISTORTED IDENTITY AND DISTORTED BELONGING

In the course of our research we have identified a number of characteristics to do with the identity and belonging of religious and faith communities in Northern Ireland that have become distorted into a pattern of relationship negatively 'over against' others that we recognise as sectarian or tending towards sectarianism. Of the possible candidates for inclusion in this section, we will focus on just three: religious-national nature of churches, separation, and superiority and self-righteousness. We choose these inter-related concepts conscious that we are leaving much unsaid, but in the hope that they can most comprehensively illustrate the temptations and therefore the challenges posed by sectarianism to Christian communities.

Religious-national nature of churches

The first characteristic concerns boundaries of identity and be-longing. Writing about Protestants and Catholics in Northern Ireland, political scientist Frank Wright perceptively observed: 'it is necessary to recognise that the "religious" communities are, for better or worse, national communities.'[62] He argues that, un-like other situations, national communities here are distin-guished by branches of Christianity and not by language and he points to the very thin line that separates the transcendental, in this case Christianity, and the national.[63] It seems ironic that the rise of nationalisms in the nineteenth century, which as the Faith and Politics Group have observed, 'seemed to offer an escape from the world of religious differences and sectarianism', has in fact proved to be a critical factor in fuelling and strengthening this sectarian divide.[64] The malign conjunction of nationalism and religion has issued in subtly different expressions of reli-gious-national community in the two traditions.

Wright notes that it is possible to maintain some distance be-tween Roman Catholicism and Irish nationalism, because the Catholic faith does not assert as sacred the political unity of Ireland. This strong relationship yet distance between religious and political dimensions is a significant but complex character-istic of the Catholic-nationalist community. There is a very real sense in which Roman Catholicism could be regarded as a sym-biotic culture in which threads of religion, nationalism, and Irish culture are intimately intertwined. We will return to this theme below in the section concerning idolatry. In writing about the expression of identity, particularly through symbols, Clem McCartney and Lucy Bryson point out:

> For many nationalists the sense of identity exists whether it is expressed or not. In any case there are many ways that Irish identity can be expressed, including identification with the wider Irish community, the language, the culture, the church in Ireland, and so on.[65]

The picture sketched by McCartney and Bryson is one of a reli-gious-national community with a fluid and confident sense of identity, which subsists in a variety of religious, political, and cultural ways, and which may or may not be overtly expressed. On the whole, they argue, nationalists appear to be concerned about overt expression of identity only when they sense that their symbols are being undermined or deemed illegitimate.[66]

The image of the Protestant-unionist community is significantly different. Some years ago Wright asserted that if the self-definition of unionists as British were to be repudiated, their self-definition would be 'forced back' on Protestantism.[67] His point was a call to recognise unionism as 'an assertion of Britishness', in order that Protestant Christianity may be freed from taint of subordination to nationality.[68] Though this might have been a way that Protestant-unionist identity developed, it has not happened. In a situation of weakening and less trustful relationship with successive British governments, and therefore declining appeal to 'Britishness',[69] there has been no religious revival or return to religious practice; church numbers have continued to fall. What appears to be emerging is twofold. Firstly, claims to religious affiliation that increasingly take the minimalist form of a relatively content-less boundary marker, and yet which continue to include an element of anti-Catholicism. Secondly, the growth of churches which are prepared to legitimate Protestant-unionist identity in a more wholehearted way than the larger Protestant churches.

The situation is further complicated in two ways. Firstly, Protestant-unionism has a much less extensive range of political and cultural means of expression than Catholic-nationalism, hence the relative importance of cultural activities such as marching. Many of their symbols are linked to Britishness or to Protestant Christianity or to both, and the appeal of both of these elements is waning. The attempt to revive Ulster-Scots language and traditions is at least in part an effort to trace another source of identity. Secondly, McCartney and Bryson have identified a need in the Protestant-unionist community to maintain their sense of identity through self-expression. They note:

> For many unionists the sense of self is very closely bound up with self expression. … [I]t is important for unionists to be able to display their symbols in public, and have them accepted by everyone.[70]

There is considerable pressure, therefore, on both the content of identity and the mechanism for maintaining a sense of identity. Some of the pressure is perceived to be coming from the Catholic nationalist community.[71] The pressure is leading to an impoverishment of identity in the Protestant unionist community and is undoubtedly a significant factor in their accelerating sense of both loss and grief around the changes coming about through implementation of the Belfast Agreement.

Idolatry

Whatever the proximity or distance in the mix of religion and politics, we are arguing that one key element in sectarianism in Northern Ireland is that both traditions have developed, what Volf calls an 'idolatrous shift in loyalty' with regard to their nation. They have allowed loyalty to their 'nation' and the movement of nationalism to either taint, distort, or in some cases subvert the being and mission of church. Christians will always have national or cultural identities but, as the Faith and Politics Group point out, 'those identities must not dominate their lives.'[72] Our contention is that for both traditions concerns about national identity and therefore their 'own' people have become disproportionately important to the point of being idolatrous. In addressing what we regard as the idolatrous shift in loyalty to the nation we are not suggesting that all forms of loyalty are idolatrous. There is a proper loyalty to the state, for example, which is asked of citizens and which, provided it remains subordinate to loyalty to Jesus Christ, is not idolatry of the state. The key element in the judgment about certain behaviour being idolatrous is whether or not it assumes an ultimacy that belongs properly to God.

We are using idolatry here in the classical sense of the Greek *eidololatria*, 'the worship of images'. This is based on the concept that 'God could neither be named nor imagined' and that therefore to name God as God of Ireland or of Ulster or of 'one tribe' is to deny the transcendence of God.[73] To name, and in so doing to claim power over, the One who is transcendent is to turn that god into an idol. This god becomes for people the god of 'their own', and their ethical concern becomes focused upon that which is not ultimate, namely a person's own people, land, nation. When people are looking towards this idol-god whom they have created, they avert their eyes from the transcendent glory, power, and demands of Jesus Christ. In averting their eyes they tend not only to betray Jesus Christ as Lord, but also to lose sight of the only source of power and love that can bring about the reconciliation of peoples, nations and churches.

Such idolatry is exemplified in the Protestant tradition in the old Ulster Volunteer Force motto, later to become a well-worn Protestant unionist slogan, 'for God and Ulster'. That this type of crude mixing of religion and politics commands the adherence of steadily fewer Protestants is undoubtedly true. At the time of the Solemn League and Covenant in 1912, the slogan would have resonated in the heart of many, if not most, who considered themselves Protestant in the north. For many it has now lapsed into part of the mythology of resistance, which gave force to the current unionist movement. Even so, some contributors to the book *Faith in Ulster*, which invites reflection on what 'for God and Ulster' means, recognise that the slogan along with accompanying expression through band music and banners still calls to something primeval in them.[74] What is described as primeval seems to be to an early sense of a community of belonging and the simplicity of childhood. The power and the subtlety of this type of idolatry is precisely that it appeals to the positive passion of people for their country and culture. Its danger lies in the fact that in a situation of ethnic religious antagonism and division such passion too easily ends up at the service of conflict and not of healing and reconciliation, a movement made easier if people do not recognise the Christianity of the other.

Attempts to defend 'for God and Ulster' from charges of promoting an idolatrous relationship with nationality are on the whole unconvincing. To justify the slogan on the basis either that it means seeking God's guidance to preserve Britishness and Protestantism rather than 'being caught up in the maelstrom of materialism' or that it provides direction and purpose in a society experiencing 'social and spiritual meltdown' strains the imagination.[75] Similarly, to suggest, as assemblyman Esmond Birnie does, that it is an expression of a biblically grounded understanding that God can use political states, even though he admits that there is no necessary link between evangelical Christianity and unionism, is a questionable reference to scripture that ignores large parts of the biblical witness.[76] Such defenders would need to provide both more cogent arguments and evidence that they could say 'for God and Ireland' or 'for God and Spain' or 'for God and Iran' with equal fervour or at the very least acknowledge that, on their own premises, these statements would be equally valid.

There seems to be no obvious Catholic nationalist or republican equivalent to the slogan 'for God and Ulster'. Once again, lack of a slogan is not necessarily a sign that such idolatry does not exist in Catholic nationalism. Indeed the logic of a slogan, which would read 'for God and Ireland', is woven right through the early days of the modern Irish nationalist movement. This is typified in the revolutionary mysticism of Pádraig Pearse and in the faith and fatherland emphases of the approach to Irish history associated with the Christian Brothers.[77] It is also evident in the quasi-sacred place accorded to the memory of Bobby Sands and other dead hunger strikers in republican folklore, and the religious imagery surrounding them.

That there is not the need currently within Catholic nationalism to sloganise this idolatry is a convergence of several threads. Firstly, it is part of the early and now largely assumed founding mythology. Secondly, it has been achieved, even if only partially, in the republic functioning until recently largely as a Roman Catholic state for a Roman Catholic people; a state, which republicans and nationalists are confident, will become a fully united Ireland in the not too distant future. Thirdly, there is increasing plurality and secularisation in the Republic and in republicanism, which makes appeal to openly religious motivation less desirable. Finally and perhaps most significantly there is the emergence of a republican political analysis of the problem as a purely political issue concerning British-Irish relationship: this of course ignores the role of religion in the situation. This analysis has been modified in the last decade to take seriously the claim to 'Britishness' made by northern unionists. There is an argument to be made for viewing republicanism itself as a religion, demanding as it does ultimate commitment to the nation even to the point of sacrifice where necessary. Irish republicanism is no different in this regard. Thus the fact that an overtly religious element is disappearing may only indicate a more subtle manifestation of idolatry.

The issue of the expression of idolatry within the Roman Catholic tradition is complex. The Catholic community, with its deliberate emphasis on the relationship between church, home, and school, creates a whole Catholic culture. The strong link between Irish nationalism and Roman Catholicism in Ireland means that this culture comprises religious, social, and political elements and that all the elements are subtly suffused with church presence. Catholic priests, for example, work on management committees of schools or hold posts in the GAA, and Catholic church halls are often the venues for Gaelic social events. While there is no overt involvement of Roman Catholic clergy in party politics in the sense of holding office at local or national level, the intimate link that has been forged between Gaelic culture and Irish nationalism carries subtle forms of politicisation into social and sporting events that are integral parts of Catholic parish life. In this context, idolatry is the failure of the Roman Catholic Church to distinguish sufficiently between the various components of Catholic culture and to give ultimacy to commitment to Jesus Christ.

The critique of these types of idolatry in our context is already documented and we do not propose to rehearse it again here.[78] We will confine ourselves to commenting that one of the central problems created by idolatrous loyalty to 'nation' is that in a situation of ethnic religious conflict it can, on the one hand, focus people, understandably, on their own, and on the other hand, serve to blind them to the subtle ways in which it draws them into constructing and then underlining their identities over against the other, in a manner which excludes them. In the rest of this section we are going to reflect on some of the subtle and not so subtle contours of this idolatry and how it, or shadows of it, have permeated the being and action of churches and faith communities in Northern Ireland. We will maintain a distinction between what we consider to be fully idolatrous behaviour and positions, which we name as idolatry, and behaviour or positions tending towards or opening the way for idolatry, which we name as shadows of idolatry, because it is not yet fully present and visible.

In the socio-political realm, churches maintain two significant roles: (1) religiously as pastors and (2) politically as advisors, critics, and encouragers of politicians and parties and sometimes as channels of communication between politicians and political or paramilitary groupings who could not otherwise relate with one another. We examine each of these roles in turn for indications of idolatry or shadows of idolatry.

Idolatry in the religious and pastoral role of churches
In discussing the pastoral role of churches we need to briefly characterise the situation in which this role was being undertaken. From the very early 1970s until 1994 there was open and violent conflict between various groups in society, including republican and loyalist terrorists and the security forces. The level of violence and threat was high. Since the ceasefires from August 1994 the level of violence has diminished considerably but not disappeared. There continue to be sporadic killing, attempts to plant large bombs, pipe- and petrol-bombings, punishment beatings,

forced evictions, and intimidation. Churches and pastors now are dealing largely with the aftermath of prolonged violent conflict and deeply antagonised religious-political division.

In the face of this situation, there is no doubt that Christians in many churches and faith communities have, at times, acted prophetically and courageously in confronting the spiral of sectarian activity. On a week to week basis, ministers and lay leaders have helped greatly to restrain or to mitigate sectarian violence through the steady preaching of a gospel of love, judgment, forgiveness, and forbearance of vengeance and through their denunciation of violence, even in the face of appalling tragedy and provocation. Individual Christians, too, have stayed the hand of reprisal by their swift and heartfelt appeals for no retaliation even in the midst of their immediate grief at loss or bereavement.[79] It is important to acknowledge also how much time and energy church people have given, and how much compassion they have shown, in responding to the trauma of those who might be termed 'victims' or 'sufferers' of the Troubles. In addition to this, priests, ministers, and lay Christians have been to the fore in pastoring those caught up in perpetrating violence and intimidation.[80] For the most part then, churches and faith communities have carried, well and willingly, a heavy and crucial pastoral burden in this society throughout the conflict.

But even here we can detect a shadow of idolatry, by which we mean the tendency for people to work with their own, for their own, and among their own. It appears most obviously in a relative lack of commitment to shared ministry to those in local areas who are enduring sectarian related suffering. Instances of ongoing commitment to shared ministry to those affected by the Troubles are still sufficiently few to be remarkable.[81] The tendency, which is entirely understandable, is for people to look after their own, especially in times of dire suffering. Even the truth that someone's ministry may be rejected by, or unacceptable to, the injured party, however, is not a reason to forego searching for ways to offer this important witness. These ways may need to be small and indirect, for example, a telephone call to the minister of the family concerned asking her or him to convey sympathy. What is crucial is only partly the action in itself. Crucial also is the fact that the action is both a manifestation of the will to reach across the sectarian boundary to the other, and an assurance that the person is not elevating the suffering of their own people above the suffering of others. Outside a context of antagonised religious and political division, people caring exclusively for their own might pass unremarked and perhaps even as the expected norm. But in the cauldron of sectarianism in Northern Ireland, people must acknowledge that this behaviour at least opens the door to and at worst is an instance of religious-political tribalism that cannot be ignored or wished away.

Our assertions are not an attempt to build a case, by subterfuge, for 'ecumenical' ministry: the parameters of such a ministry would be very different from what we have in mind here. Whatever a person's attitude to 'ecumenism', a Christian cannot avoid the twin biblical imperatives to cross boundaries towards the stranger, or even the enemy, and to be peacemakers. We will deal with these imperatives in detail below in the section concerning separation. We are pointing to the need in a religiously divided society for Christian churches to extend Christian charity, and even human empathy, towards the 'hurting' other, together and in a visible way. Such action witnesses to God's love for all, and is a means of working towards the healing of division and highlighting that violence or the threat of violence is not consonant with the gospel of Jesus Christ. We are challenging a mindset, pervasive in church circles in Northern Ireland, and born of sectarianism and subtle forms of national idolatry, that it is acceptable and possibly even desirable for Christian ministry, lay or clerical, to work exclusively within the boundaries of their religious-political tribes.

Chaplains to the tribes
The more overt face of idolatry begins to emerge, however, when this important and difficult pastoral role can be seen to have either degenerated into, or been nothing more than, what is popularly called 'chaplains to the tribes'.[82] Before examining this phenomenon, some comments on how we are using the term 'tribalism' are called for. The differentiation that we are making between what constitutes tribal allegiance and what we would deem 'healthy allegiance' is that it is characteristic of tribalism for people to think and act exclusively within, with, or on behalf of their 'own', without significant reference to any other or to their needs and problems. Healthy allegiance, on the other hand, while being appropriately concerned with 'their own', re-

tains at least an awareness of, and at best an active concern for, others and their needs.

We have remarked in other chapters the tendency in church and faith communities to be so self-absorbed, to find life within their own community so busy and so satisfying that they need not look beyond the borders of their 'own' in order to have a happy and fruitful existence. These characteristics constitute the pre-conditions for 'benign apartheid'. In a Christian ministry sense, they are also the most benevolent incarnation of the phenomenon of chaplains to the tribes; pastors tending their flocks, albeit with little heed to those not of their fold. From our research we would affirm that the oversight here is not necessarily intentional and can be more a function of ignorance, denial, self-absorption, or especially 'overload' than of sectarian intent. This finding in itself underlines the very subtle and unintended ways in which groups allow the shadow of idolatry to shape their being as churches and faith communities.

In terms of ignorance, we have found that many clergy and lay leaders are not well equipped either at initial formation or in an ongoing way to recognise the distinctive characteristics required of Christian ministry in a divided society, where denominational allegiance is a point at issue. The uneven presence of sustained and practically orientated reflection on sectarianism in either clergy training or teacher training settings in Ireland, let alone in the ongoing formation of more experienced clergy and teachers, is worrying. It is also concrete evidence of the level of denial in the churches with regard to sectarianism. Our experience in piloting sectarianism courses in seminary and teacher training settings is that it is readily welcomed, especially by ministers, who are anxious to think through and talk through approaches to situations that they know they will face when carrying responsibility for ministry in a parish or congregation. There are three main effects in parishes and congregations of clerical and lay leaders being inadequately prepared to deal with sectarianism. Firstly they are hesitant about engaging in cross-tradition initiatives, and this frustrates some church members, whilst giving power to those who either fear or actively oppose cross-tradition relationships. Secondly, they are failing to lead, challenge, and nurture their parish or congregation members about their collective and individual responsibility for overcoming sectarianism. Thirdly, there are some situations in which church members are going off independently to find training or cross tradition experiences. This is creating a widening gap and tensions among people in the pews, and between them and the church leadership.

We have come across several possible roots for the kind of denial, self-absorption, and apathy that leads to unintended tribal chaplaincy. The first, and most tragic, is a type of despairing resignation that sees the situation as totally intractable. The tragedy is particularly poignant in the case of more experienced clergy or lay leaders, who have, over long years, been witness to, and responsible for bringing comfort to, those enduring the most appalling suffering. As communities and institutions, people need to ask themselves whether at times they have left key pastoral workers, on the cutting edge of ministry, with insufficient pastoral support. This is a betrayal of the church as *koinonia*, which is called to look both inwards as well as outwards in living deep communion and support. The second root is a fear of at least disapproval, if not attack, from their own if they reach out to the other 'side'. That this intimidatory manifestation of religious-political tribalism is so prevalent in churches and faith communities is a matter of grave concern. It seems that churches have allowed themselves to develop the types of ethos that either mimic or adapt the intimidatory strategies of the society in which they live. The third root is paralysis created by the sense of inadequate training and insufficient skills to deal with the consequences of working across the community divide.

The theme of clergy 'overload' recurred frequently enough throughout our research for us to regard it as a significant factor in limiting cross tradition work in the churches sector. As one committed, but harassed, clergyman said when asked to attend a meeting of an inter-church group working on sectarianism: 'You know I am paid to minister to my flock, and there is a limit to what my parish will tolerate in terms of time given to other things.' Too often we came across committed and able ministers, carrying more than full workloads in their own congregations and parishes, who were trying to find time and energy for work across the tradition divide, usually at the expense of their leisure or family time. This raises not only questions about human resources management within churches and faith communities, but also about the model of 'successful ministry' that they espouse.

Our research shows that, on the whole, successful ministry seems to be judged in terms of how much a congregation or parish is growing or attracting new members and how vibrant is its internal life in terms of worship, prayer groups, Bible study groups, youth groups, social activities, and social justice programmes. The criteria for judgement are heavily weighted in terms of what benefits, sustains, and builds up their parish or congregation directly. In other words, judgement is made overwhelmingly in terms of issues around how effective the minister is in attending to community boundary maintenance. One strong message that this sends out is that successful ministers are those who can work with their own, for their own, among their own to build up their own. But in a society suffering antagonised religious division, the persistent re-inforcement even of healthy community boundaries, without adequate attention to cross tradition dimensions, has the unintended effect of deepening the sectarian divide.

In its less benign form, the tribal chaplain notion describes pastors and lay leaders, Roman Catholic and Protestant, who preach and act overtly as if the faith community is co-terminus with their national community and as if God blesses and ordains their social and political philosophy.[83] The danger, as theologian Emmanuel Clapsis points out, is that this has lead to:

> excluding the presence of God and therefore the recognition of human dignity of those who are different and live outside the boundaries of such communities. This is especially true in relation to those communities that are perceived to be a threat and/or abomination to the welfare and purity of specific and divinely sanctioned ethnic and national identities.[84]

Once people begin to see or to create a sense of the 'other' as being without the image of the divine, and as having less human dignity than their community, it sets up the conditions for regarding them as less than human. From there it is but a step to justifying their domination, exclusion, and in extreme cases their annihilation. This may be far from the intent of the preacher, yet it can and has been a direct consequence of their action.[85] That this type of behaviour, which is clearly contrary to the gospel, is either feebly challenged or tacitly condoned by the churches concerned is a scandal and reveals how far national idolatry has become embedded in the being of churches and faith communities in Northern Ireland. That it is allowed to pass publicly unchallenged by other churches is equally destructive and amounts to collusion with the idolatry, when a timely external challenge might have strengthened the hand of those within a church who wish to tackle the overtly 'tribal' approach of their own.

Idolatry in the political role of churches
We begin this section by asking a general question: is it appropriate for churches to have an overtly political role? One answer is that in a society riven by sectarian violence, where religion and politics are so closely and negatively aligned, it is impossible for churches not to play a political role. If, however, by political people mean party political, then our response must be 'no'. In all but exceptional circumstances, it is not the business of churches to promote one political party over another; Christian churches are sanctuaries for God's people from whatever creed, colour, or political persuasion. It can be the case, however, that a church's witness may be more congruent with the views of one party rather than another. In a deeply sectarian society, ministers of religion who are also elected political representatives are, in our view, risking seriously compromising their religious positions. If by political people mean the social, public sphere of society then our response is a qualified 'yes'. Yes, because by their nature and mission churches are called to serve as agents of transformation in society and must take their place and make their contribution to public debate of, and policy formation about, issues concerning the whole society, especially those to do with achieving peace. The 'yes' is qualified because the church, while entering the debate, needs also to try to retain its independence from societal pressures and be guided by the spirit and teachings of Jesus – to be in the world but not of it. In Northern Ireland we have ministers of religion involved in both party politics and in the realm of public debate and policy formation.

The small number of church ministers serving as elected officials of political parties stand in the Protestant tradition and on the whole represent a mindset that is either overtly or tacitly antagonistic to Roman Catholicism.[86] The expression of idolatry in their position lies not in their anti-Catholicism. They are entitled to critique Roman Catholicism provided they understand and move to mitigate the danger, prevalent in our violently divided society, of hardening the boundaries between their followers and Catholics in a manner that could encourage sectarianism. Rather, the taint of idolatry lies in their mixing of party politics and religion in such a way that they are putting allegiance to British, Protestant identity before shared identity in Christ, the *koinonia* to which the church is called, or they are making the two coterminous. The underlying logic of their position is that Roman Catholics are not Christian and therefore are to be opposed in the public and political sphere, lest the power of Rome take hold in Northern Irish society. They view, however, many liberal and conservative Protestants as also not Christian, and yet are able to make common political cause with them because they share a broader political identity. By the critique of their own standards, then, they are engaging in inconsistent and idolatrous behaviour.

Much larger numbers of ministers of religion have been, and are, involved in the realm of public debate and policy formation. It is important to acknowledge that church leaderships have, on the whole, been much more nuanced in their support of political positions during the Troubles than were their predecessors in the Home Rule crisis of 1912. There has been a development of relationship between church leaders, and they have maintained a good level of contact throughout the last thirty years. They have also been largely publicly supportive of the peace process. Other ministers too have played a very positive role, often behind the scenes and away from public recognition or support. These positive contributions have taken at least three forms. Firstly, there has been, over thirty years or more, a series of courageous initiatives by ministers, both Protestant and Roman Catholic, to enter into dialogue with paramilitaries, their political representatives, and other political parties in an effort to find a path towards understanding, and ultimately towards peace. These conversations were taking place when it was both unfashionable and even dangerous to be engaged in them. They created not only a network of relationships, but also some discreet channels of communication between people who could not meet publicly. Secondly, and also behind the scenes, as pastors to committed Christian politicians, ministers have exercised a ministry of influence and support. Thirdly, in the public realm, individual ministers, church institutions, and inter-church groups have consistently encouraged politicians to seek political accommodation for the sake of peace.

In exploring idolatry in the political role of churches it is important to acknowledge that the world of public politics is an ambiguous and tangled one. The clarity of moral certainty that churches might like to insist upon is often and necessarily muddied in the pursuit of workable accommodations and agreements. Churches are left, therefore, sometimes looking towards the greater goal of achieving peace and an end to violence and death in order to justify supporting morally suspect positions. This is never a comfortable situation for ministers of the gospel.

The shadow of idolatry in the political role of churches is evident in the way in which ministers have been subtly seduced into the 'political game'. It is expressed in two forms that are two sides of one dynamic. There has been a tendency to accept the oppositional political system and work within it instead of maintaining adequate distance and using the churches' mission of reconciliation to develop a critique that would move society in the direction of a more co-operative political model. To some degree this might be defended on the grounds of pure pragmatism. But it is striking that in constructing the Belfast Agreement, local politicians chose for the legislative assembly a model of functioning that enshrines co-operative as well as oppositional politics. Perhaps the stronger shadow is cast in the fact that churches and faith communities, while acting in a way that restrained violence, have tended to be little more than reflections of 'their' communities. To that extent they have failed to challenge their communities sufficiently to think beyond and even to cross boundaries or to expose and challenge divisive sectarian attitudes and actions in their own group. Ironically, the very process that has facilitated ministers and lay church leaders making an effective contribution in the political realm has also been a process whereby many have mirrored oppositional relationships and therefore have helped to create or sustain oppositional politics. They have invested large amounts of energy in advising their 'own' politicians and guiding their 'own' flocks in political choices without recognising that as long as churches failed to address fundamental division and difference within and between them, they not only undermined the gospel message of peace and reconciliation, which is their core mission, but also failed to give an example of a better or different way.

At this point, some may be tempted to reply that we are ignoring the huge and intractable religious problems that exist concerning doctrine and church order, problems that would at least stymie and likely prevent any attempt at closer church relationships. We would argue that in Northern Ireland it would have been, and is, possible to work at reconciliation and improved relationships between churches without necessarily becoming embroiled in contentious doctrinal issues. What is at issue here is a movement towards reconciliation of people connected with Christian traditions who have been or are killing, injuring, or intimidating one another against a background of politicised religion. It is about churches and faith communities acting to fulfil the twin biblical imperatives to cross boundaries towards those who are other and to be peacemakers.[87] These imperatives can and need to be addressed no matter what a person's view about ecumenism or worshipping together or church unity. We can distinguish reconciliation on at least three levels : (1) respectful, peaceful relationships; (2) shared basic faith commitments, particularly allegiance to Christ; and (3) the whole realm of doctrine. It is possible to work at reconciliation at levels (1) and (2) without having to open up wider doctrinal issues. This would manifest itself as inter-church co-operation in peacebuilding and the capacity to stand together and speak the gospel of reconciliation, while holding in tension the many differences between groupings. One example of such inter-church co-operation is that of Calvinist and Arminian evangelicals, who co-operate within the Evangelical Alliance while holding opposing theologies.

It is sobering to try, while acknowledging the role they fulfilled as restrainers, to imagine what the landscape of the Troubles would have looked like if the Christian churches had, at the outset, as institutions, worked seriously and consistently at improving their relationships; if they had preached a gospel of love of the enemy, a gospel of unbounded grace, accessible to all regardless of political/national considerations. One reason why this has not happened is that it would have torn churches apart and exposed covertly idolatrous mixes of religion and nationalism in attitudes, even among those in church leadership.

Conclusion
Our research has confirmed that the negative 'over against' pattern of relationship, which is characteristic of sectarianism, is manifest in a number of ways in churches and faith communities

in Northern Ireland. In particular, this identity in opposition is bound up with a directly idolatrous, or shadows of an idolatrous, relationship to nation and nationalism. Identities, modes of thinking, and leadership at the heart of churches and faith communities are sometimes coloured by concerns about the national sovereignty towards which they look in ways that detract from the sovereignty of Jesus Christ. The communion *(koinonia)* that is the fundamental being to which churches are called is fractured in many ways, among which are political fault lines that largely reflect, rather than challenge, the deep divide in wider society. This fracturing is undergirded by a model of successful ministry, in all traditions, that is focused on the growth, development, and maintenance of their own churches, with too little regard for boundary crossing and reconciling relationships. There is evidence that some ministers and local lay leaders feel too ill-equipped in terms of formation, too overloaded with internal parish or congregation duties, and too fearful of alienating certain groups within their 'flocks' to invest as much effort and creativity as they think is necessary to begin to heal relationships in their local area. All in all, this makes churches' fulfillment of their mission of reconciliation both fragmentary and a truly uphill struggle hampered by internal rifts.

SEPARATION

Another characteristic of healthy society that has become distorted into a destructive over-against pattern through sectarianism is separation. The process of forming identity and establishing belonging requires that individuals and groups understand and experience themselves as separate from others. When this gets distorted, however, healthy differentiation can take the form of an impetus towards destructive separation, which may lead to a sense of superiority and even self-righteousness. We argued earlier that separation is both a cause and an effect of sectarianism. It is also an outworking of the lie purveyed by the sectarian system that division affects every sphere of life and comprehensively separates people from those who are other. The issue of separation is complex, because it requires discernment about when the healthy boundary maintenance of distinct groups has become unhealthy and divisive separation that can fuel antagonised division. In the discussion which follows it is important to bear in mind that this impetus to destructive separation is embedded in and interactive with the religious-national nature of communities explored in the previous section. We have identified at least four types of dynamics involved in destructive separation in Northern Ireland: fear, self-absorption, disdain, and theological conviction.

Fear
In Northern Ireland, fear comes in a number of forms: fear of contamination by those who are religiously other, fear that a person's group will absorbed by, or taken over by the other, and fear for physical safety either from a person's own group or from the other. Fear of contamination is expressed largely by conservative evangelical Protestants who wish to keep themselves scrupulously separate from anyone, Protestant or Roman Catholic, who is not in their judgement Christian. Their concern is to protect the purity of their beliefs and to avoid in any way compromising the truth as they see it. This springs from theological conviction and we will address it under that section below.

Fear of being absorbed or taken over by another group is expressed predominantly by the Protestant-unionist community. They recognise themselves to be, and are fearful of their position, as a minority on the island of Ireland. Because of the growth in the Catholic-nationalist population in some urban areas, Protestant-unionists feel themselves being 'squeezed out' of areas which were traditionally theirs. This seems to come about in a spiral way. When Roman Catholics start moving into an area that is mostly Protestant-unionist, those residents begin to move out, which leaves more space for Catholic-nationalists to occupy and so the trend accelerates. This pattern is very visible in, for example, North Belfast. The movement of Protestant-unionists away from areas where Catholic-nationalists are beginning to live, even though there is no threat to them, suggests that there may be low tolerance of the anxiety that comes from living in a mixed area or minority situation, or an element of avoiding contamination that is perceived to come from living in proximity with Catholic-nationalists, or an element of disdain.

A person or group's fear for their physical safety from their own group can have a number of facets. There is direct intimidation and threat of violence from paramilitaries to prevent their own people from reaching out to the other tradition. There is also the vulnerability of those who do not 'fit in' to their community, such as mixed marriage couples.

By far the greatest source of fear has been, and is, the threat from the other tradition. The intensity of the violence of the last thirty years combined with the clear demarcation of 'sides' between nationalist and unionist, republican and loyalist, Roman Catholic and Protestant has meant that the choice to live in areas where the traditions are mixed is a precarious one. Small enclaves of one tradition living in areas largely dominated by the other tradition often feel themselves under threat, especially at times of heightened tension, such as during the marching season. This fear exists even where the custom of local relationships has been peaceful and neighbourly. Threat or even the fear of threat can be as potent a catalyst for population movement from mixed areas into ghettos of their 'own' kind as any actual physical attack. The accelerating development of segregated housing in turn re-inforces antagonised division and so the sectarian divide deepens and widens.

Much of the intimidation comes from small but powerful groups of paramilitaries in a local area; some is initiated by bored and frustrated young people caught up in the dynamic of antagonised division. It is, however, important to recognise that these groupings can only operate with tacit support from the majority local population. This support may take the form of ignorance of their existence and activities because people do not want to know, or of turning a blind eye to what is happening through fear, even if what is happening is an attack on or eviction of a neighbour whom they like and respect. The lack of a sense of collective involvement in and responsibility for this enforced separation is a feature of Northern Irish society.

In these dynamics of fear, people are treating the other as a leper to be avoided, or allowing the vulnerable to be threatened and persecuted, or allowing the stranger to be driven from their midst. Yet Jesus related with lepers, and Peter made it clear that God shows no partiality.[88] Moreover, hospitality for the stranger and for anyone who is vulnerable and in need is one of the great biblical themes. Abraham and Sarah, for example, welcomed and fed the three strangers who arrived unexpectedly at their home (Gen 18:1-8), the parable of humility and hospitality in the gospel of Luke challenges Christians to extend hospitality to those who cannot repay them (Lk 14:12-14), and the parable of the Good Samaritan shows how to care for a stranger who has been attacked (Lk 10:25-37). Making space in their tent, even physically, for the other who is different has been a fundamental tradition of the people of God from earliest times. It is one of the many practical aspects of the nature of church as communion *(koinonia)*. In Northern Ireland this will require people, not only to make space for the other, but also to face and come to terms with the hurts that the other or her/his community have caused them and vice versa, and so move towards reconciliation. Embracing and providing hospitality to the stranger is a core message of the gospel and it is central to what it means to be church and to be part of the reconciling mission of Christ.

Self-absorption
We have noted in previous chapters the tendency towards 'benign apartheid' in Northern Irish society. In part this is inspired by an unrealistic hope that if people live side by side and leave one another alone, all will be well. In part, however, it is the out-working of a self-absorbed spirit. The life of their community or their church is so time-consuming and so gratifying that people do not need or want to look beyond the boundary of their group. This is especially true when relationship with the people beyond the boundary is likely to be difficult and challenging. So they fill their time with good and worthy activities such as Bible study, prayer group, the Legion of Mary, novenas, and their calendars with events that are in themselves healthy and upbuilding: harvest suppers, youth rallies, retreats, Bible weeks, days of prayer, pilgrimages, etc. They also tend to live, to be educated, to socialise, and to marry largely with their own. Such concentration on their 'own' community or church life in a society divided along religious-political lines does, by default, foster destructive separation and thereby division. Communally they do not seem to have the will, or if there is the will, they do not have the time or the structures, to create meaningful, sustainable, and recognised bonds across the traditions. The creation and maintenance of these relationships is often left to the enthusiastic few who are willing to reach out to others and to organise periodic communal events. In the absence of sustained communal or institutional work at cross tradition relationships, separation is likely to persist and possibly deepen.

There appears to be nothing either intentional or malicious

about this self-absorption. It does raise questions, however, about people's understanding of what it means to be church, in particular, about the call to communion *(koinonia)* and to the mission of reconciliation. What does communion mean if it is exclusively with those who are within their own group? Jesus' response to the lawyer's question 'who is my neighbour?' in Luke's gospel is clear: Christians are to regard all people as neighbours.[89] The gospel call is to go beyond their boundaries and get to know and love the other. Similarly, people need to ask: whose responsibility is it to initiate moves towards reconciliation? Again Jesus' actions are unambiguous: he is the one to reach out to Peter, who denied him, and to re-establish the relationship.[90] Self-absorbed inertia, even for reasons of doing other good works, is not an option for churches living in a society riven by religious-political division, if those churches are to be true to their calling.

Disdain

A more intentional dynamic of destructive separation is that of disdain. People choose to keep themselves separate from a particular person, group, or organisation because they dislike, disagree with, scorn, or despise what they do, say, or stand for. This is not a stance that is based on specific theological or political convictions. It is not as reasoned a dynamic as that generated by clear conviction and often is fed by rumour, myth, and ignorance of the other. It can include some element of conviction, but it is a more general process of 'writing off' individuals or entire groups because people do not agree with them or have been hurt by them or see them as failing to meet criteria that they have set: for example, the mutual disdain displayed by many liberal or ecumenical individuals or groups and those who hold more conservative evangelical views.

One of the more destructive aspects of disdain is that the separation is usually so scornful or passionate that people have stopped listening to what the other has to say. They thereby cut themselves off from any reasonable opportunity to understand the other's position, or to have their erroneous and possibly dangerous myths about them debunked, or to recognise when the other has shifted position. Behind the dynamic of disdain is a sense of superiority, to which we will return in the following section, and a belief, however muted, that the other is irredeemable in any other way than becoming what they are or what they want them to be. Again, the gospel challenges this perspective by repeatedly showing the need for openness, conversation, and a willingness to be changed by the other. Jesus neither dismisses nor ignores people, even those who oppose him. He treats them with openness even when roundly condemning or physically opposing their actions and calling them to repentance. This can be seen in several conversations between Jesus and the Pharisees and Sadducees, including the cleansing of the Temple, recorded in Matthew, chapters twenty-one to twenty-three. Another example is the story of Zacchaeus, who moves to practical repentance simply through encounter and social interaction with Jesus.[91] Perhaps most instructive is the exchange between Jesus and the Canaanite woman in Mt 15: 21- 28. In the course of the conversation, Jesus shifts his understanding of his own mission from being exclusively to 'the lost sheep of the house of Israel' to include this foreigner. Such openness and dialogue does not necessarily mean agreeing with the conversation partner, but it does mean being open to receive insight in and through them and to being changed by encounter with them.

Theological conviction leading to separation
The fourth dynamic is that of destructive separation flowing from theological convictions which may be, in themselves, positive. It is important to note that the convictions concerned centre on whether, and if so how, the other can be viewed as 'church' or not. Roman Catholic and Protestant traditions respond in different ways, and for different reasons, to the need for their traditions to be distinct from one another. The drive to separation because of concern for purity in certain strands of Protestantism can be very clearly delineated. There are, however, other less overtly divisive theological stances, which can have significant outcomes in terms of separation, such as the Roman Catholic Church's refusal to recognise the validity of ordination in Protestant denominations and the negative impact on Catholics of knowing that friends or colleagues have subscribed to the Westminster Confession of Faith, with its offensive stance towards Roman Catholicism. We will look briefly at some Roman Catholic convictions and a variety of Protestant convictions.

Roman Catholic convictions

During the Second Vatican Council, the Roman Catholic Church modified its doctrinal claim to be the one true church to declare that the 'the unique church of Christ … subsists in the Catholic Church', a claim repeated in the recent document *Dominus Iesus*.[92] As we noted earlier, this modified understanding expressed in the documents of Vatican II evidences both a change in the Catholic Church's self-definition and a certain openness towards other churches, but one which is limited. The *Dominus Iesus* document, which is to be read in the light of Vatican II, makes clear that churches which have not 'preserved the valid episcopate and the genuine and integral substance of the eucharistic mystery, are not churches in the proper sense'.[93] Indeed, the text refers to them not as churches but as 'ecclesial communities'. Those churches which have maintained apostolic succession and have a valid Eucharist, but which reject the primacy of the Pope, are 'true particular churches'. All, however, are seen to suffer from 'defects'.[94] This vision of church, so central in Roman Catholicism, leads inevitably to a mode of operating that is best characterised as self-sufficiency. Believing that fullness subsists in itself, the Roman Catholic Church has no need of Protestant churches. Inter-church relationships, therefore, tend not to have a high priority in parish or diocesan life, or, if they do, it is likely to be out of the special interest of one individual or small group. The Roman Catholic Church is willing to recognise and acknowledge the spirit of God working in and through other churches and ecclesial communities but regards them as separated and deficient.

In one sense, this position entails neither hostility nor an active intent to exclude, even if effectively it does exclude. It is, rather, an acknowledgement that there is not yet basis for communion, or full communion, because of fundamental differences in doctrine. This is a serious theological position held also by Orthodox churches, but it is one that has consequences in a society divided religiously and politically. What appears to be a somewhat self-contained acceptance of separateness, when not mitigated by active institutional commitment to reach out to the Protestant community, can be unhelpful in at least two ways. Firstly, because it undermines reconciliation work and peace-building by giving the impression that these activities are marginal to the life of the Roman Catholic community. Secondly, it conveys, by silence and distance, at least a sense of ignoring, and possibly a sense of disdain for, expressions of Protestant Christianity.

These dynamics are then further accentuated by the insistence of the hierarchy of the Roman Catholic Church on maintaining a segregated education system, while largely refusing to show positive support for forms of integrated education. We acknowledge that the issue of education is sensitive for Roman Catholics who historically suffered discrimination in the under funding of their schools and who regarded good education as a means of rising above the discriminatory social and political system that pertained in Northern Ireland from partition until recently. It is also true that in a divided society, control of schooling is about the formation and transmission of cultural identity, and Protestant denominations have not necessarily wanted integrated education either. We would want to support the right of any religious group to educate their young people in an ethos consonant with their beliefs. But there are unhelpful consequences of segregated education here that issue from the context of a divided society, and they need to be given serious consideration. Without effort and careful management, segregation can cut young people off from meaningful contact with their contemporaries in other traditions and deepen the already considerable ignorance between the traditions. It can also re-inforce a sense of self-sufficiency about the Roman Catholic Church and heighten suspicion through ignorance in the Protestant unionist community. One experience during the research worried us in this regard. When working with third-year trainee teachers (twenty years old) in St Mary's University College in Belfast, the Roman Catholic teacher training college for Northern Ireland, we discovered that a number of students had either never met or never had a serious conversation with a Protestant. These young people seemed unaware that there are serious implications of such ignorance of the Protestant-unionist tradition among those who will be educating the next generation of young Roman Catholics.

In no sense are we suggesting that Roman Catholics abandon their truth claim about 'the unique church of Christ' subsisting in their church. It is their right to hold this claim. Rather, we regard gospel injunctions, to welcome the stranger and to reach across boundaries in the name of the reconciling love of Jesus, as entailing at least the need to mitigate the effects of separateness by: (1) recognising the ease with which this can veer into disdain and (2) active institutional commitment to building peaceful, respectful relationships that recognise shared identity in Christ. We are specifying the aspect of institutional commitment because the truth claim is an institutional norm that profoundly shapes the being and identity of the Roman Catholic Church. Such an institutional commitment to building relationships would include at least structural links with Protestant churches and schools.

The self-sufficiency of the Roman Catholic Church has another largely unintended effect in the religious-political realm. It can, in certain circumstances, be interpreted as having an element of secrecy or mystery about it. When combined with the fact that the Vatican is a political state, and the significant political influence that Roman Catholicism has had in the Irish Republic and in other 'Catholic' countries such as Spain, Italy, and Poland, this perceived secrecy has fuelled fears about the political agenda and intent of the Church of Rome in general, and in Northern Ireland in particular. The Roman Catholic Church may well claim that it has no strictly political agenda other than the universal Christian imperative to seek justice and peace for all in society. Nevertheless, in a society where all churches and faith communities have been involved in an 'idolatrous shift of loyalty' towards national interests, it needs to take the fears seriously and to consider discussing openly the contours of its political agenda as it sees it.

Protestant convictions
There are at least four sets of convictions within Protestantism which can potentially or actually lead to destructive separation, one which pertains to largely liberal or ecumenical Protestant constituencies and three which characterise a spectrum of more evangelical groups.

Among the larger denominations at institutional level, Presbyterian, Church of Ireland, and Methodist, there is a recognition that the Roman Catholic Church is a Christian church. This does not necessarily dispel unease about aspects of what is regarded as Roman Catholicism's unbiblical approach particularly in the place given to tradition, the Virgin Mary, the Pope, certain sacraments, the role of the clergy, and statues and images.

These denominations, however, are involved, officially or unofficially, in the ecumenical movement and maintain an openness towards Roman Catholics and all Christians, evident in the practice of an open communion table. As in the case of Roman Catholicism, this openness represents a shift of position that has taken place over the last decades, and particularly under the influence of the ecumenical movement.

The Roman Catholic Church, without saying that earlier formulations were wrong, convoked a Vatican Council that revised the standards of the faith, and altered or at least mitigated some theological beliefs that were offensive to, and derogatory about, both Protestant Christianity and Judaism. Some Protestant denominations have maintained in current force historical documents that contain assertions, which are offensive to and derogatory about Roman Catholicism, though in practice some sections of these denominations, though not all, ignore such content.[95] The Presbyterian Church in Ireland has moved to minimise the potential for hurt and divisiveness by passing resolutions at General Assembly level, which go some way to mitigating the effect of such anti-Catholic texts,[96] but without superseding them. Similarly, the Church of Ireland has acknowledged that 'negative statements' in some of its formularies do not represent the 'spirit of this church today' and regrets that some elements of its formularies might be used in a manner which is hurtful to other Christians.[97]

Such actions, while already an improvement, still leave open the path to destructive separation in two ways. The retention of texts containing formulations offensive and hurtful to Roman Catholics undermines and subtly puts in question the commitment of that denomination to positive inter-church relationship, however loud the disavowal of the content may be. Such texts leave in force within the tradition material that gives power and weight to the arguments of those who wish to pursue a blatantly anti-Catholic agenda. The implications, legal, financial, and in terms of potential for creating new ruptures within the denomination, of changing these historical documents are very serious and require close consideration. There is, however, within the biblical notion of *kenosis* (self-emptying), so central to the movement towards communion *(koinonia)* to which churches are called, a demand to let go of old loyalties that no longer serve, and to go beyond the best of ourselves in the search for communion in Christ. In this spirit, we wonder if it is not possible for these denominations to agree a revised standard of faith, which builds upon but supersedes the historical confessions. Of course, such a process would require denominations facing deep internal divisions over relationships with the Roman Catholic Church and would likely expose how ambivalent is the support for positive inter-church relationships. It would also require them to affirm that in some way their identity has changed, and this is not an easy task for any institution.

Among more evangelically-inclined Protestants, whether within the larger denominations or in smaller, new churches and other organisations, there are at least three major stances that can potentially or actually lead to destructive separation. There are some, for example, who belong to ECONI and YMCA, who accept the Roman Catholic Church as a Christian church, while at the same time remaining critical of and rejecting what they regard as unbiblical beliefs and practices of that church. They may or may not, therefore, be able to share worship with Roman Catholics, but can and do enter into dialogue with them and work alongside them in some areas. Many are particularly conscious of the need to relate with them positively over issues affecting civic life. This is a significant and effective mitigation of the potential for destructive separation in their theological stance. Those who hold such theological convictions need to be continually vigilant about the potential for divisiveness in their stance and to mitigate it by consciously building positive relationships in areas which impact upon communal, civic life.

A second stance is that of evangelical Protestants who believe that the Roman Catholic Church is not Christian, but who recognise that there is a need to, and are prepared to, interact with Roman Catholics around issues that concern the wider civic community. People taking this stance are likely to be found in the larger denominations as well as in organisations like Evangelical Alliance, YMCA, and ECONI. They too regard Roman Catholic beliefs and practices as unbiblical and in error and may or may not, therefore, be able to share worship or to enter into formal dialogue with Roman Catholics around religious issues. Many, however, accept that individual Catholics may be Christian and may be saved. This is a midway position for evangelicals who, while rejecting the Roman Catholic Church, wish to recognise that some individual Catholics live

evidently holy and Christian lives. This stance entails a significant risk of encouraging divisive separation. Those who hold
these convictions need to be aware of the risk and to mitigate it
by at least showing and actively promoting charity towards
Roman Catholics, where possible taking opportunities to learn
more about what Roman Catholics believe from Roman Catholic
sources and engaging alongside Catholics in work for the development of civic society.

A third stance is that adopted by, for example, the Free
Presbyterian Church and the Caleb Foundation, but which is
also found among some evangelicals within the larger denominations. It entails actual separation. These groups believe that
the Roman Catholic Church is not a Christian church, that it is
radically in error, that the Pope is the antichrist, and that those
who persist in Roman Catholic beliefs are doomed to hell. This
stance is usually accompanied by a deep and genuine concern
for 'truth' and a distrust of dialogue with those in error, on the
grounds that it will lead to compromise of the 'truth'. For that
reason, many, though not all, desire to remain scrupulously separate from Roman Catholics, or indeed from any person or
group, Protestant or Catholic, which might be a cause of
contamination of beliefs. Some people holding these beliefs distinguish religious and social separation and therefore, while remaining religiously separate, they would be open to entering
into social interaction with those deemed to be in error.

There are significant risks concerning destructive separation
and sectarianism in holding these convictions. The convictions
themselves are simply truth claims, which the churches and
groups are entitled to make. People holding these beliefs, however, need to recognise that they can, but need not necessarily,
open the door to destructive patterns of relating, such as actively
hardening the boundaries between their adherents and Catholics,
demonising and belittling Roman Catholicism, passively increasing ignorance and myths about Catholics, and justifying or collaborating in the domination of Catholics. Such patterns of relating
are ones that we have already identified as sectarian.

Those holding these beliefs, therefore, have to work especially
hard at mitigating the potentially destructive effects of their
stance in this society, riven as it is by antagonised religious and
political division. This cannot mean less than: (1) being careful
to learn what Roman Catholics truly believe and basing their

arguments on accurate fact, (2) actively promoting Christian charity to Catholics and others whom they consider to be in error, (3) defending full citizenship rights for Roman Catholics, and (4) refraining from mixing religiously-based opposition to Roman Catholicism with party political motivations. In a situation where, for reasons of conscience, a Christian person or group does not feel able to meet and dialogue with others whom they oppose, it is incumbent upon them to ensure that the distanced relationship that exists is as much as possible animated by the gospel injunction to charity.

Conclusion

There are destructive dynamics of separation, whether deliberate or unintentional, in operation in the churches and faith communities in Northern Ireland. On the whole, these dynamics reflect rather than challenge the antagonised divisions of the 'world' that the church is intended to serve, and in no small measure they contribute to deepening divisions. In doing so they undermine the nature of church as inclusive and welcoming, characterised by *koinonia* (communion), and they militate against the mission of the church as reconciliation. That this situation has continued in the face of a society so much in need of the message and experience of healing and reconciliation that Christianity can offer, can only be understood as a failure of the duty of stewardship. Christians, as Paul says, have been entrusted with the message of reconciliation.[98] This is a resource available to churches and faith communities to be used in the service of the Lord who calls the church into being and sends it out to proclaim the gospel to all nations indiscriminately.[99]

SUPERIORITY AND SELF-RIGHTEOUSNESS

An additional destructive element running through the characteristics of both the religious-national nature of churches and the separation of churches and faith communities is that of superiority. Enshrined, often unconsciously but sometimes consciously, in 'idolatrous shifts of loyalty', physical intimidation, self-absorption, disdain, and theological convictions are collective understandings that one group, which is defining itself over against the other group in terms of culture or power or religious belief, is superior. In religious circles this sense of superiority can also overflow into self-righteousness.

Historically it is true, as the Faith and Politics Group note, that '[n]ational superiority supported by a belief in divine sanction has been used to justify the domination of one nation over others.'[100] Moreover, as we observed in chapter three, the doctrine of 'error has no right' combined with a doctrine of 'providence' has functioned religiously to justify the belief that God wants people to persecute those who oppose them. The logic of both these assumptions of superiority has been or is evident in the conflict in Northern Ireland. Given the different status that churches and faith communities now have in society, they no longer formally have the power to exert domination. It is, however, evident that many Christians, across all traditions, behave as if belonging to their church or faith community makes them superior to others and as if righteousness does not exist outside the doors of their assembly. Indeed for some, righteousness even among those participating in the community cannot be assumed. These attitudes are predicated on a sense of individual or collective self-righteousness and on judgements made about others. Such dynamics, whether individual or collective, are antithetical to the Christian gospel. It is to the gospel, and its interpretation in the struggles of the early Christian community, that we can look for the imperative that challenges claims to superiority and self-righteousness.

The Pauline response to inter-community, inter-ethnic rivalry between Jews and Gentiles in the nascent Christian community is instructive with regard to superiority, self-righteousness, and judgment of others. Paul's letters emphasise that in Christ, through baptism, a new single humanity comes into being 'out of the two', in this case Jewish and Gentile communities.[101] In the new Israel[102] difference is not abolished by unity, but rather differences are made subordinate to identity in Christ through faith.[103] In Romans chapter three the writer makes clear that justification is by grace through faith, and that faith may be expressed in very different ways, through circumcision or not, according to the cultural background of the believer. One fundamental Pauline insight is that Christianity does not nullify cultural identity; it subordinates it to identity in Christ and therefore to the demands of the gospel of love preached by Jesus. Later in the letter to the community in Rome, Paul spells out the extent of that subordination: it is permissible to eat or not eat, to drink or not drink, to regard things as clean or not clean, as long as everything is done in honour of the Lord and with due regard for the up-building of the community.[104] The cultural freedom shown by Paul is breathtaking. His injunction is that all should live in a manner that edifies others, and if that means letting go of cultural beliefs, in this case about food laws and purity, then so be it. Moreover, Paul asserts that it is not the place of community members to judge one another; judgement is to be left to the Lord: 'For we will all stand before the judgment seat of God.' (Rom 14:10)

The notion of justice undergirding Pauline thought here is the Hebrew sense that justice is 'a style of action in a relation of fellowship between partners which is the permanent constituent of this relationship'.[105] The Pauline view of 'justification' has an inherently relational character based in God's relationship with human beings. Individual justification cannot be judged solely in terms of relationship with God; it always entails the dimension of just relationship with neighbours and between communities. This Pauline approach to the demands of new identity in Christ and its relativisation of cultural identity leaves no basis for individual or collective claims to superiority or self-righteousness. According to Paul, Christian believers, through the free gift of grace, share the identity of the one who being God emptied himself and took the form of a servant and became humbler yet, even to total self-emptying in the crucifixion.[106] In this lies the foundation of both equality and freedom in the new creation, and the imperative that Christians are not to boast of anything except Christ crucified.[107]

Use and abuse of scripture
One of the most insidious and destructive means by which religious superiority and self-righteousness can be expressed is by the use and abuse of scripture. This is a large and complex topic, to which we cannot possibly do justice, but rather will give a few illustrations of what we consider to be destructive uses of scripture that are likely to encourage or give apparent legitimacy to dynamics of sectarianism. We will focus on three in particular: uses of Old Testament scripture which ignore the fulfilment of the old covenant by the new covenant in Christ; the use of scripture to support or give authority to political ideologies; and applying scripture out of context.

A selective use of scripture is always problematic. It is particularly so when Christians appeal to texts that explicate the 'old covenant' without reference to the ways in which the 'new covenant' in Christ has fulfilled the old one. Jesus' great injunctions with regard to love were: to love the Lord your God, to love your neighbour as yourself and to love your enemies.[108] In several boundary-breaking incidents, Jesus demonstrated the universality of these commandments by, for example, offering salvation to people like the Samaritan adulteress at the well and to the tax collector, Zacchaeus, one a despised foreigner and the other a despised local, shunned by his own.[109] The rubrics of the old covenant that would separate believers from people like these (e.g. Is 52:11), or even encourage the utter annihilation of the enemies of God (e.g. Deut 7:2), are transformed in the Christian gospel. Yet such ideas and texts continue to be used in some evangelical circles to lend authority to a separatism that seems hardly to recognise the example and ministry of Jesus and to justify demonising Roman Catholicism. It is true that a strand of teachings concerning separation continues into the New Testament, nowhere more strikingly than in 2 Cor 6:17, which draws on Is 52:11 to say, 'Therefore come out from them, and be separate from them, says the Lord, and touch nothing unclean.' The few New Testament passages advocating separation have at least as much to do with the internal integrity of the church, however, as with relations with those outside, and in any case traces of separation are radically relativised, even transformed, by the thrust of all the major themes of the New Testament.

Scriptural texts can also be pressed into service to give authority or sanction to political ideologies. For example, the Deuteronomy text mentioned in the previous paragraph appears chillingly in an Ulster Volunteer Force wall mural on Sandy Row, Belfast: '[Y]ou must utterly destroy them. Make no covenant with them and show them no mercy.' (Deut 7:2) The mural depicts outlines of armed men and alongside the Deuteronomy text it reads:

They arose in those dark days
to defend our native land
for God and Ulster.

Such a crude and blatant mixing of religion and nationalism is, as we have seen, idolatrous. That the scriptures should be used, out of context, to sanction the pursuit of a political ideology by force of arms is an abuse. It is remarkable, and a sign of the ambivalence in society here, that church authorities or the Belfast

City Council have not managed to have this mural, and others like it, removed.

It is very tempting for individuals and groups to take strong and evocative biblical imagery and to use it against those whom they oppose. This process may be legitimate where the context of the biblical image matches the context of the actions of the opponent. Out of context, it can serve simply as means to demonise the other. A striking example is the use of 'antichrist' to describe the Roman Catholic papacy. Sociologists John Brewer and Gareth Higgins trace the development of the use of this image and note that its original context and use, in the book of the Apocalypse, was to describe a political power, namely the Roman Empire, and not a church.[110] They show that the application of the term antichrist to an individual pope pre-dated its use by the Reformers, Luther and Calvin, and that in fact in the schism of 1378, when there were three popes competing for power, these individuals used that term of one another. The use of biblical imagery out of context in a manner that demonises an individual, group or structure is an abuse of sacred texts in the service of sectarian dynamics.

Conclusion

Attitudes of superiority and self-righteousness are present in relationships both within and between churches, and between church people and the wider society. These are particularly corrosive agents in any community; they weaken, distort, and ultimately destroy relationships. In churches whose fundamental nature is *koinonia*, communion, they manifest the polar opposite of what churches are called to be. Moreover, they undermine the church's mission of reconciliation by inculcating distance, division, and even disdain at the heart of communities. Jesus made a very challenging response to the disciples who were arguing about who was the greatest among them:

> Whoever welcomes this child in my name welcomes me, and whoever welcomes me, welcomes the one who sent me; for the least among all of you is the greatest. (Lk 9:48)

Superiority and self-righteousness are clearly antithetical to the gospel of Jesus who expressed his own role as one of service. One of the greatest contributions that Christians can make to the life of their churches and local communities is to repent of these attitudes and to re-commit themselves to live the depth of humility that true discipleship demands.

TRANSFORMING IDENTITY AND BELONGING

However disturbing the picture of the role of churches and faith communities in sectarianism that is emerging from this research, there are two immediate sources of hope. First, the current 'peace process' offers an opportunity for all of society, including churches, to work diligently to examine and learn from the past and to use those insights to help to build a new, more inclusive society. This will mean churches and faith communities recognising and owning their distorted expressions of identity and belonging, in order to be able to transform them. The transformation will be both active and passive – a conscious re-ordering of confessional identity undertaken in a kenotic spirit. Such *kenosis* is made possible by the second source of hope, namely the promise made by God in Christ to make a new creation.[111] Herein lie the power and the biblical mandate for churches and faith communities to let go of distortions and develop new and evolving identities and a new sense of belonging. We noted above, in discussing levels of identity in church, that according to the *Groupe des Dombes*, both individual Christian identity and ecclesial identity have an eschatological dimension and are provisional to the extent that they are rooted in a constantly reinterpreted identity in Jesus Christ. The task of moving beyond sectarianism for churches, therefore, entails developing hermeneutics appropriate for being a reconciling presence in a society riven by antagonism that is religiously as well as politically motivated.[112]

What is envisaged here is firstly a journey of reconciliation within and between churches and faith communities towards a new way of being 'church'. It will be a renewal of the nature of church as *koinonia* and the mission of church as reconciliation. Such communion and reconciliation will affect and be lived by the churches at different levels; it will impinge upon both individual and confessional identities. How far the movement of reconciliation will extend must remain an open question to be determined by the churches and faith communities themselves. Flowing from this inter-church journey towards reconciliation will be a renewed engagement with society. This is not a process of churches and faith communities 'cosying up' to one another – the demands of reconciliation needed to move beyond sectarianism will feel anything but cosy – it is rather a renewal of the mission and witness of 'church' to society. In particular it will be a witness to, model of, and resourcing for genuine struggle to overcome antagonised religious and political division.

The task for churches and faith communities is threefold and entails developing certain hermeneutics in order to counter or to mitigate other predominant hermeneutical approaches. Firstly, it means moving from a predominant hermeneutic of suspicion of others towards a hermeneutic of suspicion of their own positions and motivations. It is a movement away from beginning by blaming others to first, radically, and perhaps unilaterally, taking responsibility for their own implication in sectarianism. There are signs of this happening in small ways, for example in the work of the Church of Ireland sub-committee on sectarianism. Secondly, it means moving from a predominant hermeneutic of retrieval of all that makes them different from and superior to others towards a hermeneutic of retrieval of identity in Christ and of the boundary-breaking inclusiveness lived by Jesus Christ. It is a movement away from constructing identities negatively over against others to developing identities in the kind of positive relationship that respects and leaves space for difference does not necessarily imply agreement. Thirdly, it means moving from a predominant hermeneutic of negative engagement with others, within their own church tradition, in other Christian traditions and in society, towards a hermeneutic of positive engagement with those who are different, or who are antagonistic. It is a movement away from the type of separation that augments ignorance, fear, and division to the type of engagement that brings the wisdom and the challenge of Christian discipleship to bear on differences within a tradition, differences between traditions, and on the deliberations of society.

In the sections that follow, the theological implications of these three tasks are outlined along with some of the key questions which face churches and faith communities that seek to find ways of moving beyond sectarianism. The questions can be addressed both by institutions and by individual Christians. The tasks are not necessarily sequential; they are likely to be overlapping. Tasks one and two, which comprise a journey into deeper *koinonia* and reconciliation between churches and faith communities, will be a necessary means of better equipping churches for the third task of positive engagement.

1. From blame towards responsibility and repentance

The movement from a predominant hermeneutic of suspicion of others towards a hermeneutic of suspicion of themselves has at least two aspects: one which is orientated from the present into the past, and the other which is orientated from the present into future. Earlier in this chapter we noted the 'necessary judgment' under which, according to David Stevens, all civic institutions must fall when we come to look back at what has happened in society here. Given that this conflict has had both religious and political aspects, it is crucial that churches and faith communities summon up the courage to lead the process of necessary judgment, beginning with themselves. The imperative to lead the process, rather than to be dragged unwillingly into it or left as a scapegoated bystander, derives from the richness of the models and understandings that the church has to offer to society. Christian communities have a particularly important resource in the form of a truth-telling that leads to repentance. The belief that the offer of forgiveness made by God in Christ carries with it the seeds of renewed life and identity is a gift of hope that churches can make to society. Both the truth-telling and the repentance are important. The truth-telling will ventilate emotions and contribute to the compilation of a communal 'memory suffused with moral judgement', which theologian Donald Shriver regards as one of the marks of a society moving into forgiveness. Repentance is a gift from the Jewish and Christian traditions that can help to free people and institutions from crippling burdens of guilt and shame that will remain long after the fighting has stopped.

The key theological theme of this task is repentance. Some of the questions facing churches and faith communities are:

* In what way have we been engaged in 'idolatrous shifts of loyalty'?
* In what way have we contributed to and mirrored oppositional relationships in our own communities and with others?
* In what ways have we separated ourselves from others through: not welcoming the stranger, self-absorption, disdain, or our sincerely held theological convictions?
* In what way have we been tempted into self-righteousness and assumptions about superiority?
* In what way have our models of successful ministry failed

to adequately address the antagonised religious and political divide in society?

* In what ways have we used or abused scripture or tolerated or condoned its abuse?

The orientation from the present into the future will necessitate an ongoing checklist of questions that will help churches and faith communities to expose for themselves any subtle or inadvertent sectarian implications of their proposed statements, actions or decisions, the kind of 'overlooking' which can occur when a group's attention is focussed too narrowly on their own concerns. The aim of exposing sectarian implications is not to prevent a group from taking the action considered but to alert them to the type of consequences of the action that will need to be mitigated if they are not to risk deepening the sectarian divide. Checklist questions might include for example:

* How will this decision, statement, or action be understood by others?

* Are there alterations that we could, in good conscience, make which would ease the impact?

* What types of mitigating strategy do we need to put in place in conjunction with the action?

* What do the other community or communities need to hear us say or see us do at this time?

2. From opposition towards forbearance and inclusion

The movement from a predominant hermeneutic of retrieval of all that makes them different from or superior to others towards a hermeneutic of retrieval of identity in Christ, requires churches and faith communities to open themselves to the full implications of the scandalous choice of God to give grace priority over justice. At the heart of the Christian gospel is a righteous God who, out of love, compassion, and empathy for this world, was prepared to embrace self-emptying even to the point of dying for human beings while they were yet sinners.[113] In the kenotic sacrifice of Jesus, God forbore both rightful dignity and vengeance in order to offer forgiveness, righteousness, and reconciliation to human beings. Moreover, in Christ, God has, by grace, made of the world one new creation – this is the eschatological endpoint of the boundary-breaking inclusivity which the historical Jesus lived. This is also the 'already present – not yet' future which beckons the churches. Entry into the self-sacrificing love of God calls churches and faith communities to give priority to grace over justice in forgiveness and in the forbearance of vengeance. This does not mean that rightful claims to justice are given up; they are not. It does mean, however, that justice is cleansed of any taint of vengeance and that justice is pursued within the larger context of reconciliation, specifically in relation to the forbearing possibilities suggested by forgiveness. Forbearance of vengeance and empathy for the other are two of the marks of communal movement into forgiveness identified by Donald Shriver. Shriver also argues that without these conditions, the truth-telling about which we reflected in the last section might easily fuel new sources of enmity and division.

The key theological themes of this task are forgiving and repenting. Some of the questions facing the churches and faith communities are:

* How can we help one another to face the cost of forgiveness and the forbearance of vengeance?

* How can we help one another to recognise that we are all, to differing degrees, both victims and perpetrators in this conflict, and therefore we all have things to forgive and to repent of?

* Whom do we need to forgive, and what do we need to make that possible?

* To whom do we need to repent, and what do we need to make that possible?

* What are the resources within our tradition that speak a theology of grace, a theology of repentance, and a theology of forgiveness?

* What kind of structures and processes might we put in place, within our tradition and across traditions, to help one another to let out the hurts, and to ritualise remembering, repentance, forbearance, and forgiveness?

* How might we change our patterns of worship so that they more adequately convey and reflect the message of the priority of grace and of self-emptying forgiveness and our necessary response of repentance?

3. From separation towards positive engagement
and the will to co-existence

The movement from a predominant hermeneutic of negative engagement with others towards a hermeneutic of positive

engagement with those who are different or antagonistic requires churches and faith communities to enter into a radical
process of *kenosis,* self-emptying. To do this is to pattern themselves on Christ, who, 'though he was in the form of God, did
not regard equality with God as something to be exploited, but
emptied himself'. (Phil 2:6-7) It means taking into account what
the other needs in order to be able relate to them, just as God
sent Jesus to show the face of God to human beings in a manner
that could be received and understood. It does not mean giving
up the distinctive identities of different churches and faith communities except insofar as they are distorted. It means, rather,
examining them to identify what contributes to separation and
misunderstanding or presents obstacles to fuller relationship,
and then seeking ways in which, without doing violence to the
tradition, these identities can be re-expressed. Such self-emptying has a number of effects. (1) It invites God to speak love, compassion, and reconciliation into the space created and to speak
through the churches to a society in need of healing. (2) It signals
at least a will to co-exist with the other in positive relationship.
Kenosis for the sake of better relationship, and a movement towards reconciliation with others, is a strong and counter-cultur-
al gift that churches and faith communities can give to this society. (3) It creates both the space and positive conditions of communication within which a deeper communion, *koinonia,* within
and between churches can flourish. This in turn can be a model
of positive relationship in diversity for others.

The key theological theme of this task is *kenosis,* self-emptying. Some of the questions facing the churches and faith communities are:

   * What among our truth claims or in our way of living our
   confessional identity are not essential and might be modified
   or let go?
   * Which of our truth claims and ways of living our confessional identity are not negotiable? Are these expressed arrogantly or humbly? Can they be re-expressed?
   * What strategies of mitigation could we put in place to ameliorate the effect of what is not negotiable?
   * What are our resources and strategies for dealing with difference within our own tradition?
   * What models of, or lessons about, relationship have we as
   churches and faith communities to offer to society? How best
   might these be expressed?

Conclusion

It is clear that churches and faith communities in Northern Ireland have developed distorted expressions of both identity and belonging, which contribute to and are exacerbated by sectarianism. In no small part, churches mirror the oppositional styles of relationship characteristic of sectarianism.[114] The process of redeeming these distorted expressions is a demanding one. It entails a re-orientating or retrieval of parts of the Christian tradition and resources, the living of which have become overlaid by negative elements. It will be a radical renewal of what it means to be 'church' called to live communion, *koinonia,* and to exercise a ministry of reconciliation. In particular, it requires a re-orientation of three hermeneutics in a multifaceted shift that will depend upon individual and communal repentance, individual and communal forgiveness, and individual and communal self-emptying. There are strong and vibrant resources in the Christian tradition, particularly in its biblical heritage, and in concepts of truth-telling, repentance, forgiveness, reconciliation, and self-emptying, that have much to offer to a society where genuine expressions of community and positive relationship are desperately needed.

CHAPTER 8

Moving Beyond …

Introduction
The preceding chapters map out our understanding of the nature, depth, and extent of sectarianism in Northern Ireland. Our repeated emphasis on the systemic nature of sectarianism and the unintentional ways in which people find themselves colluding with it risk, as some of our most valued friends and critics have pointed out, inducing in people a sense of hopelessness and inevitability. While we have tried to deal with this problem at points throughout the book, it is appropriate in conclusion that we address directly two questions that arise naturally in response to what we have written: If sectarianism is as portrayed here, what might a place beyond sectarianism be like? And, how can people go about bringing that place into being? These questions seek both for signs of hope and for practical pointers to the way ahead. Possible answers have been scattered along the way, sometimes implicit and sometimes in fragments. We turn now to more direct comment.

What might a place beyond sectarianism be like?
It is a fairly simple psychological truth that people will not change if they do not have a vision of what it is that they are changing to, moving toward, becoming. In the absence of such a vision, they will, to a remarkable extent, prefer the devil they know to the devil they don't. They may even prefer the devil they know and dislike to the rumour of some great thing if they cannot see how they could possibly get there. No vision, no change – even though people may rail against their present situation. When captivated by a vision, on the other hand, the changes people are capable of are amazing.

The place we have in mind will not be a utopia, and it will not be the kingdom of God fully realised. It will, we hope, be a noticeably happier and more relaxed place. But it will still be

337

Northern Ireland, people will still disagree strongly, and people will still dislike each other. The most remarkable feature of a place beyond sectarianism will not be the absence of conflict but how conflict is handled. It is possible, in fact, that every disagreement and distinction existing now will exist there. Because of the different ways that people handle their disagreeing and disliking and difference, however, they will be able to say that this is Northern Ireland transformed and redeemed. Not fully, of course, because limitations and weaknesses will still be apparent, but transformed in recognisable, significant, and satisfying part.

The relationship between action and thought, the external and the internal, between public manifestation and inner logic, is not easily determined. At the very least, however, we are persuaded that outward changes are most likely to endure when they are accompanied by inward transformation. What follows, therefore, is a sketch of some key features of the spiritual, mental, and relational landscape of Northern Ireland when it has become a place beyond sectarianism.

Northern Ireland beyond sectarianism will be marked by several key features.

Spiritual renewal, and a noticeable increase in spiritual warmth
We have always understood sectarianism as a spiritual problem in part, therefore requiring a spiritual solution in part. What we have had in mind, however, has been a fairly robust and concrete version of spirituality, focusing on the dynamics of taking responsibility, repenting, forgiving, doing justice, telling the truth, and self-emptying. In other words, being reconciled. This we would still stand over, but we have also come to see the need for a more general spiritual renewal.

Two people that Joe interviewed raised this point particularly sharply. One man, unsentimental and deeply engaged in grassroots work in the community, said simply and bluntly that unless the level of love in the community at large is raised at least a few degrees, he cannot see any possibility of a lasting peace worthy of the name. Indeed the inter-communal chill factor is in some places positively polar, even in places where obvious, overt sectarianism is not much of a problem. And when things are that cold, the laws of physics apply: things slow down and movement of any kind is much harder, if it is possible at all. A

Church of Ireland clergyman, working in a particularly difficult situation in mid-Ulster, made a similar point. For the people of his parish, he said, expectations of religion are sunk in a sense of tradition and obligation so stultifying that they simply cannot hear anything new. I can preach the ministry of reconciliation until I'm blue in the face, he said. I can explicitly apply it to our local circumstances, but right now they are simply incapable of hearing it. In these circumstances, and we suspect in more circumstances than people sometimes admit, spiritual renewal – an expanded and enlivened inner spirituality – is a necessary prelude to moving beyond sectarianism. This renewal will be both individual and communal. Spiritual renewal alone will not solve the problem of sectarianism, of course, and renewal could even be twisted in ways that strengthen sectarianism, but spiritual renewal is a necessary part of the solution.

While we have our own ideas about what such renewal might entail, we resist the inclination to be more specific. What renewal means, after all, will vary from one tradition to another. What constitutes renewal for one group might look beside the point to another. What matters most is that renewal take forms and expressions familiar enough that it can be recognised as authentic to the tradition and strange enough that it can inspire real change. For immediate purposes, then, we stick to the general definition above – spiritual renewal involves an expanded and enlivened inner spirituality.

Changes in mental habit

If a general increase in spiritual warmth is a necessary condition of moving to a place beyond sectarianism, authentic spiritual renewal will be accompanied and marked by changes in mental habit. Indeed, in the Christian tradition spiritual renewal and changes in mental habit are not neatly distinguishable, Christians being enjoined, after all, to 'be transformed by the renewing of your minds.' (Rom 12:2)

On this topic, we feel little need to elaborate. Chapter by chapter, the mental characteristics necessary to move beyond sectarianism have been either explicitly developed or else implicit in our critique of the ways of sectarianism. Distinguishing between intentions and consequences, mitigation, new ways of dealing with difference, and bifocal vision are just four of the most obvious mental habits that will characterise a place beyond sectarianism.

Transformed patterns of relationship

Sectarianism takes the form of destructive patterns of relating. These patterns – blaming, separating, overlooking, belittling, dehumanising, demonising, dominating, and attacking – are endemic in Northern Ireland. Here, the different traditions cannot hope for a future in which they just peacefully ignore one another. For the variety of reasons already examined in chapter five, benign apartheid is not likely to be a plausible option. Ongoing transformation of relationships, therefore, on a spectrum from bare civility to a full living of *koinonia* (communion), will be essential marks of a society living beyond sectarianism. Individually and corporately, people must find a will to co-existence, by which we mean some practical, applied version of reconciliation, however limited. Such co-existence makes possible sharing this limited space in a way that offers to everyone the possibility of having their identity and tradition acknowledged and given place.

Despite the current 'peace process', and while applauding what has been achieved, it seems to us that the actual will to co-existence is not yet sufficiently broadly rooted to make lasting peace a viable prospect. Evidence of a concrete will to co-existence cannot mean less than the widespread development of at least toleration and preferably empathy for others whom we find difficult or obnoxious. Toleration, in this instance, is not the expansive virtue of tolerance, but rather the minimal, and possibly even reluctant, maintenance of civility.[1] A place beyond sectarianism, then, will be one in which, proactively and without inducement or coercion, relationships of blame are giving way to taking responsibility and repentance; separating to engagement and forgiveness; overlooking to self-emptying and inclusivity; belittling, dehumanising, and demonising to mutual recognition and respect; dominating to inter-dependence; and attacking to peaceful co-existence.

As we have seen, these positive relational dynamics are central to Christian community, both to the nature of church as *koinonia* and to its reconciling mission. In a place beyond sectarianism, the Christian churches and faith communities could and would have a significant role in encouraging and assisting people to renew and transform their ways of relating. This is a core strategy of peacebuilding, which in Northern Ireland is one of the most needed and most distinctive contributions that churches and faith communities can make. It is also one for which they possess a rich variety of biblical, theological, and practical resources.

A concurrent step, perhaps even prior, must be for the churches to continue to work at transforming relationships within and between themselves. This is not an optional extra to be undertaken only by those interested in ecumenical activity. In ecumenically aware Christian circles, we regularly come across the supposition that the answer to sectarianism is more vibrant and widespread ecumenical relationships, that a place beyond sectarianism will be one big ecumenical family, with a few unenlightened begrudgers on the outside. The best theology and practice of the ecumenical movement would have no place for such a notion, but unfortunately the best does not always prevail. Certainly improved ecumenical relationships will be a valued, necessary part of the vision for a place beyond sectarianism; they are not, nor can they be, the whole vision. There are Protestant people, inclined toward and active in inter-church and cross-community work, for whom the concept of ecumenism and talk about 'Christian unity' evoke a fear of coercion. There are also people espousing separatist theologies who fear, as one chaplain to the Orange Order put it, being dragged into a big melting pot of unity and undifferentiated doctrine in which anyone who tries to stand up for what he regards as truth will be accused of sectarianism and slapped down. These concerns are real and need to be taken seriously. Moreover these concerns need not, and should not, prevent Christian churches from fulfilling, insofar as they are able, the biblical imperatives to engage in prophetic boundary-crossing activities and to be peacemakers. It is crucial that society as a whole and Christian churches and faith communities in particular broaden both the agenda and the language that they use to describe the peacebuilding necessary to bring a place beyond sectarianism into being.

The necessary broadening would involve expanding the characteristic religious language of peace in Northern Ireland from ecumenical relationship, unity, compromise, and agreement to include language – sometimes complementary but sometimes alternative – such as consultation, communication, practical co-operation, mutual respect, and dialogue. The second set of terms differs from the first in clearly valuing relationship and connection, but making no assumptions about the possibility or desirability of agreement, compromise, or unity, concepts which some conservative Protestants see as the fundamental meaning of the red-flag word 'ecumenism'. While the reality of what ecumenists believe about unity, compromise, and agreement is far more complex and diverse than popular stereotype allows, the stereotype is not without foundation. The relevance of this second set of terms, then, is that it serves as a challenge to conservative Protestants by meeting some of their basic fears around ecumenism while continuing to press for inter-church relationships. It challenges ecumenists as well, however, by honouring their commitment to inter-church relationship, but without any guarantee that their further concern for unity, in any of its varied meanings, will necessarily be met.

Liberated from tension around issues of ecumenism, more extensive inter-church communication and consultation, focused on an agenda of peacebuilding, could offer the possibility of creating new 'spaces' within which to generate creative dialogue and into which to invite others. These spaces would be new because the interplay of difference and tension, provided it was not debilitating, would create an ethos within which a variety of people or groups could find a resonance of identity or belonging and the confidence to risk thinking and relating more widely.

In such a place ministers and lay leaders would regularly review where they direct most of their energy; they would reconsider how they nurture their community's identity and what it means to do this. They would take seriously the fact that part of their identity is inextricably linked with the other tradition or traditions, even if only negatively. Whether people like others or not, or agree with them or not, they populate one another's landscape and therefore shape each other's identity.

Getting there by small steps

The broad principles of transformation of heart and mind and relationships detailed in the preceding section point toward a vision of what a place beyond sectarianism might be like. But having a vision and being able to realise that vision are two very different matters. Many enterprises fail because people lack audacity, some fail because people are imprudently audacious. Moving beyond sectarianism is going to be a matter of generational change. The process envisaged throughout this book is the kind of long, slow, patiently pursued change, with an occasional spurt of growth, typical of all living entities.

Especially in the early stages, the steps along such a path will be mostly small and unglamorous. They will not be accessible to those who must make a visible impact nor to those who are in too much of a hurry. They will require people to live long periods analogous to the liturgical season of Lent: watching and waiting, discerning and repenting. The occasional flashes of Easter, the more spectacular spurts of growth, of resurrection and new life, will serve as beacons to strengthen people's faith and courage, metaphorical pillars of cloud and of fire behind and before those on the journey.[2] The following are a few of the key small steps that we consider essential to moving beyond sectarianism.

1. Maintaining a clear and steady vision that all people are implicated in the system and that every level and structure of society is tainted by sectarianism, however indirectly.
'Implicated' can have a range of meanings here, from judicial guilt, to people doing things in the name of others, to simply being part of Northern Ireland society. This step requires that people, individually and corporately:

* Take active responsibility, not just accept responsibility, for their own sectarianism and their own complicity, working at self-awareness, self-critique, radical honesty, and developing ongoing reflective methodologies which will expose complicity.

* Develop a habit of thinking through the consequences of projected actions and decisions before they are taken, exercising an hermeneutic of suspicion about their intentions and motivations.

* Seek a critique of their significant projected actions or decisions from members of the other group and be willing to give an honest and constructive critique to others if asked, developing a sympathetic and honest relationship with at least one person from the other group.

* Be honest, at least with themselves, about their feelings, which are signposts to sometimes hidden attitudes and beliefs, and create an ethos, in groups and in society, in which it is acceptable to express feelings.

2. Maintaining a consistent and clear commitment to act
in order to challenge sectarianism.

All people have the potential to be significant agents of change in society. Having the capacity to influence change, however, and choosing to use that capacity require very different levels of courage and engagement. This step requires that people, individually and corporately:

> * Invest sustained amounts of energy and time, even if these are limited, into taking action to move beyond sectarianism: on the one hand, allocating time, space, and resources to this task within tradition groups and, on the other hand, setting aside agreed periods for cross-tradition reflection and action. Co-ordinating several sets of local church diaries is a delicate operation that would be greatly aided by agreeing one night a week in a local area which was designated for alternating sessions of within-tradition and between-tradition reflection and action.

> * Develop an understanding of their capacities, resources, and opportunities for taking action, possibly carrying out an audit of talents and opportunities in the group as well as needs in the area. It could also mean getting outside help to assist groups in identifying their capacities.

> * Network and share information about activities and problems, developing channels of communication within and between traditions at all levels.

> * Monitor actual levels of action, putting in place a definite evaluative structure or process and making a commitment to respond to it.

3. Naming and exposing sectarian dynamics,
action, attitudes, beliefs and structures wherever they are recognised.

Naming sectarianism in a way that can lead to change rather than to destructive reaction can be a sensitive process that demands both courage and discernment. This step requires that people, individually and corporately:

> * Understand the dynamics of sectarianism, putting in place educational and experiential courses at all levels.

> * Understand their own and others' religious, political and cultural traditions, creating opportunities for education, reflection, and meaningful exchange.

> * Name, expose, and oppose all forms of sectarianism, devel-

oping language skills in general, and in particular learning to communicate non-violently, to empathise and to be able to make judgments or denunciations without separating from or demonising the other, so that those to whom it is directed can hear the message.

* Be courageous and compassionate in identifying and naming sectarianism, developing adequate support structures for the people concerned.

* Understand and explore processes of mitigation, developing analytical tools for discovering the potential for mitigation in any situation.

4. Taking risks to break the cycle of antagonised division.
Stepping out of familiar territory across boundaries that carry the status of communal or quasi-communal taboos is a risky business at any time, but it is more so in a situation of inter-communal conflict. It is also true that in such a situation this type of risk-taking is absolutely crucial. This step requires that people, individually and communally:

* Enter into a process of self-emptying and developing a wider inclusivity than they traditionally countenance – on the one hand, possibly letting go of parts of their community story or identity that need to be transformed and, on the other, embracing traditions which are unfamiliar and possibly uncomfortable.

* Develop imagination for envisioning the type of boundary crossing that will be most effective – seeking inspirational input from within and without and giving time to communal reflection and discussion.

* Be prepared to take counter-intuitive action – summoning up courage and ensuring that there are sufficient support structures for the risk-takers, including possible protection by the leadership of the group or group members themselves.

* Co-operate across traditions – developing positive relationships with those whom they consider other and constantly seeking to be as inclusive and open as they are able to be.

5. Developing a vision of reconciled community in Northern Ireland.
'Where there is no vision, the people perish.' (Prov 29:18 *KJV*)
The wisdom of the sage holds true in Northern Ireland today. If

steps one to four deal with short to medium term actions, this step is based on the longer view. In the previous section we offered a few tentative suggestions about possible contours of a place beyond sectarianism, but it is the people in society who will choose, shape, and implement their vision. This step requires that people, individually and corporately:

 * Develop an ideal towards which they would be willing to strive – giving time to imagining, reflecting, and discussing what kind of a Northern Ireland they would want in the future.

 * Generate inspiration with and for one another – seeking and encouraging all inspirational expressions of renewed personal and / or communal identity.

 * Develop a theology of reconciliation based on the experiences and needs of the churches and faith communities in Northern Ireland[3] – perhaps one or more of the theological colleges commissioning such a piece of research. Ideally, this type of project would be undertaken by a team representing some of the major strands in Protestantism and Roman Catholicism.

Conclusion

The path ahead, we hope, if still daunting, is at least a little more clearly defined than when we began our research in early 1995. Sectarianism cannot be wished away, nor will it disappear of its own accord. For churches, faith communities, and people in society in general to do nothing is to continue to collude with the sectarian system. To commit oneself to the journey of moving beyond sectarianism is to find oneself, along with the magi in T. S. Eliot's poem 'Journey of the Magi', 'no longer at ease, here in the old dispensation'.[4] While the road toward a new dispensation will undoubtedly pass through hard places, we are confident that those who make the journey together will find it rewarding, at times even joyous.

Bibliography

Abbott, Walter M., SJ, ed. *The Documents of Vatican II: The Message and Meaning of the Ecumenical Council*. London: Geoffrey Chapman, 1966.

Aldridge, Alan. *Religion in the Contemporary World: A Sociological Introduction*. Cambridge: Polity Press, 2000.

Alexander, Yonah, and Alan O'Day, eds. *The Irish Terrorism Experience*. Aldershot, England and Brookfield, Vermont: Dartmouth, 1991.

Barnard, Toby. 'Improving Clergymen, 1660-1760.' In *As By Law Established: The Church of Ireland Since the Reformation*, eds Alan Ford, James McGuire, and Kenneth Milne. Dublin: Lilliput Press, 1995.

Barnard, Toby. 'The Uses of 23 October 1641 and Irish Protestant Celebrations.' In *The English Historical Review*, vol. 106 (October 1991).

Baum, Gregory, and Harold Wells. *The Reconciliation of Peoples: Challenge to the Churches*. Maryknoll, New York: Orbis Books, 1997.

Baumeister, Roy F., and Mark R. Leary. 'The Need to Belong: Desire for Interpersonal Attachments as a Fundamental Human Motivation.' In *Psychological Bulletin*, vol. 117, no. 3 (1995).

Bendroth, Margaret Lamberts. 'Fundamentalists and Us.' In *Christian Century*, vol. 113, no. 18 (22-29 May 1996).

Benson, David, and Karen Trew. 'Dimensions of Social Identity in Northern Ireland.' In *Changing European Identities: Social-Psychological Analyses of Social Change*, eds G. M. Breakwell and E. Lyons. London: Pergammon Press, 1996.

Berger, Klaus. 'Justice.' In *Encyclopedia of Theology: A Concise Sacramentum Mundi*, ed. Karl Rahner. London: Burns and Oates, 1975.

Bew, Paul, and Gordon Gillespie. *Northern Ireland: A Chronology of the Troubles, 1968-1993*. Dublin: Gill and Macmillan, 1993.

Beyond the Fife and Drum: Report of a Conference Held on Belfast's Shankill Road, October 1994. Island pamphlets, no. 11. Newtownabbey, Northern Ireland: Island Publications, 1995.

Birrell, Derek, John Greer, Duncan Morrow, and Terry O'Keeffe. *Churches and Inter-Community Relationships*. Coleraine: Centre for the Study of Conflict, 1994.

Boal, Frederick W., Margaret C. Keane, and David N. Livingstone. *Them and Us? Attitudinal Variation Among Churchgoers in Belfast*. Belfast: Institute of Irish Studies, Queen's University of Belfast, 1997.

Bowen, Desmond. *Souperism: Myth or Reality: A Study in Souperism*. Cork: Mercier Press, 1970.

Boyd, Robin. *Ireland: Christianity Discredited or Pilgrim's Progress?* Geneva: WCC, 1988.

Boyle, Kevin, and Tom Hadden. *Northern Ireland: The Choice*. London: Penguin Books, 1994.

Brady, Ciarán, ed. *Interpreting Irish History: The Debate on Historical Revisionism 1938-1994*. Blackrock, Co. Dublin: Irish Academic Press, 1994.

Breakwell, G. M. *Social Psychology of Identity and the Self Concept*. London: Surrey University Press, 1992.

Breakwell, G. M., and E. Lyons. *Changing European Identities: Social-Psychological Analyses of Social Change*. London: Pergammon Press, 1996.

Brewer, John D., with Gareth I. Higgins. *Anti-Catholicism in Northern Ireland, 1600-1998: The Mote and the Beam*. London: Macmillan Press, 1998.

Briggs, Charles A., Francis Brown, and S. R. Driver, eds. *A Hebrew and English Lexicon of the Old Testament*. Oxford: Clarendon Press, 1907.

Brown, Francis, S. R. Driver, and Charles A. Briggs, eds. *A Hebrew and English Lexicon of the Old Testament*. Oxford: Clarendon Press, 1907.

Brown, John. 'The Battle of the Diamond.' In *Steadfast for Faith and Freedom*. Belfast: Education Committee of Orange Order, 1995.

Bruce, Steve. *God Save Ulster! The Religion and Politics of Paisleyism*. Oxford: Clarendon Press, 1986; paperback ed., Oxford: Oxford University Press, 1989.

Brueggeman, Walter. *Theology of the Old Testament: Testimony, Dispute, Advocacy*. Minneapolis: Fortress Press, 1997.

Byrne, F. J., T. W. Moody, and F. X. Martin, eds. *A New History of Ireland*, vol. 3. Oxford: Clarendon Press, 1976.

Canny, Nicholas P. *The Elizabethan Conquest of Ireland: A Pattern Established*. Hassocks, England: Harvester Press, 1976.

Canny, Nicholas. *From Reformation to Restoration: Ireland 1534-1660*. Dublin: Helicon, 1987.

The Catholic Bishops Conferences of Ireland, Scotland, England, and Wales. *One Bread, One Body: A Teaching Document on the Eucharist in the Life of the Church, and the Establishment of General Norms on Sacramental Sharing*. Dublin: Veritas Publications, 1998.

Clancy, Pat, Sheelagh Drudy, Kathleen Lynch, and Liam O'Dowd. *Irish Society: Sociological Perspectives*. Dublin: Institute of Public Administration, 1995.

Clapsis, Emmanuel. 'Globalization, Nationalism and the Unity of the Church.' Unpublished paper delivered at a WCC consultation,

'Ethnic Identity, National Identity, and the Unity of the Church.' St Deniol's, Wales, September 1997.

Cole, R. Lee. *A History of Methodism in Dublin*. Dublin: printed for the author, 1932.

Congregation for the Doctrine of the Faith. *Declaration* Dominus Iesus: *On the Unicity and Salvific Universality of Jesus Christ and the Church*. Rome: Congregation for the Doctrine of the Faith, 2000.

Congregation for the Doctrine of the Faith. 'Note on the Expression "Sister Churches": A Letter to the Presidents of the Conferences of Bishops.'
Available on-line: <http://www.vatican.va/roman_curia/congregations/cfaith/documents/rc_con_cfaith_doc_20000630_chiesesorelle_en.html> [4 April 2001].

Corish, Patrick J. *The Irish Catholic Experience: A Historical Survey*. Dublin: Gill and Macmillan, 1985.

Darby, John. 'Conflict in Northern Ireland: A Background Essay.' In *Facets of the Conflict in Northern Ireland*, ed. Séamus Dunn. Basingstoke: Macmillan, 1995.

Darby, John. *Conflict in Northern Ireland: The Development of a Polarised Community*. Dublin: Gill and Macmillan, 1976.

Darby, John. *Scorpions in a Bottle: Conflicting Cultures in Northern Ireland*. London: Minority Rights Publications, 1997.

de Bhaldraithe, Eoin. 'Mixed Marriages and Irish Politics: The Effect of *Ne Temere*.' In *Studies*, vol. 77 (Autumn 1988).

de Gruchy, John W. 'The Dialectic of Reconciliation.' In *The Reconciliation of Peoples: Challenge to the Churches*, eds Gregory Baum and Harold Wells. Maryknoll, New York: Orbis Books, 1997.

Deaux, K. 'Personalizing Identity and Socializing Self.' In *Social Psychology of Identity and the Self Concept*, ed. G. M. Breakwell. London: Surrey University Press, 1992.

Deane, Seamus. *Civilians and Barbarians*. Field Day pamphlets, no. 3. Derry: Field Day, 1983.

Department of Theological Questions, Irish Inter-Church Meeting. *Being Church in the New Millennium: A Discussion Document*. Dublin: Veritas, 2000.

Driver, S. R., Francis Brown, and Charles A. Briggs, eds. *A Hebrew and English Lexicon of the Old Testament*. Oxford: Clarendon Press, 1907.

Drudy, Sheelagh, Pat Clancy, Kathleen Lynch, and Liam O'Dowd. *Irish Society: Sociological Perspectives*. Dublin: Institute of Public Administration, 1995.

Dunn, Séamus. 'The Conflict as a Set of Problems.' In *Facets of the Conflict in Northern Ireland*, ed. Séamus Dunn. Basingstoke: Macmillan, 1995.

Dunn, Séamus. *Facets of the Conflict in Northern Ireland*. Basingstoke: Macmillan, 1995.

Eames, Robin. *Presidential Address*. Diocese of Armagh, Diocesan Synod, 20 October 1998.

ECONI. *A Future with Hope: Biblical Frameworks for Peace and Reconciliation in Northern Ireland*. Belfast: ECONI, 1995.

Edwards, Ruth Dudley. *Patrick Pearse: The Triumph of Failure*. London: Gollancz, 1977; paperback ed., Swords, Co. Dublin: Poolbeg, 1990.

Eliot, T. S. 'Journey of the Magi.' In *A Christian's Prayer Book*, eds Peter Coughlan, Ronald C. D. Jasper, and Teresa Rodrigues. London: Geoffrey Chapman, 1974.

The evidence of his grace the archbishop of Dublin, before the select committee of the house of lords, on the state of Ireland. Dublin: Richard Moore Tims, 1825.

Faith and Politics Group. *Boasting: Self-righteous Collective Superiority as a Cause of Conflict*. Belfast: Faith and Politics Group, 1999.

Faith and Politics Group. *Doing Unto Others: Parity of Esteem in a Contested Space*. Belfast: Faith and Politics Group, 1997.

Faith and Politics Group. *Forgive Us Our Trespasses...? Reconciliation and Political Healing in Northern Ireland*. Belfast: Faith and Politics Group, 1996.

Falconer, Alan D. 'From Theologies-in-Opposition Towards a Theology-of-Interdependence.' In *Life and Peace Review*, vol. 4 (1990).

Falconer, Alan. 'Remembering.' In *Reconciling Memories*. Rev. ed., eds Alan Falconer and Joseph Liechty. Blackrock, Co. Dublin: Columba Press, 1998.

Falconer, Alan, and Trevor Williams, eds. *Sectarianism: Papers of the 1994 Corrymeela Ecumenical Conference*. Dublin: Dominican Publications in association with the Irish School of Ecumenics, 1995.

Falconer, Alan, and Joseph Liechty, eds. *Reconciling Memories*. Rev. ed. Blackrock, Co. Dublin: Columba Press, 1998.

Ford, Alan.'The Protestant Reformation in Ireland.' In *Natives and Newcomers: Essays on the Making of Irish Colonial Society, 1534-1641*, eds Ciarán Brady and Raymond Gillespie. Irish Academic Press, Dublin, 1986.

Ford, Alan. *The Protestant Reformation in Ireland, 1590-1641*. Frankfurt am Main: Lang, 1985; new ed., Dublin: Four Courts Press, 1997.

Ford, Alan, James McGuire, and Kenneth Milne, eds. *As By Law Established: The Church of Ireland Since the Reformation*. Dublin: Lilliput Press, 1995.

Foster, R. F. *Modern Ireland, 1600-1972*. London: Allen Lane, 1988.

Fulton, John. *The Tragedy of Belief: Division, Politics, and Religion in Ireland*. Oxford: Oxford University Press, 1991.

Gallagher, Eric. *A Better Way for Irish Protestants and Roman Catholics: Advice from John Wesley*. Belfast: Mission Board, Methodist Church in Ireland, 1973.

Gillespie, Gordon, and Paul Bew. *Northern Ireland: A Chronology of the Troubles, 1968-1993*. Dublin: Gill and Macmillan, 1993.

Giraldus Cambrensis, *The History and Topography of Ireland*. Rev. ed. Translated by John J. O'Meara. Portlaoise, Ireland: Dolmen, 1982.

Gopin, Marc. 'The Heart of the Stranger.' Unpublished paper, Boundaries and Bonds Conference, Stranmillis College, Belfast, June 1997.

Gopin, Marc. *Between Eden and Armageddon: The Future of World Religions, Violence, and Peacemaking*. New York: Oxford University Press, 2000.

Greaves, Richard. '"That's No Good Religion that Disturbs Government": The Church of Ireland and the Nonconformist Challenge.' In *As By Law Established: The Church of Ireland Since the Reformation*, eds Alan Ford, James McGuire, and Kenneth Milne. Dublin: Lilliput Press, 1995.

Green, Ian.'"The Necessary Knowledge of the Principles of Religion": Catechisms and Catechising in Ireland, c.1560-1800.' In *As By Law Established: The Church of Ireland Since the Reformation*, eds Alan Ford, James McGuire, and Kenneth Milne. Dublin: Lilliput Press, 1995.

Greer, John, Derek Birrell, Duncan Morrow, and Terry O'Keeffe. *Churches and Inter-Community Relationships*. Coleraine: Centre for the Study of Conflict, 1994.

Griffin, V. G. B. *Anglican and Irish: What We Believe*. Dublin: APCK, 1976.

Groupe des Dombes. *For the Conversion of the Churches*. Geneva: WCC, 1993. Originally published as *Pour la conversion des Eglises*. Paris: Editions du Centurion, 1991.

Hadden, Tom and Kevin Boyle. *Northern Ireland: The Choice*. London: Penguin Books, 1994.

Haddick-Flynn, Kevin. *Orangeism: The Making of a Tradition*. Dublin: Wolfhound Press, 1999.

Halkes, Catharina J. M. *New Creation: Christian Feminism and the Renewal of the Earth*. London: SPCK, 1991. Originally published as *En Alles Zal Worden Herschapen*. Baarn: Uitgeverij Ten Have, 1989.

Hamilton, George. 'A Sermon Preached at the Formation of the Evangelical Society of Ulster in Armagh, 10th October 1798.' Handwritten manuscript, held by the Presbyterian Historical Society, Belfast.

Hammond, T. C. *The One Hundred Texts of the Society for Irish Church Missions*. Seventh ed. London: Society for Irish Church Missions; Marshall, Morgan and Scott, 1966.

Hauck, Friedrich. '*Koinonia*.' In *Theological Dictionary of the New Testament*, ed. Gerhard Kittel. Grand Rapids: Eerdmans, 1977.

Hayton, David. 'Did Protestantism Fail in Early Eighteenth-Century Ireland? Charity Schools and the Enterprise of Religious and Social Reformation, c. 1690-1730.' In *As By Law Established: The Church of Ireland Since the Reformation*, eds Alan Ford, James McGuire, and

Kenneth Milne. Dublin: Lilliput Press, 1995.

Hempton, David, and Myrtle Hill. *Evangelical Protestantism in Ulster Society, 1740-1890*. London: Routledge, 1992.

Hickey, John. *Religion and the Northern Ireland Problem*. Dublin: Gill and Macmillan, 1984.

Hill, Jacqueline. '1641 and the Quest for Catholic Emancipation, 1691-1829.' In *Ulster 1641: Aspects of the Rising*, ed. Brian Mac Cuarta. Belfast: Queen's University Belfast, 1993.

Hill, Myrtle. 'Evangelicalism and the Churches in Ulster Society: 1770-1850.' Ph.D. thesis, Queen's University, Belfast, 1987.

Hoppen, K. Theodore. *Ireland since 1800: Conflict and Conformity*. London and New York: Longman, 1989.

Hurley, Michael, ed. *Reconciliation in Religion and Society*. Belfast: Institute of Irish Studies, 1994.

Hutchinson, John, and Anthony D. Smith, eds. *Ethnicity*. Oxford: Oxford University Press, 1996.

Hutchinson, John, and Anthony D. Smith, eds. *Nationalism*. Oxford: Oxford University Press, 1994.

Irwin, Henry. *Remains of the Venerable Henry Irwin*. Dublin: William Curry and Co.; London: Wertheim and Macintosh; Edinburgh: Oliver and Boyd, 1858.

Is There Room in Heaven for Billy Wright? Belfast, 1998.

Jordan, Glenn. *Not of this World? Evangelical Protestants in Northern Ireland*. Belfast: The Blackstaff Press, 2001.

Jourdan, G. V. 'The Breach with Rome.' In *History of the Church of Ireland*, ed. Walter Alison Phillips. 3 vols. Oxford and London: Oxford University Press, 1933-4.

The Kairos Document: Challenge to the Church. Rev. 2nd ed. Johannesburg: ICT, 1986.

Keane, Margaret C., Frederick W. Boal, and David N. Livingstone. *Them and Us? Attitudinal Variation Among Churchgoers in Belfast*. Belfast: Institute of Irish Studies, Queen's University of Belfast, 1997.

Kittel, Gerhard, ed. *Theological Dictionary of the New Testament*. Grand Rapids: Eerdmans, 1977.

Lambert, Ralph. *A sermon preach'd to the Protestants of Ireland now residing in London: at their anniversary meeting on October 23, 1708*. London, 1709.

Lambkin, Brian. *Opposite Religions Still? Interpreting Northern Ireland After the Conflict*. Aldershot: Avebury, 1996.

Leary, Mark R., and Roy F. Baumeister.'The Need to Belong: Desire for Interpersonal Attachments as a Fundamental Human Motivation.' In *Psychological Bulletin*, vol. 117, no. 3 (1995).

Lee, J. J. *Ireland 1912-1985: Politics and Society*. Cambridge: Cambridge University Press, 1989.

Lee, Raymond M. 'Intermarriage, Conflict and Social Control in Ireland: The Decree "Ne temere".' *The Economic and Social Review,* vol. 17 (October1985),

Liechty, Joseph. 'Historical and Theological Origins of Sectarianism.' In *Sectarianism: Papers of the 1994 Corrymeela Ecumenical Conference,* eds Alan Falconer and Trevor Williams. Dublin: Dominican Publications in association with the Irish School of Ecumenics, 1995.

Liechty, Joseph. 'Irish Evangelicalism, Trinity College Dublin, and the Mission of the Church of Ireland at the End of the Eighteenth Century.' Ph.D. thesis, National University of Ireland Maynooth, 1987.

Liechty, Joseph. 'The Nature of Sectarianism Today.' In *Sectarianism: Papers of the 1994 Corrymeela Ecumenical Conference,* eds Alan Falconer and Trevor Williams. Dublin: Dominican Publications in association with the Irish School of Ecumenics, 1995.

Liechty, Joseph. *Roots of Sectarianism in Ireland: Chronology and Reflections.* Belfast: Irish Inter-Church Meeting, 1993.

Liechty, Joseph, and Alan Falconer, eds. *Reconciling Memories.* Rev. ed. Blackrock, Co. Dublin: Columba Press, 1998.

Lindbeck, George A. *The Nature of Doctrine: Religion and Theology in a Postliberal Age.* Philadelphia: Westminster Press, 1984.

Livingstone, David N., Frederick W. Boal, and Margaret C. Keane. *Them and Us? Attitudinal Variation Among Churchgoers in Belfast.* Belfast: Institute of Irish Studies, Queen's University of Belfast, 1997.

Lucy, Gordon. 'Orange Influence in the Foundation of the Ulster Volunteer Force.' In *Steadfast for Faith and Freedom.* Belfast: Education Committee of the Orange Order, 1995.

Lucy, Gordon, ed. *The Ulster Covenant: A Pictorial History of the 1912 Home Rule Crisis.* [Belfast]: The Ulster Society, 1989.

Lynch, Kathleen, Pat Clancy, Sheelagh Drudy, and Liam O'Dowd. *Irish Society: Sociological Perspectives.* Dublin: Institute of Public Administration, 1995.

Lyons, E., and G. M. Breakwell. *Changing European Identities: Social-Psychological Analyses of Social Change.* London: Pergammon Press, 1996.

McCafferty, John. 'John Bramhall and the Church of Ireland in the 1630s.' In *As By Law Established: The Church of Ireland Since the Reformation,* eds Alan Ford, James McGuire, and Kenneth Milne. Dublin: Lilliput Press, 1995.

McCann, Eamonn. *Dear God: The Price of Religion in Ireland.* London, Chicago, Sydney: Bookmarks Publications, 1999.

Mac Cuarta, Brian, ed. *Ulster 1641: Aspects of the Rising.* Belfast: Queen's University Belfast, 1993.

MacDonald, Michael. *Children of Wrath: Political Violence in Northern Ireland.* Cambridge: Polity Press, 1986.

McGarry, John, and Brendan O'Leary. *Explaining Northern Ireland: Broken Images*. Oxford: Blackwell, 1995.

McGuire, Jame, Alan Ford, and Kenneth Milne, eds. *As By Law Established: The Church of Ireland Since the Reformation*. Dublin: Lilliput Press, 1995.

McIntyre, Alasdair. *Whose Justice? Which Rationality?* London: Duckworth, 1988.

McMaster, Johnston. 'Changing Models of the Church.' In *Being Church in the New Millennium: A Discussion Document*, Department of Theological Questions, Irish Inter-Church Meeting. Dublin: Veritas, 2000.

McVeigh, Robbie. 'Cherishing the Children of the Nation Unequally: Sectarianism in Ireland.' In *Irish Society: Sociological Perspectives*, eds Pat Clancy, Sheelagh Drudy, Kathleen Lynch, and Liam O'Dowd. Dublin: Institute of Public Administration, 1995.

McVeigh, Robbie. 'Symmetry and Asymmetry in Sectarian Identity and Division.' In *Journal: A Quarterly Journal for Community Relations Trainers and Practitioners* (Summer 1997).

Maddi, Salvatore R. *Personality Theories: A Comparative Analysis*. 4th ed. Chicago: Dorsey Press, 1980.

Marger, Martin. *Race and Ethnic Relations: American and Global Perspectives*, 5th ed. Belmont, California: Wadsworth, 2000.

Martin, David. *Does Christianity Cause War?* Oxford: Oxford University Press, 1997.

Martin, F. X., T. W. Moody, and F. J. Byrne, eds. *A New History of Ireland*, vol. 3. Oxford: Clarendon Press, 1976.

Maslow, Abraham H. *Towards a Psychology of Being*. 2nd ed. New York: Van Nostrand Rheinhold, 1968.

Miller, David W. 'Presbyterianism and "Modernization" in Ulster.' In *Past and Present*, vol. 80 (August 1978).

Milne, Kenneth, Alan Ford, and James McGuire, eds. *As By Law Established: The Church of Ireland Since the Reformation*. Dublin: Lilliput Press, 1995.

Moody, T. W., F. X. Martin, and F. J. Byrne, eds. *A New History of Ireland*, vol. 3. Oxford: Clarendon Press, 1976.

Mooney, Canice. 'The First Impact of the Reformation.' In *A History of Irish Catholicism*, vol. 3. Ed. Patrick J. Corish. Dublin and Melbourne: Gill and Son, 1967.

Moran, Séan Farrell. 'Patrick Pearse and Patriotic Soteriology: The Irish Republican Tradition and the Sanctification of Political Self-immolation.' In *The Irish Terrorism Experience*, eds Yonah Alexander and Alan O'Day. Aldershot, England and Brookfield, Vermont: Dartmouth, 1991.

Morrow, Duncan, Derek Birrell, John Greer, and Terry O'Keeffe. *Churches and Inter-Community Relationships*. Coleraine: Centre for the Study of Conflict, 1994.

Moxon-Browne, Edward. *Nation, Class and Creed in Northern Ireland*. Aldershot: Gower, 1983.

Musser, Donald W., and Joseph L. Price, eds. *A New Handbook of Christian Theology*. Cambridge: Lutterworth Press, 1992.

The Nature and Purpose of the Church: A Stage on the Way to a Common Statement. Faith and Order Paper no. 181. Geneva: WCC, 1998.

O'Brien, Conor Cruise. *Ancestral Voices: Religion and Nationalism in Ireland*. Dublin: Poolbeg, 1994.

O Connor, Fionnuala. *In Search of a State: Catholics in Northern Ireland*. Belfast: Blackstaff Press, 1993.

O'Day, Alan, and Yonah Alexander. *The Irish Terrorism Experience*. Aldershot, England and Brookfield, Vermont: Dartmouth, 1991.

O'Donoghue, Fergus. 'The Use of St Augustine's Thought: A Response to Professor Williams.' In *Milltown Studies*, no. 19/20 (Spring and Autumn 1987).

O'Dowd, Liam, Pat Clancy, Sheelagh Drudy, and Kathleen Lynch. *Irish Society: Sociological Perspectives*. Dublin: Institute of Public Administration, 1995.

O'Hanlon, Gerry. 'Justice and Reconciliation.' In *Reconciliation in Religion and Society*, ed. Michael Hurley. Belfast: Institute of Irish Studies, 1994

O'Hegarty, P. S. *A Short Memoir of Terence MacSwiney*. Dublin: Talbot Press, 1922.

O'Keeffe, Terry, Derek Birrell, John Greer, and Duncan Morrow. *Churches and Inter-Community Relationships*. Coleraine: Centre for the Study of Conflict, 1994.

O'Leary, Brendan. Review of *Biting at the Grave: The Irish Hunger Strikes and the Politics of Despair*, by Padraig O'Malley. In *Irish Political Studies*, vol. 6 (1991).

O'Leary, Brendan, and John McGarry. *Explaining Northern Ireland: Broken Images*. Oxford: Blackwell, 1995.

O'Mahony, Cornelius. *Disputatio Apologetica, de Jure Regni Hiberniade pro Catholicis Hibernis adversis haereticos Anglos*. [Lisbon] 1645; reprint, [Dublin], 1826.

O'Malley, Padraig. *Biting at the Grave: The Irish Hunger Strikes and the Politics of Despair*. Belfast: Blackstaff, 1990.

Phillips, Walter Alison, ed. *History of the Church of Ireland*. 3 vols. Oxford and London: Oxford University Press, 1933-4.

Pollak, Andy, ed. *A Citizens' Inquiry: The Opsahl Report on Northern Ireland*. Dublin: Lilliput Press, 1993.

Price, Joseph L., and Donald W. Musser, eds. *A New Handbook of Christian Theology*. Cambridge: Lutterworth Press, 1992.

Roe, Peter. *Sixth Annual Address to the Parishioners of St Mary's, Kilkenny*. Kilkenny, 1822.

Rolston, Bill. *Politics and Painting: Murals and Conflict in Northern Ireland*. London: Associated University Press, 1991.

Ronan, Myles V. *The Reformation in Ireland under Elizabeth, 1558-1580*. London, New York, and Toronto: Longmans, Green, and Co., 1930.

Ross, Kelley L. 'Morality, Justice, and Judicial Moralism.' In *The Proceedings of the Friesian School*, fourth series (1996). Available on-line: <http://www.friesian.com/moral-2.htm> [21 December 2000].

Schöpflin, George. *Citizenship, Ethnicity, and Cultural Reproduction*. Frank Wright Memorial Lecture 1997, The Queen's University of Belfast Department of Politics, Occasional Paper No. 9. Belfast: QUB Department of Politics, Belfast, 1997.

Schreiter, Robert. *Reconciliation: Mission and Ministry in a Changing Social Order*. New York: Orbis Books, 1992.

Shriver, Donald W., Jr. *An Ethic for Enemies: Forgiveness in Politics*. New York: Oxford University Press, 1995.

Shriver, Donald W., Jr. *Forgiveness and Politics: The Case of the American Black Civil Rights Movement*. London: New World Publications, 1987.

Smith, Ian Crichton. 'The Legend.' In *The Exiles*. Dublin and Manchester: Carcanet, 1984.

Smith, Anthony D., and John Hutchinson, eds. *Ethnicity*. Oxford: Oxford University Press, 1996.

Smith, Anthony D., and John Hutchinson, eds. *Nationalism*. Oxford: Oxford University Press, 1994.

The Statutes at Large, Passed in the Parliaments Held in Ireland: From the Third Year of Edward the Second, A.D. 1310, to the Twenty-Sixth Year of George the Third, A.D. 1786 Inclusive. 20 vols. Dublin, 1786-1800.

Steadfast for Faith and Freedom. Belfast: Education Committee of Orange Order, 1995.

Stevens, David. 'As We Enter a New Millennium.' In *Studies*, vol. 89, no. 354 (Summer 2000).

Stewart, A. T. Q. *The Narrow Ground: The Roots of Conflict in Ulster*. London: Faber, 1977; revised paperback ed., London: Faber, 1989.

Stewart, A. T. Q. *The Ulster Crisis: Resistance to Home Rule, 1912-14*. London: Faber, 1967.

Thompson, Joshua. 'Baptists in Ireland, 1792-1992: A Dimension of Protestant Dissent.' Ph.D. thesis, Oxford, 1988.

Thomson, Alwyn, ed. *Faith in Ulster*. Belfast: ECONI, 1996.

Trew, Karen Trew. 'What It Means to be Irish Seen from a Northern Perspective.' In *The Irish Journal of Psychology*, vol. 15, nos. 2 and 3 (1994).

Trew, Karen, and David Benson. 'Dimensions of Social Identity in Northern Ireland..' In *Changing European Identities: Social-Psychological Analyses of Social Change*, eds G. M. Breakwell and E. Lyons. London: Pergammon Press, 1996.

Ulster's Protestant Working Class: A Community Exploration. Island pamphlets, no. 9. Newtownabbey, Northern Ireland: Island Publications, 1994.

van der Zijpp, N. 'Münster Anabaptists in the Netherlands.' In *The Mennonite Encyclopedia*, vol. 3.

Volf, Miroslav. *Exclusion and Embrace: A Theological Exploration of Identity, Otherness, and Reconciliation*. Nashville: Abingdon Press, 1996.

Volf, Miroslav. 'The Social Meaning of Reconciliation.' In *Interpretation*, vol. 54, no. 2 (April 2000).

Volf, Miroslav. 'A Vision of Embrace: Theological Perspectives on Cultural Identity and Conflict.' In *The Ecumenical Review*, vol. 47 (April 1995).

Walker, Brian. *Dancing to History's Tune: History, Myth and Politics in Ireland*. Belfast: Institute of Irish Studies, 1996.

Walkington, Edward. *A sermon preach'd in Christ-Church, Dublin, on Saturday, the 23rd of October, 1703; being the anniversary thanksgiving for discovering the Irish rebellion, which broke out in the year 1641*. Dublin, 1703.

Walls, Andrew F. 'Old Athens and New Jerusalem: Some Signposts for Christian Scholarship in the Early History of Mission Studies.' In *International Bulletin of Missionary Research*, vol. 21, no. 4 (October 1997).

Weber, Max. *The Protestant Ethic and the Spirit of Capitalism*. Translated by Talcott Parsons. New York: Charles Scribner's Sons, 1958.

Wells, Harold, and Gregory Baum. *The Reconciliation of Peoples: Challenge to the Churches*. Maryknoll, New York: Orbis Books, 1997.

The Westminster Confession of Faith. Edinburgh: Blackwood and Sons, 1979.

Whyte, John H. 'The Influence of the Catholic Clergy on Elections in Nineteenth-Century Ireland.' *English Historical Review*, vol. 75 (April 1960).

Whyte, John. *Interpreting Northern Ireland*. Oxford: Oxford University Press, 1990.

Williams, Trevor, and Alan Falconer, eds. *Sectarianism: Papers of the 1994 Corrymeela Ecumenical Conference*. Dublin: Dominican Publications in association with the Irish School of Ecumenics, 1995.

Wink, Walter. *Engaging the Powers: Discernment and Resistance in a World of Domination*. Minneapolis: Fortress Press, 1992.

Winton, Tim. *Cloudstreet*, St Paul, Minn.: Graywolf Press, 1992.

N. a. 'A Word to Murthough O'Sullivan.' In *Captain Rock in London*, no. 46 (14 January 1826).

[Working Party on Sectarianism] *Sectarianism: A Discussion Document*. Belfast: Department of Social Issues, Irish Inter-Church Meeting, 1993.

Wright, Frank. *Northern Ireland: A Comparative Analysis*. Dublin: Gill and Macmillan, 1987.

Wright, Frank. 'Reconciling the Histories: Protestant and Catholic in Northern Ireland.' In *Reconciling Memories*. Rev. ed., eds Alan D. Falconer and Joseph Liechty. Blackrock, Co. Dublin: Columba Press, 1998.

Yoder, John Howard Yoder.'The Kingdom as Social Ethic.' Chapter in *The Priestly Kingdom: Social Ethics as Gospel*. Notre Dame: University of Notre Dame Press, 1984.

Yoder, John Howard Yoder. 'How H. Richard Niebuhr Reasoned: A Critique of *Christ and Culture*.' In *Authentic Transformation: A New Vision of Christ and Culture*, eds Glen H. Stassen, D. M. Yeager, and John Howard Yoder. Nashville: Abingdon Press, 1996.

Notes

INTRODUCTION: SECTARIANISM AS A SYSTEM

1. Some of the dynamics and incidents mentioned in passing here will be dealt with more carefully in chapter two, 'Where Does Sectarianism Come From?'
2. (Minneapolis: Fortress Press, 1992).

CHAPTER ONE: UNDERSTANDING SECTARIANISM

1. Brian Lambkin, *Opposite Religions Still? Interpreting Northern Ireland After the Conflict* (Aldershot: Avebury, 1996), pp. 3, 24.
2. John Hickey, *Religion and the Northern Ireland Problem* (Dublin: Gill and Macmillan, 1984); Steve Bruce, *God Save Ulster! The Religion and Politics of Paisleyism* (Oxford: Oxford University Press, 1986); John Fulton, *The Tragedy of Belief: Division, Politics, and Religion in Ireland* (Oxford: Oxford University Press, 1991).
3. Bruce, *God Save Ulster!*, p. 249.
4.John Whyte, *Interpreting Northern Ireland* (Oxford: Oxford University Press, 1990), p. 111.
5. Andy Pollak, ed., *A Citizens' Inquiry: The Opsahl Report on Northern Ireland* (Dublin: Lilliput Press, 1993), p. 101.
6. Séamus Dunn, 'The Conflict as a Set of Problems', in *Facets of the Conflict in Northern Ireland*, ed. Séamus Dunn (Basingstoke: Macmillan, 1995), pp. 7-8.
7. Robbie McVeigh, 'Cherishing the Children of the Nation Unequally: Sectarianism in Ireland', in *Irish Society: Sociological Perspectives*, eds Pat Clancy, Sheelagh Drudy, Kathleen Lynch, and Liam O' Dowd (Dublin: Institute of Public Administration, 1995), pp. 638-9.
8. John Darby, 'Conflict in Northern Ireland: A Background Essay', in *Facets of the Conflict in Northern Ireland*, ed. Séamus Dunn, p. 21.
9. John Darby, *Scorpions in a Bottle: Conflicting Cultures in Northern Ireland* (London: Minority Rights Publications, 1997), p. 55.
10. Ibid., p. 53.
11. John McGarry and Brendan O'Leary, *Explaining Northern Ireland: Broken Images* (Oxford: Blackwell, 1995), p. 213.

12. For a contrary interpretation, arguing the necessity of clearly identifying the 'fundamental nature or character (religious, political, economic, psychological etc)' of the conflict, see Lambkin, *Opposite Religions Still?*, p. 36.

13. George A. Lindbeck, *The Nature of Doctrine: Religion and Theology in a Postliberal Age* (Philadelphia: Westminster Press, 1984), pp. 33, 18.

14. The literature on ethnicity and nationalism is enormous. For an overview of and introduction to these concepts, two books from the Oxford Readers series are useful: John Hutchinson and Anthony D. Smith, eds, *Ethnicity* (Oxford: Oxford University Press, 1996), and John Hutchinson and Anthony D. Smith, eds, *Nationalism* (Oxford: Oxford University Press, 1994).

15. Marc Gopin, *Between Eden and Armageddon: The Future of World Religions, Violence, and Peacemaking* (Oxford: Oxford University Press, 2000), p. 246, n. 49.

16. Walter Brueggeman, *Theology of the Old Testament: Testimony, Dispute, Advocacy* (Minneapolis: Fortress Press, 1997), p. 430.

17. Gopin, *Between Eden and Armageddon*, p. 269, n. 14.

18. Miroslav Volf, 'A Vision of Embrace: Theological Perspectives on Cultural Identity and Conflict', *The Ecumenical Review*, vol. 47 (April 1995), p. 198.

19. For a brilliant account of the difference between proselytism and evangelism, and the significance of the difference for Christian identity and history, see Andrew F. Walls, 'Old Athens and New Jerusalem: Some Signposts for Christian Scholarship in the Early History of Mission Studies', *International Bulletin of Missionary Research*, vol. 21, no. 4 (October 1997), pp. 146–53.

20. For an excellent reflection on the meaning and implications of Pentecost and its relationship to the tower of Babel, see Miroslav Volf, *Exclusion and Embrace: A Theological Exploration of Identity, Otherness, and Reconciliation* (Nashville: Abingdon Press, 1996), pp. 226-31.

21. For Lee, see Pollak, ed., *A Citizens' Inquiry*, pp. 334-335; Frederick W. Boal, Margaret C. Keane, and David N. Livingstone *Them and Us? Attitudinal Variation Among Churchgoers in Belfast* (Belfast: Institute of Irish Studies, Queen's University of Belfast, 1997), e.g. pp. 2-3, 171-2.

22. The habit of thinking of Protestantism and Catholicism as separate or even opposite religions is analysed with care by Brian Lambkin in *Opposite Religions Still?*

23. Fulton, *The Tragedy of Belief*, p. 7.

24. Ibid., p. 8.

25. Max Weber, *The Protestant Ethic and the Spirit of Capitalism*, trans. Talcott Parsons (New York: Charles Scribner's Sons, 1958).

26. Throughout his career, the Mennonite theologian John Howard Yoder challenged and provided alternatives to the cast of mind and categories fostered by church-sect typology; see, for example, John Howard Yoder, 'The Kingdom as Social Ethic', chapter in *The Priestly*

Kingdom: Social Ethics as Gospel (Notre Dame: University of Notre Dame Press, 1984), pp. 80-101, and John Howard Yoder, 'How H. Richard Niebuhr Reasoned: A Critique of *Christ and Culture*', in Glen H. Stassen, D. M. Yeager, and John Howard Yoder, *Authentic Transformation: A New Vision of Christ and Culture* (Nashville: Abingdon Press, 1996), pp. 31-89.

27. For a recent example, see Alan Aldridge, *Religion in the Contemporary World: A Sociological Introduction* (Cambridge: Polity Press, 2000), pp. 33-55.

28. *Oxford English Dictionary*, 2nd ed. (Oxford: Clarendon Press, 1989).

29. Ibid.

30. Robbie McVeigh, 'Symmetry and Asymmetry in Sectarian Identity and Division', *Journal: A Quarterly Journal for Community Relations Trainers and Practitioners* (Summer 1997), p. 10.

31. John Darby, *Conflict in Northern Ireland: The Development of a Polarised Community* (Dublin: Gill and Macmillan, 1976), p. 126.

32. Michael MacDonald, *Children of Wrath: Political Violence in Northern Ireland* (Cambridge: Polity Press, 1986), p. 4.

33. Ibid, p. 6.

34. Ibid.

35. Ibid., p. 7.

36. Ibid., p. 8.

37. Ibid., p. 10.

38. Ibid., p. 173, n. 17.

39. Ibid., p. 36.

40. Whyte, *Interpreting Northern Ireland*, p. 104; Bruce, *God Save Ulster!*, p. 6; A. T. Q. Stewart, *The Narrow Ground: The Roots of Conflict in Ulster* (London: Faber, 1977; revised paperback ed., London: Faber, 1989), pp. 25-6.

41. David Hempton and Myrtle Hill, *Evangelical Protestantism in Ulster Society, 1740-1890* (London: Routledge, 1992), p. 180.

42. Edward Moxon-Browne, *Nation, Class and Creed in Northern Ireland* (Aldershot: Gower, 1983), p. 3.

43. Ibid.

44. Ibid.

45. Martin Marger, *Race and Ethnic Relations : American and Global Perspectives*, 5th ed. (Belmont, California: Wadsworth, 2000), pp. 500-1.

46. Frank Wright, *Northern Ireland: A Comparative Analysis* (Dublin: Gill and Macmillan, 1987), pp. 47-8.

47. Ibid., p. xv.

48. McGarry and O'Leary, *Explaining Northern Ireland*, especially pp. 354-407.

49. On the priority of institutions, ibid., pp 250-3.

50. Ibid., p. 4.

51. Ibid., p. 171.

52. Ibid., pp. 171-2. In fact they seem to find this a particularly persuasive line of reasoning, because they use exactly the same 'important

implications follow' formula near the beginning of their efforts to dismiss cultural interpretations. (p. 217) Again in the case of culture, however, their argument falls apart under examination.

53. Ibid., p. 213.

54. Ibid., p. 193.

55. Ibid., p. 197.

56. Ibid., p. 200.

57. Ibid., p. 204.

58. Ibid., pp. 243-4.

59. Ibid., p. 244.

60. Ibid., p. 248.

61. Ibid.

62. Alasdair McIntyre, *Whose Justice? Which Rationality?* (London: Duckworth, 1988).

63. McGarry and O'Leary, *Explaining Northern Ireland*, p. 244.

64. Ibid., p. 245.

65. Brendan O'Leary, review of *Biting at the Grave: The Irish Hunger Strikes and the Politics of Despair*, by Padraig O'Malley, *Irish Political Studies*, vol. 6 (1991), pp. 118-22.

66. Padraig O'Malley, *Biting at the Grave: The Irish Hunger Strikes and the Politics of Despair* (Belfast: Blackstaff, 1990), p. 117.

67. McGarry and O'Leary, *Explaining Northern Ireland*, p. 246.

68. Ibid.

CHAPTER TWO: WHERE DOES SECTARIANISM COME FROM?

1. Quoted in Brian Walker, *Dancing to History's Tune: History, Myth and Politics in Ireland* (Belfast: Institute of Irish Studies, 1996), p. viii.

2. Ciarán Brady, ed., *Interpreting Irish History: The Debate on Historical Revisionism 1938-1994* (Blackrock, Co. Dublin: Irish Academic Press, 1994).

3. The Working Party on Sectarianism's report to the churches has been published by the Department of Social Issues of the Irish Inter-Church Meeting as *Sectarianism: A Discussion Document* (Belfast: Irish Inter-Church Meeting, 1993); Joe's history chapter was separately published as a paper commissioned by the Working Party as Joseph Liechty, *Roots of Sectarianism in Ireland: Chronology and Reflections* (Belfast: Irish Inter-Church Meeting, 1993).

4. The significant exception in western societies is members of minority ethnic or religious groups which may approach history out of some sense of loss or grievance.

5. Quoted in Donald W. Shriver, Jr, *Forgiveness and Politics: The Case of the American Black Civil Rights Movement* (London: New World Publications, 1987), p. 5.

6. Quoted in Kelley L. Ross, 'Morality, Justice, and Judicial Moralism', *The Proceedings of the Friesian School*, fourth series (1996). Available online: <http://www.friesian.com/moral-2.htm> [21 December 2000].

7. Fergus O'Donoghue, 'The Use of St Augustine's Thought: A Response to Professor Williams', *Milltown Studies*, no. 19/20 (Spring and Autumn 1987), 85.

8. Quoted in Richard Greaves, '"That's No Good Religion that Disturbs Government": The Church of Ireland and the Nonconformist Challenge', in *As By Law Established: The Church of Ireland Since the Reformation*, eds Alan Ford, James McGuire, and Kenneth Milne (Dublin: Lilliput Press, 1995), p. 133.

9. Giraldus Cambrensis, *The History and Topography of Ireland*, trans. John J. O'Meara, rev. ed. (Portlaoise, Ireland: Dolmen, 1982), pp. 102-3.

10. Ibid., p. 106.

11. Ibid., p. 118.

12. Nicholas Canny, *From Reformation to Restoration: Ireland 1534-1660* (Dublin: Helicon, 1987), p. 10.

13. Toby Barnard, 'Improving Clergymen, 1660-1760', in *As By Law Established*, eds Ford, McGuire, and Milne, p. 137.

14. Ralph Lambert, *A sermon preach'd to the Protestants of Ireland now residing in London: at their anniversary meeting on October 23, 1708* (London, 1709), p. 4.

15. The most important works on the 1641 rising and its legacy are: specifically for 23 October sermons, Toby Barnard, 'The Uses of 23 October 1641 and Irish Protestant Celebrations', in *The English Historical Review*, vol. 106 (October 1991), pp. 889-920; and more generally, Brian Mac Cuarta, ed., *Ulster 1641: Aspects of the Rising* (Belfast: Queen's University Belfast, 1993).

16. G. V. Jourdan, 'The Breach with Rome', *History of the Church of Ireland*, 3 vols, ed. Walter Alison Phillips (Oxford and London: Oxford University Press, 1933-4), vol. 2, pp. 169-73, 212-3 (I am grateful to Alan Ford for showing me this material); Steve Bruce, *God Save Ulster! The Religion and Politics of Paisleyism* (Oxford: Clarendon Press, 1986; paperback ed., Oxford: Oxford University Press, 1989), pp. 220-6.

17. Seamus Deane, *Civilians and Barbarians*, Field Day pamphlets, no. 3 (Derry: Field Day, 1983), p. 11.

18. Quoted in Nicholas P. Canny, *The Elizabethan Conquest of Ireland: A Pattern Established* (Hassocks, England: Harvester Press, 1976), p. 153.

19. Quoted ibid., p. 121.

20. Canice Mooney, 'The First Impact of the Reformation', in *A History of Irish Catholicism*, vol. 3, ed. Patrick J. Corish (Dublin and Melbourne: Gill and Son, 1967), p. 33.

21. Quoted in Myles V. Ronan, *The Reformation in Ireland under Elizabeth, 1558-1580* (London, New York, and Toronto: Longmans, Green, and Co., 1930), p. 609.

22. Quoted in Cornelius O'Mahony, *Disputatio Apologetica, de Jure Regni Hiberniade pro Catholicis Hibernis adversis haereticosAnglos* ([Lisbon] 1645; reprint, [Dublin, 1826]), pp. 39-40. I am grateful to Eoin de Bhaldraithe for his translation from the Latin.

23. Ibid., p. 42.

24. Ibid., p. 125.

25. T. W. Moody, F. X. Martin, and F. J. Byrne, eds, *A New History of Ireland*, vol. 3 (Oxford: Clarendon Press, 1976), p. 292.

26. *The Statutes at Large, Passed in the Parliaments Held in Ireland: From the Third Year of Edward the Second, A.D. 1310, to the Twenty-Sixth Year of George the Third, A.D. 1786 Inclusive*, 20 vols (Dublin, 1786-1800), vol. 2, p. 526.

27. Ian Crichton Smith, 'The Legend', *The Exiles* (Dublin and Manchester: Carcanet, 1984), p. 36.

28. Alan D. Falconer, 'From Theologies-in-Opposition Towards a Theology-of-Interdependence', *Life and Peace Review*, vol. 4 (1990); Marc Gopin, 'The Heart of the Stranger' (unpublished paper, Boundaries and Bonds Conference, Stranmillis College, Belfast, June 1997).

29. Patrick J. Corish, *The Irish Catholic Experience: A Historical Survey* (Dublin: Gill and Macmillan, 1985), p. 105.

30. Alan Ford, 'The Protestant Reformation in Ireland', in *Natives and Newcomers: Essays on the Making of Irish Colonial Society, 1534-1641*, eds Ciarán Brady and Raymond Gillespie (Dublin: Irish Academic Press, 1986), p. 64; see also Alan Ford, *The Protestant Reformation in Ireland, 1590-1641* (Frankfurt am Main: Lang, 1985; new ed., Dublin: Four Courts Press, 1997).

31. Alan D. Falconer, 'Theologies-in-Opposition', pp. 3-4.

32. Alan Falconer, 'Remembering', in *Reconciling Memories*, rev. ed., eds Alan Falconer and Joseph Liechty (Blackrock, Co. Dublin: Columba Press, 1998), p. 14.

33. T. C. Hammond, *The One Hundred Texts of the Society for Irish Church Missions*, seventh ed. (London: Society for Irish Church Missions; Marshall, Morgan and Scott, 1966), pp. 85, 87.

34. Ibid., p. v.

35. Falconer, 'Remembering', p. 14.

36. V. G. B. Griffin, *Anglican and Irish: What We Believe* (Dublin: APCK, 1976), pp. 11-13.

37. Ibid., pp. 17-19.

38. Ibid., p. 24.

39. Ibid., pp. 8-9.

40. Ibid., p. 9.

41. Ibid., p. 10.

42. Ian Green, '"The Necessary Knowledge of the Principles of Religion": Catechisms and Catechizing in Ireland, c.1560-1800', in *As By Law Established*, eds Ford, McGuire, and Milne, p. 80.

43. Ibid., pp. 84-8.

44. David W. Miller, 'Presbyterianism and "Modernization" in Ulster', *Past and Present*, vol. 80 (August 1978), p. 73.

45. Ibid.

46. Green, '"The Necessary Knowledge"', pp. 74, 75.

47. Quoted in John McCafferty, 'John Bramhall and the Church of Ireland in the 1630s', in *As By Law Established*, eds Ford, McGuire, and Milne, p. 106.

48. Ibid., p. 101.

49. David Hayton, 'Did Protestantism Fail in Early Eighteenth-Century Ireland? Charity Schools and the Enterprise of Religious and Social Reformation, c. 1690-1730', in *As By Law Established*, eds Ford, McGuire, and Milne, p. 175.

50. Ibid., p. 179.

51. Toby Barnard, 'Improving Clergymen, 1660-1760', in *As By Law Established*, eds Ford, McGuire, and Milne, p. 138.

52. Ibid., p. 144.

53. Ibid., p. 146.

54. Ibid., pp. 138-9.

55. Jacqueline Hill, '1641 and the Quest for Catholic Emancipation, 1691-1829', in *Ulster 1641*, ed. Mac Cuarta, pp. 161-2.

56. Hayton, 'Did Protestantism Fail?', p. 175.

57. For example, see Edward Walkington, *A sermon preach'd in Christ-Church, Dublin, on Saturday, the 23rd of October, 1703; being the anniversary thanksgiving for discovering the Irish rebellion, which broke out in the year 1641* (Dublin, 1703), pp. 22-3.

58. Quoted in R. Lee Cole, *A History of Methodism in Dublin* (Dublin: printed for the author, 1932), p. 19.

59. Joseph Liechty, 'Irish Evangelicalism, Trinity College Dublin, and the Mission of the Church of Ireland at the End of the Eighteenth Century' (Ph.D. thesis, National University of Ireland, Maynooth, 1987), pp. 298-305, 499-501.

60. George Hamilton, 'A Sermon Preached at the Formation of the Evangelical Society of Ulster in Armagh, 10th October 1798' (handwritten manuscript, held by the Presbyterian Historical Society, Belfast).

61. *The evidence of his grace the archbishop of Dublin, before the select committee of the house of lords, on the state of Ireland* (Dublin: Richard Moore Tims, 1825), pp. 9-10.

62. N. a., 'A Word to Murthough O'Sullivan', *Captain Rock in London*, no. 46 (14 January 1826), p. 16.

63. Peter Roe, *Sixth Annual Address to the Parishioners of St Mary's, Kilkenny* (Kilkenny, 1822), pp. 2-3.

64. Quoted in Myrtle Hill, 'Evangelicalism and the Churches in Ulster Society: 1770-1850' (Ph.D. thesis, Queen's University, Belfast, 1987), p. 285.

65. Henry Irwin, *Remains of the Venerable Henry Irwin* (Dublin: William Curry and Co.; London: Wertheim and Macintosh; Edinburgh: Oliver and Boyd, 1858), pp. 237-8.

66. Quoted in Myrtle Hill, 'Evangelicalism and the Churches in Ulster', p. 283.

67. Quoted in Desmond Bowen, *Souperism: Myth or Reality: A Study in Souperism* (Cork: Mercier Press, 1970), p. 186.

68. *Baptist Irish Society Thirty-Third Annual Report* (1847), p. 26, quoted in Joshua Thompson, 'Baptists in Ireland, 1792-1992: A Dimension of

Protestant Dissent' (Ph.D. thesis, Oxford, 1988), pp. 116-7.

69. Eoin de Bhaldraithe, 'Mixed Marriages and Irish Politics: The Effect of *Ne Temere'*, *Studies*, vol. 77 (Autumn 1988), p. 285.

70. Quoted in Raymond M. Lee, 'Intermarriage, Conflict and Social Control in Ireland: The Decree "Ne temere"', *The Economic and Social Review*, vol. 17 (October 1985), p. 22.

71. Quoted ibid., p. 22.

72. Quoted in de Bhaldraithe, 'Mixed Marriages', p. 295.

73. David Martin, *Does Christianity Cause War?* (Oxford: Oxford University Press, 1997).

74. Quoted in A. T. Q. Stewart, *The Ulster Crisis: Resistance to Home Rule, 1912-14* (London: Faber, 1967), p. 49.

75. Gordon Lucy, ed., *The Ulster Covenant: A Pictorial History of the 1912 Home Rule Crisis* ([Belfast]: The Ulster Society, 1989), p. 44.

76. Quoted in Ruth Dudley Edwards, *Patrick Pearse: The Triumph of Failure* (London: Gollancz, 1977; paperback ed., Swords, Co. Dublin: Poolbeg, 1990), p. 179.

77. Quoted ibid., pp. 253, 260.

78. Quoted ibid., pp. 161-2.

79. R. F. Foster, *Modern Ireland, 1600-1972* (London: Allen Lane, 1988), p. 487.

80. Quoted in P. S. O'Hegarty, *A Short Memoir of Terence MacSwiney* (Dublin: Talbot Press, 1922), pp. 78-9.

81. Frank Wright, 'Reconciling the Histories: Protestant and Catholic in Northern Ireland', in *Reconciling Memories*, eds Falconer and Liechty, p. 137.

82. Seán Farrell Moran, 'Patrick Pearse and Patriotic Soteriology: the Irish Republican Tradition and the Sanctification of Political Self-immolation', in *The Irish Terrorism Experience*, eds Yonah Alexander and Alan O'Day (Aldershot, England, and Brookfield, Vermont: Dartmouth, 1991), p. 23.

83. Quoted in J. J. Lee, *Ireland 1912-1985. Politics and Society* (Cambridge: Cambridge University Press, 1989), p. 54.

CHAPTER THREE: WHAT IS SECTARIANISM?

1. See for example the definition put forward by sociologist Robbie McVeigh: 'sectarianism in Ireland is that changing set of ideas and practices, including, crucially, acts of violence, which serve to construct and reproduce the difference between, and unequal status of, Irish Protestants and Catholics.' Robbie McVeigh, 'Cherishing the Children of the Nation Unequally: Sectarianism in Ireland', in *Irish Society: Sociological Perspectives*, eds Pat Clancy, Sheelagh Drudy, Kathleen Lynch, and Liam O'Dowd (Dublin: Institute of Public Administration, 1995), p. 643.

2. Drumcree is a Church of Ireland parish on the outskirts of Portadown, Co. Armagh. Since 1995 it has been become a particular

flashpoint associated with a Loyal Order church parade on the Sunday prior to 12th July and has led to Northern Ireland-wide public disorder for five consecutive years. Members of the Orange Order in Portadown have been protesting for three years on Drumcree hill about being denied the right to march along the Garvaghy Road, which traverses a predominantly Nationalist area.

3. Robin Eames, *Presidential Address*, Diocese of Armagh, Diocesan Synod, 20 October 1998.

4. See the work of Croatian theologian, Miroslav Volf, especially his discussion of 'exclusion' in Miroslav Volf, *Exclusion and Embrace: A Theological Exploration of Identity, Otherness, and Reconciliation* (Nashville: Abingdon Press, 1996), pp. 57-98.

5. The concept of 'recovering sectarians' is developed in Joseph Liechty, 'The Nature of Sectarianism Today', in *Sectarianism: Papers of the 1994 Corrymeela Ecumenical Conference*, eds Alan Falconer and Trevor Williams (Dublin: Dominican Publications in association with the Irish School of Ecumenics, 1995), p. 18.

6. 'They joined the brotherhood to defend themselves, to support the Protestant religion, and to uphold the King and Constitution.' John Brown, 'The Battle of the Diamond', in *Steadfast for Faith and Freedom* (Belfast: Education Committee of the Orange Order, 1995), p. 5.

7. '"In these circumstances you have two duties to perform: You must use every effort to defeat them at the polls, neglecting no opportunity of influencing votes in Great Britain. But you are equally bound to prepare for a struggle in this country if we should fail to carry the elections. Already steps are being taken to enrol men to meet any emergency. Orangemen must set the example to other unionists by volunteering their service."' Quoted in Gordon Lucy, 'Orange Influence in the Foundation of the Ulster Volunteer Force', in *Steadfast for Faith and Freedom*, p. 91.

8. Ibid.

9. This position would be that of personality theorists who subscribe to what Salvatore Maddi describes as the 'Fulfillment Model' of core personality. See Salvatore R Maddi, *Personality Theories: A Comparative Analysis*, 4th ed. (Chicago: Dorsey Press, 1980), pp. 88-156. In particular, see the work of Abraham Maslow and his emphasis on self-actualisation and the need for belongingness, respect, and love. Abraham H. Maslow, *Towards a Psychology of Being*, 2nd ed. (New York: Van Nostrand Rheinhold, 1968).

10. Roy F. Baumeister and Mark R. Leary, 'The Need to Belong: Desire for Interpersonal Attachments as a Fundamental Human Motivation', *Psychological Bulletin*, vol. 117, no. 3 (1995), p. 522.

11. See for example, K. Deaux, 'Personalizing Identity and Socializing Self', in *Social Psychology of Identity and the Self Concept*, ed. G. M. Breakwell (London: Surrey University Press, 1992).

12. Karen Trew, 'What It Means to be Irish Seen from a Northern Perspective', *The Irish Journal of Psychology*, vol. 15, nos. 2 and 3 (1994), p. 296.

13. Karen Trew and David Benson, 'Dimensions of Social Identity in Northern Ireland', in *Changing European Identities: Social-Psychological Analyses of Social Change*, eds G. M. Breakwell and E. Lyons (London: Pergammon Press, 1996), pp. 123-43.

14. N. a., *Is There Room in Heaven for Billy Wright?* (Belfast, 1998).

15. Marc Gopin, 'The Heart of the Stranger' (unpublished paper, Boundaries and Bonds Conference, Stranmillis College, Belfast, June 1997); Alan Falconer, 'Remembering', in *Reconciling Memories*, rev. ed., eds Alan Falconer and Joseph Liechty (Blackrock, Co. Dublin: Columba Press, 1998), p. 13.

16. 'Stamp out Sectarianism' was the slogan of the Students Union anti-sectarianism campaign, 1999-2000.

17. Bill Rolston, *Politics and Painting: Murals and Conflict in Northern Ireland* (London: Associated University Press, 1991) p. 124.

18. The Catholic Bishops Conferences of Ireland, Scotland, England, and Wales, *One Bread, One Body: A Teaching Document on the Eucharist in the Life of the Church, and the Establishment of General Norms on Sacramental Sharing* (Dublin: Veritas Publications, 1998).

19. Ibid., paragraph 41.

20. Ibid., paragraphs 81-3.

21. Ibid., paragraph 83.

22. Volf, *Exclusion and Embrace*, p. 75.

CHAPTER FOUR: DYNAMICS AND VARIETIES OF SECTARIANISM

1. Quoted in Kevin Haddick-Flynn, *Orangeism: The Making of a Tradition* (Dublin: Wolfhound Press, 1999), p. 382. Some versions of the Qualifications use the wording 'towards Roman Catholics' rather than 'towards his Roman Catholic brethren'.

2. The Brook Advisory Centre offers a range of contraceptive and family planning services, including abortion referral.

3. This material is from the transcription of an interview taped on 26 October 1995.

4. Margaret Lamberts Bendroth, 'Fundamentalists and Us', *Christian Century*, vol. 113, no. 18 (22-29 May 1996), p. 579.

5. Steve Bruce, *God Save Ulster! The Religion and Politics of Paisleyism* (Oxford: Oxford University Press, 1986), p. 63.

6. Frank Wright, *Northern Ireland: A Comparative Analysis* (Dublin: Gill and Macmillan, 1987), p. 119.

7. Walter Wink, *Engaging the Powers: Discernment and Resistance in a World of Domination* (Minneapolis: Fortress Press, 1992), p. 3.

8. Quoted in Conor Cruise O'Brien, *Ancestral Voices: Religion and Nationalism in Ireland* (Dublin: Poolbeg, 1994), p. 7.

9. Ibid.

10. N. van der Zijpp, 'Münster Anabaptists in the Netherlands', in *The Mennonite Encyclopedia*, vol. 3.

11. Miroslav Volf, *Exclusion and Embrace: A Theological Exploration of Identity, Otherness, and Reconciliation* (Nashville: Abingdon Press, 1996), p. 298.

CHAPTER FIVE: TOOLS, MODELS AND REFLECTIONS

1. [Working Party on Sectarianism] *Sectarianism: A Discussion Document* (Belfast: Department of Social Issues, Irish Inter-Church Meeting, 1993), pp. 23-4.

2. The Darkley murders were claimed by the obscure Catholic Reaction Force, and the INLA was probably involved indirectly; the UDA and UFF claimed that Stone acted alone. Paul Bew and Gordon Gillespie, *Northern Ireland: A Chronology of the Troubles, 1968-1993* (Dublin: Gill and Macmillan, 1993), pp. 173, 213.

3. [Working Party on Sectarianism] *Sectarianism*, p. 23.

4. *Beyond the Fife and Drum: Report of a Conference Held on Belfast's Shankill Road, October 1994*, Island pamphlets, no. 11 (Newtownabbey, Northern Ireland: Island Publications, 1995), p. 35.

5. *An Phoblacht/Republican News* (5 November 1981), quoted in Bew and Gillespie, *Northern Ireland: A Chronology of the Troubles, 1968-1993*, p. 157.

6. Frank Wright, *Northern Ireland: A Comparative Analysis* (Dublin: Gill and Macmillan, 1987).

7. Frank Wright, 'Reconciling the Histories: Protestant and Catholic in Northern Ireland', in *Reconciling Memories*, rev. ed., eds. Alan Falconer and Joseph Liechty (Blackrock, Co. Dublin: Columba Press, 1998), pp. 131-2.

8. [Working Party on Sectarianism], *Sectarianism*, p. 23.

9. Ibid.

10. John H. Whyte, 'The Influence of the Catholic Clergy on Elections in Nineteenth-Century Ireland', *English Historical Review*, vol. 75 (April 1960), p. 248.

11. [Working Party on Sectarianism], *Sectarianism*, p. 23.

12. K. Theodore Hoppen, *Ireland since 1800: Conflict and Conformity* (London, New York: Longman, 1989), p. 188.

13. Kevin Boyle and Tom Hadden, *Northern Ireland: The Choice* (London: Penguin Books, 1994), p. 3.

14. Ibid., p. 192.

15. Ibid., chapter two and elsewhere.

16. Ibid., p. 192.

17. Ibid., p. 208.

18. Frank Wright, 'Reconciling the Histories', p. 133.

19. Wright, *Northern Ireland: A Comparative Analysis*, p. xiii.

20. Ibid.

21. Ibid., p. xv.

22. Ibid.

23. Ibid., p. xvi.

24. Ibid., pp. 289-90.

25. Miroslav Volf makes a particularly forceful and cogent case, both theological and biblical, for 'the inherent social meaning of reconciliation', (p. 160) in 'The Social Meaning of Reconciliation', *Interpretation*, vol. 54, no. 2 (April 2000).

26. Fionnuala O Connor, *In Search of a State: Catholics in Northern Ireland* (Belfast: Blackstaff Press, 1993), p. 195.

27. Ibid.

28. Walter Wink, *Engaging the Powers: Discernment and Resistance in a World of Domination* (Minneapolis: Fortress Press, 1992); for material directly relevant to our argument in this section, see especially pp. 3-10, 65-85.

29. Ibid., p. 129.

30. Quoted in Kevin Haddick-Flynn, *Orangeism: The Making of a Tradition* (Dublin: Wolfhound Press, 1999), pp. 381-2.

31. Quoted ibid., p. 382. Some versions of the Qualifications use the wording 'towards Roman Catholics' rather than 'towards his Roman Catholic brethren'.

32. Wink, *Engaging the Powers*, p. 175.

33. Miroslav Volf, *Exclusion and Embrace: A Theological Exploration of Identity, Otherness and Reconciliation* (Nashville: Abingdon Press, 1996), pp. 63-4.

34. Tim Winton, *Cloudstreet* (St Paul, Minn.: Graywolf Press, 1992), p. 402.

CHAPTER SIX: WHEN IS A RELIGIOUS IDEA SECTARIAN?

1. In this section we will speak mostly of religious ideas and truth claims and beliefs, but we do not use these terms in an exclusively intellectual or spiritual sense. Our assumption is that religious ideas are likely to be closely associated with practices and activities, and that practices and activities always have a set of ideas behind them.

2. Many of McCann's writings on religion, mostly short pieces from his *Hot Press* and *In Dublin* columns, are gathered together in Eamonn McCann, *Dear God: The Price of Religion in Ireland* (London, Chicago, Sydney: Bookmarks Publications, 1999).

3. The quotation is from the transcript of a 'Desert Island Discs' radio interview from the spring of 1995, cited in David Martin, *Does Christianity Cause War?* (Oxford: Clarendon Press, 1997), p. 24.

4. Martin, *Does Christianity Cause War?* p. 25.

5. John Whyte, *Interpreting Northern Ireland* (Oxford: Oxford University Press, 1990), pp. 67-9.

6. Congregation for the Doctrine of the Faith, 'Declaration *Dominus Iesus*: On the Unicity and Salvific Universality of Jesus Christ and the Church'. Available on-line: <http://www.vatican.va/roman_curia/congregations/cfaith/documents/rc_con_cfaith_doc_20000806_dominus-iesus_en.html> [4 April 2001].

7. Congregation for the Doctrine of the Faith, 'Note on the Expression "Sister Churches": A Letter to the Presidents of the Conferences of Bishops'. Available on-line: <http://www.vatican.va/roman_curia/congregations/cfaith/documents/rc_con_cfaith_doc_20000630_chiese-sorelle_en.html> [4 April 2001].

8. Congregation for the Doctrine of the Faith, 'Declaration *Dominus Iesus*'.

9. Luke 6:13. While most translations say 'deliver us from evil,' a more literal rendering is 'deliver us from the evil one.'

10. George Schöpflin, *Citizenship, Ethnicity, and Cultural Reproduction*, Frank Wright Memorial Lecture 1997, The Queen's University of Belfast Department of Politics, Occasional Paper No. 9 (Belfast: QUB Department of Politics, 1997), p. 3.

11. *Irish Times* (29 May 2000), p. 8.

12. Ibid., p. 16.

CHAPTER SEVEN: REDEEMING IDENTITY AND BELONGING

1. See the standing committee theological reflections, appendix K: 8.1-8.2.1.4, the Sub-Committee on Sectarianism Report, in *Standing Committee Report* (Dublin: Church of Ireland, 1999), pp. 174-6.

2. As suggested before in this book, see Alan Falconer's idea of 'identity-in-opposition' (Alan D. Falconer, 'Remembering', in *Reconciling Memories*, rev. ed., eds Alan D. Falconer and Joseph Liechty (Blackrock, Co Dublin: Columba Press, 1998), p. 13) and Marc Gopin's notion of 'the need for a threatening other' (Marc Gopin, 'The Heart of the Stranger' (unpublished paper, Boundaries and Bonds Conference, Stranmillis College, Belfast, June 1997)).

3. Miroslav Volf, *Exclusion and Embrace: A Theological Exploration of Identity, Otherness, and Reconciliation* (Nashville: Abingdon Press, 1996).

4. David Stevens, 'As We Enter a New Millennium', *Studies*, vol. 89, no. 354 (Summer 2000), p. 163.

5. *Koinonia* is a Greek term meaning 'communion' or 'participation' and is an increasingly important concept in conversations between churches at local and global level. 'The notion of *koinonia* (communion) has become fundamental for revitalising a common understanding of the nature of the Church and its visible unity.' *The Nature and Purpose of the Church: A Stage on the Way to a Common Statement*, Faith and Order Paper No. 181 (Geneva: WCC, 1998), section 48.

6. 'The Church belongs to God. It is the creation of God's Word and Holy Spirit. It cannot exist by and for itself. The Church is centred and grounded in the Gospel, the Word of God. The church is the commu-

nion of those who live in a personal relationship with God who speaks to them and calls forth their trustful response – the communion of the faithful. . . . Faith called forth by the Word of God is brought about by the action of the Holy Spirit. . . . As the communion of the faithful, the Church therefore is also the creation of the Holy Spirit.' *The Nature and Purpose of the Church,* sections 9-11.

7. Ibid.

8. Ibid., section 12.

9. Groupe des Dombes, *For the Conversion of the Churches* (Geneva: WCC, 1993), section 192; originally published as *Pour la conversion des Eglises* (Paris: Editions du Centurion, 1991).

10. Johnston McMaster, 'Changing Models of the Church', in Department of Theological Questions, Irish Inter-Church Meeting, *Being Church in the New Millennium: A Discussion Document* (Dublin: Veritas, 2000) p. 45.

11. For a fuller description of these positions, see *The Nature and Purpose of the Church,* sections 20-1.

12. Groupe des Dombes, *For the Conversion of the Churches,* section 189.

13. Ibid., section 190.

14. Ibid., section 192.

15. McMaster, 'Changing Models of the Church', p. 45.

16. *The Nature and Purpose of the Church,* section 12.

17. Groupe des Dombes, *For the Conversion of the Churches,* section 192.

18. McMaster, 'Changing Models of the Church', p. 45.

19. Groupe des Dombes, *For the Conversion of the Churches,* sections 189-90.

20. McMaster, 'Changing Models of the Church', p. 45.

21. Glenn Jordan, *Not of this World? Evangelical Protestants in Northern Ireland* (Belfast: The Blackstaff Press, 2001), p. 61.

22. Alwyn Thomson, *Beyond Fear, Suspicion and Hostility* (Belfast: ECONI, 1994), p. 17.

23. Jordan, *Not of this World?,* pp. 69-75.

24. Ibid., p. 85.

25. Thomson, *Beyond Fear, Suspicion and Hostility,* p. 11.

26. Jordan, *Not of this World?,* p. 63.

27. Ibid., p. 12.

28. Thomson, *Beyond Fear, Suspicion and Hostility,* p. 22.

29. These three identities and their corresponding calls to conversion are the whole content of *For the Conversion of the Churches.*

30. Groupe des Dombes, *For the Conversion of the Churches,* section 16.

31. Ibid.

32. Ibid., section 19.

33. '[T]he irreversible and unfailing presence of the gift God has given of himself to human beings in Jesus Christ.' Groupe des Dombes, *For the Conversion of the Churches,* section 22.

34. They see themselves as Confessions only from an historical and so-

ciological point of view. In the Vatican II document *Lumen Gentium* the Roman Catholic understanding is clear: 'This is the unique Church of Christ. ... This Church, constituted and organized in the world as a society, subsists in the Catholic Church, which is governed by the successor of Peter.' *Lumen Gentium*, section 8, in Walter M. Abbott, SJ, ed., *The Documents of Vatican II: The Message and Meaning of the Ecumenical Council* (London: Geoffrey Chapman, 1966), pp. 22-3.

35. Groupe des Dombes, *For the Conversion of the Churches*, section 29.

36. Ibid.

37. For a summary of uses of *koinonia* in the Christian Scriptures and philosophical Greek writings, see Friedrich Hauck, '*Koinonia*', in Gerhard Kittel, ed., *Theological Dictionary of the New Testament*, vol. 3 (Grand Rapids: Eerdmans, 1977), p. 798.

38. *The Nature and Purpose of the Church*, section 49.

39. *The Nature and Purpose of the Church*, section 51. For a summary of some uses of *shalom* in this sense, in particular *shalom* as 'a covenant of peace' in Is 54:10, see Francis Brown, S. R. Driver, and Charles A. Briggs, eds, *A Hebrew and English Lexicon of the Old Testament* (Oxford: Clarendon Press, 1907), section 5, p. 1023.

40. The biblical basis for *kenosis* is Phil 2:5-8.

41. For fellowship with the Son, see 1 Cor 1:9; for communion in the Holy Spirit, see 2 Cor 13:13; for participation in the body and blood of Christ, see 1 Cor 10:16-7. Greek text: Nestle-Aland, *Novum Testamentum Graece*, 26th ed. (Stuttgart: Deutsche Bibelstiftung, 1981).

42. 2 Cor 8:3-6.

43. *The Nature and Purpose of the Church*, section 26.

44. 2 Cor 5:19-20.

45. For Paul's vision of reconciliation, see especially Col 1:19-20 and Eph 1:9-10. For the creation waiting to be set free from bondage, see Rom 8:19-23.

46. Whilst Paul would not have thought in ecological terms, theologian Robert Schreiter has argued that Paul's vision of reconciliation, especially as expressed in Col 1:19-20 and Eph 1:9-10, likely reflects Jewish or possibly Hellenistic cosmologies, and therefore an awareness of reconciliation as wider than just the inter-personal. Robert Schreiter, *Reconciliation: Mission and Ministry in a Changing Social Order* (New York: Orbis Books, 1992), pp. 56-9.

47. See for example the work of Catharina J. M. Halkes, *New Creation: Christian Feminism and the Renewal of the Earth* (London: SPCK, 1991); originally published as *En Alles Zal Worden Herschapen* (Baarn: Uitgeverij Ten Have, 1989).

48. Miroslav Volf, 'The Social Meaning of Reconciliation', *Interpretation*, vol. 54, no. 2 (April 2000), p. 160.

49. Ibid., p. 159.

50. *The Kairos Document: Challenge to the Church*, rev. 2nd ed. (Johannesburg: ICT, 1986), article 3.1, p. 9.

51. Volf, 'The Social Meaning of Reconciliation', p. 169.

52. 'No peace is possible within the overarching framework of strict justice for the simple reason that no strict justice is possible.' Ibid.

53. One of the best examples of the priority of reconciliation over justice is found in Nelson Mandela's decision to seek reconciliation. South African theologian John de Gruchy observes, 'It had become abundantly clear to him [Mandela] that there was no alternative. ... The path of reconciliation was not only the goal of liberation but also a means to achieve that end.' John W. de Gruchy, 'The Dialectic of Reconciliation', in *The Reconciliation of Peoples: Challenge to the Churches*, eds Gregory Baum and Harold Wells (Maryknoll, New York: Orbis Books, 1997), p. 18.

54. Volf, 'The Social Meaning of Reconciliation', p. 163.

55. Gerry O'Hanlon, 'Justice and Reconciliation', in *Reconciliation in Religion and Society*, ed. Michael Hurley (Belfast: Institute of Irish Studies, 1994), pp. 50-1.

56. Ibid., p. 51. The idea of the injured party absorbing the offence by his or her suffering is very similar to Miroslav Volf's notion of the 'will to embrace'. See Volf, *Exclusion and Embrace*, p. 29.

57. O'Hanlon, 'Justice and Reconciliation', p. 53.

58. Schreiter, *Reconciliation*, p. 43.

59. Donald W. Shriver, Jr, *An Ethic for Enemies: Forgiveness in Politics*, (New York: Oxford University Press, 1995), pp. 7-9.

60. A similar approach is taken by the Faith and Politics group. See *Forgive Us Our Trespasses...? Reconciliation and Political Healing in Northern Ireland* (Belfast: Faith and Politics Group, 1996) p. 19.

61. Shriver, *An Ethic for Enemies*, p. 7.

62. Frank Wright, 'Reconciling the Histories: Protestant and Catholic in Northern Ireland', in *Reconciling Memories*, rev. ed., eds Falconer and Liechty, p. 134.

63. Ibid., p. 138.

64. Faith and Politics Group, *Boasting: Self-righteous Collective Superiority as a Cause of Conflict* (Belfast: Faith and Politics Group, 1999), p. 11.

65. Clem McCartney and Lucy Bryson, *Clashing Symbols? A Report on the Use of Flags, Anthems and Other National Symbols in Northern Ireland* (Belfast: Institute of Irish Studies, 1994), p. 73.

66. Ibid.

67. Wright, 'Reconciling the Histories', p. 134.

68. Ibid.

69. See for example the comments of one speaker at a series of discussions in mid-1994 on the Shankill Road, Belfast, which were aimed at assisting the Protestant working class communities to articulate their needs and aspirations: 'We know that the British don't care tuppence for us, but sure they don't even care about their own people—half of England has become an industrial wasteland. When I watch the Tories on the box I ask myself – do I *really* want to be loyal to yon crowd?'

Ulster's Protestant Working Class: A Community Exploration, Island pamphlets, no. 9 (Newtownabbey, Northern Ireland: Island Publications, 1994), p. 15.

70. McCartney and Bryson, *Clashing Symbols?*, p. 73.

71. See the comments of a working class Protestant during the Shankill Road discussions in 1994. 'The Protestant community has little left to give up – except its identity. And it looks increasingly that that's what the Nationalist community are waiting for, that's all that will satisfy them.' *Ulster's Protestant Working Class*, p. 25.

72. Faith and Politics Group, *Boasting: Self-righteous Collective Superiority as a Cause of Conflict* (Belfast: Faith and Politics Group, 1999) p. 20.

73. This is the basis on which the meaning and pronunciation of the Hebrew name for God, symbolised by YHWH, remains a mystery. See 'Idolatry', in *A New Handbook of Christian Theology*, eds Donald W. Musser and Joseph L. Price (Cambridge: Lutterworth Press, 1992), p. 246.

74. Alwyn Thomson, ed., *Faith in Ulster* (Belfast: ECONI, 1996). See in particular the contributions of Arthur Aughey, p.17, and John Dickinson: 'Even after a quarter of a century that slogan, along with the sight of an Orange banner or the sound of a flute band, still calls to something primeval in me.' P. 46.

75. The first is the position of Billy Kennedy, religious correspondent of the *Ulster/Belfast Newsletter*; the second is the argument of DUP assemblyman Gregory Campbell. Both are taken from Thomson, ed., *Faith in Ulster*, pp. 72-3 and 36-7.

76. See Esmond Birnie's contribution, ibid., p. 25.

77. See the oath-prayer of Pádraig Pearse, quoted in full in chapter two, in which he combines prayer to God including invocation of Christ, the Virgin Mary, and the saints, with an oath: 'That we will free our race from bondage, Or that we will fall fighting hand to hand. Amen.' Quoted in Ruth Dudley Edwards, *Patrick Pearse: The Triumph of Failure* (London, 1977; paperback ed., Dublin: Prometheus Books, 1990), pp. 161-2.

78. See for example, the work of ECONI (Evangelical Contribution on Northern Ireland), especially *A Future with Hope: Biblical Frameworks for Peace and Reconciliation in Northern Ireland* (Belfast: ECONI, 1995), p. 14, and the work of the Faith and Politics Group, especially *Doing Unto Others: Parity of Esteem in a Contested Space* (Belfast: Faith and Politics Group, 1997).

79. The moving declaration of Gordon Wilson after the death of his daughter Marie in the Enniskillen bombing in 1987 has in some way assumed the proportions of a symbol of Christian forgiveness in the Northern situation and was acknowledged by Loyalist paramilitary leaders to have actually prevented reprisals.

80. For example, the role of many chaplains to the prisons who, over the years, have helped perpetrators of sectarian violence to reflect on and turn away from that path.

81. For example, the work of communities like Cornerstone, Corrymeela, and Currach in Belfast; congregational initiatives such as the Clonard/Fitzroy group; and the work of some clergy groups, such as in Ballynafeigh, Belfast.

82. First use of this term is attributed to Robin Boyd, Presbyterian minister and former director of the Irish School of Ecumenics. See Robin Boyd, *Ireland: Christianity Discredited or Pilgrim's Progress?* (Geneva: WCC, 1988), p. 30.

83. For example, Rev Ian Paisley, leader of the DUP and moderator of the Free Presbyterian Church, said following the Ulster workers strike in 1974: 'There are those who mistakenly analyse the Ulster situation in terms of social and economic factors, in terms of politics, or philosophies. These theories and analyses collapse because they ignore, deliberately or otherwise, the main key and to us the most obvious factor: Protestantism versus popery. The war in Ulster is a war of survival between opposing forces of Truth and Error, and the principles of the Reformation are as relevant today in Ulster as they were in Europe in the sixteenth century.' *Protestant Telegraph* (15-28 June 1974).

84. Emmanuel Clapsis, 'Globalization, Nationalism and the Unity of the Church', unpublished paper delivered at a WCC consultation, 'Ethnic Identity, National Identity, and the Unity of the Church', St Deniol's, Wales, September 1997, p. 1.

85. See for example the heated exchange with Iris Robinson, DUP, during a conference held on the Shankill Road in Belfast, in which speakers from the floor, some of whom had served time in prison for fighting Republicans, accuse her, her husband (DUP deputy leader Peter Robinson), and DUP leader Ian Paisley of 'encouraging others to do it'. *Beyond the Fife and Drum: Report of a Conference Held on Belfast's Shankill Road, October 1994*, Island pamphlets, no. 11 (Newtownabbey, Northern Ireland: Island Publications, 1995), pp. 35-6.

86. For example, Rev Ian Paisley, who is also leader of the Democratic Unionist Party, and Rev Martin Smyth, former Grand Master of the Orange Order.

87. See for example Jesus reaching out to Zacchaeus in Lk 19:1-10 and the lepers in Lk 17:11-19, and the beatitude 'Blessed are the peacemakers' in Mt 5:9.

88. Lk 17:11-19 and Acts 10:34.

89. Lk 10:25-37.

90. Jn 21:15-19.

91. Lk 19:1-10.

92. See *Lumen Gentium*, section 8, in Abbott, ed., *The Documents of Vatican II*, p. 22, and *Declaration* Dominus Iesus: *On the Unicity and Salvific Universality of Jesus Christ and the Church* (Rome: Congregation for the Doctrine of the Faith, September 2000) paragraph 17.

93. *Declaration* Dominus Iesus: *On the Unicity and Salvific Universality of Jesus Christ and the Church*, paragraph 17.

94. Ibid.

95. For example, the Westminster Confession of Faith describes the Pope as 'that antichrist, that man of sin, and son of perdition, that exalteth himself in the church against Christ, and all that is called God.' *The Westminster Confession of Faith* (Edinburgh: Blackwood and Sons, 1979), chapter 25, paragraph 6. The Anglican Articles of Religion say of the Catholic mass offered for the dead: 'Wherefore the sacrifices of Masses, in which it was commonly said, that the Priest did offer Christ for the quick and the dead, to have remission of pain and guilt, were blasphemous fables, and dangerous deceits.' Available on-line: <www.churchofireland>, paragraph 17 [February 2001]. In *Notes on the New Testament*, John Wesley refers to the Pope as the 'man of sin'. See Eric Gallagher's reflections on Wesley's stance in Eric Gallagher, *A Better Way for Irish Protestants and Roman Catholics: Advice from John Wesley* (Belfast: Mission Board, Methodist Church in Ireland, 1973), pp. 7-8.

96. For example, the General Assembly of 1988 declared: 'The General Assembly, under God, reaffirm that this historical interpretation of the Pope of Rome as the personal and literal fulfillment of the biblical figure "Anti-Christ" and the "Man of Sin" is not manifestly evident from Scripture.' *Minutes of the General Assembly* (Belfast: Church House, 1988) p. 54.

97. 'Historic documents often stem from periods of deep separation between Christian churches. Whilst, in spite of a real degree of convergence, distinct differences remain, negative statements towards other Christians should not be seen as representing the spirit of this Church today. The Church of Ireland affirms all in its tradition that witnesses to the truth of the Gospel. It regrets that words written in another age and in a different context should be used in a manner hurtful to or antagonistic towards other Christians.' Appendix K, the Sub-Committee on Sectarianism Report, in *Standing Committee Report*, p. 199.

98. 2 Cor 5:19.

99. Mt 28:19.

100. Faith and Politics Group, *Boasting*, p. 12.

101. Eph 2:15.

102. Gal 6:16.

103. Rom 3:29-30.

104. Rom 14.

105. Klaus Berger, 'Justice', in *Encyclopedia of Theology: A Concise Sacramentum Mundi*, ed. Karl Rahner (London: Burns and Oates, 1975), p. 788.

106. Phil 2.

107. Gal 6:14-15.

108. Mt 22:37 and Mt 5:44.

109. Jn 4:1-42 and Lk 19:1-10.

110. John D. Brewer with Gareth I. Higgins, *Anti-Catholicism in Northern Ireland, 1600-1998: The Mote and the Beam* (London: Macmillan Press, 1998), pp. 200-2.

111. 2 Cor 5:17-18.

112. 'Hermeneutics deals with the principles or theory of interpretation. This involves understanding and communication of values, meaning and truth through not only a text, but also through language and symbols. Hermeneutics involves the interaction between two contexts or two worlds, that of the text and that of the hearer. The dynamic of interpretation and the disclosure of meaning take place in such contextual interaction. All texts, language and symbols require interpretation and therefore hermeneutics.' Johnston McMaster, personal communication, 3 April 2001.

113. Rom 5:8.

114. See the research by Duncan Morrow, et al, which reflects this. Duncan Morrow, Derek Birrell, John Greer, and Terry O'Keeffe, *Churches and Inter-Community Relationships* (Coleraine: Centre for the Study of Conflict, 1994).

CHAPTER EIGHT: MOVING BEYOND ...

1. For a fuller explanation of these dynamics see the section on 'Approaches to Dealing with Difference' in chapter five.

2. Ex 13:17-22.

3. This call was made also by the Inter-Church Working Party on Sectarianism in 1993. See *Sectarianism: A Discussion Document* (Belfast: Department of Social Issues, Irish Inter-Church Meeting, 1993) p. 102.

4. T. S. Eliot, 'Journey of the Magi', in *A Christian's Prayer Book*, eds Peter Coughlan, Ronald C. D. Jasper, and Teresa Rodrigues (London: Geoffrey Chapman, 1974) pp. 75-6.